SCA

In memory of
my mother, a devout Catholic,
and my father, a devout Protestant,
both of whom would have enjoyed the story

SCALAN:
The Forbidden College, 1716–1799

John Watts

With a Foreword by Right Rev.
Mario Bishop Conti, K.C.H.S., D.D.,
F.R.S.E., President of the
Scottish Catholic Heritage Commission

TUCKWELL PRESS

First published in 1999 by
Tuckwell Press Ltd
The Mill House
Phantassie
East Linton
East Lothian EH40 3DG
Scotland

ISBN 1 86232 061 6

A Catalogue record for this book
is available on request from
the British Library

Typeset by Hewer Text Ltd, Edinburgh
Printed and bound by Cromwell Press, Trowbridge, Wiltshire

It is not without reason
That this hollow
Has been put away in a wilderness . . .
The road that leads to its retreat
Is a hard and toilsome road.

Gottfried von Strassburg, *Tristan*

Contents

List of Illustrations

List of Maps and Figures

Foreword

Dr. John Watts has done us all a timely service. For the historian he has gathered from various sources all that is essental to the story of Scalan. It will be an invaluable reference book. For the general reader he has told a tale of courage in the face of enemies both within and without which is truly engaging. For those who have inherited or embraced the faith of such stalwart precursors, he has produced a work of piety – and the Romans among them would know the full sense of that familiar word.

The book is timely because its publication coincides with the tercentenary of Scalan's first precursor, as well as the bi-centenary of the transfer of the staff and students to Aquhorties by the lower reaches of the Don, and the centenary of the laying of the foundation stone oft eh chapel of Blairs College, on the banks of the Dee, which was the inheritor of Scalan's traditions and hopes. The latter was, until its recent closure, the repository also of books and other objects which remain as a tangible witness to a breadth of culture out of all proportion to the straitened circumstances of the Seminary by the Crombie Burn.

The book is timely also for the reason that in recent years there has been an increasing interest in what remains of the 'Forbidden Seminary'. The progressive repair of the abandoned buildings and their increased accessibility to the roamer and tourist, as well as the waning of religious bigotry, have all conspired to make the place better known, and its history more fervently sought.

Dr. John Watts has produced a book which his many readers will appreciate, and which his many friends will admire and applaud.

Mario Conti

Bishop of Aberdeen

Acknowledgements

The author wishes to express his grateful thanks, first of all, to the Society of Antiquaries of Scotland for their award of a research grant to him during 1997; and to the Catholic Bishops of Scotland, and Bishop Conti of Aberdeen personally, for their generous support of the publisher, without which publication would not have been possible.

I am especially indebted to Bishop Conti, President of the Scottish Catholic Heritage Commission, for his faith and encouragement through-out; and also to Mgr. John McIntyre, formerly Rector of Blairs College and the Scots College Rome, and Alasdair Roberts, historian and editor of the *Scalan News*, who read the manuscript, pointed out a number of errors, omissions and infelicities, and made many valuable suggestions: the text is certainly the better for having passed before their critical eye.

Among others who have given valued help special mention should be made of Veronica Gordon Smith, formerly of Drumin and a descendant of the Gordons of Lettoch; Ann Dean; Fr. Colin Stewart, parish priest of Tomintoul-Tombae-Chapeltown; Mr. and Mrs. Normile Baxter of Aqu-horties House; Stuart Mitchell; Rev. John Woodside, Keeper of the Blairs Museum; John Joseph Watts; Paul Jackson; and Gordon McGillivray of Achnascra, Braes of Glenlivet.

I should also like to record my gratitude to the staffs of the Scottish Record Office, the Scottish Catholic Archives, the National Library of Scotland, the Edinburgh University Library, the Library of the Royal Museum of Scotland, and the Local History Department of the Elgin City Library, for their ready assistance.

Lastly, for their moral support and patience, a heartfelt 'thank you' to my wife Moira and our children.

Introduction

> The time by the goodness of God will come, when the Catholic religion will again flourish in Scotland; and then, when posterity shall enquire, with laudable curiosity, by what means any sparks of the true faith were preserved . . . Scalan and the other colleges will be mentioned with veneration, and all that can be learned of them will be recorded with care.

With these oft-quoted words Bishop Geddes concluded his *Brief Historical Account of the Seminary at Scalan*,[1] written in 1777 when the little college was still open and the Penal Laws which decreed it illegal were still in force.

The record begins on a late summer evening of 1716, when a young, scholarly, and by no means robust priest, with three or four boys entrusted to his care, arrived foot-weary at the door of an obscure turf house, high in the Banffshire hills. Theirs had been an arduous journey from the West. They did not know how long they were to remain in this new home, but they knew why they had come. Their task was to set up a clandestine college there, in defiance of the Law, where would be trained the priests needed to restore their Church in Scotland, all but exterminated at the Reformation. The boys were to be the first of those priests. Perhaps, as they fell into grateful sleep that night, they were vaguely aware that they were making history.

It has been my endeavour to chronicle that history, and the pursuit of that goal; to follow the fortunes of the seminary, from its secret foundation "in as remote a place as is in Scotland", when secrecy and remoteness were a necessity, to its closure eighty-three years later, when changed conditions within Scottish society had rendered those qualities needless and an obstacle to further progress.

Scalan was not an entirely new idea. At least two abortive attempts had already been made to establish a seminary on the Scottish Mission, the first of them in 1699. The publication of the present volume is therefore doubly timely, since it coincides not alone with the bicentenary of the closure of Scalan in 1799, but with the tercentenary of its first precursor.[2]

It is by no means the first work on the subject, and owes much to a number of previous studies. Ninety years ago Dom Odo Blundell surveyed the site, and gathered important documentary and other information.[3] Forty years later Mgr MacWilliam wrote useful articles on the subject, based mainly on first-hand sources.[4] In 1963 Fr W. J. Anderson made crucial manuscripts available in published form,[5] in the hope that they might be used for a "serious study" of the college. "It is very desirable that someone should undertake this task at some future date," he wrote. Mgr MacWilliam himself went some way in this direction with a valuable historical account written in the 1970s, which unfortunately remains in typed manuscript.[6] More recent research – notably by Johnson, Doughty, Roberts, Dean and Mitchell[7] – has covered particular aspects of Scalan. And the lively biannual magazine, *Scalan News*, edited by Roberts,[8] continues to provide a wealth of information on the seminary and the unique area of North-East Scotland in which it was sited. But to date no general history has been written which is at once comprehensive, detailed, and accessible.

The present work attempts to fill that gap. It is considerably larger in scope than previous studies and is based as far as possible on original documentary sources. It seeks to give a dispassionate account of the seminary, identifying its shortcomings and blemishes along with its virtues, its failures as well as its successes. Sharing the affection that everyone feels for Sclan – for the glamour of its remote, often parlous existence and the courage of its youthful community – I have consciously tried to resist the temptation to romance.

Forbidden College aspires to fulfil Fr Anderson's hope for a "serious study", but it lays no claim to have recorded "all that can be learned" of Scalan as Bishop Geddes envisaged, and that for good reason. Quite apart from the requirements of the publisher in regard to length of text, it has been written for the general reader as much as the specialist, and as such seeks to provide the kind of detail that would inform and interest, and just enough context to make the narrative meaningful.[8] Some material has been omitted, therefore, and the keen-eyed will be able to find lacunae here and there, and places where the treatment is cursory. Certain aspects of Scalan's story undoubtedly merit fuller attention than I had space to give,[9] and these must await a more detailed treatment elsewhere. Meantime, a comprehensive general history of Scalan has long been needed, and the present volume attempts to meet that need.

In the chapters that follow the reader will be taken into the daily life of the seminary, but not – it is hoped – so as to lose sight of the wood among the trees. Scalan's own masters and boys, as they lived their lives and faced immediate problems, must have constantly had to remind themselves to keep sight of their original vision, lest it become forgotten in the day-to-day. And so here, it is intended that the details should illuminate, not obscure, the underlying purpose that drove and sustained them.

It was this original purpose, this vision, that had led the boys and their young master to their new home in the first place. To best understand it, and the circumstances that brought them there – the road to Scalan, as it were – we need first to look at the condition of the Catholic Church in Scotland at the time, and the previous attempts that had been made to establish seminaries to serve the struggling Scottish Mission.

NOTES

1. Geddes, Bishop J. 'A Brief Historical Account of the Seminary at Scalan', transcript of lecture given at Valladolid, 1777; CS 1/3, para. 40, SCA.
2. By a further coincidence, and as if pointing up the continuity of the tradition, 1999 also marks the centenary of the opening of the seminary church at Blairs College (1829–1986), the most important and long-lived of Scalan's successors.
3. Blundell O. *The Catholic Highlands of Scotland*, vol. 1 (Edinburgh, 1909).
4. MacWilliam A. S. ('Glenlivetensis') 'Scalan 1717–1799', *Claves Regni*, (*St Peter's College Magazine*), vol. xvii, no. 67, Dec. 1944 and no. 68, June 1947.
5. Anderson W. J. (ed.) 'The College for the Lowland District of Scotland at Scalan and Aquhorties: Registers and Documents', *IR*, vol. xiv, no. 2, autumn 1963.
6. MacWilliam A. S. 'The Scottish Seminaries Loch Morar to Aquhorties 1714–1829', 1977, typescript, SCA.
7. Johnson C. *Developments in the Roman Catholic Church in Scotland 1789–1829* (Edinburgh, 1983); and 'Three Scottish Seminaries', *The Deeside Field*, 18, 1986. Doughty D. 'Chapeltown, Braes of Glenlivet, and Tombae, the Debris of the Old Scalan Library', *The Deeside Field*, 19, 1987. Roberts A. *passim* in *Scalan News*, espec. 'Tombae and Scalan: *Status Animarum*', no. 10, June 1995. Dean A. and Taitt M. 'Scalan Reconstructed: Architectural and Documentary Evidence', *IR*, vol. lxvi, no. 1, spring 1995. Mitchell S. 'Scalan in the Eighteenth Century: A Postscript – The 'Forty Five', *Scalan News*, no. 14, June 1997.
8. *Scalan News*, ed. Roberts A., published twice yearly by the Scalan Association, first issue Dec. 1990, eighteen issues to date (June 1999).
9. There was also some documentary material – notably the holdings of the Propaganda Archives in Rome – that the author was only able to consult through printed sources, and which may contain further information in the originals. The same applies to the Archives of the Scots College Rome, though the Archives catalogue (Flanagan Catalogue, SCA) suggests that they contain very little material directly relevant to Scalan that is not accessible elsewhere.
10. In particular, perhaps, Scalan's relationship with the Scots Colleges abroad, the impact that the Scottish Mission's precarious financial position had upon it over the years, and the students' family backgrounds. Nor was it possible to make more than passing reference to the seminaries that came after Scalan down to the present time, or of its re-discovery in recent years as a monument and a place of pilgrimage. These last two themes are of importance, since they emphasise Scalan's place in the on-going story of Catholicism and in Christian and Scottish heritage, and highlight its unbroken link with and profound relevance to today's Church. But they fall outside the scope of the present account.

1

The Road to Scalan 1:
The Catholic Church in Scotland
Three Hundred Years Ago

In 1677 the priest Mr Alexander Leslie received a commission from the Vatican's Congregation *de Propaganda Fide* to undertake a fact-finding tour of Scotland, in order to assess the state and needs of the Catholic Church there. His purpose was to discover where, and to what extent, it was still surviving, a century and more after the catastrophe of the Reformation.[1]

In his report he estimated the number of communicants in the whole country to be no more than 14000, a figure that would suggest a total for all baptised Catholics, adult and child, of something close to 24000, a mere $2\frac{1}{2}$% of the national population.[2] But even this figure was deceptive, since their distribution across the country was far from uniform.

In certain areas – Moidart, Arisaig, Morar, Knoydart, Glengarry, Barra, Uist, Benbecula, and several of the small Hebridean islands – he found that all the people were Catholics; and in others, notably Strathglass, Coll, Tiree and Eigg, nearly all. He came upon considerable numbers in Lochaber, Aberdeenshire, Banffshire, Buchan and Galloway; smaller groups in Inverness town, Perthshire and beside the Solway Firth, and tiny minorities in Lowland districts such as Clydesdale and Lothian. But in vast areas of the country he found that the Church had in effect ceased to exist altogether.

A glance at Map 1 reveals with stark clarity this unevenness of distribution. In the South and the Central Lowlands small Catholic communities can be seen "scattered here and there" – in Mr Leslie's own phrase – and far apart from one another. Some had gathered around the seats of the few great families that had remained loyal to the Old Faith in these parts of the country. But in total they must have amounted to less than two thousand persons.

To the north the picture appears quite different. Here were to be found at least 90% of Scotland's Catholics, but they are seen to be almost entirely confined within a quite narrow band of country stretching from the North-East coast to the Western Isles, in some parts of which they

MAP 1
Areas of Catholic Population
c. 1680-1700

n

Enzie

Benbecula

S. Uist

Barra

Strath-
Glass

Strathbogie

Inverness

Garioch

Skye

Canna

Glen Morriston

Glenlivet

Aberdeen

Rum

Strathavon

Mearns

Glengarry

Upper Deeside

Coll

Lochaber

Tiree

Mull

Clydesdale

Lothian

Traquair

Kintyre

Terregles

New Abbey

Munshes

① Knoydart   ■ All/nearly all

② North and South Morar   ▨ Many

③ Arisaig   ◨ Some

④ Moidart   ⁚ Few/very few

---------------- Highland Line

formed the majority or even the entire population. Apart from the Enzie, Strathbogie and the Garioch, all the Catholic areas in this swathe lay within the Highlands and Islands, within whose feudal clan society the people were bound by ties of kinship as well as by their common faith. Everywhere else the map is blank.

At this time the Lowlands and the Highlands were two quite separate worlds. The latter were remote and almost impenetrable, and their inhabitants primitive and poor to a degree that rudely shocked the few outsiders who ventured to visit them. Such visitors were struck by their stunted growth, their susceptibility to illnesses brought on by cold, damp and malnutrition, and their wretched chimneyless homes that dotted the landscape like smoking dunghills.[3] Their dress and Gaelic language further emphasised their difference.[4] Mr Leslie took an interpreter with him when he entered the mountains, and his party donned the Highland garb because, as he explained to Propaganda, Highlanders were quite unlike the men of the Lowlands and dressed in garments similar to the toga of the ancient Romans. To most Lowlanders, not to say the English, they were indeed an alien people – "rude, warlike, quarrelsome and mischievous", as one described them – and hardly less exotic than the savages of the New World.[5]

We might therefore in a real sense speak of two Catholic Churches in Scotland three hundred years ago: one English-speaking, scattered, and – except in a few areas of the North-East – nowhere numerous; the other far more widespread and numerically perhaps six times as large,[6] Gaelic-speaking, for the most part desperately poor, and – in its main strongholds – forming almost the entire local population.

Survival and Recovery

Still struggling to recover from its near-extinction after the Reformation, the Church had few resources and little manpower to call on. There was a chronic shortage of priests: Mr Leslie found just five secular clergy and four Jesuits in the whole country when he made his tour. In the Highlands and Islands he was everywhere struck by the fervour and simple piety of the people, who "in spite of their natural ferocity were as lambs in the presence of a priest, and as firm in their Faith as rocks". But their thirst for teaching and the sacraments could nowhere be satisfied, for lack of manpower. "Their cries for priests of their own never left our ears," he reported, and wherever he went the people tried every means to persuade him to stay. In Barra they even tried to take him hostage, hoping to use him to bargain with the Pope himself to be given a permanent priest of their own! He believed he would be haunted for the rest of his life by the memory of the harvest of souls in the Highlands "going to waste for want of workers".[7]

These communities had remained Catholic after the Reformation in the sense that, resistant to Protestantism as they were, they had never been seriously penetrated by Presbyterian missionary activity.[8] But such was the shortage of priests that in some of them at least Catholic worship had itself become little more than a distant memory for a while in the early part of the seventeenth century, and something close to a religious vacuum had obtained there, in practice if not in sentiment.[9] It was only through the efforts of a handful of Irish Franciscans, who in a few years in the 1620s and 1630s had received and baptised as many as 10000 people in these very areas, that recovery had been achieved.[10] These men were afterwards withdrawn by their Order, but their spectacular success had shown the desire of the people, and suggested that rebuilding might be possible elsewhere also, if only priests could be made available.

Even in places where the Kirk was already organised and active there was potential for some limited recovery, but here too it hung upon the presence of a priest. Thus when the Jesuit Fr Forsyth arrived in Upper Deeside in the late 1660s, on the estate of the Protestant Earl of Mar, his local flock comprised – as far as he knew – just two persons. It was several years before he learned by chance of a further forty or so on his doorstep, who did not attend the kirk and had been secretly waiting and praying for the arrival of a pastor of the Old Religion. Fr Forsyth stayed to serve the district around Braemar for thirty more years, and under his care the number of Catholics there grew to several hundred.[11]

Unfortunately, not every shepherd remained so faithfully with his flock. For most of the seventeenth century there was no authority structure within the Scottish Mission to ensure that they would. There was no bishop to decide an overall plan, issue instructions, and allocate fixed stations to them, with the result that each came and went largely as he pleased or as he thought best. The secular priests were at least bound by oath to the Mission as a whole, but not even this safeguard applied to those in orders – the Benedictines, Vincentians, Franciscans and Jesuits – and it was all too common for them to be withdrawn by their superiors with little or no warning, from their stations or even from the country.

We can therefore point to three great handicaps under which the Catholic Church laboured in Scotland three hundred years ago: its poverty, its shortage of priests, and its lack of organisation. These were the very shortcomings that Mr Alexander Leslie himself identified as the main obstacles to its recovery, and which he urged Rome to address if it was to survive and grow.[12]

Obstacles to Recovery

The problem of organisation was largely solved by the end of the century.
A start had already been made in 1649 with the appointment of an Agent
for the Mission, a Scottish priest resident in Rome who could deal face-to-
face with the Cardinal Protector and the officials of Propaganda in
representing the needs of a poor and distant country. Four years later
a Prefect had been appointed for the Mission, with some limited authority
over the clergy at home. But the decisive step was taken in 1694 when
Thomas Nicolson was consecrated bishop, Scotland's first since the
Reformation, with full episcopal authority.[13]

Arrested and imprisoned on his return to Britain, it was three years
before Bishop Nicolson was able to take up office. And because of a
devastating famine in the Highlands it was a further three before he could
attempt a visitation to the West where most of his people lived. By then
his own experience and the local reports he was receiving had convinced
him that the only priests worth having were those with a lasting
commitment to Scotland, and that this could not be guaranteed from
foreigners.[14] As far as he was concerned, the Mission would in future
need to rely on producing its own native clergy.

When he finally made his journey to the West in 1700 he met his
Highland priests and assigned them to fixed stations. In the same year he
drew up a set of *Statuta*, instructions regarding the duties of priests which
clarified their work and consolidated his own authority. He also appointed two Pro-Vicars (one for the mainland, and the other for the Isles),
a team of Administrators to look after matters spiritual and temporal, and
Procurators to receive and dispense the finances, such as they were.[15] The
authority structure that he thus established did not as yet adequately
reflect the very different needs of the Church in the Highlands and
Lowlands, but in every other respect it could be said that the essential
elements of organisation were now in place.

The second problem, the shortage of priests, proved more intractable.
Before the Reformation most priests, in Scotland as elsewhere, had
received their education in the universities. But the Council of Trent
had decreed that in future they were to be trained in seminaries set up for
the purpose by the Church, where they could receive a more suitable
preparation and so avoid the widespread clerical laxity and ignorance
that had been a main cause of the Reformation.

This was the laudable theory, but such arrangements were in fact out of
the question in many Protestant countries, and the Scottish Mission, like
its English and Irish counterparts, had been forced to set up its training
colleges abroad, in European countries where Catholicism flourished.

Scots Colleges had been opened at Douai in the late sixteenth century, at Rome in 1600 and at Madrid in 1627, to complement the long-established College in Paris which could trace its origins to the fourteenth century.[16]

But they were far from being the ideal solution. Their distance from home, their financial independence, and the conditions of their foundation made them all too often unsympathetic to the needs and deaf to the pleas of the Mission they existed to serve. The College at Paris, for instance, was in the overall control of the Prior of the local Carthusian monastery, and being part of the university could never be used solely as a seminary for training priests.[17] The other three colleges were run by the Jesuits who, it was claimed, often tempted the most able students to join their own Society, with the result that many never returned to Scotland. And this was only one of a number of criticisms levelled against them. When Propaganda made formal inspections of the Rome and Madrid colleges at the urgent request of the Scots Agent, their reports were damning.[18]

For Bishop Nicolson the most serious drawback of the Scots Colleges was their failure to prepare men for the harsh realities of life on the Scottish Mission. The students' way of life was too comfortable, he believed, and their courses of study far too theoretical – "scholastic subtleties, considered by our own wisest men as mere intellectual trifling",[19] and hopelessly irrelevant in the mountains.

A further drawback was the difficulty of sending students abroad. Travel overseas for Catholic schooling was illegal, under Acts of the Scottish Parliament passed in 1609 and 1625.[20] Few ships' captains were willing to risk prosecution, and students were often forced to get aboard in the guise of cabin boys. For lads of twelve or even younger, perhaps without any adult companion, the journey was never less than an ordeal and sometimes a nightmare, and if the ship carrying them was driven off course they might be set ashore in a completely unknown place. Once on land they were at risk from anyone ready to prey upon their innocence. Even if they were lucky and the journey passed without mishap, it might take four months,[21] so that they would arrive at their destination utterly exhausted. And the cost of such journeys was crippling to a Mission without funds, as witness the tediously regular correspondence between Scotland, Rome and the Colleges disputing responsibility for the payment of 'viatics'.

For one reason or another, therefore, the Scots Colleges were by no means solving the problem of Scotland's shortage of priests as the seventeenth century drew to a close.

The poverty of the Scottish Mission was to remain a severe obstacle to advancement for close to another hundred years. Central responsibility for giving financial aid to Mission countries belonged to Propaganda. But Scotland's was a small Mission on the far edge of Europe, and never high among the Congregation's priorities. It had been Propaganda's reluctance to guarantee fixed, regular support that had prompted the Irish Franciscans to pull out of the country in the 1630s.[22] Since the appointment of the Mission's first Prefect in 1653 Rome had been sending 500 Scudi per year, the equivalent of £125 Sterling, a figure barely adequate then when less than ten priests were to be supported, but still not increased three-quarters of a century later[23] when the workforce had trebled. Propaganda was more than once warned that priests were on the point of deserting the Mission, because they simply could not exist on their meagre incomes. "Too little, too late" is the judgment upon Rome's financial support of one modern commentator, who concludes that had it given a real commitment many other parts of the North and West of Scotland could have been held or recovered for the Church.[24]

The Mission received additional monies from time to time from legacies and gifts, including a fund endowed by James II/VII. Donations came from the few persons of wealth within the Church, great landowners, or people like Lewis Innes, the Principal of the Scots College Paris, who received a considerable income for his services to the exiled king and remembered his homeland generously over many years, especially in its times of crisis.

Under these circumstances it is perhaps not surprising to find the bishops and priests of the time giving disproportionate attention in their correspondence to the few gentlemen and men of property within the Church. The common people were usually too close to the edge of starvation to support them with anything other than goodwill.

The three great obstacles to recovery described above were internal matters, shortcomings that the Church itself could at least try to address. But to them we must add a fourth, an external obstacle, which Mr Leslie did not highlight in his report because it was too self-evident to require comment, and because it was a matter that both Rome and the Mission were at the time powerless to remove. This was the illegal standing of the Catholic Church in Britain. It was in fact *the* fundamental obstacle to the Church's recovery, greater than the others and indeed itself a main underlying cause of them.

The Illegal Status of the Church

The Acts of 1609 and 1625 preventing travel abroad were only two in a series of laws passed in the hundred years after the Reformation by successive Scottish Parliaments intent on severing the arteries of the Catholic Church. Following the Restoration of 1660, it is true, Scottish

Catholics were to some extent shielded from the force of this legislation during the reigns of Charles II and James II/VII, and according to Mr Leslie's report suffered "no noteworthy persecution" at this time. But James' attempt to shield them further by his Declaration of Indulgence in 1687 contributed to his downfall the following year, and the accession to the throne of William III, during whose reign the existing laws were enforced with renewed vigour and new and more effective ones were enacted. William's very first legislation for Scotland confirmed and extended the Acts of 1609 and 1625.[25] Eight years later he issued an Edict for the seizure and banishment of "all priests, Jesuits and trafficking papists", and in the fury that followed it perhaps as many as 10000 Catholics were driven or fled from Britain and Ireland, including hundreds from Scotland itself.

The prime targets of the Law were the clergy. Fourteen Scottish secular priests were imprisoned or banished in as many years after William's accession, a huge number for a small Mission, and several regulars were also jailed.[26] Priests were vulnerable at all times, but doubly so when undertaking certain essential duties – in particular celebrating the Mass, corresponding with fellow priests and bishops, and making journeys.

They always celebrated the Mass in the safety of private homes or outhouses whenever possible, their churches having been either confiscated or destroyed. But where none was to be had, or a large crowd was to be accommodated, they were forced to hold services in the open fields. The survival of several Mass stones in the Highlands dating from the Penal era, and the large number of local place names alluding to the outdoor celebration of Mass, bear witness to the custom.[27] But such occasions were all too visible, and the very opportunity that spies and informers might be waiting for.

Priests never sent letters by the public post, but entrusted them to the care of friends. And in case they might still be intercepted and arouse suspicion if bound for a 'Catholic' destination, they almost always carried false addresses. Those for delivery in Paris, for example, would be addressed to 'Amsterdam', while a 'Hamburg' or 'Constantinople' address indicated to those in the know that a letter was bound for Rome. Coded language was used in any correspondence that concerned 'trade' (that is, the work of the Mission): thus priests were referred to as 'labourers', the seminaries as 'shops', and their students as 'prentices'. Personal names were never used, but indicated by initials or aliases; so Bishop Nicolson was variously 'Mr Bell', 'Mr Nisbet', 'Mr Bruce', or 'Mr Beaton'; the Scots Agent William Leslie was 'Don Gulielmo' because he lived in Rome, and that city was 'Old Town' or 'Hill Town' when it was not 'Hamburg'. The Pope was 'Mr Cant'.

When a priest was at home he could usually count on the discreet silence of his neighbours of whatever faith, especially if – as was common Mission policy – his station was in the district where he himself had been born and raised. But whenever his work took him further afield he was at once at risk, a stranger on the road, and perhaps carrying in his saddle-bags the portable Mass kit that would betray his true identity. Vivid accounts have come down to us of the life of priests travelling incognito during the reign of William III, adopting one disguise after another, on the move only by night, hiding up by day in byres, or caves, or forests.[28]

So long as the laws stood and were enforced with vigour the art of survival for priests and people lay in bypassing them. And crucial to this, in the North and West, were the power and protection of the clan chiefs. At this time the Highland chiefs exercised a jurisdiction on their own lands which afforded some protection even against the national Law, so that on the estates of the great Catholic landowners – as Bishop Nicolson explained to Rome – the faithful enjoyed a certain freedom even in the worst of times.[29]

The bishop himself took refuge at Preshome on the estate of the Duke of Gordon after his release from prison, and in effect put himself under His Grace's protection, confident that his whereabouts would not be betrayed.[30] In the West there was similar safety on all the lands of Clanranald,[31] and on the estates of Chisholm in Strathglass,[32] Glengarry in Knoydart, Glengarry and North Morar,[33] and MacNeil on Barra.[34]

In 1700 the Scottish Parliament passed a new law, the 'Act for Preventing the Grouth of Popery',[35] which went beyond all previous legislation. It empowered the Lords of Privy Council to sentence any person proved or even suspected of being a priest, to banishment, and to death should he ever return "being still papist". It extended the same punishments even to lay persons attending Catholic services. It outlawed all instruction in the Faith, disqualifying Catholics from posts as chaplains, governors or teachers, and required that Catholic children be sent to Protestant relatives or teachers for their education. It barred Catholics from inheriting or even renting land or property. For the Church's enemies it offered the incentive of 500 Merks reward for information leading to conviction; for those convicted it offered one last chance of escaping sentence – to solemnly deny the doctrines of Rome in the presence of God.

The new Act promised to be more effective than any to date, in two respects particularly. Firstly, whereas previous legislation had particularly targeted the clergy, it extended its reach to the laity also. By the threat of disinheritance it aimed to frighten off the men of property, whom it saw as a key to the survival of Catholicism in Scotland. And in this it seems to have met with some immediate temporary success, for though conversions continued among the common people they pretty well dried up among the well-to-do who had most to lose.[36]

Secondly, it was new in that it targeted minors. By instructing that Catholic children be given a Protestant education away from home, and by disqualifying Catholics from all posts as teachers or governors, it sought to stifle the future of the Church by preventing the religious formation of its youth.

In both these aims the instinct of the lawmakers was unerring. For, as we have seen above, the Church itself recognised its wealthier, influential members as being a key to its present survival; and, as we shall see below, it viewed the education of the young as a crucial condition of its future growth.

The Education of Catholic Youth

Up to the time of the Reformation children's education had been in the hands of the Church. In many parishes there were 'little schools', more often than not set up to train young boys as choristers, and offering instruction in plainsong and chant, along with basic reading and arithmetic. After two years at such a school a boy might move on to one of the Grammar Schools that had been established in the centres of population, so named because they taught the Grammatica – Latin language and literature – mastery of which was a prerequisite for entry to University. Although these had originally been set up by the Church, many had already been handed over to the local burgh councils long before the Reformation. By the mid-sixteenth century there were at least forty Grammar Schools, ecclesiastical or civic, in Scotland.[37]

At the Reformation of 1560 the schools attached to the cathedrals and collegiate churches perished with them, but the Reformed Church took over the existing parish and burgh schools, and increased their number. The reformers' vision of a school in every parish in Scotland was enshrined in law as early as 1616, and many new schools were opened, though it would take a further two centuries for their ideal to be fully realised.

Meantime, education remained as firmly in the hands of the New Religion as it had previously been in the control of the Old. The parish schools continued to teach reading, writing and the (now Protestant) catechism. The burgh schools still provided a syllabus based on the Grammatica, again with Scripture and the Westminster catechism.[38] In parish and burgh schools alike enrolment was normally conditional upon weekly attendance at the Sunday service of the local church, where – in many cases – the pupils were publicly tested in religion in the presence of the congregation.[39]

Catholic children attending the schools were in no way exempt from these regulations, of course, which it was hoped might be a means of their conversion. And this presented Catholic parents with a dilemma. For them the choice was Protestant education, or no education.

To answer the problem the Church made some attempt to set up schools of its own in the second half of the seventeenth century, in defiance of the Law, in parts of the Highlands and Islands where it enjoyed some protection. The earliest was probably the school on Barra which the Vincentian Fr White opened in 1654, and another is recorded in Glengarry in the 1660s.[40] Alexander Leslie reported that there had been two Catholic schools at the time of his visitation, but that one of them had been "broken up" in 1680, leaving only one in the whole country, the former Glengarry school now re-sited on Barra. And this school was so poor that Catholic parents were reluctant to send their children to it. Leslie recognised the vital importance of good Catholic schools, and good Catholic private tutors, for the future of the Church. He blamed the Prefect of the Scottish Mission for failing to support them, with the result that many Catholic gentlemen chose to "send their children to the schools of the heretics, or maintain heretical masters in their homes".[41]

A few sought a solution abroad. The Scots College at Douai, though primarily a seminary, did accept lay boarders and probably also ran a preparatory class for younger boys.[42] And there were in addition a number of schools established by religious orders who had fled from England.[43] All of these offered an alternative for the handful of Scots parents wealthy enough to pay, and willing to defy the Law.

The best that others could hope for was that their children might receive instruction outside school hours to counter the teaching in the classroom, if they happened to live near to the home of a priest; or, if they lived beside one of the Catholic great houses, that they might join the children of the house to receive instruction from the resident chaplain there. But arrangements such as these again only touched a tiny minority.[44]

So it was that when Bishop Nicolson made his episcopal visitation at the turn of the century, he saw what Alexander Leslie had seen a generation before. Time and again he came upon families of the tacksman class who had chosen to send their sons to the local schools, only to see them "imbibe there not alone learning but heresy, which they then passed on to their friends and dependants". He tried to combat the trend by decreeing in the *Statuta* that parents permitting their children to be raised in heresy should do public penance and be deprived of the sacraments.[45] But it was an invidious choice he left them. And the Government Act of the same year, 1700, only made it the more so.

In practice, some parents must have managed to get round the problem, judging by several reports to be found in the records of local presbyteries of the Kirk about this time. In the Gordon lands of the North-East, for instance, the Synod of Moray was told that Catholic children in the parish schools were being kept out of prayers and catechism, despite all the efforts of inspectors. Sympathetic teachers were being prevailed upon to allow the practice. The Synod ordered it to be stopped forthwith, but apparently with little success for it was an order that had to be repeated more than once.[46]

For his part, Bishop Nicolson now faced fresh difficulties. The several new schools that had been opened since Alexander Leslie's report, he found, had already folded. It had proved impossible to keep them going, much less to open others, because of the army garrisons now stationed in many parts of the Highlands which prevented priests and teachers remaining long in any one place.[47]

At the turn of the century in fact, despite his efforts, there may still only have been two schools open in the whole country. One was the same school that Leslie had visited on Barra twenty years before. The other had been set up on Canna by George Panton only the previous year: its site was well chosen, for the island lay midway between the mainland and the outer isles, and Panton himself, a fluent Gaelic speaker, proved a first-rate teacher.[48]

As Thomas Innes explained in a latter of 1699 to his brother Lewis the Principal of the Scots College Paris, schools like these served two purposes: first and more generally, they offered an alternative education where the sons of gentlemen would be taught Catholic doctrine without being exposed to heresy; second and more particularly, it was to be hoped that they might prepare 'prentices' for the Mission's 'shops' abroad, who would in time return to serve as priests in their homeland.[49] But it was obvious that the second purpose could only apply in the case of a small minority of boys. There would be great advantage, he realised, in establishing some kind of "litel shop" in Scotland itself, which could concentrate specifically on training for the priesthood, and where every boy would have a serious intent to try his vocation.

This then was the condition of the Catholic Church in Scotland three hundred years ago – or at least those aspects of it that were relevant to the setting up of a seminary at home. To men of vision like Thomas Innes the need was already clear. It was time to make a start, and that same year he did so, opening his own "litel shop" in Scotland, the first of two which – though short-lived – would pave the way for Scalan.

NOTES

1. Report of Alexander Leslie, 4. 3. 1681, English version SM 2/9/3, SCA. *Congregatio de Propaganda Fide* – The Congregation for the Propagation of the Faith – was normally referred to as 'Propaganda', and is hereafter referred to as such in the present work.
2. If, as has been proposed by Darragh (Darragh J. 'The Catholic Population of Scotland Since the Year 1680', *IR*, vol. iv, no. 1, spring 1953), we multiply the number of communicants by a factor of 1.75 to give the *total* Catholic population, the figure would be close to 24 500. Though no firm statistical evidence is available it is generally accepted that the population of Scotland at this date stood at c. 1 000 000 – cf., eg., Pryde G. S. *Scotland From 1603 to the Present Day* (London and Edinburgh, 1962), pp. 77ff.; Donaldson G. *Scotland: the Shaping of a Nation* (1974; Nairn, 1993 ed.), p. 219.
3. Burt Capt. E. *Letters From a Gentleman in the North of Scotland* (London, 1754; reprinted Edinburgh, 1974), vol. I, pp. 83f.; vol. II, p. 87. Burt was writing of the 1730s.
4. For the extent of Gaelic at this time see Withers C. W. J. *Gaelic in Scotland 1698–1981* (Edinburgh, 1984), p. 47, map fig. 7 'The Gaidhealtachd in 1698'.
5. The description is from Macky J. *A Tour Through Great Britain* (London, 1723), vol. III, p. 127. Though writing more than 40 years after Mr Leslie, Macky was one of the earliest of the gentlemen tourists into the Highlands. Like the others he thought of himself as an explorer. Unlike Mr Leslie these men only saw a fraction of the country, and very little of the islands, since they never strayed far from the few well recognised mainland through-routes. As early as the 1690s Martin Martin made a much more thorough tour, which he wrote up into his *A Description of the Western Islands of Scotland*, but he was himself a Gaelic-speaking Highlander.
6. Mr Leslie estimated that 12000 of the 14000 communicants were from the Highlands and Islands.
7. Itinerary of Alexander Leslie, 1677-78, English version SM 2/9/1, p. 7, SCA.
8. The headquarters of the Kirk seemed only vaguely aware of some of these districts: cf., eg., *Lists of Popish Parents and their Children in Various Districts of Scotland as Given to the Lords of the Privy Council and to the Commission of the General Assembly MDCCI – MDCCV*, p. 42, where the authors describe Moidart, Arisaig, Morar and Knoydart as islands!
9. Cf., McHugh M. 'Kirk, State and the Catholic Problem in the Western Highlands and Islands of Scotland 1690–1760', unpublished M. Litt. thesis, Univ. Strathclyde, 1982, pp. 8ff.
10. Giblin C. (ed.) *Irish Franciscan Mission to Scotland 1619–1646: Documents from Roman Archives* (Dublin, 1964), pp. 120-64, and espec. section 47, evidence of Fr Cornelius Ward, and section 48, report of Fr Patrick Hegarty, 1633, pp. 147ff.
11. Fr Charles Farquharson MS, SCA. Re this MS and the re-establishment of

Catholicism in the area, see MacWilliam A. 'The Jesuit Mission in Upper Deeside 1671–1737', *IR*, vol. xxiii, 1972.

12. Report of Alexander Leslie, p. 2.

13. For a readily accessible account of his life and career, see Doran W. 'Bishop Thomas Nicolson, First Vicar-Apostolic 1695–1718', *IR*, vol. xxxix, no. 2, autumn 1988.

14. He went so far as to instruct that no more Irish priests were to be allowed to work in the country – Walter Innes to Lewis Innes, 25. 5. 1699, BL, relaying an instruction from Bishop Nicolson.

15. Bishop Nicolson Report to Propaganda, 1700, SM 3/1, SCA; and 'Statuta Missionis', 1700, SM 3/2/1, SCA (both in Latin). Re Pro-vicars, Procurators etc., Thomas Innes to William Leslie, 13. 10. 1701, BL.

16. Re Rome, see Abbé Paul McPherson 'The History of the Scots College, Rome (1600–1792)', MS, 1810, CA 3/18, SCA, also printed under same title in Anderson W. J. (ed.), *IR*, vol. xii, 1961; and Brown W. E. et al. *The Scots College Rome* (London and Edinburgh, 1930). Re Madrid, see Taylor M. *The Scots College in Spain* (Valladolid, 1971); and McGoldrick W. 'The Scots College Madrid', *IR*, vol. iv, no. 2, autumn 1953. The Paris College was originally founded at Grisy-Suines in 1326; a second house was established in 1603, and the two were united in 1639 – cf., Halloran B. M. *The Scots College Paris 1603–1792* (Edinburgh, 1997), pp. 1-5. For a useful summary of all the Colleges, see Johnson C. *Developments in the Roman Catholic Church in Scotland 1789-1829* (Edinburgh, 1983), pp. 48ff.

17. New Statutes drawn up in 1707 attempted to confine admission to students for whom there was a hope of a religious vocation, but they were not adhered to and lay students continued to be admitted, not least for the fees they brought in: cf., Halloran B. M. *Op. cit.*, p. 6. Halloran calculated that over the years lay students outnumbered seminarians by about 5:3.

18. Re the Madrid inspection (1674) and report, see McGoldrick W. *Op. cit.*, p. 103; re the Rome inspection (1693) and report, see Abbé Paul McPherson *Op. cit.*, pp. 141-151 (MS)/ pp. 58ff.(Anderson ed.) At Madrid the inspectors found not a single student enrolled; at Rome they were highly critical of the curriculum, spirituality, economy and discipline.

19. Bishop Nicolson Report to Propaganda 1697, printed in Bellesheim A. *History of the Catholic Church of Scotland* (London and Edinburgh, 1890), vol. IV, Appendix VI.

20. 'Anent nobilmen who sendis thair sones oute of the cuntrie', 1609, Acta Parliamentorum Jacobi VI, *APS*, vol. IV, p. 406; and 'Ane Act anent the childrene of noble men and otheris remaning in seminaryis of popishe religioun beyond sea' etc., 1625, Acta Parliamentorum Caroli I, *APS*, vol. V, p. 177.

21. In the mid-18C Mr John Geddes took four months to reach Rome, and longer on the return journey – cf., his account in Anderson W. J. 'The Autobiographical Notes of Bishop John Geddes', *IR*, vol. xviii, no. 1, spring 1967, pp. 41f. and 43f.

22. Giblin C. (ed.) *Op. cit.*, p. xiv.

23. Cf., eg., Thomas Innes to William Leslie, 13. 10. 1701, BL; and Report of Bishops Gordon and Wallace to Propaganda, 4. 7. 1730 (in Latin), BL.

24. Hay M. 'Too Little and Too Late', *IR*, vol. vi, no. 1, spring 1953. Re the 18C specifically, Macmillan J. F. ' "The Root of All Evil"? Money and the Scottish Catholic Mission in the Eighteenth Century', *Studs. in Church Hist.*, vol. 24, 1987.

25. 'Declaration of the Estates of the Kingdom of Scotland', etc., 11. 4. 1689, Acta Parliamentorum Gulielmi et Mariae, *APS*, vol. IX, p. 39.

26. See Dilworth M. 'The Scottish Mission in 1688–1689', *IR*, vol. xx, 1968.

27. Re Mass stones, MacDonell A. and McRoberts D. 'The Mass Stones of Lochaber', *IR*, vol. xix, 1966.

28. Eg., Report of Fr John Innes, SJ, Stoneyhurst MS, printed in Forbes-Leith W. *Memoirs of Scottish Catholics during the XVIIth and XVIIIth Centuries* (London, 1909), vol. II, pp. 195f. Re placing of priests, see, eg., Stewart J. A. 'The Clan Ranald and Catholic Missionary Successes, 1715-1745', *IR*, vol. xlv, no. 1, spring 1994; and examples in Blundell O. *The Catholic Highlands of Scotland* (Edinburgh, 1909), vol. 1, p. 83.

29. Bishop Nicolson Report to Propaganda, 1697, printed *loc. cit.*

30. Bishop Nicolson to Duke of Gordon, n.d., GD 44/43/332/12, SRO.

31. Bishop Nicolson Report to Propaganda, 1697. He considered Allan, the current chief, to have done more than any other man to bring the Highlands and Islands back to the Faith.

32. Chisholm had been converted to Catholicism about thirty years before: cf., MacWilliam A. 'A Highland Mission: Strathglass 1671–1777', *IR*, vol. xxiv, 1973.

33. Glengarry was also converted in the mid-17C, according to a 1652 letter from Fr Dermot Dugan to Vincent de Paul, quoted with many other details in Blundell O. 'St Vincent of Paul and the Highlands of Scotland', *Dublin Review*, cxlix, 1911.

34. When Bishop Nicolson visited Barra in 1700 he noted that the aged chief MacNeil not only protected his people but instructed them in the faith – Bishop Nicolson Report to Propaganda, 1700, SM 3/1 (in Latin), SCA. The power of the landlord could be equally effective *against* the Church, as in the case of Rum. The island was 100% Catholic when Mr Leslie visited it, but half a century later the male inhabitants were coerced into embracing Protestantism by their landlord MacLean of Coll, and the rest of the island soon followed. The Kirk saw MacLean's "prudent endeavours" as a model for the conversion of other areas of the Highlands and Islands where Catholic tenants lived under Protestant landlords – cf., Register of the Actings and Proceedings of the Committee of the General Assembly of the Church of Scotland for Reformation of the Highlands and Islands of Scotland, And for managment of the King's Bounty for that end, Annis 1725-1729, 'Memorial Concerning the Growth of Popery' presented to meeting of 10. 5. 1726, and approved; CH 1/5/51, p. 79, SRO.

35. 'Act for Preventing the Grouth of Popery', 1700, Acta Parliamentorum Gulielmi, *APS*, vol. X, pp. 215ff.

36. Thomas Innes to Cardinal Barberini, 13. 10. 1701, BL.

37. Durkan J. 'Education in the Century of the Reformation', *IR*, vol. x, no. 1, spring 1959 (also printed as chap. 6 of McRoberts D. (ed.) *Essays on the Scottish Reformation 1513–1625* (Glasgow, 1962); and Dealy M. B. *Catho-*

lic Schools in Scotland (published PhD thesis, Washington, 1945), chap. 1. The Grammar schools charged a fee plus seasonal collections, but these were often waived in the case of poor scholars.

38. Grant J. *History of the Burgh Schools of Scotland* (London and Glasgow, 1876), espec. pp. 332ff. Any other subjects such as Geography or Science were incidental, and derived merely from what the Roman authors had written on these themes. By the late 17C some schools had begun to teach basic Arithmetic.

39. Eg., at Aberdeen G.S., Simpson H. F. M. (ed.) *Bon Record – Records and Reminiscences of Aberdeen Grammar School* (Aberdeen, 1906), chap. 6; and at Edinburgh, Steven M. W. *History of the Royal High School of Edinburgh* (Edinburgh, 1849), p. 69.

40. Fr White to Propaganda, 1665, quoted in Blundell O. 'St Vincent of Paul and the Highlands of Scotland', *Loc. cit.*

41. Alexander Leslie Report, pp. 19 and 29.

42. Hay M. V. *The Blairs Papers (1603–1660)* (London and Edinburgh, 1929), pp. 52ff.

43. Notably, St Gregory's Douai (Benedictine), opened 1618; Bornhem (Dominican), opened 1673; St Omer's nr. Calais (Jesuit), opened 1592; the English College Douai, originally opened as a seminary 1579, and re-opened as a lay school 1593. Cf., Barnes A. S. *The Catholic Schools of England* (London, 1926), passim.

44. Examples included John Wallace (the future bishop), who tutored the children of the Duke of Perth; and John Irving, who was tutor to the son of the Earl of Traquair until 1672, when the Privy Council ordered that the boy be taken from home and put in the care of a Protestant tutor.

45. Bishop Nicolson Report to Propaganda, 1700, section 16; and 'Statuta Missionis', 1700, section 6.

46. Synod of Moray Records of Meetings, meeting of 31. 10. 1704, with further instructions at meetings of 26. 5. 1708, 1. 6. 1709 and 10. 5. 1710, CH 2/271/IV, pp. 48, 199, 224 and 263 respectively, SRO. Some but not all of the references to the Synod records in the present work are more easily accessible in published form in Crammond W. *Extracts from the Records of the Synod of Moray* (Elgin, 1906).

47. Bishop Nicolson Report to Propaganda, 1697.

48. Thomas Innes to Lewis Innes, 9. 8. 1698, BL.

49. Ibid.

2

The Road to Scalan 2: Of Litel Shops and Prentices (1699–1716)

Thomas Innes had returned to Scotland from the Scots College Paris in 1698. His work in France had convinced him that his talent lay in teaching, and before returning to the Mission he had told the Scots Agent William Leslie of his "inclination above all other things" to train young people of the Highlands for the priesthood. His hope was to prepare them for the Colleges abroad, or even if possible to give them their entire training at home:

> I am and always have been of that mind . . . that for our highlands the surest way & most canonicall & naturall to establish the Religion among them is to educate these on the place & instruct & form Church men without ever bringing them abroad from their own hardships, to feel the ease & (in regard of the poor & hard life they lead at home I may say) the delicacies of our Colledges abroad.[1]

He arrived at Glenlivet in Upper Banffshire at the height of the worst Highland famine in memory. At least two thirds of his flock had been wiped out, and the rest were on the brink of starvation.[2] When he wrote to his brother Lewis the following summer the destitution throughout the whole country was such that it was quite out of the question to send any students abroad in the meantime.[3] Because of this he had opened a "shop" himself in Glenlivet, to which he hoped to bring "some of the most hopefull of them". As yet he had only one or two boys, but with money that his brother had sent him he hoped to expand that autumn. "Prentices" were already gathering, and others were "ready to come on a call from farr off". Glenlivet was well placed for both Highlands and Lowlands, and Lowland boys could learn Gaelic there, both from their fellow students and from the local community.[4]

He knew the risk he was running and the danger of house raids,[5] and was therefore doubly careful to keep a low profile and hide his association with the little seminary: "Underhand Campbel [Thomas Innes himself] directs all, above board it has a face to please the worst sett of the times at least not to irritate them", he wrote.[6] He believed that if he could only shelter it from the public gaze and keep it open, it might in time "be something more than [had] yet been done of the kind here & not much inferiour to some abroad". Perhaps, if developed, it could eventually meet all the Mission's requirements for seminary training, and solve all the shortcomings of the existing system. His only other fear was that he himself would be called away:

> if he be removed it immediately sinks & with it all hopes of doing any thing worth the while here of a long time. for the truth is the rest of our people have not their genious that way, not haveing been bred to it.[7]

He hoped to spend the rest of his life in Glenlivet, where he was content "in his hills on his butter and cheeses". But much against his will he was recalled to Paris in 1701, and his embryo seminary closed.[8]

There were now three Catholic lay schools in the Highlands. The school on Barra was still open, though it only taught English, and must have been on a par with a typical parish school. George Panton's school on Canna now had a roll of thirty, and was teaching the Grammatica. And its success had prompted the priest of South Uist to open a similar school on that island earlier in the year, with an experienced master brought from Ireland.

But there was no guarantee that they would last. That summer George Panton had to move his school from Canna to Arisaig, partly perhaps because of his own poor health. He must have taken most of his pupils with him, for his new school was described as having "above thirty schollars off the best Gentlemens children of the highlands".[9] But it was not long opened when the priest of Arisaig was arrested, imprisoned and transported, and Panton was forced to close up again, this time for good.

Such schools were all too obviously at the mercy of circumstance. And in any case they were no real substitute for the kind of seminary that Thomas Innes had been developing. His success, though shortlived, had shown what could be done. When Mr James Gordon wrote to Propaganda on behalf of the bishop in 1703, giving a detailed account of all the issues relating to the Mission, he again put the case for having a seminary in Scotland.[10] Nothing could be "more useful or more to be wished", he argued. Quite apart from the failings of the existing Colleges, young men trained at home would not be exposed to temptation as were those trained abroad; they would be more committed to the Mission; and they would be "less obnoxious" to the Protestant authorities, since the Penal laws were aimed primarily at priests trained in foreign countries, on the grounds that they might have learned there sentiments disloyal to their own.

In 1702 Mr Gordon had been sent to Rome to assist the Scots Agent. In his four years there he saw at first hand the shortcomings of the Scots College. It had declined still further at this date, being now under the control of Italian Rectors who had little understanding of the Scottish language and character or the needs of the Scottish Mission. In the year before he left he wrote officially to the Society of Jesus describing the College as a nuisance, a reproach and a scandal to the nation, and threatening to appeal to the Pope himself to have it taken out of the Society's hands.[11] His experience could only have made him more convinced of the need to establish a permanent seminary at home.

In 1706 he returned to the Mission as Co-adjutor Bishop, with particular responsibility for the Highlands and Islands. The word from the Scots College Paris that year gave him further cause for concern. Not only had standards fallen badly in the long-term absence of the Principal, Lewis Innes; the house had now slipped into debt through mismanagement, news that distressed but did not greatly surprise him.[12]

The following year he made his first episcopal visitation to the West, where the penury of the people and their priests made a deep impression on him. He saw how demoralised the priests were. Many were "wedded to their own judgment, posts or conveniency", and unwilling to obey instructions. Even the Administrators hand-picked by Bishop Nicolson he found "so opinionate" that he could barely either guide them individually or get them to agree among themselves.[13] Again, these experiences, at home and abroad, only added to his conviction that the Mission needed its own seminary, where it could train priests from their youth, under close supervision and according to its own needs and principles.

His journey took him through Morar, where he made an over-night stay in the house on Eilean Bàn, one of the little islands in the loch, as Bishop Nicolson had done before him.[14] Perhaps in his mind he earmarked it then as an ideal site for a seminary, should the day come when one could be set up. That day was not yet, for though Lewis Innes offered him a grant to finance the training of students he could not find a single priest on the Mission with the qualities needed to take charge of them.[15] But he did not abandon the idea, and continued to discuss it with the Paris Principal.

He was in fact beginning to think of living permanently in the West himself. With Bishop Nicolson's blessing he stayed there for seven months in the winter of 1710-11, in order to learn the Highlanders' ways and at least something of their language, and found that the mountains greatly suited his health. He confessed to the Scots Agent that he longed to shut himself up forever among them, and to serve the poor people there, and even asked that Rome might send a second assistant for Bishop Nicolson, in order to free him to do so.[16]

Early in 1712 he wrote again to Lewis Innes, to tell him that he believed the time for a seminary had now arrived, and that he hoped to prepare the ground during his visitation to the Western Highlands that summer. The Paris Principal at once sent him a handsome donation, which arrived shortly before he set out.[17] On his return in July he was able to report that he had "taken measures about beginning the nursery", which was now dependent only upon his finding a suitable priest to run it. He urged that the Innes' nephew George could be sent home to fill the post. He had recently been ordained after fourteen years at the Scots College, and seemed more suitable than anyone available in Scotland:

> all cry to get <u>M. Geo</u>: M. Debrie's [Lewis Innes'] nevew home after so long time spent in shop, & I am persuaded none we can get will be so fitt <u>to direct</u> the dessignd Sem^y, for the Western tongue [Gaelic] is not nec^y, & he seems to have all the other qualifications much better than any we can pitch on.[18]

George Innes sailed to England at the end of the summer, and after an overland journey from Newcastle reached Bishop Gordon's home at Glastirim in October. But the bishop was shocked when he saw him: the journey up had "disordered him to a pitch could hardly be imagined", and he wondered how he would ever cope with the hardships of the Highlands.[19] It was in any case too late in the year to do anything further meantime.

The following March found the young priest still "very ill of a shortness of breath" and at his parents' home at Balnacraig trying to recover his health. But despite the setback the bishop was determined to pursue his plans. "I am going in a few days to begin my Western journy", he told Lewis Innes,

> and when there will use all possible means to bring that good dessign (towards which your generous charity & zeal has so farr extended itself) to something, & am resolv'd by the help of God to dispose things so that I may spend the most of my time in it.[20]

He clearly had it in mind to make Eilean Bàn his main, if not his permanent home. It would suit his own desires, and perhaps better serve the needs of the Church, so many of whose members were in the West. But his thinking also reflects the high priority he gave to the seminary, his recognition of its need for effective supervision and support, and his difficulty in finding a suitable man to take sole charge. He was not at all sure that George Innes was up to the task, or whether he would be able to come. If not, he hoped to persuade Gregory Farquharson to take up the post as a stand-in. Farquharson was a layman, but he had spent some time at the Scots College in Paris and had some experience as a tutor.[21]

* * *

But the autumn came, with Farquharson still undecided, George Innes' health still not improved, and nothing done. Bishop Gordon felt that time was being wasted, and that he could no longer wait for others. "If I could get that length", he wrote to Thomas Innes, "I would strive still to be doing something in it one way or other & not lose time; for my life is passing off, & 'twill be long ere any fruits can be expected thence however diligent we be."[22] He made up his mind to make a start himself come the spring, alone if need be.

In March 1714 he set out for the West, probably reaching Eilean Bàn about the end of the month. He took occupation of the house there, and brought his first students in.

He only stayed three months, enough time to put the seminary on a firm footing. George Innes was now much improved in health, and by the summer he was ready to take over. He left Balnacraig near the end of June, about the same time that the bishop was setting out for the East, and arrived at the island early in July.[23]

We have little firm information about the seminary on Eilean Bàn. We know that the house itself dated from the late seventeenth century. The aged priest Mr James Cahassy had lived in it until his death in 1704, and it had also been used by Bishop Nicolson during his visit in 1700, and several times by Bishop Gordon, before he opened it as a seminary.

Today the island is thickly overgrown, but remains of the stone base of a building are still just visible on it, of a kind that suggests that the house was turf-built. Such a house would have had a frame of crucks, roof cabers, and possibly an interior dividing wall of wattle. According to the building habits of the day it would have been adapted, as required, for each successive use, and re-roofed from time to time.[24] The remains that survive today would in that case be the founds of the original late-seventeenth century building used by the seminary in 1714.[25]

Whatever the curriculum at Eilean Bàn we can be sure that it was based upon "true, solid and zealous piety" and the "knowledge of things not nice, sublime and speculative, but practical, popular, and edifying", for these were Bishop Gordon's stated priorities. The language of instruction would necessarily have been English, because George Innes did not speak Gaelic and nor, perhaps, did several of the boys. But those students who had the language were actively encouraged to keep it up.[26]

There were seven students in the first year. Not all their names are recorded, but two of them at least were MacDonalds, sixteen year old Allan from Stoneybridge in South Uist; and Hugh, a year younger and a son of the Laird of Morar, who had been raised almost within sight of the island. A third boy was John MacLachlan, and like Allan he had arrived with a good level of education. Already by the first autumn the bishop had plans to send the two of them to Paris, but in fact early in 1715 he received a request from Rome for two students and agreed, with some reluctance, to let the boys go there.[27] They were Eilean Bàn's first and only graduates to the Colleges abroad.

With the seminary only in its infancy at this date, boys were still occasionally also being sent to the Colleges direct from the Highland schools or (especially in the Lowlands where such schools were out of the question) from lay tutors.[28] The schools on Barra and South Uist were still open.[29] And we know from a Church of Scotland report that the priests of Glenlivet and Strathavon in the Eastern Highlands had recently established schools in their areas and brought in women to teach in them.[30]

The Glenlivet priest whom the Kirk singled out for particular mention was Mr John Gordon of Cairnborrow. His was the one name identified by the local presbytery in October 1714 among the "traffiquing priests" whom they believed responsible for recent defections to Catholicism in the area.[31] They were authorised by their synod to do whatever they could to remove him.

The Kirk was by now in fact growing ever more alarmed at the activity of the Scottish Catholics. Only the previous year the General Assembly had thought it necessary to publish *A Seasonable Warning Concerning the Dangers of Popery,* one of a rash of pamphlets printed officially or privately at this time which pointed to the supposedly growing menace.[32]

If these publications appeared almost hysterical in regard to any real religious threat posed by Catholicism, in terms of its political threat to Crown and Government they were in fact accurate. The Church's links with the Jacobite Court in Exile at Saint Germains were well known. The Scots College in Paris was fervently Jacobite. Its long-serving Principal, Lewis Innes, had been a member of James' Cabinet for more than twenty years, and in 1714 was appointed his Lord Almoner.[33] And at home that autumn Bishop Gordon himself was writing remarkable coded messages to Paris, expressing his hopes for an early Rising.[34]

A year later, when the Rising began, nearly all the Catholic gentlemen in Scotland, particularly in the Western Highlands and the North-East, the bishops, and the bulk of the priests and the laity supported it, and many took up the sword.[35]

Mr John Gordon of Cairnborrow, the priest of Glenlivet, remained active in his community throughout the '15, and even towards the end he was still openly supporting the rebels.[36] But after their defeat he was no longer safe on his farm at Minmore at the lower end of the glen, where he had a

number of Hanoverian neighbours. About Easter, 1716, he left his home
and moved up to the head of the Braes of Glenlivet, where – according to
Bishop Geddes' account – he "staid commonly in a barn which was on the
Southwest corner of the Tom [Hill] of Scalan."[37] This afforded him a few
weeks' respite, while he looked around for a suitable place to build a
house of his own. He approached the local tacksman, Grant of Tomnavoulin, who gave him permission to build on a shelf of ground at the foot
of the hill beside the west bank of the Crombie burn. The precise location
of his house is not known for certain, but received tradition has it close to
a natural spring in the river bank (Plate 1). The site was exactly what he
needed, in a hollow of the land and largely hidden from view.

In June Bishop Gordon got a letter out to Paris with news of the
hardships the Catholics were now suffering.[38] Several members of his
own family were under house arrest. Bishop Nicolson, who was now over
seventy and a sick man, had been arrested and imprisoned; his release had
only been effected with difficulty, and it was still not safe for him to stay
in his own house. Most of the priests in the North were "constantly
threaten'd & sought after" and had left home. Many were broken in
health through sleeping rough in the hills. Some were even talking of
abandoning the Mission. In all, times were very hard "for any kind of
trade". His letter continued with news from the Western Highlands,
where George Innes was still managing to keep the seminary open on
Eilean Bàn:

> I can't get to West, thogh Long extreamly, that country is allmost
> desperate & will probably do something very odd; & my friends can
> hardly have access to me or I to them, the ways are so unsafe; nev. Geo:
> is pretty well, but has not been able to do much for the stirr of folks
> about him, yet the shope is kept in some manner, at least some of the
> prentices together; & I make Greg^y do nearer hand what I can with
> some few.

'Greg^y' was Gregory Farquharson, whom he had tried to persuade to
become the master at Eilean Bàn three years before. He was now teaching
at the public school at Huntly, and he may well have enrolled the students
there. The school was close beside the former seat of the Gordons, and
with the Duke's influence it would have been quite possible to enrol
Catholic boys, excuse them from Protestant prayers and Catechism, and
even give them instruction in their own faith.[39] He probably also gave
them extra tuition outside school hours, and may well have lodged them
at his own home. But the arrangement was at best a stop-gap.

Bishop Gordon also knew that the seminary on Eilean Bàn could not be
kept open indefinitely, because it lay too close to the coast and was
vulnerable to surprise attack from the sea. Since the defeat he had been

MAP 2
Glenlivet and the Braes of Glenlivet
with the place-names mentioned in the text

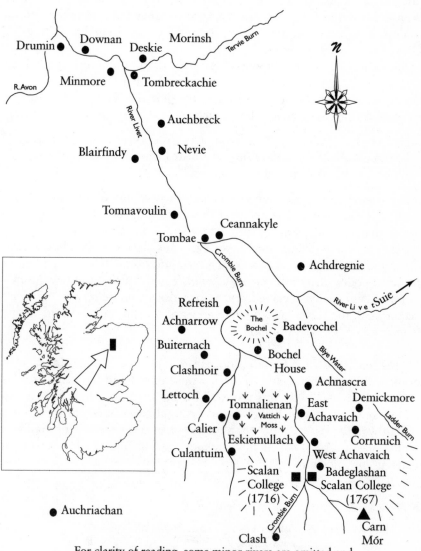

For clarity of reading, some minor rivers are omitted and
only those hills mentioned in the text are marked.

Note:

looking out for a suitable place to re-locate it, and now with the summer well advanced there was some urgency for him to do so: not only were master and boys living with daily danger, but to move house with all their possessions would be impossible once the bad weather set in.

Mr John Gordon's turf house at the foot of the *Tom* of Scalan was as safe and suitable a place as he was likely to find meantime. It must have been at his request that the priest agreed to move out and take over the station at Mortlach near Huntly, leaving his new-built house free for George Innes and his boys.

We do not know exactly when they arrived, but they were certainly in and settled by the early autumn, because in October the bishop was able to tell Rome about the new location, now not in the West but the North – "You will think it strange," he wrote,

> that M. Fife [himself], that is so harrass'd, keeps still in a more convenient place the shop you have heard of in the West, & reservs still in it some very hopefull prentices.[40]

His guarded words did not reveal the whereabouts of this more convenient place, for fear that his letter should be intercepted, but there is no doubt that he was referring to the new site at the Scalan.

From this letter, and others, we can thus date the founding of the College of Scalan with certainty to 1716, and not 1717 as is implied in Bishop Geddes' *Brief Historical Account*,[41] and which – following him – is the date usually accepted, even in serious and otherwise accurate accounts:[42] the date, indeed, that appears on the notice board at the front gate of the restored College today.

On the road that led to Scalan three names stand out: Thomas Innes, who pointed the way; his brother Lewis, whose moral and financial support made progress possible; and above all Bishop Gordon, whose persistence and dogged pursuit of his goal had brought the Church to this point. Scalan was *his* vision, more than anyone's; and for the rest of his life it would play a central rôle in his plans for the Mission, and hold a special place in his affections.

NOTES

1. Thomas Innes to William Leslie, 27. 1. 1698, BL.
2. Thomas Innes to Lewis Innes, 27. 3. 1699 and 9. 5. 1699, BL.
3. Thomas Innes to Lewis Innes, 15. 7. 1699, BL.
4. Thomas Innes to Lewis Innes, 15. 10. 1699, BL.
5. It was about this time that his house was raided, and though he himself escaped by leaping through a window, all his research papers – the fruit of

ten years' work – were seized and burned: McLaren R. 'Father Thomas Innes: Lost Papers', *IR*, vol. v, no. 1, spring 1954, quoting Thomas Hearn's *Reliquiae Hearnaniae*, vol. ii, diary entry for 26. 2. 1721.

6. Thomas Innes to Lewis Innes, 15. 10. 1699, BL.
7. Ibid.
8. Thomas Innes to William Leslie, 13. 10. 1701, BL.
9. Ibid.; and Thomas Innes to Lewis Innes, 11. 3. 1701, BL. There even seemed to be a possibility that he would be appointed to oversee the schools in the Highlands and Islands, to bring some coherent overall plan to Catholic education.
10. James Gordon 'Narratio', 1703 (in Latin), SM 3/8, SCA, espec. section 25.
11. Abbé Paul McPherson 'History of the Scots College Rome (1600–1792)', 1810, CA 3/18, SCA (also printed under same title in Anderson W. J. (ed.), *IR*, vol. xii, 1961, pp. 102ff).
12. Bishop Nicolson to Thomas Innes, 5. 5. 1707, BL. The following year new Statutes were drawn up for the College in an attempt to right its ills.
13. Bishop Gordon to Lewis Innes, 12. 10. 1707, BL; and to Thomas Innes, 20. 11. 1707, BL.
14. Bishop Gordon 'Diary' (in Latin), SM 3/9/1, SCA; and 'Itinerary', SM 3/9/2, SCA.
15. Bishop Gordon to Thomas Innes, 20. 11. 1707, BL.
16. Bishop Gordon to William Stuart, 19. 6. 1711, BL.
17. Bishop Gordon to Lewis Innes, 15. 4. 1712, BL.
18. Bishop Gordon to Lewis Innes, 23. 7. 1712, BL.
19. Bishop Gordon to Lewis Innes, 9. 10. 1712, BL.
20. Bishop Gordon to Lewis Innes, 23. 3. 1713, BL.
21. Bishop Gordon to Thomas Innes, 1. 7. 1713 and 4. 7. 1713, BL.
22. Bishop Gordon to Thomas Innes, 17. 10. 1713, BL.
23. Bishop Gordon to Thomas Innes, 13. 8. 1714, BL.
24. Cf., eg., Fenton A. and Walker B. *The Rural Architecture of Scotland* (Edinburgh, 1981), pp. 44ff. and 59ff.
25. The remains of an earthen dyke are also visible. This apparently enclosed a garden, but is more likely to date from the 1730s when the site was again used for a seminary.
26. Bishop Gordon to William Stuart, 8. 12. 1713, BL.
27. Bishop Gordon to Thomas Innes, 7. 9. 1714, BL; and to William Stuart, 9. 2. 1715, BL. Bishop Gordon was reluctant to send them to Rome, fearing that the Jesuits "would have interest to draw them over to them selves", and he particularly asked the Scots Agent to guard against this and take the boys under his care.
28. Bishops Nicolson and Gordon to Propaganda, 12. 12. 1711, BL, copy of a similarly worded letter cited in Blundell O. 'Bishop James Gordon and the Highlands of Scotland', *Dublin Review*, vol. clix, 1916, p. 143.
29. Re the Barra school, which had been "establish'd of new" during Bishop Gordon's visit in 1707, Bishop Gordon to Lewis Innes, 12. 10. 1707, BL; re the Uist school, George Gordon to Cardinal Sacripanti, 28. 8. 1714, BL.
30. Church of Scotland Report, 29. 5. 1714, MS 976, p. 143, NLS.

31. Synod of Moray Records of Meetings, meetings of 28. 10. 1714 and 20. 4. 1715, CH 2/271/VI, p. 14, SRO.

32. *A Seasonable Warning by the Commission of the General Assembly Concerning the Danger of Popery* (Edinburgh, 19. 8. 1713) – copy SM 3/25/2, SCA. Cf. also, eg., *Popery Reviving* (printed by John Moncour, Edinburgh, 1714).

33. Ruvigny and Raineval, Marquis of, (ed.) *The Jacobite Peerage, Baronetage, Knightage and Grants of Honour* (Edinburgh, 1904), p. 224. Lewis Innes was appointed on 17 March. He had been made 'Secretary of State for Scotland' in 1689 (*Ibid.*, p. 214), and Almoner to the Queen in 1697 (*Ibid.*, p. 217). The issue of the Scots College Paris and the Jacobite cause is covered in detail in Halloran B. M. *The Scots College Paris 1603–1792* (Edinburgh, 1997), chap. 6

34. Bishop Gordon to Thomas Innes, 7. 9. 1714, BL.

35. Re the North-East, Tayler A. and Tayler H. *Jacobites of Aberdeenshire and Banffshire in the Rising of 1715* (Edinburgh and London, 1934), passim, espec. pp. 214ff.

36. Synod of Moray Records of Meetings, meeting of 24. 4. 1716, CH 2/271/VI, SRO.

37. Bishop Geddes 'A Brief Historical Account of the Seminary at Scalan', 1777, CS 1/3, para. 5, SCA. His reference to a barn suggests that some land nearby was cultivated, but this seems unlikely. The building no longer existed when he was writing, and he must have been going on word-of-mouth. In view of the use of the Hill of Scalan in 1716 (cf. p. 36) the building is surely more likely to have been a shieling hut. If so, it would have been 'available' until the shieling season started in early June.

38. Bishop Gordon to Thomas Innes, 1. 6. 1716, BL.

39. Re Farquharson, and George Panton at the public school at Fochabers, see Synod of Moray Records of Meetings, meetings of 24. 4. 1716, 16. 4. 1717 and 18. 4. 1717, CH 2/271/VI, pp. 49f.; and previous report re both men, meeting of 1. 6. 1709, CH /271/IV, p. 224, SRO.

40. Bishop Gordon to William Stuart, 22. 10. 1716, BL.

41. Bishop Geddes 'Brief Historical Account', para. 6. He does not in fact explicitly state an opening date, merely that students attended in 1717.

42. Eg., MacWilliam A. ('Glenlivetensis') 'Scalan 1717–1799', *Claves Regni (St Peter's College Magazine)*, vol. xvii, nos. 67 and 68, Dec. 1946 and June 1947; Blundell O. *The Catholic Highlands of Scotland*, vol. 1 (Edinburgh, 1909). On the other hand Johnson C. *Developments in the Roman Catholic Church in Scotland 1789–1829* (Edinburgh, 1983) has 1716.

3

The Scalan in the Braes

Where, and what, was this place Scalan to which they had now come?

From time immemorial Banffshire had been divided, in men's minds, into two parts, Lower and Upper, Lowland and Highland. It was a division not of topography alone but of a whole way of life – of the kind and seasons of agriculture, of customs, of language, and even of race.[1] The rivers of Banffshire flowed north, and from them the people took their bearings: they looked northwards to the Low Country, and southwards to the Highlands.

Scalan lay in the parish of Inveravon, one of the two most southerly and most completely upland and Gaelic-speaking in this county of two halves. And Inveravon was itself a parish of two halves. The lower part, which began as its name suggests where the river Avon flows into the Spey, was land that belonged to the Protestant and Hanoverian family, the Grants of Ballindalloch. The upper half, which began at the confluence of the Avon and Livet and followed the latter and its tributaries, lay within the estates of the Duke of Gordon, and was considered by the Kirk as something of an adjunct. A contemporary Synod report typically referred to "the upper End of the paroch" as a separate district, eight miles from church and school and "abounding in popery".[2] In 1713 the Synod had erected a meeting house at Drumin, and put in an assistant minister to serve Glenlivet, but he and his successors only had licensed status and rarely stayed long. Not for another century-and-a-half would it be made a parish in its own right.[3]

But even Glenlivet was divided into two halves, because the lower glen and the Braes were very distinct communities, separated by the dome-like hill of the Bochel – 'the Shepherd' – which filled the middle of the valley, guarding the entrance to the Braes and setting them apart. The lower glen was well wooded – with birch, alder, hazel and aspen abounding – but the tree line was drawn pretty well at the Bochel, and the Braes were largely bare of timber at this date, though many great trees had flourished there in times past.[4] The division held also in the matter of religion, Lower Glenlivet being of more mixed faith. Even to this day the cottage in the narrow throat of land at the foot of the Bochel is known locally as 'the Kirkie', for it used to be a small church, the last place of Protestant worship before one entered the traditionally Catholic Braes.

The Scalan lay a further three miles beyond the Bochel, at an altitude of over 1250 ft, and was the very last habitation in the valley. Not far from its walls the heathery Ladder Hills rose to south and east, out of which flowed the Crombie burn that ran beside its door. The watershed, 2650 ft above sea level and the boundary between Banffshire and Aberdeen, was little more than a mile away.

In 1716 the district was barely accessible. Throughout the North of Scotland surfaced roads were almost unknown. In the oft-quoted words of Sir Archibald Grant of Monymusk there were at this time "no coach, chariote or chaise and few carts benorth Tay". A coast road ran from Inverness to Cullen, but inland the ways were so rough that, so one visitor believed, "no wheel had ever turned upon them since the foundation of the globe".[5] There were a few inland 'roads' in the North-East, of course, notably the one linking Inverness with Aberdeen which passed through Fochabers and Huntly and skirted the eastern edges of the hills. But they did not carry wheeled vehicles. They were used by runners carrying the post, and by travellers on horseback, who carried their luggage in paniers slung beside the saddle, or in baskets attached to poles in the manner of the travois of the Native Americans.[6]

In the Grampian Highlands the Minigaig Pass between Ruthven and Blair Athol was the main recognised north-south through-route at this date. Other ancient bridle paths ran east-west, linking Speyside with Strathdon, Deeside and Forfarshire. None of these Highland ways followed the glens like a modern road, but took the most direct route, sometimes over plateaux close to 3000ft high, climbing which posed no problem for the sure-footed garrons of the travellers who used them.[7]

Such roads as there were more often than not came to an abrupt stop at the rivers. When Daniel Defoe travelled through Lower Banffshire about this time he was able to cross the Isla at Keith by the "exceedingly high and steep Stone Bridge of one Arch" there, but at the county town itself he found only a ford over the river Deveron.[8] In the whole upper part of the county there was but one stone bridge, built in the sixteenth century to give access to Blairfindy Castle, which crossed the Livet about a mile above its confluence with the Avon.

Half a century of legislation promoting road building and repair had in fact produced no visible results whatever in Banffshire by the date that Scalan opened. Only after the Act of 1718 would a start be made, and not for several decades thereafter would anything be done in the uplands of the county.[9]

In the immediate neighbourhood of Scalan itself there were four recognised routes in and out (Map 3). One led south over the hill to the Conglas Water, and from there west to Strathavon, Abernethy and

Speyside. A second climbed up over the Ladder, branching either into Glen Nochty or Glen Buchat, and thence on into Strathdon and the East. A third led north-eastwards up past the Suie, over to the Blackwater and so down into Strathbogie. The last took the traveller northwards down the Braes, to join the two bridle paths that crossed Lower Glenlivet and linked with the route to Glen Rinnes.[10] The first three of these routes were hill paths, and those using them could only move slowly and would have been visible from afar. The fourth kept to low ground, but again no sudden approach was possible on it, because it crossed the great open Moss of the Carrachs, known also as the *Féithe Bhadach* – the Vatich Moss – less than a mile from the house.

Remote, hard to find and harder to reach, the Scalan was indeed as one author has aptly expressed it, "a retreat, and about as non-apparent to the busy world as was compatible with real existence".[11] And this, in the year after the '15, was of course precisely its recommendation.

The house itself was built, according to Bishop Geddes, "almost entirely of turf".[12] His description could actually apply to any one of several types of vernacular construction to be found in the uplands of the North-East of Scotland in the early eighteenth century, but the type it probably best fits is of a house built on a foundation of stone, with wooden frames, and walls and roof of turf.[13]

Such a house could be run up in a matter of days. A single course of stones would be laid first, following the contours of the outer walls and often rounded at the corners. This provided a base for the walls and also for the couples, the rough-hewn poles set some six to ten feet apart that formed the frame of the house. Between the latter the walls were then built to a height of about five feet with layers of feal – turfs cut large – packed together and left to harden before cutting out the spaces for the door and windows. The roof frame was then built up with couple arms, fixed at an angle to the couples and meeting at the ridge, where they were tied or pinned to a ridge pole or 'roof tree' that ran the length of the house. Between the couple arms slimmer poles or cabers were attached, and across both of them pirlins were laid at right angles to complete the frame. Thinner divots of turf were used for the roof covering, either alone or as a foundation for a thatch cut from whatever material was to hand. Broom, whin, rushes and straw all made an efficient thatch, but the most permanent material was heather, and of this there was no shortage close by the Scalan.

The chimney was a hole in the roof, perhaps with an open-ended cone of sticks and turfs above it, but more likely without, for even a hundred years later chimneys were almost unknown in the Braes. In the construction of such houses by far the most valuable item was the roof timber, and

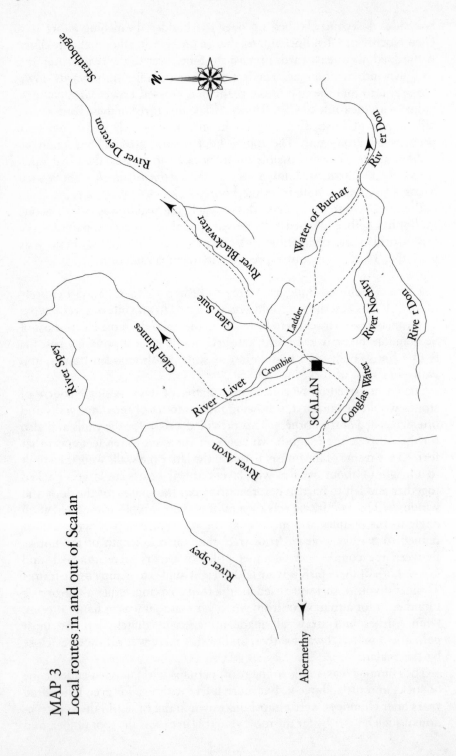

MAP 3
Local routes in and out of Scalan

in the tradition of the Braes this would have been cut from the giant trees that had lain submerged as long as memory in the Carrachs and the other mosses there.[14]

The house at the Scalan must have been small, perhaps comprising two rooms only, since it had been built for one priest, and its new owners no doubt extended it almost at once. But it should certainly not be thought of as a wretched hovel. Turf was considered a very suitable building material at the time and houses built of it could be both comfortable and durable – it was not unknown for them to last a hundred years or more.[15] A simple turf house was also particularly suitable for a seminary whose purpose was to prepare boys for the conditions that they could expect to meet as priests on the Scottish Mission.

In 1716 there were no farms adjacent to the house. The nearest were those of East and West Achavaich and Tomnalienan, with Achnascra beyond (see Map 2).[16] These were traditional 'farm towns', that is, nucleated farms of several families who shared the land and whose dwellings were set close together. Each farm town was in the hands of a tacksman or principal tenant, who rented it directly from the Duke of Gordon and himself subleased portions of it to the other tenants, according to the runrig system whereby each held a number of small strips interspersed among those of his neighbours.

The land under cultivation was ploughed in long ridges shaped like a stretched-out 'S', wide enough to take the heavy wooden plough and its team of oxen. The Infield, nearest to the dwellings, was manured before sowing and bore good crops of bear or oats. The more distant Outfield was sown without nourishment or rest, and abandoned when the yield fell below the input. Grain was still sown broadcast at this date, and in the summer the growing crops vied with the weeds – scabious, corn marigold, wild mustard, thistle and dock – that threatened to smother them.[17] Through the winter cattle were allowed to roam the ridges and graze the 'balks' or strips of grass among them as best they could. Systematic drainage was unknown, so that for much of the year stagnant water lay in the ditches between the rigs and on any unploughed, low-lying land. Between one farm and the next the land lay waste, for the modern concept of contiguous farms was unknown to the Highlander of the early eighteenth century.

The farm's hill grazing land was held in common. It extended to the highest slopes close to the watershed, which were suitable for sheep and horses, but included also the shielings, areas of better grazing lower down to which cattle and other livestock were taken in the summer. A farm's shieling land might extend to 300-400 acres or even more. It was often situated too far from the farm town for the milk to be brought home

daily, in which case it was churned on site and the butter and cheese
stored in the shieling huts. Since the purpose of a shieling was to provide
good grass it was important that it should not be over-grazed, and for this
reason its use was confined to a season of about six weeks every year,
beginning in early June.[18] All the farms in the Braes had their own hill
pasture and shieling grounds. Achnascra had their shieling on the slopes
of the Ladder burn, with rough pasture above it up to the summit.
Tomnalienan shieled two miles away above Corrunich, and pastured on
the high slopes of Carn Mór. Lettoch farm traditionally had the shieling
rights of the Clash.[19]

   Just such a shieling ground was the Scalan. We know from later
documents relating to its subsequent development that it extended to
some 345 acres in all, and included not only the *Tom* or Hill of Scalan
itself, but the land about it west of the Crombie and the Slochd burn.[20]
Traditionally it belonged to Tomnalienan farm. Since 1700 the tack for
Tomnalienan had been held by John Grant of Tomnavoulin, one of
several tacks in his name. His original contract made no specific reference
to rights to Scalan, but since the shieling belonged to the farm by tradition
he naturally assumed such rights. When his tack came to be renewed in
1722 the new contract made reference to this ambiguity:

> he is in possession of a Shieling called Scalen which he alleadges to be a
> pertinent of the af mend [aforementioned] Lands of Tomylennan but is
> not mentioned in the Said Contract.[21]

But despite the doubt John Grant kept his shieling and had it written into
later contracts. It was at the foot of this shieling, on the west bank of the
Crombie, that the turf house lay. The outlook was Upland, rather than
Highland – rough grass and heather, the underlying rock rarely breaking
the skin; dark, rounded hills often curtained with cloud, rising suddenly a
few hundred yards from the house; in front of them dun muir and green
water-meadow, strangely flat; and across it the Crombie flowing, not like
the tumbling Highland burns the boys remembered in the West, but like a
silver ribbon laid upon the land. To the west the *Tom* of Scalan rose
barely two hundred and fifty feet above them, enough to hide from their
view the higher land that lay beyond. Among the junipers upon its slopes
'black' cattle, the colour of dark wine, were perhaps still to be seen,
enjoying the last days of summer shieling. And to the north, a dozen miles
beyond the saucer of the Braes and the round dome of the Bochel, Ben
Rinnes thrust up its rocky edge, steep on its east side, shallow on its west,
the one unmistakable mountain on their horizon. It was a landscape to lift
the heart in the summer, but one that in the long months of winter could
eat into the soul.

Shortly after the seminary took the house over, John Grant sub-let a piece of the shieling gound to the new arrivals, extending almost to the top of the hill and covering some seventeen acres.[22] The tack brought him in new income, and both he and his tenants could well afford to lose the use of it, since it only amounted to a tiny proportion of the whole shieling, and they in any case held other shieling grounds above the Corrunich.

In the chapters that follow, therefore, 'Scalan' is used with two different meanings: more commonly, to denote the seminary itself; but also upon occasion the whole tract of land – at this date a shieling, but in later years a farm town supporting several tenant families – from which the seminary took its name.

At a very early date the seminary also acquired a smaller piece of land on the east side of the Crombie. Bishop Geddes states in his *Brief Historical Account of the Seminary at Scalan* that this was "granted" to them by Grant of Ruthven's brother, who was factor to the Duke and farmed at Demickmore nearby.[23] He adds that it strictly lay within the bounds of Badeglashan farm, which extended as far as the Crombie, but that it had been separated from it "by sufficient authority" and at the time of his writing (1777) was considered as belonging to Scalan.

He does not specify the nature or the terms of the original "grant", but in fact it was a gift, made directly to the seminary and probably without any written contract. No rent was ever paid for it.[24] The Duke's factor was able to donate the land because in 1716 Badeglashan was in fact still unused moor, and not the cultivated farm that it had become by the time that Bishop Geddes was writing. It was not yet leased to any tenant, and not in demand. No attempt was made to cultivate it until the perhaps the 1730s or 1740s, and only then were tacks drawn up for it.[25]

The seminary's original land on both sides of the burn can still be identified by aerial photography (see Plate 16). Its acquisition enabled the community to keep dairy cattle and sow a few crops from the outset,[26] though on a small scale at first. Scalan became in fact a working farm, as well as a College, and would remain so throughout its eighty-three years; and it is necessary to understand this in order to fully understand its history.

NOTES

1. Cf., Bannerman W. *On the Extinction of Gaelic in Buchan and Lower Banffshire* (Banff, 1895), p. 27.
2. Synod of Moray, Record of Meetings, 1. 11. 1710, CH 2/271/IV, p.281, SRO.
3. Cf., Dunnett H. *Invera'an A Strathspey Parish* (Paisley, 1919), pp. 103ff.
4. Anderson M. L. *A History of Scottish Forestry* (London, 1967), vol. 1, p. 424; and William Roy Map of Scotland (1748-53), Brit. Mus., copy NLS.

5. Burt, Capt. E. *Letters from a Gentleman in the North of Scotland* (London, 1754), vol. I, pp. 77f.

6. Re posts by foot and horse, Haldane A.R.B. *Three Centuries of Scottish Posts* (Edinburgh, 1971), pp. 38ff.; re panier and travois, Fenton A. 'Wheelless transport in Northern Scotland', in Fenton A. and Stell G. *Loads and Roads in Scotland and Beyond* (Edinburgh, 1984).

7. Kerr J., 'Old Grampian Highways', *TGSI,* vol. xlix (1974-6); and Ross A., 'Old Highland Roads', *TGSI,* vol. xiv (1887-8).

8. Defoe D. *A Tour Through the Whole Island of Great Britain,* (1724; London, 1769 ed.), pp. 224, 226.

9. Cf., Grant J. *Banffshire Roads During the First Half of the Eighteenth Century* (Banff, 1905), *passim.*

10. Based on surviving tracks; local tradition; and Map of Strathavon and Genlivet, showing existing and proposed roads, n.d.(18C), RHP 1755, SRO.

11. Stark J. *Priest Gordon of Aberdeen* (Aberdeen, 1909), p. 16.

12. Geddes Bp. J. 'A Brief Historical Account of the Seminary at Scalan' (1777), CS 1/3, SCA, para. 8.

13. Walker B. 'The Vernacular Buildings of North East Scotland: An Exploration', *Scot. Geog. Mag.,* vol. 95 (1979), pp. 46f.; Fenton A. and Walker B. *The Rural Architecture of Scotland* (Edinburgh, 1981), pp. 75f.

14. Re chimneys, cf., Phillips J.G. *Wanderings in the Highlands of Banff and Aberdeen Shires* (Banff, 1881), p.81, remembering childhood in 1820s; re cutting timbers, p. 113.

15. Walker B. *op. cit.* (1979), p. 48.

16. Achnascra was traditionally the most important farm in the neighbourhood, and the only one mentioned in Blaeu's *Atlas Novus* of 1654.

17. For detailed accounts of local wild flowers, see espec. Dickie G. *The Botanist's Guide to the Counties of Aberdeen, Banff and Kincardine* (Aberdeen, 1860), and Gibb W. G. *The Flora of Banffshire* (Aberdeen, 1912).

18. See Bil A. *The Shieling 1600–1840* (Edinburgh, 1990), pp. 175ff. The shieling season lasted six weeks in the case of dairy cattle, but longer for other stock.

19. A Short Description of Glen Livet (1761), RHP 2487, SRO.

20. Ibid.

21. Rentall of 1722, Grant of Tomvulne, GD 44/51/745/2/1, SRO.

22. Geddes Bp. J. *op. cit.,* paras. 5 and 8. Acreage calculated from descriptions of tacks after land divided, in 'Contents and Estimates, Duke Gordon Estates' (1772-3) CR 8/185, SRO.

23. Geddes Bp. J. *op. cit.,* para. 8.

24. Bishop Cameron to James Sharp, 9. 9. 1807, PL.

25. Cf., pp. 84f. below.

26. Geddes Bp. J. *op. cit.,* para. 8.

4

Laying the Foundations (1716–1722)

In 1716, however, it was not yet clear whether Scalan was destined to have a history. Eilean Bàn had lasted only two years, after all, and in the unsettled state of the country who could say that Scalan would survive longer? Bishop Gordon's correspondence at this time shows that he was still thinking of it, not as a new seminary but rather as a temporary continuation of Eilean Bàn, the same seminary but on a different site meantime.

Nor was the question of its supervision in any way settled. George Innes did not move in with the students, and it is not even certain that he played any part in setting up the seminary. Bishop Gordon wrote to his uncle Thomas Innes in December, three or four months after the boys' arrival, telling him that he had now brought the young priest Mr Alexander Smith from Aberdeen to fill "the post nevew. Geo: had".[1] But it is not clear whether he meant by this that George Innes had held the post of master for the first few weeks at Scalan, or merely that he had held it previously at Eilean Bàn. What is clear from other letters is that George Innes was simply not willing to live in at Scalan, mainly because of his poor health,[2] and that Bishop Gordon had no choice but to change his original plans. Hence his decision to send in Mr Smith, and to give him an assistant at least until the place became established; and also, since both men were inexperienced, to "reside with them as much as possible" himself.

Alexander Smith, later bishop and Vicar Apostolic, was thus the first Scalan master for whom we have definite evidence. Small of stature – one of his aliases was 'Mr Short' – and of unimposing mein, weak voiced, his face and hands marked with the King's Evil, disorganised himself and a poor organiser of others, he was nonetheless a highly intelligent man, an inspiring teacher, and a model of upright living and piety.

Bishop Nicolson fully approved of the new arrangements. The fact is that the Mission had no fixed plan for the supervision of its little seminary at this date. The typical pattern of later years – of a single resident priest as master, in charge of all matters temporal, spiritual and academic – had not yet evolved, and it was apparently assumed that the work would be shared by several people, not necessarily all resident. In the condition of the times long-term planning was in any case out of the question.

*   *   *

The following summer Bishop Gordon made a visitation of all the Catholic communities of Scotland. It was his first since before the Rising, and he found the people in the most miserable condition in living memory, desperate for comfort and support. He confirmed many hundreds, and helped wherever he could with their material needs, giving away every penny he had and himself returning home in debt. His journey only confirmed the need for the new seminary. But as he explained to the Scots Agent in Rome, between lack of funds and the dangers of the times, he could barely keep it going:

> I do all I can to pitch on hopefull youths that may be able in time to serve these poor people that deserve to have good laborers as well as any people that I know in the world. I keep the Sem^y still on foot with great difficulty & charges, & I hope God will make it very usefull. I strive to keep likewise on foot litle shops in the West.[3]

The 'litle shops' were of course the lay schools in the Western Highlands and the Isles, which the Mission continued to support by supplementing the pupils' fees, in order to keep them afloat. It is significant that he mentioned them in the same breath as the seminary: in his mind their work was quite closely related, in that he still saw them as a source of recruits for the Colleges abroad and the priesthood, and remained committed to supporting them, so long as his meagre resources would allow.

In the case of Scalan itself Lewis Innes again came to the bishops' assistance that autumn, donating 300 Livres for its upkeep and pledging a further 150 Livres annually during his own lifetime.[4] But as a benefactor he felt entitled to make certain requests of them. The first was that they should release Alexander Smith to become Procurator of the Scots College in Paris. He was well aware of the difficulties that this would pose for them so soon after the young priest's arrival at Scalan, but felt that the needs of the College should take priority. That he could "insist" on the move (the word was his own), and get his way, tells much of the power of the purse over a poor Mission. But it tells us also of his own standing. Though no longer Principal of the College he was still taking the important decisions.[5] And Bishop Gordon looked to him, not alone because he himself had studied under him, but on account of his personal qualities – his noted humility, diplomacy and generosity, and his reputation for good counsel from which many in Paris, Rome and Scotland had benefited over the years.

Mr Smith left Scalan in the new year of 1718, and finally set sail for France in May. In the words of a colleague, he "left a great blank behind him".[6] George Innes took his place as master, but still not in residence.

Lewis Innes' second request was that Scalan students should not be sent

on to Paris until they had reached at least the level of subdeacon. He had
become concerned at the poor calibre of boys sent abroad in recent years,
and had finally become convinced of the need for change after John
MacLachlan, the student sent to Rome from Eilean Bàn, had been
dismissed in disgrace. He believed that the young man had been sent
out too early and untried. His own proposal would prevent any such
mistakes in future, and perhaps help repair the good name of the Scottish
Mission. He recognised that it would involve extra costs, and therefore
proposed to provide a fund of 100 Livres annually for his nephew at
Scalan (or whoever succeeded him), over and above his Mission quota.

Grateful and anxious to support the Scots College as he was, Bishop
Gordon saw that the second request would present "insuperable diffi-
cultys".[7] It would be quite impossible to bring boys to the required level
in five years at Scalan when this could not be done even in Paris, with all
its advantages, and where teachers with the talents of Thomas Innes and
now Alexander Smith were on the staff. He had no-one near to their
ability to call on in Scotland, and was having "all the difficulty in the
world" persuading anyone even reasonable to stay at Scalan. George
Innes himself was far from ideal on a number of counts:

> for nev. Geo: besides that we could never as yet get him accommodated
> where the shop is, & we will have great difficulty still to do it, he has so
> litle health, & is so timorous and helpless in these hard times, is not of
> that genius entirely that were necessary for that post, not having much
> discretionem spirituum, & he understands so litle oeconomy, that
> another must be with him to help him.

And yet, he concluded, "with all his infirmity we have not another laborer
so fitt".

A further difficulty was the lack of space and the small number of boys
at Scalan. At present, some were being kept there for their entire training,
and the rest given a preparatory education prior to being sent abroad, and
this was manageable. But to keep this second group on longer, and give
them part of their senior training for the priesthood at Scalan, would not
be feasible: the two groups would be so different in their purposes and
their training that they would not easily co-exist in the same small house.
It might actually be easier, and worth consideration, he suggested, to open
a second seminary specifically for preparing students for the Colleges,
leaving Scalan solely as an all-through seminary, which was after all its
"first dessign."

His letter was touching on a fundamental question that was already
beginning to emerge – what exactly was Scalan's rôle to be? He himself
was clear that the Mission required a seminary of its own, in which it
could control the training of its future priests from start to finish, and that

this should always be Scalan's priority. Yet he recognised that it could not entirely replace the Colleges, certainly not at present, and that meantime part of its work must be as a provider of students for them.

If he could have looked into the future he would have seen that a separate junior seminary was never to be a practical proposition, and that Scalan would always have to serve the two purposes. In time, in fact, it would come to serve a third, when he and his successors began to admit lay students, in the face of parental pressure and their own need for funds. As such, Scalan would remain something of a hybrid for most of its days, seeking to meet needs that were not always easily compatible, and successive masters would face the problem of trying to keep the balance right.

The Society in Scotland for Propagating Christian Knowledge had been founded in 1709 with four professed aims – to spread the English language in the Gaelic-speaking Highlands and Islands, to teach the young people there loyalty to the British Sovereign and Government, to bring them up in the Protestant faith, and to instil in them habits of virtue and industry.[8] Put another way, its mission was to destroy the language, superstition, disaffection and indolence that Whig Scotland saw as the way of life of the Highlander. The SSPCK's main programme was to set up and maintain schools in the North and West, particularly in areas where parish schools did not exist. Its first school was opened on the remote island of St Kilda, and in time 133 more were established under its auspices. The eleventh opened its doors at Kinmichly, Glenlivet in 1713, moving up to Tomnavoulin the following year. Since there were no other schools in the area, its presence at once posed a problem for the local Catholic parents. Many must have decided that any education was better than none, for by the spring of 1717 more than half of the 51 pupils on roll were Catholic.[9]

When Bishop Gordon visited the area in the summer of 1719 he faced a dilemma. Was he to forbid the children to attend, or tacitly support a school whose textbooks included *Dangers of Popery, Protestant Resolution,* and the oddly titled *Funeral of the Mass*? He contacted the senior priests in the North-East and called them to a meeting at Scalan to decide how to respond. On their advice he decided to invoke the *Statuta* and announce that parents enrolling their children would be liable to excommunication. But he found, as Bishop Nicolson had found before him, that such action did not deter some parents, who simply chose to ignore it.[10] This was obviously not the time for a trial of strength, which the Church could never entirely win and which would only give scandal to its enemies: a far better solution would be for it to provide alternative Catholic schooling in the area. And this Bishop Gordon sought to do.

That autumn two Catholic schools were opened nearby. One was at Auchriachan in Glen Conglas, and the other in Glenlivet itself, where Gregory Farquharson was brought in as master.

Of course these new establishments did not go unnoticed by the Kirk, whose committee *Report* of 1720 cited them as examples of the growing arrogance of Catholics and Jacobites sheltering under the protection of the Duke of Gordon. The *Report* also warned of the existence of the seminary, of which it had this to say:

> there is a famous popish School in the forsaid Scalla in Duke Gordons Countrey under the Inspection of one father Innes who Still resides there, and keeps a Correspondence with fforeign Popish Colleges; To this nursery are sent Children from the Isles and many other places, and Such as father Innes Judges promiseing are educated and maintained here, and afer [*sic*] sometimes study at his School sent abroad.[11]

The *Report* shows that George Innes was now living in at Scalan – and the word 'still' (that is, constantly) suggests that the arrangement was permanent. Its claim that he was sending students abroad was also accurate. Only that July four boys – the first as far as we know – had sailed down to Sunderland, and were awaiting a ship that could take them to France, from where they were to travel overland to Rome. One of them, Lachlan MacIntosh, was a Highlander, while the other three, James Leslie, James Duffus and John Godsman, were from the North-East.[12] It is not known how long they had been at the seminary. It is very doubtful whether much of their training had been received there, and more likely that they had only gathered there at the beginning of the summer so that Bishop Gordon could test them and assess their readiness when he visited in June. (His visit had another purpose also: he had been very ill that spring, and his doctors had strongly advised him to spend some time in the hills for his health's sake. He made a remarkable recovery on the fresh air and goats' milk of the Braes.[13])

The three Lowland students went on to be ordained in Rome at the end of the decade: in so far as they can be claimed as Scalan boys, therefore, they can be claimed as the seminary's first 'successes' abroad.

That summer also Bishop Gordon brought Archibald Anderson to Scalan to assist with the teaching. The new man had been trained for the priesthood in Paris, and had been ordained deacon there, but had been forced to leave after suffering a brain fever that left him with a permanent disability. The bishop was doubtful whether he could ever be ordained to the priesthood, and asked Thomas Innes as to the practice of the Church in France in similar cases. He feared that as a priest he could be a cause of scandal, because of the ever-present danger of a relapse, and what he termed the "insolidity" of mind that often developed with this particular illness (Mr Anderson apparently swore like a dragoon when angered). It was for this reason that he had placed him in Scalan, no doubt with strict instructions to the boys on no account to rouse his ire. He planned to keep him there for some time at least, and eventually send him to the West Highlands to continue his studies and learn the Gaelic language. His background was not known in the West, and he thought it might be possible to ordain him to the priesthood there: "If ever he could be raised," he told Thomas Innes, "it w^d be for that country."[14] In the meantime Mr Anderson was "extremely" happy at Scalan.

In 1721 the Church of Scotland returned to its now perennial theme of the resurgence of Catholicism in Moray and Banffshire, and the General Assembly set up a special Commission to look at the problem. The Commission's Report,[15] presented the following year, revealed that children were still receiving a Catholic education in many places on the Gordon estates, from private tutors in the case of the sons of land-owners, and in the case of the common people in the "great number" of small schools that had been set up recently. It was able to name seven of these new foundations, of which one was Gregory Farquharson's in Glenlivet. He was said to be teaching English, Latin and French there: the reference to Latin suggests that his was more than a rural 'little school', while the fact that he taught French, which was unheard-of at this date even in the Burgh schools, must have fuelled the Kirk's conviction that the true loyalty of the Highland Catholics was not to London or Edinburgh but to the Court of St Germains. They would have been even more convinced had they known that the boys also learned Gaelic,[16] the language of the disaffected Highlands.

The commissioners also referred at some length to Scalan, from where, they claimed, students were "sent regularly every year to Germany, ffrance & other places in great numbers to be farder taught"! Apart from this compulsive need to exaggerate the strength of the opposition their description of the seminary is revealing:

> And there is in the Scallay of Glenlivet a famous Popish Nursery taught by Mr Archibald Anderson A Papist & others under the inspection of ffather Innes & M^r McDonald Priests And for the better accommoda-tion of this College, There is lately built a fashionable House with suitable office houses, A large Garden and great Park for graseing well fenced about, this Place belongs to Duke Gordon and thither are brought Youths from diverse Corners of Scotland to be educat.

From the details they were able to produce, and their use of the word "famous", it is obvious that they were well acquainted with Scalan.

Despite its retired and unfrequented location, and for all its efforts to avoid the public gaze, it could never have succeeded in remaining for long an unknown, secret hideaway. It was by now all too well known to the Kirk authorities, and attracting attention as a prime example of the alarming "increase of popery".

The Report also confirms how much progress had already been made in developing the seminary in the six years since it had opened. Its reference to a "fashionable" house supports the contention made earlier (p. 35 above) that the main building was no hovel, and had a good outward appearance. Its use of the phrase "office houses" – the eighteenth century term for farm buildings – indicates that several outhouses had already been erected by this date, a byre for cattle certainly, and perhaps barns for hay and grain.

It also provides evidence that quite a large area was already under cultivation as a garden. This was probably laid out formally in symmetrical patterns, in accordance with contemporary practice, and contained both flowers and herbs.[17] Gardens were hardly to be found outside the towns and the estates of the well-to-do in the 1720s. They had certainly not reached the Uplands of Banffshire, and this one among the muirs must have been a wondrous sight. As we shall see in Chapter 8, it was apparently sited some distance from the house on the seminary's land on the east side of the Crombie.[18]

The "great Park for graseing well fenced about" undoubtedly refers to this land to the east of the burn. ('The Park' was indeed the name always given to it by the Scalan community itself.) According to Bishop Geddes' *Brief Historical Account* the fencing or turf dyke surrounding it was at an early date extended on the west side of the burn also, to form a single enclosure for the whole of the seminary's land, which served to keep their own beasts in and other people's out.[19] This 'head-dyke' would become even more necessary in future years, as larger areas of their land were put under the plough.

By 1722, in short, much had already been achieved in developing the seminary. The enclosure, garden and outhouses all point to a well-established property, developed at some expense by a community that felt its future secure and now saw Scalan as a permanent home.

That community now also had six years' experience of the needs, possibilities, problems and pitfalls of a seminary. It had laid the foundations, and was aware of all the issues, the do's and the don't's. What was needed now was for these to be drawn up into a formal and coherent set of *Rules*, with episcopal authority. And this was the task that Bishop Gordon set himself that summer.

NOTES

1. Bishop Gordon to Thomas Innes, 1. 12. 1716, BL.
2. Bishop Gordon to Lewis Innes, 25. 3. 1718, BL.
3. Bishop Gordon to William Stuart, 16. 10. 1717, BL.
4. Lewis Innes to Bishop Gordon, 27. 1. 1718, copy SM 3/22, SCA.
5. He had resigned in 1713 when King James insisted that he accompany him to Lorraine – cf., Halloran B. M. *The Scots College Paris 1603–1792* (Edinburgh, 1997), p. 80.
6. James Carnegy to Thomas Innes, 25. 2. 1718 and 5. 6. 1718, BL.
7. Bishop Gordon to Lewis Innes, 25. 3. 1718, BL.
8. Belches A. *An Account of the Society in Scotland for Propagating Christian Knowledge* (Edinburgh, 1774) GD 95/11/1, p. 53, SRO.
9. 'Register of Society's Schools', 13 March 1710–7 May 1761, Account of Glenlivet SSPCK school, GD 95/9/1 (microfilm), SRO. It must have been in response to the opening of this school that the Catholic priests of Glenlivet and Strathavon had attempted to set up schools of their own in 1714 (see p. 25).
10. MS 68, f. 31, NLS.
11. *Ibid.*
12. Bishop Gordon to Thomas Innes, 23. 7. 1720; and Bishop Gordon to Rome, 18. 9. 1720 (in Latin), BL.
13. Bishop Wallace to Thomas Innes, 7. 6. 1720; and Robert Gordon to Thomas Innes, 15. 6. 1720, BL.
14. Bishop Gordon to Thomas Innes, 26. 9. 1720 and 8. 11. 1720, BL. For an account of Archibald Anderson, see Anderson W. J. 'The College for the Lowland District of Scotland at Scalan and Aquhorties: Registers and Documents', *IR*, vol. xiv, no. 2, autumn 1963, Appendix IV.
15. 'Representation by the Committee of the Commission of the General Assembly of the Church of Scotland Anent the Growth of Popery in the North' (1722), MS 3430, pp. 239f., NLS.
16. Cf., Bishop Gordon to Thomas Innes, 8. 10. 1724, BL, where he mentions a student learning Gaelic "by the by at Greg$^{y's}$ school".
17. Cox E. H. M. *A History of Gardening in Scotland* (London, 1935), espec. pp. 34-60.
18. See pp. 89f. It was common practice on 18C estates to site the garden some distance away from the house.
19. Geddes Bp. J. 'A Brief Historical Account of the Seminary at Scalan' (1777), CH 1/3, SCA, para. 8. Local tradition is that the dyke was built of turf and stones, bound on top by planting juniper (Phillips J. G. *Wanderings in the Highlands of Banff and Aberdeen Shires* (Banff, 1881), p. 91.

5

Bishop Gordon's Rules

The *Rules* for Scalan, compiled by Bishop Gordon in June 1722, defined its principles and practice and covered every aspect of its daily life. Though later extended and revised, they were never changed in their essentials and remained to the end the foundation upon which the seminary was built, and the touchstone against which it was judged. To read them in full is to gain a vivid insight into the ideals and hopes of Scalan's founders, and the day-to-day world of those who lived there.[1]

Rules

The dessign of the house being to educate a few youths in piety & learning & to fitt them to instruct others, it seems necessary to keep off all such company as may give them wrong impressions or disturb them in their business; & to put them upon such methods as are most proper for attaining what they aim at.

For keeping the house quiet and orderly

1° The schollars must converse as little as possible with strangers, & therefor when any come to the house let them be entertain'd in another room & not where the scholars are.

2° They should shun the company of women entirely, & women should not be allowed to enter the house as farr as it can be avoided.

3° Strangers should not be invited to the house, especially to stay nights, unless it be churchmen, when is there any necessary occasion for it, or when it can't be avoided.

4° Servants or workmen should not be allow'd to eat or play or discourse with the scholars, unless the master approve it or be present, and they should be less allowed to lye in the same room. And the scholars should be very carefull never to go to the Kitchen.

5° Let the house be allways kept quiet without any noise quarrel or disturbance, & let silence be kept during the time of studys, at night after the evening prayer is over, & in the morning till the prayers be said.

Of the Master

6° The master should be with the scholars constantly, as much as is possible, & particularly in time of studys, in the night, & even at play or recreation: and when he can't be with them, he should have at least one with them he can trust, were it but one of themselvs who is of age & has prudence discretion & vertue, & who can give him account how they behave.

7° Seeing he should allways have them under his eye as much as he can, he should not allow them to speak to friends or parents without leave; & should not easily permit them to go to parents houses to stay nights.

8° Being to be with them ordinarly when they go abroad, are at recreation, or divert themselvs at any litle work; he should take care to keep them in the spirit of concord Love and charity; & to take occasion without affectation to say now & then some usefull things to them, but without restraint & not by way of lesson.

9° It depending on him to instruct them & keep them in order; he must be obeyed by all equally young & old; & where there arises any difficulty it belongs to him to determine it.

Of piety

10° The house being chiefly dessign'd to educate them in piety, more regard must be had to it then to learning, & more care must be constantly taken to instill it into them, as certainly it is infinitely more valuable than learning, & without it learning is but a sword in a madmans hand. So if any appear remarkably vitious he must immediately be put away, because entirely unfit for the dessign, and for the hurt he may soon do to others.

11° Care should be taken that they pray not only evening & morning, but now & then in the day time, as a little before dinner & supper, & when after recreation they fall again to study; & they should be well taught to pray allways seriously & from the heart, to seek Gods blessing upon every thing they do, & never to think to do any thing well by their own meer human industry without Gods particular help & grace.

12° They should make some pious lecture every morning & afternoon; nay I think fitt every one young & old should get by heart every morning some parcel of the holy scripture.

13° They should be taught to meditate in an easy & solid manner; & as soon as they can be made capable, they should meditate at least a quarter every morning.

14° They should confess every fortnight, & communicate once a moneth at least.

Of studys

15° Let the dayly time of their studys be proportion'd to what their health can bear; & let them never be dull'd with keeping them too Long close; but let them seek leave, when they want it, to go out a litle even out of time of recreation, to refresh their spirits by walking.

16° Let them get something by heart every morning; & then study at least about two hours at the most serious study every one is fitt for. They should apply about as much time in the afternoon to the most serious studys: & what other time remains either before or after noon may be applyed to easier studys, as the Master shall judge proper. It is of importance that they study allways alltogether in the same room.

17° They should be taught from the very beginning by way of recreation or easy study something of Ecclesiastick history, especially of the Lives of the Saints. It were fitt also that they should all learn by way of diversion or easy study something of the French & Irish or highland language; which they may learn a good deal of that way without constraint & with litle trouble; & they may be afterwards of very great use to them.

18° They may learn also according as they advance something of Geography, Chronology, History & Critick, by the by, without much trouble or application. It is fitt that all learn some litle of the Greek, & likewise of Rhetorick, when they know the Latin pretty well. And those who are well advanc'd in philosophy or divinity may learn somewhat of the Hebrew, if they have a genius for tongues. But all this must be left to the prudent management of the Master.

Of the order of the Day

19° They should rise in summer at five & in winter at six, & accordingly go to bed at nine or ten at night; for eight hours of rest & sleep is thought generally to be sufficient for any body in health.

20° A quarter of hour or litle more may serve for putting on their cloaths (wch should be done quickly & modestly,) for combing their heads, & washing their hands.

21° Immediately after about half an hour should be employed in the morning prayer & meditation.

22° About eight such as please may take breakfast.

23° At twelve they should dine; & after dinner they should be allowed at least about an hour of recreation. And at dinner & supper there should be reading of the scriptures, & other edifying books, at least of some good historys. After supper near an hour of recreation should be likewise allowed.

24° Before nine or ten at night according to the time of year evening prayer should be made; & the subject of meditation for next morning should be read immediately after. And all should go to bed at nine or ten, with great silence & modesty.

25° When Mass is said, & 'tis fitt it be said several days a week besides Sundays & holy days; the fittest hour for it is before breakfast.

26° It is fitt that the scholars read weekly by turns at table, & do any other litle thing they shall be order'd to keep the house neat & decent.

For Sundays & Holy days

27° It is fitt they say on these days some part of the Church Office both in forenoon and after noon; which 'tis necessary the master should say with them to direct them.

28° It is proper that on these days their master catechize them, & give 'em such instructions as he finds they want most. And they should be caus'd make some Catechism or Instruction themselves on these days as soon as they grow capable to do it.

29° On these days no studys are to be allowed but such as relate to Religion & piety.

Of Recreation

30° It is necessary that the Master or some body he can trust have still an eye over them when they are at their walking, diversions or plays: yet they should ever have all manner of innocent liberty allowed them; nay they should be encouraged & obliged to take corporal exercise & diversion; because it is not possible for young folks who study much to keep their health without a great deal of exercise, walking & diversion. The regulating of all these things relating to diversion must be left to the Masters prudence; but he must certainly be desir'd in the general to cause them walk & exercise & play much, according to the proper times & seasons, & to every one's age, state of health & genius.

31° Besides dayly recreations they must be allowed one whole afternoon weekly, that they may have such a continuance of diversion & exercise as may reasonably refresh them after their studys: And it seems proper to chuse rather the day of recreation in the middle of the week than in the end of it; so that wednesday or thursday may be pitch'd on, unless there fall an holy day on them. It seems fitt notwithstanding that a whole afternoon be not spent without something to raise their minds to God; & therefore some edifying history may be related or read to them, or some other pious lecture made.

The modern reader will immediately be struck by the strictness of Rules 1-4, concerning the company the boys should and should not keep; but if so, we might bear in mind that similar rules applied in junior seminaries in Scotland until very recently, and also that they were in accord with the rules of any Catholic boarding school of the day. Certain events in later years would prove their wisdom, and also vindicate the apparently harsh Rule 7 concerning visits to and by parents.[2]

The insistence in Rules 6 and 30 on close and constant supervision again reflected the thinking of the time: it was the practice in the Jesuit schools of Europe, for instance; but it also echoed a more general trend in the educational thinking of the day, secular as well as religious, which argued that children, being weak and prone to temptation, should be left to themselves as little as possible.[3] The master was to be given unquestioned authority, but this he must exercise through care and good counsel (Rules 8-9). According to the spirit of the *Rules*, at least, corporal punishment had no place at Scalan, in notable contrast to school régimes the length and breadth of Scotland at the time, where the tawse was standard issue.[4]

Similarly, the regulations concerning homilies, meditation and prayers at set times of the day (Rules 11-13) – and indeed the daily timetable as a whole – had parallels in the English-speaking boarding schools run by the religious orders in Europe.[5] And these in turn owed something to the centuries-old division of the monastic day. The regulation of silence between evening and morning prayers, for example, (Rule 5) had its origin in the Great Silence of the monasteries, while the monastic practice of edifying reading at mealtimes, taken up in the boarding schools and seminaries abroad, gave Scalan Rule 23.

The daily timetables of some of the English-speaking boarding schools of the eighteenth century have survived on record, and they all reveal a similar pattern. That of St Gregory's, the school of the English Benedictines at Douai, is a typical example, and is of particular interest since it is exactly contemporary with the Scalan *Rules*. The two provide a striking comparison – in each case, though the environments were utterly different the order of activities was almost identical, and even the times of them were quite closely similar: (Fig. 1)[6]

Fig. 1. The Timetables at Scalan and St Gregory's Douai

Scalan		St Gregory's Douai
(Summer timetable)		
05.00	Rise and prayers	05.00
05.30?	Studies	05.30
c. 07.15	Mass (certain days)	c. 06.45
08.00	Breakfast	07.30
08.40	Lessons/Studies	08.00
11.40	Prayers	11.00
12.00	Dinner	12.00
12.30	Recreation	–
13.30	Lessons/Studies	13.00
16.00	Recreation	16.30
16.30	Lessons/Studies	17.00
19.00	Supper	18.00
19.40	Free time	19.00
20.40	Prayers	20.40
21.00	Bed	21.00

If the early hour of rising strikes us as one of Scalan's most 'monastic' rules, it is worth remembering that all schools in Scotland began the day early at this time. Burgh school pupils faced a 7 a.m. start and eight hours at their desks, at least in the summer. The SSPCK schools also normally began lessons at 7 a.m. in the summer months. And in the few boarding schools – such as Watson's in Edinburgh, which was founded just two years after the Scalan *Rules* – the pupils were called from their beds at 6 a.m. in summer and an hour later in winter.[7] Scottish society as a whole rose and began its business early, of course: whether the farmer in the country or the town lawyer, who might be at his desk and meeting his clients at 5.00 or even 4.00 in the morning.

We might wonder what growing boys thought of Rule 22! Breakfast was traditionally the main meal of the day in Scotland, and that is what the boys would have been used to before they came to Scalan. But now, when they had already been up three hours and studying, breakfast was something to be opted into! But here again we need to see the rule in context. All the meals at Scalan were in any case frugal – kail and mashlam porridge were the staple diet except on feastdays[8] – not least because the boys were preparing for the hardships of the Mission. And the older students, especially, would be developing their own spiritual routines, which could include fasting. They might well choose to forego breakfast once or twice in the week, if their health allowed it, and if their spiritual adviser consented. For we may be sure that each would be given prudent counsel in the matter of meals, as in every other aspect of their daily lives.

Prudence and commonsense are apparent throughout the *Rules*, in fact. Bishop Gordon recognised that growing boys, studying hard, needed times of lighter study also (Rule 17), as well as sufficient physical exercise, rest, and time to themselves (Rule 30). Again, this was not new: something similar could be found in the *Ratio Studiorum* of the Jesuits, for example, and ultimately in the old monastic ideal of the balanced day. But it was novel for Scotland, and enlightened when compared with practice in the Grammar Schools, with their long hours at the desk and minimal recreation. Enlightened too was its attempt to tailor the amount and kind of study to the individual (Rule 30), at a time when the science of pedagogy was in its infancy and the concept of 'individual needs' almost unknown.

I have referred to some of the sources that may have influenced Bishop Gordon, but as a seminary Scalan was also and more particularly modelled on the existing Scots Colleges, and the *Rules* reflect this. The Statutes of the Scots College Paris, for instance, offer close parallels – in the requirement of constant vigilance and supervision by the master; in authority through exhortation, timely correction and example; in tailoring academic and spiritual education to age and individual need; in the emphasis on piety, etc. The daily timetable differed, of course, since Paris students were bound by the university courses, but the general shape of the day was similar, with a 5 a.m. rise, study and Mass before an 8 a.m. breakfast, supper at 7 p.m., and lights out at 9.15.[9]

Bishop Geddes, who himself studied at Rome, remarked how closely the Scalan *Rules* resembled those of his and the other Colleges: the only differences he noticed were a few adaptations to meet the particular circumstances of the Braes, or which were "thought useful for giving the youths a due command of themselves".[10]

What he implied by the latter becomes clear when we look at the context of the summer of 1722, when the *Rules* were compiled. Just a week or two beforehand, Bishop Gordon had received a letter from Thomas Innes complaining of the poor calibre of students sent to Paris of late. He at once wrote back a very pointed reply, justifying the Mission's choice of students, and throwing the blame for any failures squarely back at the Scots College and in particular at Innes himself. (Brilliant scholar as he was, Innes was inclined to neglect the students for his own studies.) The letter is revealing, for it seems certain that the dispute influenced Bishop Gordon in his framing of the Scalan *Rules*.

my opinion is, that the defect lyes not in the choice made of such as are

sent to you (for a great many that have miscarryed have been the very
hopefullest that ever I knew sent,) but in the manner they are care'd for
there, for of those who are best dispossd most ruine their health by
excessive studys, & for want of corporal exercise; (& both these
defects are essential in point of health, & yet little look'd after w^t
you;) & another the most considerable of all defects is that a proper
Director does not take sufficient care of them, leaves 'em allmost
entirely to 'emselvs, or if good advices once or twice given be not
followed, they are allmost utterly abandon'd, wch can't be but of most
pernicious consequence, & above all things I have ever been astonish'd
that M. Fleming [Thomas Innes], who has a call to that (to Direct) by
his post, & has much genius & capacity for it, has little applyed to
it . . . & unless his advices be followed readily by the young ones, he
gives 'em quite over . . . it can't be expected while better measures are
not followed that things can thrive as we would wish.[11]

Bishop Gordon had always thought of Paris as the least flawed of the
Colleges, but it was still short of what he wished his new seminary to be.
In the light of his letter we cannot but think that he had its present
shortcomings in mind when he wrote the *Rules* for Scalan; and in
particular those sections that stressed the need for a balance between
study, physical exercise and wholesome recreation, for study matched to
age, health and aptitude, for consistent and positive supervision, and even
(as in Rule 15) for listening to the views of students.

The section of the *Rules* entitled 'Of Studys' did not pretend to offer a full
description of the Scalan syllabus – that was not its purpose – but it does
give us a glimpse of what was taught. The standard course followed by all
the students was similar to that taught in the Scottish Grammar Schools in
that it was based on the study of Latin language and literature – these
were the "serious studies" referred to in Rule 15. Religious subjects –
Scripture, Church History and the Lives of Saints – had their place on the
curriculum, but were to be learned "by way of diversion or easy study": a
phrase that did not imply that they were unimportant, but that they were
acquired through reading, without the drills and rote learning of the Latin
lessons, and often in the students' own language. Knowledge of other
matters – French, Gaelic, Chronology, History and Critick – might also
be acquired "by the by": that is, as we would say today, they were not
part of the core curriculum. But even in giving them this much attention
Scalan was probably ahead of its time, as we have seen.[12] In the case of
Gaelic, indeed, it was almost certainly the only school in the country
(apart from Gregory Farquharson's) to teach it at this date; and this with
good reason: it was preparing its future priests to master and use the

language of the Highlander, while the other schools of Scotland were dedicated to destroying that language.

In the five-year classical syllabus of the Grammar schools the names given to the classes varied according to local usage, but typically they might begin with Figures in first year, and progress through Grammar, Syntax and Poetry to the final class, Rhetoric, in the fifth.[13] Scalan used a similar division, with Rhetoric completing the course (and with Greek available to those who had made good progress). But the small number of students meant that the arrangement had to be flexible. In practice, the seminary hardly ever enjoyed the luxury of five separate classes. Adaptability was the watch-word, with the course sometimes extended beyond five years, or compressed into four, depending on the aptitude of particular students and the general level of the group.[14]

The boys transferring to the Scots Colleges, (and in future years the lay students), left at the end of the Classical course. Those staying on to complete their training for the priesthood at Scalan now proceeded to a course of study similar to that provided at the Colleges themselves, a five- or six-year programme usually comprising two years' Philosophy followed by three or four of Divinity.[15] It was to these senior students that Rule 18 referred; those among them who had shown a special aptitude for languages as juniors might now also take the opportunity to acquire Hebrew.

Thus a young man receiving his entire training at Scalan would spend ten or eleven years there, and take his education from the beginning of elementary Latin to a level of Philosophy and Divinity comparable with that of the Scots Colleges in Europe. And for Bishop Gordon, who had fought so hard and long for a seminary at home and now with his *Rules* had completed its foundations, it was important that the comparison would be a favourable one. The little seminary must match the standards of the Colleges; but with few of the resources they could call upon. The task he set it was remarkable – to be a Paris or a Rome and more, on a shoe string, with a handful of students, in a small turf house, in the remote uplands of Glenlivet. It had none of their traditions, their libraries, their cultural resources. And where they had religious communities at their disposal, and a staff team of Principal, Procurator and Prefect of Studies, it would often only have one man: a young man, more often than not, only recently ordained.[16] He must be everybody – academic director and polymath, spiritual guide and confessor, guardian of the house, bursar, farmer, priest. No wonder that the bishop had been hard put to find such a man for the post; not surprising some men's reluctance to take it on: it would daunt the strongest.

NOTES

1. Bishop Gordon *Rules*, June 1722, CS 1/2, SCA; also printed, with slightly different spelling and punctuation, in Anderson W. J. 'The College for the Lowland District of Scotland at Scalan and Aquhorties: Registers and Documents', *IR*, vol. xiv, no. 2, autumn 1963, Appendix I.
2. Re keeping company, see the events leading to the dismissal of Jamie MacIntyre in the 1790s (pp. 196f. and 219f.); for an example of the harmful effect of a parental visit, see the incident involving Tom Robertson in 1770 (p. 141).
3. Cf., Beveridge C. 'Childhood and Society in Eighteenth Century Scotland', chap. 11 of Dwyer J., Mason R. A. and Murdoch A. (eds.) *New Perspectives on the Politics and Culture of Early Modern Scotland* (Edinburgh, 1982).
4. As to whether corporal punishment was in fact used at Scalan, I have found no evidence in the correspondence. We do know that Bishop Hay, who was master between 1788-93, had no hesitation in beating the future Bishop Murdoch when he was his student at Aquhorties in the early 1800s.
5. Barnes A.S. *The Catholic Schools of England* (London, 1926), espec. the accounts of St. Omer's (pp. 67f.) and St. Gregory's Douai (pp. 78ff.).
6. Recollections of Gilbert Langley, who joined the school in 1721, in Barnes A.S. *Op. cit.*, pp. 80f.
7. Re Burgh schools in 17C, Scotland J. *The History of Scottish Education* (London, 1969), vol. 1, pp. 77f.; re 18C, Grant J. *History of the Burgh Schools of Scotland* (London and Glasgow, 1876), p. 166; re SSPCK, Scotland J. *Op. cit.*, p. 99; re Watson's, Waugh H. L. *George Watson's College: History and Record 1724–1970* (Edinburgh, 1970), p. 36 (the pupils rose one hour later in the winter months). In the 17C most burgh schools had opened at 6 am, with pupils facing an 11 hour day!
8. Bishop Hay, in Notes re proposed union of seminaries, 1778, CS 1/1/4, SCA.
9. 'Statuta Collegii Scotorum Parisiensis', 1707, (in Latin) CA 1/10/2, cap. iv and cap. vii. 1, 3, 4, 5-6, SCA.
10. Geddes Bp. J. 'A Brief Historical Account of the Seminary at Scalan', 1777, CH 1/3, para 10.
11. Bishop Gordon to Thomas Innes, 15. 9. 1722, BL.
12. Cf., chap. 1, note 38.
13. Egs. of curricula in Grant J. *Op. cit.*, pp. 336ff. and 404ff.
14. We have documentation from the 1780s for four classes: Bishop Hay 'Distribution of the Hours at Scalan', n.d., CS 1/1/14, SCA.
15. The Scots College Rome's five year Classics syllabus comprised Figurae, Grammatica, Syntaxis, Poesis and Rhetorica, followed by Philosophy, Dialectic, and Junior and Senior Divinity: *Records of the Scots Colleges at Douai, Rome, Madrid, Valladolid and Ratisbon,* New Spalding Club (Aberdeen, 1906).
16. Cf., p. 232, for the average age and post-ordination experience of Scalan masters at the time of appointment.

6

Under Attack (1722–1732)

In May 1722 George Innes moved out of Scalan. His uncle Walter, who had been living at the family home at Balnacraig, acting as chaplain to the house and priest to the local population, was about to leave for France, and George was asked to take his place. He seems to have left the seminary against Bishop Gordon's express wish that he should stay. The annual grant he was now receiving from his uncle Lewis gave him a certain independence, since he no longer had to rely solely on his Mission quota. The bishop responded by stopping his quota,[1] and brought Mr John Alexander Grant in to replace him at Scalan.

Mr Grant was only three years a priest, and just back from Paris. He was recognised as a man of great virtue, but with his piety went a nervous and scrupulous temperament, and with his humility a sense of his own unfitness for office. When he realised the burden of his new post, he later admitted, his very bones shook and tears many times filled his eyes. As well as looking after the seminary he was expected to act as priest to the local community. Though he shouldered his burdens with goodwill he was plagued with anxiety over the problems he encountered – questions of mixed marriages, children's education, and the witholding of the sacraments. And it was not the responsibility alone that weighed upon him: he felt crushed by the desolate landscape of the Braes, and longed for the beauty of Paris again.[2]

During his first winter he had the benefit of a lengthy visit from Bishop Gordon, who at this time had it in mind to spend his winters at Scalan whenever possible. The two most senior students, George Gordon and Hugh MacDonald, had been at the seminary since it opened, Hugh having come there from Eilean Bàn. Both had already completed Philosophy were now due to receive Minor Orders. The bishop wanted to be at Scalan to give them their final preparations personally and satisfy himself that they were ready.[3]

The following June (1723) he returned to prepare them for advancement to the order of subdeacon,[4] and after a month at the College headed for the Western Highlands and Islands where he confirmed more than 2000 people, most of them converts to the Faith. He was able to report more conversions than for many years, in fact, but he also had to warn Rome of the growing opposition to Catholics everywhere. Parliament had recently passed an 'Act of Abjuration', and he feared that this would be used as a pretext for further harrassment by the Church's enemies. Scalan was already being targeted, as were the Catholic schools.[5]

One of the latter was Gregory Farquharson's school in Glenlivet. He was still managing to make it pay, by boarding some of the pupils at his home to supplement the fees which alone would not have supported himself and his family. But in the summer of 1724 he moved to Fochabers, to become private tutor to the Duke of Gordon's oldest son. Bishop Gordon decided that Archibald Anderson would have to be released from Scalan to keep the school going.

The deacon went with some reluctance, for he did not think himself "carv'd out for a Dominie".[6] And as a single man it was beyond him to keep the boarders on. Nor could he hope to be supported by his own family, for his older brother had squandered every penny of their money. Bishop Gordon knew his circumstances, and had been giving him an annual allowance of £30 Scots just to keep him in clothes. But he could not make ends meet at the school and in any case, when his father died the following year, he was needed back at the farm, and had no choice but to close it.[7]

Though George Innes was still at his parents' home at Balnacraig he continued to play some part in training boys for the priesthood. He was preparing one boy for the Scots College Paris at his parents' house, and keeping contact with one or two others whenever possible, and reporting to Paris as to their suitability.[8] His views carried weight with Charles Whytford, the College principal, who ideally would have liked to have him on the staff there, to succeed his uncle Thomas as Prefect of Studies.[9]

At the end of July he paid a hurried visit to Scalan to see for himself how the young master and the students were surviving in the new hostile climate. He found things better than they might have been:

> These few dayes bygone I have been in Sc which I longd much to sie, [he wrote to Paris] and am to leave it to morrow. I'm overjoyd to see y^m subsist & floorish considering the violent oppositions of their numerous adversaries who thought utterly to undoe them.[10]

Although the local Kirk was stepping up its opposition, and the Synod of Moray were preparing a report concerning the Catholic menace in Banffshire which they intended to bring to the attention of the King himself,[11] this had not actually resulted in any direct harrassment of Scalan. And ironically it was their co-religionists, the Protestant gentlemen of Glenlivet, who were thwarting their attempts to do real damage: these good neighbours knew that the seminary was harming no-one, and they used their influence to shield it from direct attack.

*   *   *

George Innes left Scalan on 1 August, being now urgently needed in Aberdeen to care for the elderly priest Mr Robert Strachan in his last illness.[12] He was there barely three weeks, for the old man was declining fast, and died on 20 August. Bishop Gordon was now faced with the problem of finding someone to serve Aberdeen and decided to send John Alexander Grant, despite the fact that he had already taken Archibald Anderson out of Scalan. He may well have felt that the young master would be better away from the seminary for a while, given the growing threats against it and his own scruples as to his fitness.

The man he sent to cover for him, John Tyrie, was hardly the ideal replacement. Even as a newly ordained priest he had appeared to colleagues over-forward and too great a lover of company, and these and other faults would emerge even more clearly in later years, to the distress of the Mission.[13] But Bishop Gordon had little room for choice, and in any case only intended the arrangement to be temporary.

Mr Grant probably stayed in Aberdeen about six months. Certainly, the wording of a letter written by him from Scalan on 16 March 1725 suggests that had returned shortly before that date.[14]

Once back at the seminary his immediate task was to prepare four of his students for the next stage of their careers. Two of them, his own brother James and Peter Grant of Blairfindy, were due to transfer to Rome. They set out in September, bearing his letter of recommendation to William Stuart the Scots Agent, which particularly asked him to take them under his wing, since they could hope to receive little support from the College staff. "You are to them in that place where their neerest nighbours are not their best friends (inimici hominis domestici) as Father, Master, &c," the letter urged.[15] Mr Grant was aware that the success rate of Scots students in Rome was low. But in these two cases his worries were needless: James went on to complete his course and become a priest and eventually a bishop of the Mission; and Peter would in time succeed William Stuart as Scots Agent, and hold that post for forty-five years.

The two other students were George Gordon and Hugh Macdonald, who were being prepared for ordination at Scalan. The date set for the event was Ember Sunday, but Bishop Gordon arrived at the beginning of the summer to oversee the last three months of their preparation.[16] For him the ordinations were hugely important, because they would see his original hopes for the seminary coming to fruition at last. And for the Mission they would be a watershed, for these young men were the first since the Reformation to have received their entire training for the priesthood in Scotland.

After their ordination the two new priests were given posts in the Highlands, as they had requested. George Gordon was assigned to assist Mr William Shand, the priest of Strathavon, by covering the Glenlivet end of his extensive station: the placement made Glenlivet in effect a separate station for the first time. Hugh MacDonald was sent to learn his trade as assistant priest in Moidart, and after a year was given a station of his own in his home country of Morar, where he resided in the turf house on Eilean Bàn in which he had begun his training for the priesthood.

Bishop Gordon was now over sixty, and his assistant Bishop Wallace in his seventies. Over the past twenty years his visitations to the West had met with much success, but they were becoming ever more arduous. How much more could be achieved by a bishop based permanently in the Western Highlands, and who spoke the Highlanders' language as a native! He was already pressing Rome to consider appointing such a "Western Physician", and he had earmarked John Alexander Grant as "incomparably the fittest" for the position.[17]

Mr Grant was an Enzie man and not a native Gaelic speaker, but he had learned something of the language during his time at Scalan. And his piety was beyond dispute. But he himself had no desire for the mitre, and was as diffident as ever of his own worthiness. And though he had found Scalan daunting at first, he had by now grown into his work there. He had discovered a real talent for teaching and guiding young people, and had no ambition to leave the College where, he believed, he could happily live and die. But Bishop Gordon continued to press Rome to agree to his appointment, and even wrote to ask King James to use his influence in the matter.[18]

The Kirk had stepped up its harrassment of Catholics in 1725, encouraged by George I's grant of 1000 Crowns "for the reformation of the Highlands and Islands", which not only gave them the wherewithal, but seemed to give the nod of approval for a more aggressive approach.

The Committee appointed to manage this 'King's Bounty' decided to make their prime target the areas of Catholic population, and above all the Gordon country of the North-East. This they believed was now *the* nerve centre of Catholicism in Scotland, the seat of its bishop and the hub of its "intelligence, counsel and direction".[19] There Catholics were openly employed as school teachers, in administration and the courts, and many had recently bought lands, all in defiance of the Act of 1700. There too, they particularly noted, was sited the Church's national "Nursery or College" at "Scalla", whose student roll they were able to quote with some accuracy.[19]

When the persecution began in earnest in the spring of 1726, therefore, it was inevitable that the Gordon lands would bear the brunt of it, and that the seminary would not be spared. On the eve of Pentecost Mr Shand was seized in Strathavon and thrown into "an abominable prison with thieves and whores, in summer devoured with rats and vermin, and in winter killed with cold".[20] And over at Scalan, every day the little community awaited the knock at the door.

Then towards the end of August there was an unexpected lull, and the worst seemed to be over.[21] Bishop Gordon paid a visit to Scalan, despite the dangers, and stayed long enough to satisfy himself that the community was safe.[22] But barely a month after he left the attacks were renewed. As word came of the Independent Companies returning to Glenlivet, the master and boys packed their clothes and whatever else they could and took refuge in houses nearby, so that when a detachment of soldiers arrived at the seminary they found the place deserted. Bishop Gordon's letter to Paris provides the details:

a party went by orders to S . . .n, & threatn'd to lodge thereabout all winter, & to send some of their number every other day; & as the storm had been foreseen all who used to stay there had scatter'd; after some weeks M. Fife made the prent[es] return, & sometimes the shop-keeper was with them; they are still threatn'd but especially he; & there is never quiet because of the restless & unrelenting malice of the p . . . ers [preachers?]who clamour without end; & make the Capt[s] in spite of them in a manner strive to do mischief.[23]

Although the master resumed his duties during the day, it was some time before he dared sleep overnight at Scalan, and Bishop Gordon did not know whether he would be able to continue doing so in the long-term. He even thought seriously about taking over himself for a while – this might be safer, because their enemies would hesitate to touch him. He was close to the Duke of Gordon, and His Grace had already intervened on the Catholics' behalf, apparently at the personal request of the Pope: it was in fact only through the Duke's influence, the bishop believed, that greater harm had not been done.[24]

Shortly before Christmas John Alexander Grant was called to Rome to be consecrated bishop, and Bishop Gordon apparently saw this as an opportunity to ease the situation at Scalan. His solution was to reinstate George Innes as master, but allow him to continue living at Balnacraig. How this was managed in practice, and who took direct charge at Scalan under his authority, is not known. But not having a priest on the premises may well have helped to quieten their enemies. By the end of the year, though things were in no way back to normal, at least the lessons were taking place regularly again. The seminary had also received donations from Lewis Innes and the Duchess of Perth, enabling it to recover and even take in more boys: there were now actually thirteen students in residence, twice as many as ever before, and the house was stretched to the limit to accommodate them.[25]

* * *

In the spring of 1727 the Prefect of Studies post at the Scots College Paris fell vacant. Thomas Innes was planning to return home to publish his seminal *Essay on the Ancient Inhabitants of Scotland*,[27] and he and his senior colleagues all favoured George Innes as his successor. They believed that with his quiet and studious temper he would be the best man for the post, "if his parents would part with him" and let him leave Balnacraig.[28]

At home, Bishop Wallace felt he was too valuable to lose. "If it depended on me," he told Paris, "I w^d think my selfe oblidged in conscience to keep him in this harvest."[29] But the decision was Bishop Gordon's, and though he recognised George Innes' worth as a scholar and teacher he did not share his Assistant's unqualified regard for him. "His chief fault," he told his uncle frankly, "is to be easily discourag'd especially in temp^{ls}, in which he is one of the most shiftless & least skillfull you know."[30] However, as Prefect of Studies he would be taking little to do with 'temporals' – financial and other worldly matters – and Bishop Gordon decided to let him go. He knew that Alexander Smith would probably be returning to Scotland, and that George Gordon, the young priest whom he had ordained at Scalan, was also returning from a brief visit abroad and could be slotted in at the seminary.

George Innes left Balnacraig at the beginning of the summer and travelled down to Aberdeen, intending to sail as soon as he could take ship. He must have been delighted and relieved to be returning to Paris, where he had found life so congenial and so well suited to his health.

It cannot be said that he had got Scalan off to a good start. He was painfully aware of this himself, in fact, and his feelings of guilt had brought on a general crisis of confidence in his vocation the previous year, when he had confessed to his uncle Thomas not only a sense of failure in regard to the seminary, but a conviction that he had been "wholy incapable and insignificant" throughout his priestly life.[31]

It was November before he finally got away.[32] It is good to know that after his problems on the Mission he settled happily to his new work in Paris, and undertook it with energy and wisdom to the pleasure of his uncles and the great comfort of his bishop.[33] In seven years he became Procurator (despite his shortcomings regarding 'temporals'), and four years later he was made Principal, a post he would hold until his death in 1752.

When George Gordon arrived to take over at Scalan in June 1728, it was hoped that his stay would be longer than that of his predecessors. The seminary had had six changes of master in its first eleven years and its greatest need now was for continuity. But he could hardly have come at a more difficult time. On 20 November, just five months after his arrival, the Duke of Gordon died. His widow Henrietta at once made arrangements to have the children, including Cosmo George his heir, taken from their Catholic tutors to be brought up in her own Episcopalian faith. Her action spelled the end of the Catholic House of Gordon. It was a body blow to the Church in the North-East, indeed throughout Scotland, and a bitter disappointment to Bishop Gordon. His meeting with the Duchess, in which she promised fair treatment to the Catholics on her estates, only partly reassured him. His great fear was that the faithful in the North-East, who had hitherto been shielded from the worst effects of persecution, would from now on be "exposed to continual vexations".[34]

He was particularly concerned with the danger to Scalan. He would have preferred to be there himself through the autumn and winter, he told Bishop Wallace, had not other duties prevented him:

> I never had greater need than I have just now to stay some considerable time at Sc: where I fear things will go quite wrong because I am not allowed to stay longer & oftener with them; pray much for them I beseech you.[35]

He had very possibly learned of the plans of the area Kirk Synod against the seminary. On its agenda that very month was a plan of action for Glenlivet, which among other things recommended that the local Presbytery "lay out themselves" to suppress the College,[36] just as they had done two years before.

But it was not only threats from without that caused him to fear that things might "go quite wrong". This was a time of flux for Scalan, with a young master who lacked experience, and with an unusually large number of students not only transferring to the Colleges abroad but also returning from them.

In November Allan MacDonald arrived from Douai. He was thirty-one, and had been one of the original students at Eilean Bàn, and – along with John MacLachlan – the first to transfer to Rome. But despite taking the Mission oath he had left the College in 1721, plagued by ill health and doubts about his vocation. Six years later he had sought to try again at Rome but had been refused admission, and after unsuccessfully approaching the Scots College in Madrid had finally enrolled at Douai. His career there had ended in dismissal after barely a year, and now, on his return to Scotland in October, he had gone straight to Bishop Gordon. He had given him a frank account of his previous failures, but begged to be given one last trial at Scalan. "He seem'd so penitent & submissive, & conjur'd so earnestly" that the bishop agreed to let him stay at least for the winter.[37]

Another student also recently returned from Paris was Alexander

Gordon, dubbed 'Coffurich' after his birthplace to distinguish him from the host of other Gordons. He was now in his late teens, and being so much older than the other boys was more like an assistant than a student. When Bishop Gordon paid his next visit to Scalan in the autumn of 1729 he found that the young master was now relying heavily on him, and was unwilling to let him resume at Paris as planned.[38]

The bishop decided that Alexander Gordon must return to France. But he agreed that Allan MacDonald could stay, at least for the following year. Unlike so many students returning from the Colleges abroad he had settled well, and not unsettled the younger boys: "Scarce ever any came hither from ab^d who has been so exemplary," he reported to Thomas Innes, "very pious, submissive, humble, tractable, & docile; & behaves so that he gives no handle to press him away."[39] The only concern was his poor health, which made his future uncertain.

In the new year of 1730 Ranald MacDonald arrived home from Rome, having left without completing his studies, and was enrolled at Scalan. His admission marked an immediate change in the atmosphere there. He seemed to have no serious intent, and in no time became a disruptive influence on the others.[40] His arrival also brought the number of High-landers at the seminary up to six, so that they were no longer a minority. They now spent all their free time together, away from the rest and speaking their own language. Before long the student body had split into two hostile camps, Highland and Lowland.[41]

Allan MacDonald himself seems to have become infected by the changed atmosphere, and to have been drawn into the disputes. There was a new tone to Bishop Gordon's letter to Paris in February – Allan was not applying himself to his studies, he reported, and his relations with his fellow students had changed; he was even thinking of moving him if possible:

> He has so litle health that he can't apply, & therefore we are endeavouring to get him employ'd some other way: but in the main he is uneasy to others in the meantime, & we think by the experience we have had of him & others we will be forc'd to take a resolution not to medle hence forth with Hamb^{gers} [ex-Rome students]; they doing no good to them selvs, & eating the bread of others, & creating no small uneasiness.[42]

The Highland clique were now not only quarrelling almost daily with the other boys, but showing scant respect for the master himself, and their challenge to authority had reached such a pitch that it seemed Scalan might have to be closed entirely. Bishop Gordon was forced to step in, and in order to save the seminary he decided to dismiss Ranald, Allan, and two of the other Highland students.[43]

(Allan went back to the West, where for the next twelve years he worked as a teacher in the Catholic schools, with a brief spell in 1738 in the Highland seminary at Gaotal. He finally had his wish and was ordained to the priesthood in the summer of 1742.[44])

Scalan's unhappy experience with its students in the spring of 1730, and the dismissal of several who were well advanced in their training, was the more unfortunate in view of the crying need for priests in Scotland. The bishops' report to Rome that year warned that the number of missioners was falling – between illness, overwork, or sheer poverty – and was likely to fall further yet, since every day others were threatening to quit.[45]

But there were reasons for the high failure rate of Scottish students, both at home and abroad, which were largely beyond the bishops' control, as they were at pains to point out in a lengthy letter sent to the Cardinal Protector the following year. The choice of candidates was very limited, they explained. Nearly all the Catholics of Scotland were of low birth, poor and lacking education. Since boys of such a background would be despised by their own people if they were ever to return as priests, the bishops had been forced to restrict their choice to the small number of sons of higher birth. And their choice was further limited by the practice of the Benedictines and Jesuits of taking boys of this class at a young age – sometimes younger than ten – and sending them to their own houses abroad. They themselves were thus forced to search for even younger recruits.But the younger the boys, the longer the training they required, and this must take place either at Scalan or abroad. And since it was beyond the Mission's means to provide an extended education at Scalan to any but a very few, they had been obliged to send most boys abroad when still far too young and immature.[46]

The result, of course, was that a high proportion were giving up their studies – probably through home-sickness more often than not – and returning to Scotland. And some, like Allan and Ranald, were ending up at Scalan. The little seminary now had a polarised student body, made up of young boys and adult 'returners', and neither was good for the other. The older ones were often disenchanted, and resented finding themselves back among children; and the youngsters were becoming infected by the talk of their elders and their criticisms of the Colleges abroad.[47] It is not surprising that the 'failure rate' at this time was high.

One returner who did persevere to the end was George Duncan. He had been sent to Paris in the spring of 1726, where his goodness and piety were soon noticed by the staff. He showed admirable goodwill and diligence in his studies, although he was very much a plodder – "longsome (wee call it Lambin)" as his teacher described him.[48] But his health had suffered in France. At this time the Paris College was a hazardous place for those of weak health. Several students had already been sent home, one had died there, and – incredibly – two more were to die within the next three years.[49] In young George's case the physicians advised that he would only grow worse unless he was sent home, but this he was reluctant to agree to, for he was desperate to pursue his vocation. He was only persuaded after Bishop Gordon promised him that he could continue his training in Scotland, where he would be given all the books he needed, and special tuition and care, even if it meant the bishop himself providing it.[50]

The following spring he returned to Scotland and continued his training in the care of a priest of the Mission. The individual attention he received, and his own determination, brought him through. His progress was very slow, but steady,[51] and he was eventually able to enrol as a student at Scalan. The exact date of his admission is not known, but he almost certainly missed the dissensions of 1730. He was by now well advanced in his training, and within about a year was judged ready for the priesthood. In March 1732 Bishop Gordon travelled up to the seminary to ordain him, after which he sent him to gain experience teaching in the Highlands.[52]

NOTES

1. George Innes to Thomas Innes, 29. 1. 1723, BL.
2. John A. Grant to Bishop Gordon, 1. 8. 1723, BL.
3. Bishop Gordon to ?, 17. 10. 1722, BL.
4. Bishop Gordon to Thomas Innes, 28. 9. 1723, BL.
5. Bishop Gordon Report to Propaganda, October 1723 (in Latin), BL 2/249/7; and Bishop Gordon to Thomas Innes, 28. 9. 1723, BL. Act of Abjuration – 'An Act to oblige all Persons, being Papists, in that Part of Great Britain called Scotland, and all persons in Great Britain, refusing or neglecting to take the Oaths appointed for the Security of His Majesty's Person and Government, by several Acts herein mentioned, to Register their Names and Real Estates', etc.: 9 Geo I c. 24, 1723, *The Statutes at Large*, vol. v, (London, 1763), p. 475.
6. Archibald Anderson to Thomas Innes, 31. 7. 1724, BL.
7. James Carnegy to Thomas Innes, 8. 9. 1725, BL.
8. George Innes to Thomas Innes, 13. 7. 1724, BL.
9. Thomas Innes to Bishops Gordon and Wallace, 10. 6. 1724, copy SM 3/22, SCA.
10. George Innes to Thomas Innes, 31. 7. 1724, BL.
11. Synod of Moray, Record of Meetings, meeting of 29. 10. 1724, CH 2/271/VI, p. 223, SRO.
12. George Innes had previously stayed at Aberdeen to assist Mr Strachan in 1723 – cf. Bishop Wallace to Thomas Innes, 19. 8. 1723, BL.
13. Robert Gordon to Thomas Innes, 15. 6. 1720, BL. Re the future cf. Chap. 7 below.
14. John A. Grant to Bishop Gordon, 16. 3. 1725, BL.

15. John A. Grant to William Stuart, 28. 8. 1725, BL. His words of concern echoed those of Bishop Gordon when sending students from Eilean Bàn to Rome – cf., Chap. 2, note 27.
16. James Carnegy to Thomas Innes, 8. 10. 1725, BL.
17. Re Bishop Gordon's opinion of Mr Grant, Bishop Gordon to Thomas Innes, 8. 9. 1725 and 10. 9. 1726, BL.
18. Bishop Gordon to Propaganda, 20. 1. 1726; and to King James, 15. 8. 1726, BL.
19. 'Register of Actings and Proceedings of the Committee of the Church of Scotland for the Reformation of the Highlands and Islands of Scotland, And for managment of the King's Bounty for that end', Annis 1725-9; 'Memorial' presented to meeting of 10. 5. 1726, and approved: CH 1/5/51, pp. 73ff., SRO.
20. James Carnegy to Thomas Innes, 19. 12. 1726, BL.
21. George Innes to Thomas Innes, 26. 8. 1726, BL.
22. Bishop Gordon to Thomas Innes, 26. 8. 1726, BL, sent from Scalan.
23. Bishop Gordon to Thomas Innes, 6. 12. 1726, BL. A number of Independent Companies had been formed the previous year, so called because they operated in their own local areas. They were later combined into an official force that came to be known as the Black Watch. Cf., Forbes A. *The 'Black Watch', the Record of an Historic Regiment* (London, 1896), chap. 12 'The Genesis of the Regiment'.
24. Ibid.
25. Ibid.
26. John A. Grant to Bishop Gordon, 13. 1. 1727, BL. His appointment had been approved by Propaganda on 17 December, but was not ratified until July 1728.
27. Innes T. *Critical Essay on the Inhabitants of the Northern Parts of Britain or Scotland,* 2 vols. (London, 1729). This work confirmed Innes as a scholar of international standing.
28. Thomas Innes to Bishops Gordon and Wallace, 16. 4. 1727 and 23. 4. 1727, copy SM 3/22, SCA.
29. Bishop Wallace to Thomas Innes, 18. 4. 1727, BL.
30. Bishop Gordon to Thomas Innes, 10. 1. 1727, BL.
31. George Innes to Thomas Innes, 26. 8. 1726, BL.
32. George Innes to Thomas Innes, 14. 8. 1727, 2. 9. 1727, 9. 10. 1727, 16. 10. 1727, BL.
33. Thomas Innes to Alexander Smith, April 1729, copy SM 3/22; Bishop Gordon to Thomas Innes, 6. 8. 1729, BL.
34. Bishop Gordon to Propaganda, 29. 3. 1729 (in Latin), BL.
35. Bishop Gordon to Bishop Wallace, 19. 10. 1728, BL.
36. Synod of Moray, Record of Meetings, meeting of 23-24. 10. 1728, CH 2/271/VI, pp. 284f., SRO.
37. Bishop Gordon to Thomas Innes, 15. 2. 1729, BL.
38. Bishop Gordon to Lewis Innes, 4. 11. 1729, BL.
39. Bishop Gordon to Thomas Innes, 6. 11. 1729, BL.
40. Bishop Gordon to Thomas Innes, 28. 2. 1730, BL.
41. William Reid to Bishop Grant, 16. 12. 1763, BL, recalling events from his own student days at Scalan.

42. Bishop Gordon to Thomas Innes, 28. 2. 1730, BL.
43. William Reid, loc. cit.
44. Cf., Clapperton W. *Memoirs of Scotch Missionary Priests*, transcibed Wilson G. (Elgin, 1901), pp. 2045ff., SCA, based on Bishop Geddes' *Memoirs* and Mission Quota Accounts. Re his being i/c Gaotal, Bishop Hugh MacDonald to George Innes, 20. 10. 1738, BL.
45. Report of Bishops Gordon and Wallace to Propaganda, 4. 7. 1730 (in Latin), BL.
46. Bishops Gordon and Wallace to Cardinal Falconieri, 13. 11. 1731 (in Latin), BL.
47. Bishop Gordon to Lewis Innes, 12. 8. 1732, BL.
48. Thomas Innes to Bishops Gordon and Wallace, 25. 9. 1726, copy SM 3/22, SCA.
49. Cf., Halloran B. M. *The Scots College Paris 1603–1792* (Edinburgh, 1997), p. 152.
50. Bishop Gordon to Thomas Innes, 6. 12. 1726, BL.
51. Bishop Gordon to Thomas Innes, 27. 2. 1729, BL.
52. Bishop Gordon to ?, 15. 4. 1732, original not located, cited in Clapperton W. *Memoirs*, p. 2047.

7

Wounded from Within (1732–1738)

The "heats and seditions" that had come to a head at Scalan in the spring of 1730 were at heart a clash of cultures and temperaments. But they were more than this. The Church had still not really addressed the quite different needs of the Highlands and Lowlands, either in its own structures or in the training it provided for its priests. Scalan was not geared to cater for these differences, any more than the Scots Colleges abroad. The pious hope that it would foster Gaelic, for instance, though enshrined in the *Rules,* was not likely to be realised where English was the medium of learning and all serious business, and where, moreover, the Highlanders and Lowlanders were barely speaking to one another.

It was in order to address the problem, at least in terms of the authority structure of the Church, that Bishop Gordon had argued for a separate bishop for the Highlands, and won the Vatican's agreement, as long ago as 1726. But his original choice, the Scalan Master John Alexander Grant, though he reached Rome had disappeared before the date fixed for his consecration – it is still not known for certain how or why – and years of delay had followed. It was not until January 1731 that his replacement, Hugh MacDonald, was nominated, and – after visiting Paris to broaden his ecclesiastical experience – finally consecrated in Edinburgh by Bishops Gordon and Wallace in October.[1]

After the ceremony the three men agreed a draft document for dividing the country into Highland and Lowland Districts. It was a division that broadly followed the geographical divide, but, since it was based on language rather than terrain, the areas that lay close to the Highland Line were assigned to one or other District according to the predominant language of the local people.[2] Their proposals were accepted in Rome, and ratified almost verbatim in a Decree issued by Propaganda. But minor changes in the wording of this final document had important implications for the areas on the edge of the Highlands. The Decree included within the Highland District those parts of Dumbartonshire, Angus, Perthshire, Stirlingshire, Mar and Moray where Gaelic was generally spoken, but (unlike the draft) with no specific mention of Banffshire.[3] The result was that in the North-East, areas such as Upper Deeside, Glengairn and Corgarff were included in the Highland District, whereas Glenlivet and Strathavon – which on grounds of language were equally strong con-

MAP 4
The Highland and Lowland Vicariates
1732

Note: Orkney and Shetland were for convenience
sake counted within the Highland Vicariate
despite being English-speaking

Shetland

Orkney

n

Strathavon
Glenlivet

Corgarff
Glengairn

Upper Deeside

—————————— Boundary of Lowland Vicariate

– – – – – – – – – – Boundary of Gaelic-speaking area

tenders – were not (Map 4). According to the eighteenth century historian
of the Mission, John Thomson, it was Bishop Gordon himself who
persuaded Propaganda to make the emendment, in order to keep these
two stations within his own Vicariate, and particularly in order to hold on
to Scalan.[4]

Bishop Hugh MacDonald at once made a tour of the mainland parts of
the Highland District, and on his return wrote to Propaganda giving his
first impressions of the task before him.[5] The situation was wretched, he
reported, and the needs of the people pitiable. The gravest problem was
the shortage of priests, and for this he laid some of the blame on the Scots
Colleges, since many Highland boys had abandoned their vocation while
studying abroad. The solution, he argued, would be to set up a seminary
within his Vicariate, which would allow some youths to be trained at
home, and others to be sent to the Colleges only after preparatory training
and trial of their serious intent.

He did not single out any College by name, but we know from other
evidence that he was especially unhappy with Paris, which he felt was
biassed against Highland boys,[6] and where at this date the teaching,
supervision and economy were at a low ebb.[7]

Nor did he make any mention of Scalan, or of the recent problems of
the Highland students who attended it. But the fact that he was now
arguing for a separate seminary for the Highlands must suggest that he
did not consider Scalan could meet his needs, despite the fact that he had
received his own training there. Above all, he wanted a place under his
own sole control. Later in the year he got his wish, when a new, separate
seminary for the Highlands was opened, in the house on Eilean Bàn that
he had known so well as a student and priest. Scalan now lost its rôle as
national seminary, and would remain for the rest of its days the College of
the Lowland Vicariate.

The Highland Church had long felt itself the poor relation of the Scottish
Mission, second best in power and voice, its people poorer and its priests
more overworked than those in the Lowlands. Now its clergy saw the
creation of a separate Vicariate, and the appointment of their own bishop,
as the chance to put this right. They were counting on his youth and
energy, and some perhaps were also counting on his inexperience. Before
the end of his first year in office they had persuaded him to press for a
change in the method of dividing the Mission funds between the two
Districts, based not on the number of priests but of people within them.[8]
The change would have robbed the Lowlands to pay the Highlands, and
Bishop Gordon would not entertain it.

Already signs of friction and suspicion were beginning to appear, and if the 'Westerns' felt themselves ill-used some Lowland clergy feared a takeover by the far more numerous Highland Church. Two clear camps were now emerging within the Mission, based broadly on the traditional Highland-Lowland animosity, but in which a number of other factors – individual friendships and antagonisms, genuine hardships and grievances, long-standing friction between secular priests and Jesuits, and hopes for personal gain – also played a part. For this reason the two sides did not exactly match the division of the two Vicariates. Several secular priests from the Lowland District, and virtually all the Regulars across the country, allied themselves with the 'Highland' camp.

The split was becoming focused around two specific issues – those of authority (including the control of funds), and of doctrine. The first concerned in particular the crucial posts of Procurator of the Mission, who held and dispensed the funds, and Co-adjutor Bishop (since it was known that the man presently in post, Bishop Wallace, had not long to live). The second concerned an allegation of Jansenist error against a section of the Lowland clergy.

Jansenism had first emerged within the Catholic Church in the seventeenth century. Reaction against the triumphal optimism of the Counter-Reformation, together with close studies of the works of St Augustine, had given birth to a movement among certain deeply pious Catholics, which placed a strong emphasis on personal unworthiness and the concepts of predestination and 'the elect'. Its followers practised an ascetic spiritual régime, with infrequent and carefully prepared recourse to the Sacrament, in a spirit not entirely unlike that of traditional Calvinism. It was a complex and many-sided movement.[9] For its adherents it represented an emphasis in belief and spirituality rather than a hard-and-fast system. If theirs was an uneasy position within the Church, they in no way thought of themselves as heretical. But the issuing of the Bull *Unigenitus Dei Filius* by Pope Clement XI in 1713, condemning the movement, had had the effect of placing many beyond the line of heresy, and in a position of confrontation with the Church's authority that they had never wished. Jansenism had first been mentioned in reference to the Scottish Mission at the turn of the century, when Jesuit priests had made accusations against a number of missioners,[10] but it was only now that it emerged as crucial issue.

Both issues were in fact being made a nail to hang one's coat on and, for a few of the clergy, to forward their personal ambitions. One such, without doubt, was Colin Campbell, a convert from one of the great Highland Protestant families. He had hoped to be the original choice as bishop for the Highlands, and after the disappearance of John Alexander Grant had actually been promoted to Pro-Vicar by Bishop Gordon pending a permanent appointment. But when that appointment was made he had again been passed over. Now in 1732 he was emerging as the prime focus for both issues, on the one hand as a main contender for the post of Coadjutor Bishop, and on the other as the recognised leader of the group crusading against Jansenism within the Mission.[11]

In May 1732 the Scalan master George Gordon wrote to Colin Campbell's brother James, explaining his own views on doctrine. It was a letter that, with hindsight, he believed he had been tricked into writing, and which would later return to haunt him. In it he declined to come out firmly in favour of *Unigenitus,* which he believed the Pope had issued under pressure, or to condemn outright the 101 Propositions of the Jansenists.[12] Only after sending it did he realise that it might be used against him, and this fear helps to explain his subsequent behaviour.

Early the following spring he received a visit at Scalan from Colin Campbell himself, from whom he learned that his own name was being mentioned for the post of Coadjutor. He was dismayed, particularly because the word was going round that he was ambitious for such promotion. He at once wrote to Alexander Smith, who had proposed his name, urging him to undo the damage, which if allowed to continue might "crush him entirely, and ruine the whole company".[13] He was clearly anxious not to incur the displeasure of Colin Campbell, who he knew was a candidate for the post, and whom he hopefully described as his "dearest friend".

In late May (1733) Bishop Gordon visited Scalan, where on 6 June he chaired a meeting that would have profound implications for the Mission, the Scots College Paris, and Scalan itself. Also in attendance were Bishop Hugh MacDonald, three Highland and four Lowland priests, including Colin Campbell, George Gordon, and the former Scalan student George Duncan who had recently returned to the seminary as assistant master.

At the meeting three letters were penned to Rome – the first two from the bishops to the Pope and the Cardinal Protector respectively; the third from the seven priests to the Cardinal Protector, claiming to be written on behalf of "the whole clergy" of the Mission.[14] The content of all three was similar – a warning that Jansenist heresy was being taught at the Scots College Paris, and an urgent request for reform of the College and the removal of its senior staff. At the end of the meeting all present subscribed in writing to the Constitution *Unigenitus,* and took the decision that every priest in Scotland should be required to do the same.

In his recent history of the Scots College Paris, Halloran has provided a detailed account of the meeting – including a full transcription of the letters – and has shown conclusively that it was held at Scalan, and not at Clashnoir as had previously been supposed.[15]

Bishop Gordon himself gave two different explanations of how the meeting came about, which do not square with eachother. In the bishops' letter to the cardinal, which he himself penned, he implied that it was pre-arranged by himself and his colleague, with "other serious and select" priests invited.[16] On the other hand, he afterwards assured Thomas Innes at the Scots College that he had in fact been up at Scalan for his health, "not dreaming of such a meeting", and recalled the circumstances thus:

> On a sudden there came upon him greater number of Laborers than could be expected both from Highl & Lowlands and all crying of many Laborers being suspected of Jansen[m] and nothing would satisfy them till a new order was made by Nicopol. & Dianen. [himself and Bishop MacDonald] that all Laborers, Birlies [Jesuits] and Traders (Crows) [clergy in religious orders] in Scotl[d] should subscribe Const[n] Unigen. and all other Constit[ns] which was done by nine and I hope will be done by all the rest.[17]

This account appears to be an attempt to play down his own part in the affair, and to mislead without actually lying. (No doubt he *had* gone to Scalan for his health, as was his custom, and probably he had not expected *such* a meeting, even though he had arranged it himself.) Those present certainly put pressure on him, and he confided to one of his senior clergy that he felt isolated, harrassed, and forced into rushed decisions without "the sedatness and maturity that weighty affair required".[18]

But as senior bishop he should not have ceded to their demands unless he agreed with them. And the letters to Rome are quite explicit and leave no room for doubt as to where he stood. Furthermore, when he wrote to Propaganda again a week later, by which time the clergy had dispersed and he was no longer under direct pressure, his letter showed no sign of a change of opinion.[19]

If the meeting was more than he had bargained for – in the number present, their unanimity and vehemence – this was mainly due to the work of the two Campbells. Colin Campbell had been recruiting priests to attend – it was apparently he who had told Bishop MacDonald that his attendance was expected[20] – while his brother James had come to Scalan ten days early, in order to "sift" Bishop Gordon and work on the priests of the North-East as to the line they should take.[21]

George Gordon and George Duncan were really only roped in to the meeting to make up numbers, because they lived on the premises. It was ironic that they put their names to the third letter. For two days later a second meeting was held down the road at Clashnoir, in the house of Alexander Grant the priest of Glenlivet, with neither Bishop Gordon nor the two Scalan masters present, at which George Gordon was himself accused of heresy. This second meeting, which claimed a certain authority from the presence of Bishop MacDonald, passed a number of resolutions: among them, that all priests in Scotland be required to subscribe in writing to a Formula accepting *Unigenitus*; that the present Procurator be dismissed (James Campbell being recommended as his replacement); that all clergy should have a vote in the election of a Lowland Co-adjutor; and that six Mission priests including George Gordon and Alexander Smith (dubbed the 'Paris Club' on account of their association with the Scots College) stood accused of heresy and should be barred from any promotion.[22]

Shortly after the meeting Bishop MacDonald sent letters to those Lowland clergy who had not attended, urging them to subscribe to the Formula, an action that nettled Bishop Gordon since it encroached on his territory, and only widened the split. For his part the Scalan master saw no reason to subscribe again, and did not do so.[23]

The death of Bishop Wallace on 30 June (1733) brought the issue of his successor to the fore again. Alexander Smith still favoured George Gordon, and even suggested that he himself could be sent to Scalan, to take his place as master and free him for promotion.[24] George Gordon himself was totally against the proposal, and as anxious as ever not to upset the Campbell camp. He wrote to Colin Campbell that autumn, to scotch rumours that he was responsible for a campaign against him. He frankly admitted his belief that "only a Low-country-man born" should be appointed to what was a Lowland post, and that as such he could not support Campbell. But he deplored the "internal war" that seemed to be developing, and made a plea for freedom of opinion and no hard feelings once the appointment was made – "However it be," he wrote, " sicut fuerit voluntas in caelo, sic fiat; and no more of it".[25]

At the same time he organised a *Memorial* to Bishop Gordon, arguing not only that the new Co-adjutor must be a Lowlander, but that only Lowland clergy should have a vote in the election.[26] It was signed by himself, his assistant at Scalan George Duncan, and two other priests from the North-East.

The bishop still seemed to favour Colin Campbell, and in February 1734 wrote at length to George Gordon and Mr Duncan in an attempt to convince them that they should give him their vote.[27] The Scalan master sent him an equally lengthy reply, urging that if he appointed Campbell it would be "the thing that ever he did in this life that would be most blamed and cryed out against".[28]

At the same time he was writing to several known allies, trying to organise a tactical block vote at the forthcoming meeting of clergy in Edinburgh, where the election was to take place. In these letters he played the part of arch-conspirator. Failure was now unthinkable. "We are now so far advanced that we can not retire or be worsted but with great loss", he warned his friends.[29]

The loss that he feared was partly personal, and his fears were not groundless. Just weeks before the Edinburgh meeting his letter to James Campbell of two years before was leaked to a number of priests of the Mission. The timing was no coincidence. He was sure that it would be the end of him as far as Bishop Gordon was concerned, and that the bishop would certainly prevent him attending the meeting, on the pretext that the boys needed him at Scalan, but really in order to boost Campbell's chances of success.

But in fact Bishop Gordon may not have been so set on Colin Campbell as he supposed; he may indeed have had reservations about him since the Clashnoir meeting. In any case, no appointment was made at Edinburgh, and some months afterwards George Gordon was able to report to his friends with some satisfaction that through their continued efforts Campbell was now "as good as ousten".[30]

In the spring of 1735 Bishop Hugh Macdonald made a visitation to the eastern boundaries of his Vicariate. His presence there highlighted the vulnerable position of Strathavon and Glenlivet. The Highland clergy were pressing for these upland, Gaelic-speaking stations to be transferred into his Vicariate, in order to tip the balance of power in its favour,[31] and George Gordon was convinced that he was planning to raise the matter formally when he met Bishop Gordon after Easter. If so, the Scalan master and his fellow priests were resolved to acknowledge no authority but that of their own bishop, "till he expressly either by word or write give them up entirely", and even then they would resist any move into the Highland District.[32]

They contacted Bishop Gordon in advance of the meeting, urging him to surrender no territory. But their letter was in fact needless. He had no intention of giving up their stations, and above all the important resource of Scalan, for – as we saw – it was he who had been responsible for the final wording of the Vatican's Decree, which had ensured their inclusion in his Vicariate in the first place.[33]

Almost a year had now passed since the Edinburgh meeting and the question of the choice of Co-adjutor remained unanswered. Some favoured a young, energetic appointment, to match Bishop MacDonald, but George Gordon's preference was for an older man, precisely because of Bishop MacDonald's youth: "An Elderly man," he argued, "would be more regarded abroad than the Westerns' young D^r, and they themselves, not withstanding their obdurance, would be forced to shew respect to hoary hairs."[34] For this reason he was strongly opposed to Alexander Smith, who – word had it – was now the likely choice, and he believed that all the Lowland priests would share his view: "I doubt if any, whither South or North, whither Eccl[ks] [members of religious orders] or Seculars, will be content with the choice," he was telling friends in May.[35]

Three months later Alexander Smith was elected. The Scalan master, hunting with the hounds and running with the hare as usual, at once wrote to congratulate him: "I doubt not but you are fully perswaded there are few better pleased than myself with the choice M[r] Fife has made of you for his Helper," he wrote; and this, he assured him, was "the common sentiment of all of us".[36]

By now Colin Campbell and his colleague the one-time Scalan master John Tyrie were on their way to Rome, deputed to present recommendations to Propaganda for improving conditions in the Highland District, and at the same time to provide details of alleged Jansenism within the Mission. George Gordon learned that they planned to make a "very heavy charge" against him personally. He wrote at once to William Stuart, the Scots Agent in Rome, explaining in some detail his letter of 1732, for he knew that they intended to produce it as evidence.[37] The responsibility for it was his alone, he assured him, and in no way Bishop Gordon's, "who neither knew nor so much as suspected it"; indeed, it was the bishop who had since brought him from his errors. He was writing, in fact, to clear the bishop's name, because he believed that Campbell and Tyrie intended to implicate him also, and so if possible bring him down: they were planning, he wrote, "to drive the thrust they make at me into M[r] Fife's very heart".

He also reassured the Agent that he had never promoted Jansenism at Scalan:

> I likewise took care not to let my sentiments be known to any under my care, both because I ever had some dread they were not warrantable enough, and for fear of their coming that way to M[r] Fife's knowledge. So, blissed be God for it, I did harm to nobody by them: nay those who have studied under my care and direction have ever shewn the greatest horror of of Jans[m], and all the doctrines and propositions censured by H. See[Holy See].

But his defence was not entirely accepted in Rome, or in Scotland.[38] In particular, it was held against both himself and his assistant George Duncan that they had never explicitly condemned Jansenism in their lessons at Scalan, even if they did not actively propound it. To this charge they countered that they had thought it better to leave the boys entirely innocent of these scandals and divisions within the Church.[39]

George Gordon was now sure that his days as master were as good as over. "I'm perswaded, you must part with me very soon, upon account of the complaints against me," he wrote to his bishop.[40] But if so Scalan would need a replacement, because George Duncan had already left to take over the station at Angus. His own recommendation was Francis MacDonell, a student from Glengarry who had received his entire training at Scalan and had been made subdeacon the previous year. He was now a valuable support at the seminary, an assistant in all but name. Mr Gordon judged him almost ready for ordination, and suggested that Bishop Smith visit Scalan for that purpose in time for Advent. Both bishops supported the proposal, but the Co-adjutor could not make the journey until the following March (1736), because of heavy snow that lay for weeks in the Braes that winter. When he did arrive he decided that Mr MacDonell needed more time before his ordination, and that Mr Gordon would have to stay on meantime.

The master's health had suffered with the disputes of the last few years.[41] And soon more work came his way. His neighbour the Benedictine Fr Kilian Grant was forced to leave his station in Strathavon, and with no other priest available as a replacement it was arranged that he would go across to celebrate Mass there on Sundays. To ease the situation the bishops agreed to bring Francis MacDonell's ordination forward to October. The measure solved Strathavon's problem, but exacerbated Scalan's, since Mr MacDonell's new duties regularly took him away from the College. So broken was the master's own health that he feared he must sink under the burden before the year was out.[42]

That autumn Pope Clement XII issued a formal Decree instructing that all priests in Scotland, whether or not suspected of Jansenism, must subscribe to the Formula. The papal Decree was a direct result of the Scottish bishops' letters from Scalan of 6 June 1733. Bishop Gordon welcomed it, for he saw it as the Mission's chance to "stop for ever the mouths of all calumniators" and emerge from the shadow of suspicion. This was his argument when he wrote to Paris to persuade Thomas Innes to sign.[43] He particularly wanted his signature because the Vatican's legate Mgr Lercari was at that time conducting an examination of the Scots College there, also as a result of the Scalan letters.

Mgr Lercari presented his report in March 1737.[44] It was highly damaging, finding the College guilty of teaching heresy, for which it laid the blame personally on Thomas, Lewis and George Innes, whose removal it recommended as a first step to complete reform. It also named certain priests on the Scottish Mission as being "infected with Jansenism", among them George Gordon of Scalan, as author of "a letter contesting the authority of the Church", and George Duncan, "brought up in the seminary of Scalan, and taught by Innes at Paris". This last reference strongly implied that the Scottish seminary, as well as the French, stood accused of teaching error, though it did not go so far as to make the accusation explicitly.

The report was also highly critical of Bishop Gordon, as being a Jansenist sympathiser, and of Bishop Smith, who was "much suspected" and would greatly harm the Mission if ever made Vicar Apostolic. Bishop MacDonald, on the other hand, was judged blameless and deserving of the highest praise for orthodoxy and zeal. Mgr Lercari also reported that many of the clergy in Scotland now believed that the division of the Mission had been a failure, and favoured a re-uniting of the two Vicariates.

The three bishops arranged to meet at Scalan in June to discuss the implications of the report. Before their meeting George Gordon made an urgent call for Mr Duncan to meet him.[45] He must have guessed that the bishops had chosen Scalan as their venue partly in order to assess the situation there and judge whether there was substance in Lercari's implied criticism of the seminary. If so, it was important that the master and his former assistant prepare a joint defence, and when questioned speak as one.

Certainly also on the bishops' agenda was the question of re-uniting the two Vicariates. All three knew that, were this to happen, the only possible choice for Vicar Apostolic would be Hugh MacDonald. They would have known, too, that this was the reason why the Highland clergy were pressing for amalgamation, and why most of the Lowland priests were totally against it.

George Gordon felt so strongly about the matter that he had made up his mind to "lay down his charge" at Scalan if the two Districts were not kept separate.[46] He was convinced that if the Mission amalgamated "all would run into confusion and ruine." And he himself had much to fear under a Highland bishop. But there was more than this. The truth was, he wanted out. The years of infighting had sapped his strength, and the damning report all but broken his will. His only desire now was to be sent to "some by-Corner out of sight", the meaner and the more obscure the better, with a small flock, and time to devote himself to study and private meditation.[47]

But he was not to get his wish yet. Indeed, more work now came his way. For the past few months he had been covering for Mr Alexander Grant, the priest of Glenlivet, who had pretty well abandoned his charge on the excuse of supposed illness. So far he had been just about coping because he still had Francis MacDonell to help him at Scalan. But at the June meeting Bishop Gordon agreed to allow Mr MacDonell, a Glengarry man and a native Gaelic speaker, to move back to the Highland District to ease the desperate shortage of priests there.[48]

With his departure the situation at Scalan became impossible. Bishop Smith wrote to Paris urging them to send their most senior student William Duthie home before Christmas.[49] His hope was to send Mr Duthie straight to Scalan. He was almost ready for ordination. If he could be sent back already ordained he could help cover the Glenlivet station also; failing that he could finish his studies at the seminary while acting as assistant master.

The bishop also asked that Alexander Gordon 'Coffurich' be released from the College, where he had been teaching since his ordination at Scalan three years before and was currently Prefect of Studies, since the Mission stood "in greatest need" of him.[50] The young priest had already made a name for himself as a dedicated teacher in Paris. But he had also been criticised in Mgr Lercari's Report – quite unfairly, and apparently in a case of mistaken identity – and at a meeting of Propaganda in December 1737 it was decided that he should be relieved of his post.[51] The decision at least helped Scalan, though it was not until the following summer that he set sail from France.

For Lewis and Thomas Innes the Lercari Report marked a bitter end to two long and outstanding careers. In June 1738 Lewis died, and with his death Scalan lost a great friend and benefactor. And though Thomas was to live on for another six years he was now, in his own words, reduced to "almost quite a non agendo", whose only wish was to be allowed to die in peace.[52]

When that same year the Scottish bishops sent Rome a list of Mission priests subscribing to Pope Clement's Decree, George Gordon's name was on it.[53] He himself left Scalan in the autumn and was sent to serve in the station at Aberdeen. He had come out of the events of the past half-dozen years with little credit. No-one could accuse him of having been a slave to openness and truth. Bishop Gordon had certainly seen enough not to be too free with him in future.[54]

His long term of office had given Scalan the continuity, but hardly the stability or the chance to consolidate, that had been hoped for when he was appointed. What effect the disputes and accusations had had upon the college we can only guess at, but surely they must have done it great harm. Much time and energy had been spent on infighting and intrigue, that should have gone to the real work of the seminary. Its good name had been seriously damaged, by association, in Scotland and abroad. Probably this had affected its recruitment of students, and perhaps even lost it precious financial support. Whether any students had been drawn to heresy, either through direct teaching or implicit encouragement, we shall never know. But of this we can be certain – it would now take years to undo the harm, win back the seminary's reputation, and emerge out of the shadow of suspicion.

NOTES

1. The most detailed account of Bishop Hugh MacDonald is Dorrian G. M. 'Hugh MacDonald 1699–1773 – First Vicar-Apostolic of the Highland District in His Religious and Social Context', unpublished M. Phil. thesis, Univ. of Strathclyde, 1990.
2. 'Divisio variarum in Scoticae Regno regionum inter duos Vicarios Apostolicos', Edinburgh, 20. 10. 1731 (in Latin), SM 3/26/1, SCA.
3. 'Decretum', Propaganda Fide, 7. 1. 1732 (in Latin), SM 3/26/2, SCA.
4. Thomson J. 'Some Account of the state of religion and of the Mission in Scotland since the Reformation', c. 1790, typescript of MS, TH/10, vol. 2, p. 3, SCA. (We might speculate whether Braemar being traditionally a Jesuit station was a factor in its inclusion within the Highland Vicariate).
5. Bishop Hugh MacDonald to Propaganda, 20. 3. 1732 (in Latin), BL.
6. 'Instructions for Mr John Tyrie', etc., (taken to Rome on behalf of Highland Vicariate) April 1735, Article V; a copy of the whole document was seized by Govt. forces in 1746, along with four other documents, and published in *The Scots Magazine*, Appendix for the year 1747, pp. 614ff.
7. Thomas Innes to Bishop Gordon, 17. 10. 1732, copy SM 3/22, SCA. At this date the total student roll was two.
8. Lewis Innes to Bishop Gordon, 1. 11. 1732, copy SM 3/22, SCA.
9. Macmillan J. 'Scottish Catholics and the Jansenist controversy: the Case Reopened', *IR*, vol. xxxii, no. 1, Spring 1981; and 'Jansenists and Anti-Jansenists in Eighteenth Century Scotland: the *Unigenitus* Quarrels of the Scottish Catholic Mission, 1732-46', *IR*, vol. xxxix, no. 1, spring 1988, provide an excellent account of Jansenism's particular development in Scotland.
10. Robert Strachan, James Carnegie and Alexander Drummond to Bishop Nicolson, 12. 8. 1702, BL, appealing against complaint concerning themselves and Robert Monro, as well as accusations against "some of our departed Brethren" and "severals yet alive".
11. Re Campbell's rôle, Macmillan J. *Op. cit.* (1988).
12. George J. Gordon to William Stuart, 4. 12. 1735, BL.
13. George J. Gordon to Alexander Smith, 17. 4. 1733, BL.
14. Bishops Gordon and Hugh MacDonald to Pope; and to Cardinal Protector; seven priests to Cardinal Protector; all 6. 6. 1733, CP 86 ff. 269, 270, 274, Propaganda Archives, Rome, quoted in full in Halloran B. M. *The Scots College Paris 1603–1792* (Edinburgh, 1997), pp. 110ff.
15. Halloran B. M. *Op. cit.*, pp. 109ff.
16. *Loc. cit.*, note 14.
17. Thomas Innes to Lewis Innes, 27. 7. 1733, BL, transcribing Bishop Gordon's letter.

18. James Carnegie to William Stuart, 30. 8. 1733, BL.
19. Bishops Gordon and MacDonald to Cardinals of Propaganda, 13. 6. 1733 (in Latin), BL; the letter written by Bishop Gordon and addressed "Prope Livetum fluviem in Montanis Scotiae".
20. Bishop H. Macdonald to Bishop Smith, 24. 7. 1744, BL, stating that Colin Campbell brought him a "verball comission" from Bishop Gordon and claimed that Jansenism was "spreading south and north, and this did give me the alarm, who never heard such thing before".
21. James Carnegie to William Stuart, 31. 8. 1733, BL.
22. 'Intended Resolutions for Meeting at Clashnoir Glenlivet', 8. 6. 1733, transcribed 5. 7. 1733, signed John Tyrie, SM 4/1/4, SCA.
23. George J. Gordon to George Gordon (Mortlach), 10. 12. 1733, BL. His signature does not appear on original list of subscribers for 1733, 'Subscription to the Unigenitus Formula' (in Latin), SM 4/1/23, SCA; but he had already subscribed at the 6 June meeting at Scalan, and perhaps did so again before the end of the year – cf., 'Declaration by Bishop Gordon', etc., 13. 4. 1743, SM 4/11/2, SCA.
24. Alexander Smith to Bishop Gordon, 14. 9. 1733, BL.
25. George J. Gordon to Colin Campbell, 17. 11. 33, copy, BL.
26. 'Memorial to Bishop Gordon', n.d., SM 4/1/5, SCA.
27. George J. Gordon to George Gordon (Mortlach), 9. 2. 1734, BL.
28. George J. Gordon to George Gordon (Mortlach), 15. 3. 1734, BL, giving details of his letter to the bishop.
29. Ibid., and cf. the conspiratorial tone of his letters to George Gordon (Mortlach), 14. 5. 1734 and 10. 6. 1734, and to Robert Gordon, 8. 6. 1734, BL.
30. George J. Gordon to George Gordon (Mortlach), 18. 12. 1734, BL.
31. The main motive behind the Highland clergy's attempt to change the boundaries, and thus alter the relative size of the two Vicariates in favour of the Highland, was to strengthen their case for having the next Co-adjutor bishop assigned to the *Highland* Vicariate – cf., Thomson J. 'Some Account of the state of religion and of the Mission in Scotland since the Reformation', c. 1790, TH/10, vol. 2, pp. 3 and 64, SCA.
32. George J. Gordon to George Gordon (Mortlach), 9. 4. 1735, BL.
33. A month later George Gordon was able to tell his colleague that Glenlivet and Strathavon were safe, and he hoped that Corgarff, Glengairn and Braemar might even be recovered for the Lowland district since Bishop MacDonald would soon find them too remote to administer – George J. Gordon to George Gordon (Mortlach), 6. 5. 1735, BL.
34. George J. Gordon to George Gordon (Mortlach), 18. 12. 1734, BL
35. George J. Gordon to George Gordon (Mortlach), 6. 5. 1735, BL.
36. George J. Gordon to Alexander Smith, 24. 9. 1735, BL.
37. George J. Gordon to William Stuart, 4. 12. 1735, BL.
38. Thomas Innes had used the same arguments to the Scots Agent in defence of himself and the staff of the Scots College Paris – Thomas Innes to William Stuart, 21. 9. 1733, BL.
39. 'Memorandum', defending against the accusations of Campbell and Tyrie,

n.d., SM 4/7/1, SCA.

40. George J. Gordon to Bishop Gordon, 5. 12. 1735, BL. The master also sent the bishop an exhaustive apologia of his past and present position – 'Statement', n.d., SM 4/7/4, SCA.

41. George J. Gordon to Bishop Gordon, 19. 2. 1736, BL.

42. George J. Gordon to George Gordon (Mortlach), 24. 10. 1736, BL.

43. Bishop Gordon to Thomas Innes, 7. 12. 1736, BL.

44. 'Report' of Mgr. Lercari, extracts in English in Bellesheim A. *History of the Catholic Church of Scotland* (Edinburgh and London, 1890), vol IV, Appendix XVIII, pp. 408ff.

45. George J. Gordon to George Gordon (Mortlach), 13. 5. 1737, BL.

46. Ibid.

47. George J. Gordon to ?, n.d., but spring 1737, BL 3/29/10.

48. Bishop Smith to Thomas Innes, 20. 8. 1737, BL.

49. Ibid.

50. Alexander Gordon ('Coffurich') had come from the Scots College Paris to Scalan, where he had studied from 1729-30 (see pp. 63f.); he had then returned to Paris; in 1732 he was re-admitted to Scalan to complete his studies, and was ordained there in 1734.

51. Halloran B. M. *Op. cit.*, p. 129.

52. Thomas Innes to Bishop Gordon, 11. 11. 1738, copy SM 3/22, SCA. For a full account of Thomas Innes' position re Jansenism and the effects of the controversy upon his career, see Macmillan J. 'Thomas Innes and the Bull *Unigenitus*', *IR*, vol. xxxiii, 1982; also Halloran B. M. *Op. cit.*, espec. pp. 122ff.

53. 'Subscription' of bishops and priests to Apostolical Decree, 1738 (in Latin), SM 4/1/14, SCA.

54. Bishop Gordon to Thomas Innes, 4. 12. 1738, BL.

8

To *the* 'Forty-Five (1738–1746)

Mr Alexander Gordon ('Coffurich') arrived at Scalan in the August. It was a time of change in the neighbourhood. When the seminary had opened in 1716 the nearest cultivation was at Achavaich and Tomnalienan, all the land in the immediate vicinity being either shieling or muir. Almost from the first the College community had started growing corn on the Hill of Scalan, and the proof that this could be done successfully may well have given other local tenants the idea of acquiring and working portions of similar land nearby.

'Improving' barren land and making it fit for cultivation was a laborious task, involving burning and paring the top surface, and then using the ashes mixed with dung or marl to enrich the under-soil.[1] But it was an attractive proposition for tenants, especially for young men, for it offered them the chance to acquire their own land, rather than merely take a share of sub-divided land. And it appealed to the landlord also, as a source of new income.

We do not know the exact date at which the land on and around the Hill of Scalan was leased out as new tacks for 'improvement', but such evidence as we have suggests that it may have been a piecemeal development from the middle of the 1730s, or even earlier. We know that Demickmore, one-and-a-half miles to the north-east, was being improved by Grant of Ruthven's brother as early as 1716,[2] but – given his position as the Duke's factor – it is most likely that this was the first land to be developed in the district, probably several years ahead of the rest. It is also known that people were living close to the seminary from at least the early 1720s, for the Inveravon Kirk Session makes reference to one Thomas Hutchison, "taylor in Scala", in its minutes of March 1723, and his home must have been semi-permanent for it is recorded again four years later.[3] But as a tradesman he probably possessed a house without land, and the same may apply to any other habitations at this early date. The Gordon Estate papers do not record any new tacks in this part of Glenlivet in the period up to 1738,[4] but they are incomplete, and we can be fairly sure from other sources that some land had in fact already been leased out by the middle of the decade. Entries in the Parish Register for Inveravon strongly suggest that tacks had been created at Scalan from at least as early as 1735, for John Stuart of 'Scala' recorded the baptism of his son in

July of that year, and Thomas McKay of 'Scala' did likewise three years later. The fist reference in the Register to a tenant of Badeglashan occurs in the year 1738.[5] After this the development must have been quite rapid, for when the Duke's Chamberlain drew up his accounts ten years later Badeglashan and Eskiemullach had already been divided up among several tenants.[6]

In the 1730s-40s, therefore, as new tenants took up and improved their tacks, the old shieling grounds and barren land were slowly transformed into farms. In the case of Badeglashan and Eskiemullach the tenants were apparently allotted their own separate portions of land from the outset. But in Scalan's case the land was at first shared according to the traditional runrig system, and only some thirty years later divided into discrete lots.[7]

Since the farm was runrigged it is likely that the new tenants' houses were built quite close together, in the traditional 'farm town' manner. No trace of them now remains, and no exactly contemporary documents exist, but a detailed map of the area based on a survey of 1761 shows a scatter of buildings along the west bank of the Crombie.[8] Several of these must be the seminary and its outhouses, but the others may possibly be tenants' houses, sited in what would be an obvious place for a farm town, close to the burn. Some at least of these (or their successors) were still standing in the nineteenth century, when they were recorded on photograph (Plate 2).

In the spring of 1738, just months before the new master's arrival, much needed funds had come into the hands of the Scottish Mission from two separate sources. The first was a grant of 2000 Crowns made by Pope Clement XII at the request of the exiled James VIII, supplementing monies already received from Rome three years before. The second was a substantial sum from the will of the late Lewis Innes. When the Administrators met in July they agreed to lodge the papal grant in stocks, in order to create an annual fund for Scalan and its Highland counterpart, and to divide the Innes legacy equally between the two Vicariates.[9]

The Administrators must also have discussed how the seminary money should best be spent, in Scalan's case apparently recommending a rebuilding programme, which was now badly needed. Bishop Gordon travelled straight from the meeting to Scalan to discuss their recommendations with the newly-arrived master. After looking at the site and the state of the buildings, the two men decided to replace the old turf house with a more adequate building adjacent to it. No trace remains of this new house, but it was described by one who remembered it as being built "of stone and lime for the greatest part".[10] The description could be interpreted in several ways. Lime was at this time used as a mortar (an alternative and cheaper mortar being clay), and also as an exterior finish. The description might therefore indicate a stone-built house with lime mortar, or lime harling, or both.[11]

Building work began that autumn, and was probably completed before the winter set in, or by spring 1739 at the latest. The new house was certainly ready for inspection when Bishops Smith and MacDonald visited during Holy Week, and occupied well before Bishop Gordon made his prolonged stay in the summer and autumn. The old turf house was probably kept as a byre, though it is quite possible – bearing in mind the expense of roof timber – that its roof was dismantled and used for the new house.

The building work was timely, because the winter of 1739-40 turned out to be as bad as any in the century so far. Many rivers froze in the North of Scotland and remained frozen for six weeks. The frost never left the land until the end of April, so that the fields could not be ploughed and sown until May. And the late sowing was followed by a summer of little sun.[12] When the bishops visited Scalan for their annual Administrators' meeting in August (1740) they saw the corn hardly above the ground, and that autumn the crop was late, stunted, and barely fit for cattle. When the very minimum had been set aside for the next sowing, hardly any was left to grind for the year's meal.

By the spring of 1741 Banffshire was already in the grip of a famine, so bad that in March the local Justices of the Peace issued an order prohibiting all exports of bear, oats, grain or meal from the county.[13] It was a disastrous year for everyone, and none more so than those trying to win a living from their new tacks on the Hill of Scalan.

Bishop Gordon again witnessed the state of the harvest in the Braes that autumn, when he made another prolonged visit to the seminary. He stayed five weeks, and did not leave until the end of October. His purpose in staying so long was to oversee the change of master, since Mr Alexander Gordon was being moved to Edinburgh. His replacement was William Duthie, who had in fact been living at Scalan for the past three years and assisting the priest of Glenlivet, and therefore knew the house and the area well.

The new master was nearly forty, and had come late to the priesthood. He had been brought up an Episcopalian, and had actually been ordained a deacon in that Church. It was while studying at the University of Aberdeen that he had met Mr William Shand and been converted to Catholicism by him. He had chosen to continue his religious vocation in his new Faith, and had been sent to Paris to complete his studies in 1732.

Although he was already familiar with the seminary, there were certain matters that Bishop Gordon was anxious to impress upon him. In particular, he wanted him to pay strict attention to the *Rules* and the ethos, and to restore order among the boys, which had slipped under the perhaps too kind leadership of his predecessor.[14] Before he left the bishop made it clear that Mr Duthie's first task was to rebuild good practices, and to lead quietly but firmly. He was looking for a stability at the seminary that for various reasons it had never really yet enjoyed. Ironically – for reasons beyond either man's control – the new master's long term of office was to take Scalan through the most traumatic years in its history.

In August 1742 Bishop Hugh MacDonald attended a meeting at Scalan with Bishop Gordon and seven other members of the clergy, to judge a most serious and painful matter concerning the former assistant master Francis MacDonell.[15] After he left the seminary in 1737 Mr MacDonell had been given the station at Moidart. The following year his sister Catherine had moved into his house, and rumours soon began to circulate of an incestuous relationship between them. In February 1740 the girl had had an abortion, using (so it was alleged) the herb Fairy Flax which her brother himself had gathered for the purpose. When word of this reached Bishop MacDonald he had ordered the priest to leave her company, but they had continued living together, moving from place to place where they were not known. A year later Catherine gave birth to a baby boy in a house in Knoydart, and though she denied that her brother was the father, a strange circumstance following the birth seemed to suggest otherwise: when the placenta failed to come away, he is said to have given her his own urine to drink "from a silver Tass", which was taken by those present as proof that he was the true father, since drinking the father's urine was a well known remedy in such a case.

Bishop Hugh had called him to a meeting in February 1742, where he was invited to admit his guilt in front of witnesses, since the story had by now become public knowledge. When he refused, but seemed ready to admit it in private confession, the bishop suspended him from all priestly functions. A second meeting on Holy Thursday confirmed the decision, but on MacDonell's appeal it was agreed that the matter be brought to a further meeting at Scalan, with Bishop Gordon in attendance.

When he met the bishops at Scalan on 2 August MacDonell again failed to deny the charge. Worse, he succeeded in bribing a local shoemaker, William Rattray, to claim responsibility for both pregnancies. Rattray died soon afterwards, but not before confiding the whole story on oath to Mr Duthie who was tending him in his last illness.

Bishop Gordon judged that Mr MacDonell's suspension should be made permanent. He also strongly urged that he should go abroad to begin a new life, and even gave him a letter and money to enable him to do so. The young man pocketed the money, but he had no intention of going abroad. He had other plans. The following February he formally renounced his Catholic faith before the Presbytery of Edinburgh. The Kirk officials, who had no idea of his past history, accepted him, and it was not until the year after, by which time they had already ordained him a minister and appointed him to the parish of Strontian, that the truth came out.

When Bishop Gordon visited Scalan for the meeting, and when he returned in 1743, he must have met his nephew William, his brother Alexander's son, who was one of the students at this time. We know the names of several others also – Charles Farquhar, James Gordon and Peter Leith[16] – but since little correspondence has survived from the seminary for the years immediately preceding the '45, it is impossible to know how many more there were. None apparently completed their studies to become priests of the Mission: almost certainly several had their education interrupted by the Rising, and never returned in the upset days of its aftermath.

One to whom this certainly applied was Andrew Arrol. He was at Scalan from 1743, but did not return after Culloden, despite his father's wishes, and made it his excuse that Mr Duthie was teaching the students Jansenist heresy in the years 1743-45.[17] Mr Duthie denied the charge, as the "groundless calumny . . . of a giddy headed confus'd boy",[18] and his denial is certainly to be believed. He was staunchly orthodox, and indeed doubly careful to teach only accepted Catholic doctrine from his first day at Scalan. He knew that he was the object of close scrutiny, as having been a student at Paris at the time of the Lercari report, and – worse – secretly ordained into minor orders by the Jansenist Bishop Bossuet of Troyes. Since then he had been at pains to leave no room for doubt as to his orthodoxy, and had signed the Formula – by his own account – "five or six times" over the years![19]

He knew too that there was still much salvage work to be done to restore Scalan's good name. The old controversy had in fact by no means evaporated. The accusations against Mr George Gordon had actually increased[20] and by the spring of 1743 the matter had reached such a pitch that Bishop Gordon was forced to take a firm stand. Fortunately, the real motives behind the machinations of Colin Campbell and John Tyrie had emerged well before this date, and he was able to judge the events of the past decade more clearly.[21] At Easter he issued a Declaration completely exonerating the former Scalan master from any taint of heresy, past or present, and instructing that all documents written on the issue be suppressed forthwith, and all accusations cease.[22] The Declaration settled the matter for George Gordon, and must incidentally also have been of some help to Mr Duthie in his efforts to restore confidence in Scalan, and undo the damage that it had suffered, by association, under his predecessor.

In August 1743 Bishop Gordon paid his usual visit to Scalan and remained there for several weeks. It was to be his last prolonged stay. He was now seventy-eight, and his health had taken a turn for the worse. He could no longer keep up his non-stop way of life. From the autumn he made Drummond Castle his usual home, and only occasionally and for very important business ventured far away from it. The following year it was not he but his Co-adjutor who paid the 'annual' visit to the seminary.

He knew that his own death would not be long coming, and with this in mind drew up a statement of his own financial position in the new year of 1745. His intention was to set a fixed sum aside for the poor of the Lowland District, and to allocate most of the rest of the annual income on his capital to the upkeep of Scalan. In February he wrote out his will, confirming the seminary as the sole beneficiary. "I order", he wrote

all the free goods that now belong to me or are at my disposal . . . or which may pertain to me at my death . . . be employed for the maintenance, use, and support of the little seminary which I have begun, and is now at Scalan.[23]

In addition, he bequeathed to the College all his own books, as well as those that had belonged to Bishops Nicolson and Wallace, bequests that strengthened the library's holdings and laid the foundation for the outstanding facility that it would one day become.[24]

To the spring of 1745, at latest, can be dated a worked site on the seminary's land on the east side of the Crombie. The evidence for this is the map of Scotland drawn up by William Roy between 1748-55.[25] Roy surveyed the Glenlivet area no later than 1753, and, as we shall see in chapter 9, any development of the land at Scalan would have been quite out of the question in the six years after Culloden. The spring of 1745 thus represents the *terminus ante quem* of the development of the site shown on his map. The section of the map that covers the neighbourhood of Scalan is reproduced below (Map 5).

Like the whole work, this section is in Roy's own words a "military sketch" rather than a "very accurate map"; it does not mark every farm town, and those that it does record are not depicted with any precision: the scatter of buildings, for example, is impressionistic, so that one farm town looks much like another. It is certainly not a map that one would

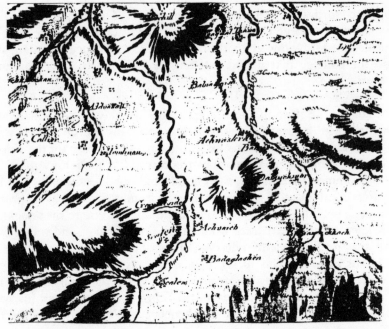

Map 5. Part of William Roy's Map of c. 1750, showing development on the E. side of Crombie.

normally draw precise conclusions from. But in fact this very quality makes its depiction of the 'Scalen' on the east side of the Crombie the more striking. It is quite unlike any other part of this section, and clearly indicates an enclosed rectangular area, surrounded by trees or a hedge. It looks very much like a garden surrounded by a dyke. If so, it may very well in fact be the "large garden" that, on the evidence of the Kirk report of 1722 (see p. 45), had been laid out in the seminary's early days.

On 23 July 1745 Prince Charles Edward Stuart landed on the coast of Eriskay. Within a month he had gathered his small army and raised the standard at Glenfinnan. Before the end of September he had taken Edinburgh, and routed the army of General Cope at Prestonpans. Early in November he crossed the border into England.

The House of Gordon did not rally to the Jacobite cause as it had thirty years before. Cosmo George, the 3rd Duke, distanced himself from the Rising, and two of his brothers actually held commissions in the army of the Government. But his brother Lewis played a leading rôle in the campaign of the Prince, by whom he was given the title Lord Lieutenant of Aberdeen and Banffshire, and Gordon Castle was for some months used as a headquarters by the Jacobites.

The people of the Gordon estates were Jacobite in sentiment, but many had been disillusioned by the events of the '15, and particularly by the Earl of Mar's betrayal of his men. When Lord Lewis began active recruiting in the autumn he met with a less warm response than he had expected, and was (as he himself expressed it) "obliged to use great threatenings" in order to get the quotas he needed from each district.[26] But with Banffshire and Aberdeen under his control, especially after his victory at Inverurie at the end of the year, some 1200 men were nonetheless recruited from the two counties, more than one sixth of the entire Jacobite army.[27]

In Upper Banffshire the influence of Gordon of Glenbuchat – whose home was at St Bridget's in Strathavon, just five miles over the hill from Scalan – ensured a strong base of support. Even before the Prince marched into England the minister of Glenlivet had abandoned his church services, on the grounds that the people were "in arms in Rebellion against the King".[28] Exactly how many were eventually recruited from Strathavon and Glenlivet into Glenbuchat's Regiment is not known, but it may well have been 300-400. They included a sizeable contingent from the Braes, among them tenants from the farms of Demickmore, Achnascra, Tomnalienan, Badeglashan, Calier, and Scalan itself.[29] Mr John Tyrie and Fr Kilian Grant OSB, the priests of Glenlivet and Strathavon, also joined the regiment, Mr Tyrie being appointed chaplain after drawing lots with his colleague.

On 17 January 1746 Bishop Gordon died, mercifully three months before the defeat of his Prince's forces at Culloden. The large numbers from Banffshire who had followed the royal standard made it certain that the county would now feel the full force of Government retribution in defeat. The well-known participation of a number of priests and leading laity made it likely that Catholics, and their churches and homes, would be given special attention in the aftermath. And the involvement of so many from Glenlivet and the Braes guaranteed that the area would be garrisoned by Government troops, and at the mercy of its enemies. In the spring of 1746 Scalan had everything to fear. And so it turned out.

NOTES

1. Cf., Wight C. *Present State of Husbandry in Scotland* (Edinburgh, 1784), p. 68.

2. Geddes Bp. J. 'Brief Historical Account of the Seminary at Scalan',1777, CH 1/3, para 8.

3. 'The Register of the Parish of Inveravine since the Year 1703', Session meetings of 4. 3. 1723 and 9. 4. 1727, CH 2/191/2, pp. 214 and 245, SRO.

4. Gordon Estate Tacks late 17C to 1738, including Glenlivet, GD 44/23/2, SRO.

5. Inveravon Parish Register, MF A In 1 55, ECL.

6. Chamberlain's Accounts 1742–1745, GD 44/51/124/2, SRO. The dates were 7 July and 21 September respectively.

7. 'A Short Description of Glen Livet', 1761, RHP 2487, SRO. Divided into separate lots when new tacks drawn up in 1767 – see 'Contents and Estimates', 1772, CR 8/185, ff. 86-88, SRO.

8. 'Plan of Glenlivet', 1761, RHP 1774, SRO.

9. George Gordon (Kirkhill) to Thomas Innes, 1. 5. 1738; and Thomson J. 'Some Account of the state of religion and of the Mission in Scotland since the Reformation',1780, typescript of MS, TH/10, pp. 60 and 109, SCA. The 1735 grant of 1000 Crowns for the legacy of Cardinal Falconieri was allocated by King James to the seminaries.

10. Geddes Bp J. *Op. cit.*, para 18.

11. Cf., Fenton A. and Walker B. *The Rural Architecture of Scotland* (Edinburgh, 1981), p. 85.

12. Walton K. 'Climate and Famines in North East Scotland', *Scot. Geog. Mag.*, vol. 68, no. 1, April 1952, p. 16.

13. Grant J. *Records of the County of Banff 1660–1760* (Aberdeen, 1922), p. 411.

14. Geddes Bp. J. *Op. cit.*, para 18.

15. Present account based on record of proceedings of Presbytery of Mull, meeting of 7. 3. 1744, including 'Complaint' placed before meeting by Bishop Hugh MacDonald and MacDonald of Kinlochmoidart, 'The Registred Acts of the Presbytery of Mull commencing anno 1729', CH 2/273/1, pp. 83ff., SRO. The herb Fairy Flax had been used as an abortifacient from early times, as its Gaelic name *miosachan* ('monthly herb') shows.

16. Re William Gordon, Geddes Bp. J. *Op. cit.*, para 21. Other students included James Gordon – Bishop Gordon to Bishop Smith, 31. 8. 1744, BL; Peter Leith – William Duthie to George J. Gordon, 3. 8. 1749, BL; and Charles Farquhar, who had been expelled from the Scots College Paris in 1740 for naïvely acting as a spy for John Tyrie at the College – Thomas Innes to Bishop Gordon, March 1740, BL, and George Innes to Bishop Gordon, 30. 5. 1740, BL.

17. William Duthie to Bishop Smith, 7. 4. 1747, BL.

18. William Duthie to ?,1. 4. 1748, BL; and William Duthie to Bishop Smith, 1. 5. 1748, BL.

19. Ibid.

20. He was named in an anonymous paper passed to Bishop Gordon in 1739– Paper, anonymous, n.d., 1739, 3/48/11(2), BL. The paper was in the possession of Patrick Gordon SJ, who claimed that Mr John Leslie had stolen it out of his pocket (Patrick Gordon to Bishop Gordon, 26. 11. 1739, BL). Mr Leslie on the other hand claimed that he found it in Corgarff "dropt" by Fr Gordon (note at end of paper – 3/48/11(2), BL). George Gordon's 1732 letter and subsequent apology were both referred to in the paper, though he was not the main target of accusation.

In 1740 Fr John Riddoch SJ made further accusations against him, and when he failed to withdraw them and was suspended by Bishop Gordon the laity were drawn into what was now becoming a public scandal – ANGLIA 5, Missio Scotica, Epistolae 1740-49, f. 262, Jesuit Archives, Rome, cited in Halloran B. M. *The Scots College Paris 1603–1792* (Edinburgh, 1997), p. 140.

21. See, eg., Bishop Gordon to Cardinal Rivera, 7. 1. 1740, and 1742 (n.d., 3/73/4), (both in French), BL.

22. Bishop Gordon 'Declaration' to priests and laity of Lowland Vicariate, 13. 4. 1743, SM 4/11/2, SCA.

23. Bishop Gordon Will, 22. 2. 1745, verbatim text in Clapperton W. *Memoirs of Scotch Missionary Priests*, transcibed Wilson G. (Elgin, 1901), vol. II, no. 1, pp. 1063ff., SCA. He added the rider that if Scalan ever closed the money was to be used for maintaining the Catholic schools and supporting the priests of his Vicariate.

24. Cf. pp. 192f.

25. Roy W. *Map of Scotland*, 1748-55, BL; slide copy, NLS Map Lib.

26. Lord Lewis Gordon to Moir, Laird of Stoneywood, 10. 12.1745, in Spalding Club *Miscellany* (Aberdeen, 1841), vol. I, p. 410.

27. Tayler A. and Tayler H. *Jacobites of Aberdeenshire and Banffshire in the Forty Five*, (Aberdeen, 1928), p. 418.

28. 'The Session Register of the Parish of Inveravon', 1740-66, meeting of 8. 9. 1745, CH 2/191/3, p. 70, SRO.

29. Tayler J. and Tayler H. *Op. cit.*, List, pp. 417-447; also Mitchell S. 'Scalan in the Eighteenth Century: A Postscript – the 'Forty five', *Scalan News*, no. 14, June 1997.

9

Hanging by a Thread (1746–1753)

At least ten priests were arrested in the North of Scotland in the first few weeks after Culloden, of whom two later died in captivity and four others were banished. The people were in a state of alarm, and many believed the rumour that the Government was planning to transport all Catholics to America. In Lower Banffshire four chapels were razed to the ground, and in the upper county the troops were hunting down activists in Glenlivet and Strathavon. Mr John Tyrie saw his house by the Bochel ransacked and all his possessions burned, and had his church not been so close to other houses nearby it too would have been put to the torch.[1]

The troops soon moved up into the Braes, destroying the house at Achdregnie on the way, and then burning Clashnoir. There was no chance that Scalan could escape their attention. Knowing this Mr Duthie and the students carried away out of the house all their own belongings and everything that could be moved – furniture, bedding, crockery, cutlery, vestments, clothing, books and documents – and left them in various hiding places nearby. The master then sent the boys to a number of different houses in the neighbourhood, while he himself went up into the hills to wait and watch.

On 16 May the troops arrived. Their orders were to destroy the seminary. They surrounded the main building. Some entered, reconnoitred, and reported it empty. Then they set fire to it, and stepped back to watch the effects of their work. The heather roof went first. Soon the cabers, beams and ridge pole collapsed and were consumed. Before the soldiers departed only the charred and smoking walls were left standing. The house completed only seven years before was "reduced to be a habitation proper only for Owls and wild beasts".[2]

From his vantage point Mr Duthie could see at once that there was only one thing for him to do. He descended the hill, gathered the boys, and sent them all home. He himself went into hiding close by, to await instructions from the bishop and consider the future. At least their possessions were secure meantime. At least the crops were already in the ground. But the peats which should have been cut that month would have to remain uncut.

In the autumn Bishop Smith journeyed north, to see the situation for himself and try to bring comfort to the people. He did what he could to support and re-deploy his depleted team, and rebuild some semblance of regular practice.[3] On his journey he took in the Braes, and secretly visited Mr Duthie in his temporary home, which – according to Bishop Geddes' *Brief Historical Account of the Seminary at Scalan* – was at Culantuim, a mile-and-a-half to the north-west of the ruined seminary.[4]

One of the students, Johnnie Gordon, was a local boy from down the glen, and he was able to keep in touch with the master. As soon as it was safe to do so he returned to live with him, perhaps at the and of the year and certainly before Mr Duthie's letter to the bishop of 6 February 1747.[5] The letter was addressed from 'Burnside', an address vague enough to prevent detection, but sufficient to let the bishop know that they were still at the same house – Culantuim beside the Fanich burn – where he had previously met Mr Duthie during his visitation. It was, the master reminded him, "a bad house and no fire", because he was still without winter fuel.

Bishop Smith had already contacted Mr Duthie with instructions to hold onto the lease of Scalan and to do whatever he could to keep the property going. The lease appeared to be safe, at least as far as the Duke was concerned, and their local landlord Grant of Tomnavoulin had also promised that it would not be cancelled. The master therefore made a start at the ploughing, his neighbours rallying round to save him the expense of hiring labour. But he was not through it when word came to him that the Duke of Gordon intended to prevent any moves to re-open the seminary, at Scalan or anywhere else on his lands. He at once wrote to warn the bishop of this new turn.[6] It was in any case impossible to make repairs to the house without money to hire a manservant and horse, and he therefore could not consider bringing the students back, nor living in himself. He believed that with doubt now hanging over Scalan's future it would be "lost labour to begin any settlement in that place all considered".

The Duke's new hard line seems to have been a response to pressure from the authorities. The Kirk were dismayed to see priests already "trafficking openly" again so soon after the Government's punitive action, and in April (1747) sent a formal *Representation* to His Grace complaining that Mass houses had been re-erected on his lands in Glenlivet and Strathavon.[7] Whatever the Duke's private views it was prudent that he should been seen publicly to oppose anything connected with Catholicism.

Sometime in the late spring Mr Duthie moved from the Braes to assist Mr Tyrie in Lower Glenlivet, taking Johnnie Gordon with him and making a temporary home near Tombreckachie. Mr Tyrie's station lay next to that of Thomas Brockie OSB in the Cabrach, but the boundary between the two was in some places unclear. Fr Brockie was notoriously touchy about anything that seemed like interference in his territory. The two men had long enjoyed a warm dislike of eachother, and now their old jealousies erupted again over the question of demarcation. Mr Duthie soon found himself caught up in the quarrel. He bore it as well as he could until the end of the year, waiting for instructions from the bishop. But when January came he had still received no word. The weather just then happened to be unseasonably mild, and the roads passable. On a sudden resolution he seized his chance, and he and Johnnie Gordon gathered their few possessions together and carried them back up to the Braes. He informed Bishop Smith that he had returned, explaining that he would obediently go wherever he was sent but that he was not willing to be "ill us'd" or to be a mere "supernumerary" for someone else. He had not dared to return to Scalan but had set up home in "a poor sheep coat" at Culantuim, where he intended to await instructions and meantime continue to supervise and teach Johnnie Gordon.[8] His new home must have been close to his temporary dwelling of the previous year, perhaps indeed the very same hut.

In their determination to ensure that there would never be another '45 the Government had introduced a whole range of measures aimed at undermining the Highland way of life. They had struck at its wealth by confiscating the land of the Jacobite leaders; at its authority by abolishing the heritable jurisdictions; at its symbols by outlawing its dress and music; at its ability to fight by prohibiting the bearing of arms.

But they recognised that any law against weapons would be of little effect unless they also tackled the underlying causes of the Highland tradition of arms bearing. They were advised in particular that the time-honoured practice of cattle stealing was a critical cause of arms bearing and the forming of gangs, and that if it could once be suppressed the reasons and excuses for self-defence and for enlisting bands of armed men would disappear.[9]

The main victims of the thieves were the farmers of those parts of Aberdeen, Banff, Angus and the Mearns that bordered on the Highlands. The most notorious raiders made their strikes from their strongholds in the West, with active support from smaller bands in Upper Glen Avon in the Highlands of Banffshire.[10] Since these were Jacobite areas and centres of the Catholic faith the Authorities found the identification 'cattle stealing/arms bearing/rebellion/Catholicism' an easy and credible one to make.

It would take the full force of the Law, an intelligence network and a presence of troops for the hornets' nests to be destroyed. Local magistrates sympathetic to the rebels would need to be frightened into line, and loyal magistrates protected. The Highland routes would have to be garrisoned, especially those on the southern borders of Banffshire through which much of the traffic passed.

One of the most frequented of these led up the Blackwater and along the slopes of the Ladder Hills, passing right above Scalan, and then either dropping into Glen Conglas or keeping to the heights and crossing the Avon nearer its source, and so on through Abernethy to the West (see Map 3).

It was to cover this route that troops of Lord John Murray's Regiment were sent from Ruthven Barracks to Upper Donside in 1747. They set up their main base at Corgarff, with outposts at Inchrory and elsewhere close to the mountain passes.[11] It was early in 1748 that Mr Duthie first became aware of them. "I am to tell you worse news," he wrote to Bishop Smith in March,

> we have got a garrison at Corgarf who are to remain there. this will in all appearance entirely disconcert and dissapoint Poor M^r F^s [Forbes – ie., himself] from settling in his old quarters, for there are but short 4 miles betwixt him & them and not one house between them being all hill so that they could surprise him at any time.[12]

It would be pointless to re-open Scalan as they had planned, he added, because in the present situation "scarce any body would venture their children with him." He had almost no money, no fuel, and was weary of wandering; he begged the bishop to instruct him what to do.

Bishop Smith wrote back giving him authority to take whatever action he thought best, advice that though well intended was exactly what he did not want to hear. "You give me a chart. blanche as to my settlement," he wrote again; "this perplexes me much for I cannot determine my self. I fear I will not be able to do it till I see you."[13] The garrison at Corgarff was now permanent, he reported. He was not afraid for himself, but any moves to set up a seminary, "tho' in the privatest manner", would certainly reach the ears of the local ministers. They would complain to the Authorities, who would probably make the recent Disarming Act their excuse for a raid. In his view it would be best to "hover a little" until the situation became clearer and perhaps make a start nearer the end of the year. The greatest problem in the meantime was keeping track of their possessions, which were still scattered in a number of hiding places. He had it in mind to build a small hut for them – "a house of one couple" – close to the home of a trusted friend who could be relied upon to light a fire in it from time to time and keep everything dry.[14]

*　　*　　*

Early in 1749, as soon as the worst of the weather was past, he had a new house hastily thrown up at Scalan, using part of the existing foundations and walls, and he and Johnnie Gordon moved in.[15] By the summer the main building was habitable, but there remained a great deal of work to be done on the rest of the property. It was almost three years since it had been occupied and every one of the buildings needed to be re-thatched. Mr Duthie had recently hired a servant, so that it would be possible to start repairs, but there were other problems to consider. Men were operating "an aquavite pot" – a small whisky still – right beside the house, and another close by at Eskiemullach, and they were sure to attract attention. And their landlord Rothmais, the son of Grant of Tomnavoulin, had cooled towards them in the prevailing anti-Catholic climate, and there was a real fear that he would not renew their lease which had only four years to run. Mr Duthie was even ready to abandon Scalan altogether and make a fresh start somewhere else. There was a plot of land available down the glen near Belnacoul, where they would be guaranteed security of tenure, and where they would be two miles further away from Corgarff. "I know well the plague & expence of flitting & pulling up houses," he told the bishop, "& shall be sorry to remove if we can stay, but I scarce think we can."[16] It looked as if Scalan's days might be about to end. But, by offering Rothmais part of the grassum for a new lease along with the half-yearly rent at Michaelmas, he finally managed to persuade him to extend their tack by a further year. They would now be secure at least until the autumn of 1754.[17]

The situation seemed to be growing calmer at last, and at the turn of the year (1750) he was able to report that the little seminary was "in great peace w^t every body and very quiet." They were now a family of five – master, man servant, maid servant and two students. Johnnie Gordon was there as ever, making steady progress and soon to begin Philosophy. It had originally been intended that he would go to Paris, but this had proved impossible in the recent circumstances, and now they had every hope that he would complete his training at Scalan and be ordained there. There was no such hope for the second boy, John Drummond, who had joined them recently, for he was a mute and could never be raised to the priesthood.[18]

Bishop Smith paid a visit to Scalan in September, as he had the previous year, and as usual the man servant was sent down with the horse to bring him up from the coast. This left Mr Duthie to wrestle with the harvest alone, at a time when he was already under great pressure. An epidemic was running through the district, and he was answering sick calls in the whole country from Strathavon to Glen Rinnes, for there was no other priest available. Fr Kilian Grant had been driven out of Strathavon, and

Mr Tyrie had abandoned his station in Glenlivet. Mr Duthie explained to the bishop how he had tried to dissuade him from going:

> I found M^r T^y ready for the Garrioch I ask'd him when he was to return his answer was not till the soldiers were gone I asked who was to take care of his people he said God, I told I would not. he said he did not bid me.[19]

Mr Tyrie's behaviour, though hard to excuse, is not impossible to understand. He had been so badly wounded at Culloden that he had been left for dead on the field; and in the aftermath he had already lost his house and all his possessions once. For the past four years he had been living under the eye of the military, and his nerve was gone.[20]

Strathavon was a different problem. Because the route of the cattle thieves lay right through it the whole area was now under constant surveillance. That summer troops of General Pulteney's Regiment stationed in Strathbogie had been sent to Upper Banffshire to support the Corgarff garrison, and had established their headquarters at Tomintoul.[21] They were now roaming through Strathavon "like locusts", Mr Duthie reported, and had a network of spies and informers, and no priest could enter the area without immediately attracting attention. And even if he did get in he would be almost useless to the people because he had no Gaelic. The English language had not yet penetrated into upper Strathavon – as it had begun to do in Glenlivet and the Braes – and knowledge of Gaelic remained essential for any priest stationed there.

With such an area to cover he felt himself "at every bodys command". He was being called away from Scalan almost every day, and it seemed pointless to continue there when the boys' studies were being badly neglected. He urged the bishop to take him away:

> I beg of you against next spring to settle me in some place you judge fit for my strength & capacity. that I may know my Work & do it . . . & youll easily find one fitter for Scal. than I.[22]

Bishop Smith decided not to grant him his wish, and in the new circumstances he was probably wise. Any coming and going at Scalan would certainly have been noticed. The Tomintoul garrison maintained outposts and made regular route marches from one to another. Their commanding officer's Report at this date referred to outposts at Auchnahyle two miles further up the Avon, at Downan in Lower Glenlivet, at the Cabrach, and at "Shelan [Scalan] and Achnascra."[23] The last comprised one sergeant and six men, and since the farm towns of Scalan and Achnascra were a mile apart it is likely that several men were billeted in each. Those at Scalan were only yards from the seminary door, their station obviously having been chosen to enable them to watch it constantly.

It looked as if the College community would have to keep a low a profile for the foreseeable future, and the master at first kept within-doors and only ventured out at nightfall, if at all.[24] But it soon became clear that although the soldiers had to follow their orders, they themselves had no real desire to harass the seminary, and in fact treated Mr Duthie with all civility.[25] In the summer of 1752 he even felt safe enough to rebuild and enlarge his house,[26] making substantial use of Bishop Gordon's legacy for the first time. And by the beginning of 1753 he was able to report that "trade was going on without trouble or molestation", with only occasional threats of storms that soon blew away."[27] Nonetheless, the hardships of Scalan had begun to tell on him. He suffered a long illness that winter, and would never enjoy good health for the rest of his life.

That winter also he first heard word that he might be sent to fill the post of Prefect of Studies at the Scots College Paris. The rumour was going round the clergy in the North-East,[28] but he heard nothing from Bishop Smith all spring, and finally wrote to him to find out his position. If the rumour was true he would be concerned for Scalan's future, and especially for Johnnie Gordon who was at a critical stage in his training. He was also worried for his own father who lived at Demickmore close by – he was old and infirm, and had recently lost his house in a fire and was now living in a barn there. The whole neighbourhood was under close surveillance again, and no-one could leave the seminary without being observed.[29]

Cosmo George, the third Duke of Gordon, had died in August 1752, and since his first son Alexander was only nine years old and was not immediately served heir, his widow had assumed temporary responsibility for the estate. In the spring of 1753 she instructed her chief factor to examine all leases on the estates that had a connection with the Catholic Church, and to require the tenants concerned to forward a statement of their holdings.[30] Mr Duthie drew up a summary of the lands in possession of the seminary and of rents paid, as requested, but thought it more prudent to send it in Johnnie Gordon's name rather than his own. 'Gordon' would be a far less eye-catching name on a letter from the Braes than 'Duthie', and he even hoped that it might replace his own name on the factor's official list. But Her Grace was far too well informed to be deceived, his name remained on the list, and in August he was called to the court hearing for renewal of leases to be held at Hardhaugh in Lower Banffshire.

To all outward appearance the hearing went badly for Scalan. The Duchess expressed strong opposition to Mr Duthie holding a lease of any land on the estate, and was highly critical of Grant of Rothmais for having allowed him the tack. The master's letter to the Church's Administrator in Aberdeen described the scene:

> To be short she publickly chid Rotmaise for having such a person here as I. Rotmaise assur'd her I was a very quiet peaceable man, a good neighbour &c. so did some others. yet she insisted and told him he incurr'd a penalty by it. This gave me some ineasiness tho' I still thought it was rather a boast by way of formality in a publick court than a real threat. this made me soon enquire of the chamberlain what was meant who assured me that no harm was intended & that I was safe enough. but this to be a dead secret so I shall communicate it to no more but to Mr Rob. [Mr Robinson – ie., Bishop Smith] and you.[31]

Again it is clear that the Duchess, like the Duke before her, was putting on a public front of anti-Catholicism in the face of pressure. The minister of Inveravon parish, James Grant, who had only arrived the previous autumn, and James Innes his recently appointed assistant for Glenlivet, were new brooms sweeping clean. They had spent the summer visiting every house in their area and had compiled a list of over 700 Catholics which they forwarded to the Sheriff Depute for the County, and he in turn presented to the Duchess.[31] Her response in the court was calculated to satisfy him, and mollify the ministers. But this would not be the end of their efforts.

NOTES

1. Bishop Geddes 'Some Account of the State of the Catholic Religion in Scotland During the Years 1745, 1746 and 1747', copy B JG 2/5, SCA. Also eye-witness account in Forbes R. *The Lyon in Mourning* (Edinburgh, 1895–6), vol. 2, p. 333.
2. Bishop Geddes 'Brief Historical Account of the Seminary at Scalan', 1777, CH 1/3, paras. 23-4, SCA.
3. Report of Bishop Smith to Propaganda, 13. 12. 1747, translation in Bellesheim A. *History of the Catholic Church of Scotland*, (Edinburgh and London, 1890), vol. IV, Appendix XVI.
4. Bishop Geddes, *Op. cit.* para 24.
5. William Duthie to Bishop Smith, 6. 2. 1747, BL.
6. William Duthie to Bishop Smith, 7. 4. 1747, BL.
7. Synod of Moray, Record of Meetings, meeting of 21. 4. 1747, CH 2/271/VII, p. 348, SRO.
8. William Duthie to Bishop Smith, 24. 1. 1748, BL.
9. 'Memoriall Anent the True State of the Highlands' etc., c. 1747, probably written by Forbes of Culloden, in Allardyce J. (ed.) *Historical Papers Relating to the Jacobite Period 1699–1750* (Aberdeen, 1895), vol. I, pp. 166-76.
10. Cf., 'Report' of Lieut. Col. Watson, 8. 8. 1747; 'Proposals Offered to Maj.

Gen. Blakeney', 1747; and 'Advertisement' re giving/witholding intelligence, 1747; in Allardyce J. (ed.) *Op. cit.*, vol. I, pp. 490ff. The main western strongholds were Lochaber and Glengarry.

11. Re route and posting of troops, see 'Description of the Hills, Glens and Passes in the Counties of Aberdeen &c', 9. 7. 1747, in Allardyce J. (ed.) *Op. cit.*, vol. II, pp. 506ff.

12. William Duthie to Bishop Smith, 26. 3. 1748, BL.

13. William Duthie to Bishop Smith, 1. 5. 1748, BL.

14. Ibid. Disarming Act – 'An Act for the more effectual disarming the Highlands in Scotland; and for the more effectually securing the Peace of the said Highlands; and for Restraining the Use of the Highland Dress', etc.; 19 Geo II 39, 1746.

15. Scalan Accounts 1750-62, CS 1/7/1, SCA.

16. William Duthie to Bishop Smith, 3. 8. 1749, BL.

17. William Duthie to Bishop Smith, 14. 1. 1750, BL.

18. Ibid.

19. William Duthie to Bishop Smith, 13. 9. 1750, BL. Paragraph also based on his letter of 10. 9. 1750, BL.

20. The bishops had issued a 'Declaration on Duties' in the late 1740s (copy SM 4/11/11, SCA); in their Report to Rome for 1753 they asked that Pope Benedict's 'Regulations for the English Mission', issued earlier that year, be extended to the Scottish – cf., Bellesheim A. *Op. cit.*, vol IV, Appendix XVII. Since 1746 the priests had been under huge pressure, and some were badly demoralised. Times of particular stress had been occasions of demoralisation and loss of discipline before – cf., eg., Bishop Gordon's experience in 1707 (p. 22) – but the danger was to some extent ever-present; thus, it has been calculated that some 8.7% of secular Mission priests apostatised in the 100 years after1653 – Szechi D. 'Defending the True Faith: Kirk, State, and Catholic Missioners in Scotland, 1653–1755', *Catholic Historical Review*, July 1996.

21. Report of Lieut. Ogilvie from Tomintoul, sent to Col. Napier, 23. 6. 1750, 'Deposition of the troops under the command of lieut. Ogilvie', in Allardyce J. (ed.) *Op. cit.*, vol. II, pp. 546f.

22. William Duthie to Bishop Smith, 10. 9. 1750 and 13. 9. 1750, BL.

23. Allardyce J. *Loc. cit.*

24. William Duthie to Bishop Smith, 28. 8. 1751, BL.

25. Fr Kilian Grant OSB (alias 'John Scott') to Bishop Smith, 10. 11. 1753, BL; and George Gordon to Bishop Smith, 14. 11. 1751, BL.

26. Scalan Accounts 1750-62, CS 1/7/1, SCA.

27. William Duthie to Bishop Smith, 3. 3. 1753, BL.

28. William Duthie to George Gordon, 23. 3. 1753, BL.

29. William Duthie to Bishop Smith, 16. 7. 1753, BL.

30. Fr Kilian Grant OSB to Bishop Smith, 10. 11. 1753, BL. Alexander was served heir in February 1754 – details from Paul, J. Balfour *The Scots Peerage*, vol. iv (Edinburgh, 1907).

31. William Duthie to George Gordon, 26. 8. 1753, BL. Hardhaugh is close to the modern Dufftown.

32. William Duthie to George Gordon, 12. 10. 1753, BL. Re James Innes, cf.

Rev. S. Ree in Calder R.H. *Glenlivet Gleanings* (Banff, 1914), pp. 44ff. James Grant was minister of Inveravon parish from Oct. 1752 until his death in Feb. 1795–cf. Scott. H. *Fasti Ecclesiae Scoticanae* (Edinburgh, 1926), vol. VI, pp. 344f. The Duke (Cosmo George) had died in August 1752.

10

Mr Duthie's Last Years as Master (1753–1758)

The detachment of Pulteney's Regiment that had been stationed in Upper Banffshire for the past three years had by now given up their post at Scalan and Achnascra, leaving Downan as their only remaining outpost in Glenlivet. The seminary no longer had soldiers just over the wall, but there was still a military presence in the neighbourhood because the Corgarff garrison had also been redistributed, with a detachment of some half-dozen men now stationed at the upper end of the Braes. This group did not have a single billet but were lodged in pairs in several farms in the district. Their sergeant and one private were quartered at Demickmore a mile-and-a-half from Scalan. The only real change, as far as the College was concerned, was that they did not have the authority to make raids except by special orders because Banffshire was strictly speaking outwith their jurisdiction.

On 4 October, following several months of calm, Mr Tyrie received word from an inside source that a raid was imminent. The other priests were warned at once. Mr Duthie left Scalan immediately, and made a home for himself at Lettoch farm, close enough to visit the seminary secretly every day and keep it going. The little community knew that raids usually took place after nightfall, and each night they waited up, expecting the knock. At 11pm on 11 October it came.[1] Johnnie Gordon answered the door and was confronted by the corporal and three of his men from the Downan post, with the Sheriff's Constable at their side. He insisted on seeing their written order before he would admit them, and kept them waiting while he slowly read it over. It was signed by the Sheriff Depute of the county and addressed to the C.O. at Tomintoul, instructing him to go to "Scala or Scalan", apprehend the person of William Duthie and bring him to the gaol at Banff. (A similar order had been issued for Mr Tyrie at Achnarrow and the Jesuit Fr William Scott at Auchriachan in Strathavon). But the raiding party found that their bird had flown.

The Braes detachment of the Corgarff garrison played no part in the incident. But their corporal happened to meet up with the soldiers from Downan that night, and he joined them in a celebration. He returned to his lodging at Demickmore in the early hours very drunk, and ordered one of his men to stand guard with fixed bayonet at the door of the barn where Mr Duthie's father had been living since his own house burned down. Either he mistook the father for the son, or more likely he hoped to gain information from him as to the son's whereabouts. The old man slept on unawares, but when he later learned of the bayonet at his door he was so shaken that he dared not stay at the farm while the troops were lodged there.

It was generally believed locally that the list sent by the Kirk ministers to the Sheriff Depute had prompted the raids;[2] certainly the Duchess had played no part in them. But Mr Duthie's fear was that they might be repeated at any time from Downan, or even from Corgarff, because their detachment in the Braes were "piqued" at not having been used in the first raid and were now looking for any excuse. It was still out of the question for him to go near Scalan at night.[3]

In November he got a letter out to Bishop Smith.[4] He was still at Lettoch, but the news was better at last. The soldiers stationed in the Braes had been withdrawn to Corgarff for the winter, and the Downan detachment were also about to be withdrawn to headquarters, so that there was every hope of peace at least until the following spring. Scalan had remained unscathed. Its little family were in good health. He himself had managed to stay in the neighbourhood throughout, though only with great hardship –

I can assure you I never had such difficulty even in 46 . . . I thank God notwithstanding I have not been in my own bed but two nights since our troubles began, lying many times in a cold barn. at other times in a rainy drafty hole, going to it in the silence of the night and coming away before day.

In the New Year of 1754 William Gray arrived at Scalan on the recommendation of Bishop Smith. He was in his mid-fifties, a single man and a convert. He had worked as a private tutor for much of his adult life, and had also spent two years studying at the Scots College Paris. He was joining the seminary now as both student and teacher: he would be studying for the priesthood himself, while his experience of teaching the Classics would make him a useful assistant for Mr Duthie. He seemed a serious, honest man, biddable, hard working and quite ready to accept the frugal life.[5]

Young John Drummond was persevering with his books and Mr Duthie asked to be allowed to keep him at least until the end of the year: he was loath to waste the time and effort that had already been put into his education, and still believed that something might be made of him. He himself had given hundreds of devoted, patient hours to help him master the rudiments of reading and writing – reading, that would enrich his life; and writing, a key to unlock the prison door of his solitary world. Surely the boy deserved to be given every chance, for he had shown great courage where "a dozen of others would have given it over long ago."[6]

Johnnie Gordon had at last reached the stage when he was to be sent to Aberdeen to be tested by the bishop as to his readiness for ordination. A suit had been ordered for him from the city, but it had missed the post, and to have one made locally would take months. It was the end of May before it finally arrived and he set out, carrying with him a written report from the master. Mr Duthie had the highest regard for his character. He thought him "an excellent virtuous young man" with "the least of the sallies and impetuosity of youth" of anyone he had known; everyone who met him was edified by his "regular prudent conduct". There were some problems regarding his studies, however. He was particularly "lame as to history." He was a plodder, who might have achieved reasonable standards with the advantages of Paris or Rome, but had suffered from the limitations of Scalan and the difficult times.

He was ordained in Edinburgh in June. George Gordon – the former Scalan master – wanted him as his assistant at Aberdeen, but Mr Duthie had come to rely on him almost as a member of staff, and was determined to hold onto him as long as possible. He argued that he needed him to help with the harvest, especially as he himself might have to go into hiding again at any time, for he still had the "two red neighbours opposite to his door".[7] Bishop Smith agreed to let him return to Scalan, on the understanding that he would move to Aberdeen once the harvest was in. But November found him still at the seminary, and it was only after a second appeal to the bishop that the master was forced to let him go.

At the end of the year Mr Gray left to resume his old post as a private tutor. He would have preferred to stay at Scalan, and his departure also came at a bad time for the College.[8] Mr Duthie had been suffering ill health for much of the year, and now the least exertion exhausted him and brought on "uneasie fits". His housekeeper Betty Grant had also been in poor health for several years and was hardly up to the work. She had wanted to leave at Michaelmas, and he had only with difficulty persuaded her to see out the winter. And his farm servant, an excellent worker, had fallen into fornication and he had been left with no choice but to dismiss him. The farm buildings were in a bad state of disrepair, every one of them letting in the rain and needing to be re-thatched. The repairs should have been made the previous summer but had been postponed because Bishop Smith had required the servant and horse at that time: "You that live in towns have little notion of a country life", Mr Duthie gently reminded him.[9]

The ever-present military threat only added to his worries in the spring

MAP 6
Seminary lands as revealed by aerial photography
showing also part of the boundaries of Easter Scalan,
Wester Scalan and Fuarandearg farms (divided late 1760s)

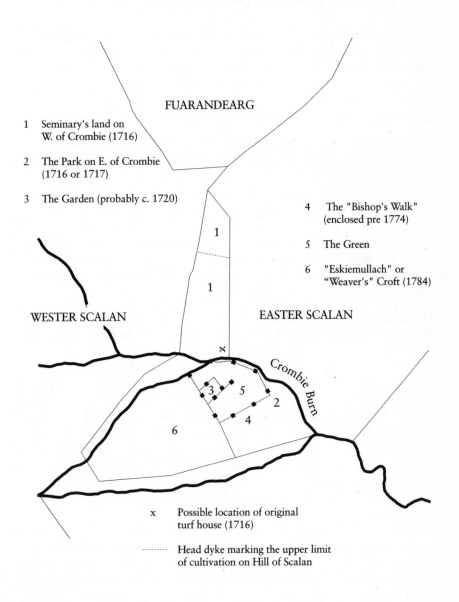

FUARANDEARG

1   Seminary's land on
    W. of Crombie (1716)

2   The Park on E. of Crombie
    (1716 or 1717)

3   The Garden (probably c. 1720)

4   The "Bishop's Walk"
    (enclosed pre 1774)

5   The Green

6   "Eskiemullach" or
    "Weaver's" Croft (1784)

WESTER SCALAN   EASTER SCALAN

Crombie Burn

x   Possible location of original
    turf house (1716)

....   Head dyke marking the upper limit
        of cultivation on Hill of Scalan

of 1755. A "severe" search was made of the priest's house at Auchriachan in March, and near the end of May Scalan itself was visited again by soldiers of the Corgarff garrison. Fortunately the Commanding Officer had talked in the neighbourhood about the imminent raid, and even let slip the date, and word of it reached the master in time so that he was able (once again) to be away when the troops arrived.[10]

The Prefect of Studies post at Paris had now fallen vacant again, and again Mr Duthie appeared to be the preferred choice of the bishop and the College principal. He protested his unsuitability as before, arguing that he had neither the learning nor the leadership qualities that the post demanded, and that his health and memory were failing. Furthermore, his leaving could well spell the end of Scalan:

> But in relation to M^r $D^{y's}$ going to Grisy [the Scots College Paris], I cannot forbear to observe, that the necessary consequence seems to be the giving up of Scal: altogether . . . 'Tis true that at present it seems to be of no consequence, but time and circumstances may soon favour it's recovery by slow degrees: but if it is once given up, there will be litle hopes remain; and the droping it would not, I beleive, be well lookt upon at $Hamb^g$ [Rome]. Now I cannot help concluding that M^r $D^{y's}$ removal must infer the giving it up, as there is no appearance of any other belonging to $comp^y$ [Company – ie., the Mission] that could in any degree be fit for that place.[11]

He recalled that Bishop Gordon had always resisted sending pupils abroad at the expense of Scalan, and urged his successor not to allow the wishes of Paris to win the day now.

The death of Mr Tyrie in May left Glenlivet without a priest and so postponed any possibility of Mr Duthie being taken from the Braes. But it also added to his burdens there. He warned that if any further load fell to him his health would be destroyed entirely. He had previously advised Bishop Smith not to post John Gordon to the Glenlivet station, because there were certain problems in that close-knit community that could "founder" a newly ordained priest and give their enemies an excuse to "make a great noise".[12] But the bishop was desperately short of man-power and had no choice but to draft the young man in, despite his inexperience.

Mr Gray made a welcome return to Scalan at the beginning of the new academic year, but it was feared that he would not be allowed to stay long, for the bishop wished to hasten his ordination to ease the chronic shortage of priests. Mr Duthie warned against raising him to the priest-hood, on the grounds that he was not yet sufficiently grounded in Divinity and that his shortcomings as a priest would be a cause of scandal.[13]

In the summer of 1756 John Drummond finally left the College. Through sheer dogged will he had mastered reading and writing and even made progress in Doctrine. He had shown remarkable courage. Mr Duthie was disappointed to lose him, and he was heartbroken to be leaving.[14]

But the master had some other more cheering news to report to the bishop – "I see the two pieces of cloath [uniformed soldiers] a little below us are calld for and are making ready", he wrote.[15] The army had more pressing work elsewhere, for Britain was now at war with France, and the war promised to bring peace to Scalan. But it would also again delay any plans to send Mr Duthie to Paris, leaving him still unsure from month to month where his future lay.

The uncertainty continued through the following year (1757), and it seemed to him that his efforts to run the seminary were neither understood nor appreciated. He was expected to make quite unrealistic economies, and criticised if he failed. If he had been given ready money at Martinmas, when prices were low, he could have made savings on meal, but the bishop had held back: it was a false economy, Mr Duthie told him frankly, adding with a touch of irritation, "If you have a mind to keep house here we could not be less".[16] He had now been at Scalan for sixteen hard and uncertain years, and his letters were beginning to betray more than a hint of bitterness and disappointment.

That autumn Bishop Smith called William Gray to Aberdeen for examination prior to his taking the last step to the priesthood. But he was surprised to receive a reply from the deacon making excuses not to make the journey. Mr Duthie believed that Mr Gray's response only proved his unfitness for ordination. Could not the bishop see that he was nothing but "a careless impertinent piece whom neither town nor country would please?" Both the master and the assistant were thrawn men in their own way, and the friction between them, thrown together within the close confines of Scalan, was beginning to affect the whole house. It was a relief when the deacon finally left for Aberdeen in December.[17]

Among the new students at this time was Alexander ('Sandy') Geddes, who was later to prove one of the most celebrated of all Scalan's alumni. He had joined the College at the beginning of 1755, and it had at once been obvious that he was a boy of unusual promise. Since then he had amply fulfilled all the master's hopes, and had already progressed far enough to move on to Philosphy. Mr Duthie judged him the most able Latin student he had ever had at Scalan, and excellent also at Greek. In later life he would earn a national reputation as a biblical scholar, and be held in high regard by the leading figures of the Enlightenment.[18] But already his health was suspect – he had been "extremely bad of a stranguary" the previous summer – and Mr Duthie feared that it might yet prevent him from completing his studies. He would have taken him home to recuperate if either of them had been strong enough to make the journey.[19]

The boy bore the Scalan winter as well as he could, and even managed to joke about it to a fellow student who was departing for the milder climate of the coast – "While you are there", he asked him earnestly, "pray be so kind as to make very particular enquiries after the health of the sun, and do not fail to present my compliments to him. I live in hope of one day renewing our personal acquaintance". But in later years – by which time he had been dismissed from the Mission and moved to London – he claimed that the climate and the austere conditions at Scalan had permanently damaged his health, and he seems to have retained a hearty dislike of the place for the rest of his life.[20]

Suddenly that December news came from Glenlivet that John Gordon was gravely ill. The young priest had been working day and night without sparing himself, and in his weakened state what started as a cold had soon turned into a raging fever. Mr Duthie went down to look after him, and arranged for a "bleeder" to visit him. When the phlebotomy was carried out the blood was found to be "so viscid that it was more in the nature of glue than blood". For two nights he never slept, with the fire in his body and an unbearable pain in his head. Twice more he was bled, but the symptoms only appeared worse. By now he had temporarily lost the power of speech. His eyes were blood red. Mr Duthie stayed by his bed talking to him, then prayed with him and gave him Extreme Unction. But he was now delirious, and somehow he seemed to have seized on one particular phrase that Mr Duthie had used and had become convinced that he had no hopes of salvation. He began to throw off his bed-clothes and could barely be restrained and held down in the bed. Mr Duthie slipped out, for he could see that his presence was only kindling the poor man's distress. The delirium lasted through the next day, but the following night he fell into a peaceful and refreshing sleep in which, during a lucid waking interval, he murmured regret at having spoken amiss. Mr Duthie stayed at his side throughout his last agony. At nine the following night he died.

His death at the age of twenty-eight was a body blow to the Mission, and a devastation to Mr Duthie who had been teacher and friend to him since his boyhood:

we are depriv'd of one of the most usefull most innocent young men I ever knew [he wrote] . . . he was indefatigable in cultivating a large field the fruits were appearing in a remarkable manner. had all the authority one could have wish'd and exercis'd w^t such charity & discretion that it was surprising to see a young man obeyd w^{t}out murmur & esteem'd at the same time.[21]

His only fault was too great a neglect of himself, he added, and that neglect had killed him.[22]

His death re-opened the question of who should serve Glenlivet. Mr Duthie could certainly take on no more. His old nervous ailment had returned, and a few weeks caring for his dead colleague's flock on winter roads soon "reduced him to nothing". Writing to George Gordon in February (1758), at his lowest ebb and at the low ebb of the year, he feared he could scarcely shoulder even his charge at Scalan, for the seminary seemed incapable of shaking itself free of problems which mounted daily. "If I were allowed I would willingly retire it is high time", he wrote. He wished someone "more proper" could be found for Scalan, and for Paris.[23]

That spring the local minister introduced compulsory catechism instruction for the Braes children during school hours, setting Bishop Smith the familiar problem that was always liable to recur where there were Protestant schools in Catholic communities. The bishop responded by forbidding Catholic parents to enrol their children, a tactic that bishops before him had tried and found unworkable, because it in fact meant that children would lose their only chance of education. Mr Duthie advised him that his order was unnecessary and dangerous: unnecessary because he had never in all his years in the area heard of a single conversion to Protestantism, and because the school was in any case soon to be moved to Lower Glenlivet; and dangerous because it left the Church open to accusations of being anti-education and of keeping its people in ignorance. It might even provoke a backlash that could close Scalan, because recent national legislation requiring all schoolteachers to be qualified had left the seminary vulnerable. He explained that the children should be safe enough at the Protestant school because he was catechising them himself at the weekends "as a ballance", and this was proving effective without causing confrontation. He was enjoying the task and felt he had never done anything as a priest "more agreeable or more usefull to old and young". It was helping to raise his own spirits as the spring days lengthened.[24]

In September Bishop Smith at last gave him the call for Paris, and he was ready to face the challenge. He bade a hasty farewell to Scalan and set out at once for Edinburgh – ever mindful of the farm – so that his servant and horse could be back in the Braes in time for the harvest. He took Sandy Geddes with him, as the young man was also going to the Scots College to complete his studies there. He stayed in the city, waiting for a ship, lodging above Bishop Smith in the World's End Close and dining with him daily. He had every reason to be content, he felt, though he would have been more use at the seminary, and found "the captious censoriousness of the polite folks" of the capital less to his liking than "the blunt simplicity" of the Banffshire uplands.

There were few ships making the crossing to Holland now, because of the war, and the bishop advised that for safety's sake he should not embark upon the first to sail, but wait for one with an armed escort.[25] The winter came and went, and it was April before he finally arrived in Paris.

He could look back on his time at Scalan with mixed satisfaction, and so also we might judge his stewardship. On the one hand, only three boys from all his sixteen years became priests of the Mission, and as a master he was not without his faults, of which intransigence was not the least. On the other, his best judges should be the college community themselves, and on this count – on the evidence of Bishop Hugh MacDonald writing shortly after his departure – the verdict is clear and wholly positive. The bishop was staying in the Cabrach at the time, close enough for his words to be more than mere hearsay. The new master was doing very well, he reported, and receiving every assistance. But things were not the same, and "there was great regrate for Mr Duth".[26]

In any case, William Duthie's place in Scalan's history is assured, and deservedly, if only because his term of office was the longest of any master, and because it was he who in its days of greatest jeopardy kept the thread unbroken.

NOTES

1. William Duthie to George Gordon, 12. 10. 1753, BL. The present account based on this letter, which is unsigned and bears no address.
2. Fr Kilian Grant OSB (alias 'John Scott') to Bishop Smith, 10. 11. 1753, BL. "All was done and hatched by ye Mn^rs to Sheriff Pringl"; the C/O was "a most civil Gentleman" and only made a "shame [sham] search" in compliance with orders.
3. William Duthie to George Gordon, 12. 10. 1753, BL.
4. William Duthie to Bishop Smith, 11. 11. 1753, BL.
5. William Duthie to Bishop Smith, 25. 2. 1754 and 27. 5. 1754, BL.
6. William Duthie to Bishop Smith, 27. 5. 1754, BL. Following paragraph also based on this letter.
7. William Duthie to George Gordon, 11. 6. 1754, BL.
8. William Duthie to George Gordon, 11. 12. 1754, BL.
9. Ibid., and William Duthie to Bishop Smith, 3. 1. 1755, BL.
10. William Duthie to Bishop Smith, 1. 4. 1755, and to George Gordon, 25. 5. 1755, BL.
11. William Duthie to Bishop Smith, 1. 4. 1755, postscript, BL.
12. William Duthie and Thomas Brockie to Bishop Smith, 21. 5. 1755, and William Duthie to George Gordon, 25. 5. 1755, BL. Mr Duthie did not specify the problems, but they almost certainly included questions of special

dispensation for marriage of relatives, which required special faculties and needed an experienced priest.

13. William Duthie to Bishop Smith, 23. 8. 1755, BL.
14. William Duthie to Bishop Smith, 1. 4. 1755 and 6. 9. 1756, BL.
15. William Duthie to Bishop Smith, 6. 9. 1756, BL.
16. William Duthie to Bishop Smith, 5. 5. 1757, BL.
17. William Gray to Bishop Smith, 8. 11. 1757, with postscript by William Duthie, BL. Re Mr Gray leaving – William Duthie to George Gordon, 11. 12. 1757, BL.
18. For a contemporary account of his life, compiled by a friend, see Good J. M. *Memoirs of the Life and Writings of the Reverend Alexander Geddes LLD* (London, 1803). For a modern biography, see Fuller R. C. *Alexander Geddes 1737–1802, A Pioneer of Biblical Criticism* (Sheffield, 1984).
19. William Duthie to George Gordon, 11. 12. 1757, and to ?, 11. 1. 1758, BL.
20. Alexander Geddes to Bishop Geddes, 14. 8. 1784, BL.
21. William Duthie to ?, 11. 1. 1758, BL.
22. Ibid. Mr Duthie took an active layman's interest in Medicine, and possessed a copy of *Praxis Medica* (which later became part of the Chapeltown library). His belief that John Gordon's constant labour without relaxation had thickened his blood until "it could not circulate thro' the capillary arteries of the brain" offers a fascinating glimpse of eighteenth century thinking on the subject.
23. William Duthie to George Gordon, 2. 2. 1758, BL.
24. William Duthie to Bishop Grant, 14. 4. 1758, BL.
25. William Duthie to George Gordon, 20. 11. 1758, and to ?, 30. 11. 1758, BL.
26. Bishop H. MacDonald to Bishop Smith, 13.10. 1758, BL.

11

Nadir (1758–1762)

Mr Duthie's successor, George Duncan, was not able to take up his post until well into October. His first task on arrival was to restore order, because the boys had been doing much as they pleased for the three weeks that no-one had been in charge.[1]

Mr Duncan was very well fitted for the post of master. He was familiar with Scalan from his days as a student and assistant master there in the '20s and '30s.Since his ordination he had had a wealth of varied pastoral experience, in rural Angus, at Traquair House in the Borders where he had also served the tiny Catholic community in the neighbourhood, and in his home town of Edinburgh. He had been imprisoned in '46, and after his release had undertaken a dangerous mission at Bishop Smith's request smuggling the Blessed Sacrament into Carlisle Castle to prisoners awaiting execution, talking his way in and out again and making good his escape back into Scotland. If experience, courage, perseverance and inventiveness were qualities required of a master of Scalan, he was not short of them. Having been a 'plodder' himself he was sympathetic to the needs and problems of students. And at fifty years of age there was every reason to believe that he could still give several good years to the College.

Sadly for Scalan he stayed only six months. William Gray returned in the spring, now sixty and still not ordained, and shortly after his arrival Mr Duncan was sent to assist Mr Guthrie at the Glenlivet station. He made his home at Tomnalienan, building a turf house onto the gable end of the mains farm house there. Scalan boys were sent to lend a hand with the building – it was their task to stamp down the earth floor – and the whole work from foundation to ridge-pole was completed in a single day.[2]

He left the College in good order and solvent, but with serious doubts as to Mr Gray's fitness to take charge. The servants had made it plain that they had no confidence in the older man, while the local community were even more outspoken and never mentioned his name without contempt. Mr Duncan doubted his capacity to run the seminary alone, and believed that he would need an assistant. But he doubted even more Bishop Smith's proposal to send him Alexander Kennedy. Kennedy had trained in Rome, where he had taken the vows of sub-deacon, but he had been refused further promotion. He had a reputation for causing friction, and Mr

Duncan was sure that he and Mr Gray "would never hitt it".[3] It was no doubt the outgoing master's advice, and similar counsel from Mr Guthrie the priest of Glenlivet,[4] that persuaded the bishop that whatever the shortage of priests Mr Gray must never be ordained.

On 12 September 1760, when Mr Gray had been master about sixteen months, two Kirk ministers, Dr Hyndman and Mr McFarlane, paid a visit to the seminary. They were members of a Church of Scotland Commission gathering information on the state of religion in the Highlands and Islands. Word had gone ahead of them, and as they they drew up on horseback before the door Mr Gray was waiting for them and invited them in. But they did not so much as dismount, and soon rode off, expressing surprise that so great a noise should have been made about a place that had such a poor appearance and seemed to be of so little consequence.

In their official Report to the General Assembly they referred to the seminary as "a sort of a college at a place called Skalon, where a Priest Teacheth",[5] apparently not realising that Mr Gray was a deacon. Their somewhat dismissive description serves to remind us how small, ill-housed and poorly resourced Scalan was compared with the facilities available to its adversaries, and of the need for its students to accept sacrifice and disadvantage in the name of their Faith. 'A sort of a college' was probably the best that could be said of it at this time.

Bishop Geddes, who was personally told of the ministers' visit by Mr Gray, relates in his *Brief Historical Account of the Seminary at Scalan* that their Report claimed that there were three priests resident at the College,[6] but this is in fact an error. He may perhaps have been confusing it with another written the same year, a *Petition by Heads of Protestant Families in Glenlivet,* which was presented to the Synod of Moray, and through the Synod's Moderator to the Duke of Gordon.[7] This claimed that Scalan was staffed by three priests as well as a professor! How such exaggerated claims could be made by local people – assuming they were not deliberate lies – and how they could be believed, we can only wonder.

The *Petition* also stated that Scalan was frequently visited by two bishops and other priests, and this at least was accurate. Bishop Smith and his assistant Bishop Grant were in fact visiting the College as often as possible at this time, and encouraging their senior priests to do the same. They were using it as a venue for Administrators' meetings, and taking the opportunity to stay over for several weeks at a time. They had serious concerns as to whether Mr Gray was up to the task at Scalan, and their purpose in visiting was to give him support, and also to observe his management and the condition of the seminary.

Their reservations regarding him remained and they would have preferred to move him from Scalan. The man Bishop Smith would have chosen to succeed him was Mr John Geddes, who had been ordained only the previous year and was now in charge of his first station at Shenval in the Cabrach. But he had not a single Mission priest whom he could spare to take Mr Geddes' place. The one man who might have been available was Fr Alexander Menzies from the Benedictine monastery at Ratisbon in Germany, but he was unwilling to commit himself to any Mission station at this time, and particularly perhaps to the Cabrach which was one of the coldest and least popular in Scotland and known as 'Siberia' among the clergy. The bishop was forced to abandon the plan meantime, but he did arrange for Mr Geddes to visit Scalan to make an assessment of the students – he obviously valued the young priest's judgment more than William Gray's.[8]

The shortage of priests was to grow even more acute over the next two years. There were too few new men coming through to replace the old. The Scots College Paris, in particular, was completely failing in its function of providing new priests. The Scottish clergy had become so concerned at its shortcomings that they sent a jointly signed *Formulaire* to the Principal in 1760 with proposals for improvement, and the following year Bishop Smith himself wrote to the Prior of the Chartreuse, who had overall charge of the College, begging him to effect remedies. The College was now as good as "lost to the Mission", he wrote: only two priests had come back to Scotland from it in the past thirty years, and not one in the past twenty; there was just one student presently on roll; and the abuses and the slackness there were a cause of scandal.[9]

The bishop also wrote to Rome, warning Propaganda that the Mission was "in great tribulation" for lack of workers, with old priests dying or becoming too infirm to undertake their duties.[10] His problems were compounded by the failure of the religious orders to give assistance. The Scottish monasteries and religious houses in Europe were in fact still taking some of his most promising boys and keeping them abroad after their ordination, while at home many of the faithful were falling away for lack of a priest. In the North there was now only one to serve them from Aberdeen to the Enzie.[11]

His workforce was further reduced by the untimely death of George Duncan in November 1761, and then by the loss of Mr James Duffus (one of Scalan's earliest alumni) the following March. Writing to him with news of this latest death Bishop Grant expressed his own fears for the future of the Mission -

When I consider how fast we are droping away one after another I am very much alarmed, and the more that I see no means left to supply our

Plate 1. The Crombie burn, the spring, and the shelf of ground traditionally the site of the first Scalan house of 1716. Photo: John Watts.

Plate 2. Buildings from the 18th-century farm town of Scalan on the west bank of the Crombie, still standing in the 19th century. Photo: Ann Dean.

Plate 3. Scalan today, looking east with the Ladder Hills behind. Photo: John Watts.

Plate 4. View from the Hill of Scalan, showing the emptiness of the landscape today. The trees to the left of the house mark the 'Bishop's Walk'. The water mills by the burn date from the 19th century. Photo: Alasdair Roberts.

Plate 5. North wing, with kitchen of 1772-3, converted to a public chapel in 1786-8; and remains of the wall which enclosed the yard on the west side still visible in this 19th-century photograph. Photo: Mgr J. McIntyre.

Plate 6. House and part of south wing, showing thatched outhouse of 1772-3 and slated kitchen of 1786-8, still standing at time of this 19th-century photograph. Photo: Mgr J. McIntyre.

Plate 7. Portrait of Bishop Hay, from the Scots College, Rome. It was in Bishop Hay's time as master that Scalan reached its high point of excellence. Photo: Mgr J. McIntyre.

Plate 8. The attic added when the roof was raised in 1788-9. Photograph, taken from the head of the stair, shows the north half of the attic. Photo: John Watts.

Plate 9. North side of the house, with door to upstairs chapel (originally reached by an outside stair). Photograph, taken during restoration (1992-4), also reveals line of original roof. Photo: Ann Dean.

Plate 10. South side of the house. Photograph, taken during restoration (1992-4), reveals line of original roof, original double ridge poles, and second window in boys' dormitory. Photo: Ann Dean.

Plate 11. Brass alarm clock (1758) acquired for Scalan 1770. Wanting its original wooden surround. Blairs Museum. Photo: Rev. J. Woodside.

Plate 12. Bishop Hay's chalice and paten, acquired in 1792 while he was master at Scalan. Blairs Museum. Photo: John Watts.

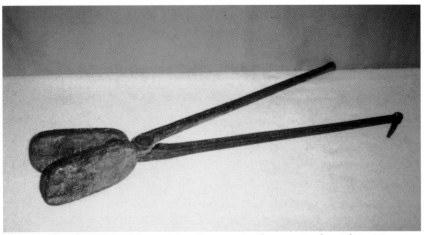

Plate 13. Bread irons used for making Communion hosts at Scalan. Blairs Museum. Photo: John Watts.

Plate 14. The College of Aquhorties, 1799, now a private house. Photo: John Watts.

Plate 15. Excursion to Scalan by students of Blairs College, 1986. Such visits had become regular events by the 1980s. Photo: Rev. Stephen Robson.

Plate 16. Aerial photograph revealing Seminary lands and other 18th-century boundaries. Compare with Map 6. Photo: Royal Commission on the Ancient & Historical Monuments of Scotland.

wants, the ordinary resources being in such a dismal situation that little good can be reasonably expected from them.[12]

The "ordinary resources" to which he was referring were the seminaries, and in paricular Paris and Scalan.

"Dismal" was indeed a fair description of the state to which the latter had fallen in the three years since Mr Gray took charge. The house itself was now in a deplorable condition, for the restoration work of thirteen years before had only been makeshift. There were only three students, Sandy Cameron of Braemar and two local boys, Alexander Gordon of Minmore in Lower Glenlivet, and John Gordon from Clashnoir in the Braes. Standards of learning and discipline had slipped badly. All the books were old and many were damaged. There was a general air of decline and disorder. There was friction among the servants, and Ann Greenlaw the housekeeper was threatening to leave.

There was a real danger that if matters were allowed to drift further the seminary could die a natural death, and Bishop Smith had seen and heard enough to make him determined to replace Mr Gray. On his behalf Bishop Grant contacted Fr Menzies in August, and this time was able to persuade him to accept the Cabrach mission. John Geddes at once left Shenval for the Scalan and moved in at the beginning of September.[13]

NOTES

1. William Duthie to George Gordon, 20. 11. 1758, BL.
2. Account of building of house related by Bishop Alexander Cameron (one of the students involved) to Bishop Kyle, and by him to Canon Clapperton – see Clapperton W. *Memoirs of Scotch Missionary Priests* (c. 1860), transcribed Wilson G. (Elgin, 1901), vol. IV, part 1, pp. 2320f.
3. George Duncan to Bishop Smith, 5. 6. 1759, BL.
4. William Guthrie to John Geddes, 26. 7. 1760, BL.
5. 'Report of Drs. Hyndman, Dick, et al. to General Assembly', 1760, copy CH 8/212, p. 73, SRO; later printed in *The Scots Magazine*, Nov. 1766, p. 574.
6. Bishop Geddes 'Brief Historical Account of the Seminary at Scalan', 1777, CH 1/3, SCA, para. 29.
7. 'Representation by Heads of Protestant Families in Glenlivet', in Synod of Moray, Record of Meetings, meeting of 22. 4. 1760, CH 2/271/VIII, pp. 4f., SRO; and Aeneas Shaw (Synod Moderator) to Duke of Gordon, 23. 4. 1760, GD 44/43/18/61, SRO.
8. Bishop Smith to Bishop Grant, 7. 1. 1760, BL; and Bishop Grant to Bishop Smith, 6. 2. 1760, BL.
9. Bishop Smith to Prior of Chartreuse, Paris, n.d. 1761, (in French), BL; and further letters, n.d. 1762 and 1. 8. 1762 (in French), BL.
10. Bishops' letter to Rome, 30. 6. 1761 (in Latin), BL.
11. Bishop Smith to Bishop Grant, 19. 12. 1761, BL. The situation had eased two years later, though two stations were still without priests and Perth was being

served from Aberdeen – Bishop Smith 'Account of the Mission' to Abbé Peter Grant, 1763, SM 4/13/9, SCA.

12. Bishop Grant to Bishop Smith, 25. 3. 1762, BL.

13. Bishop Geddes 'Dates of Some Things to be Remembered', B JG 1/1, SCA. The date was 3 Sept. Also Bishop Grant to Bishop Smith, 14. 9. 1762, BL.

12

Building Anew (1762–1767)

Mr John Geddes was twenty-six years old, and still only three years a priest, but he was already showing more that ordinary promise. Humble, sweet tempered and courteous, he had the gift of being at ease with all men without compromising his own principles. To these personal qualities were added a fine mind, a facility for languages, and the fruits of nine years' study in Rome. His student days at the Scots College had coincided with a new breadth and openness of the curriculum there, and he had been fortunate to have several outstanding scholars among his teachers. The course had brought him into contact not only with Theology and the Classics but with the latest advances in Philosophy, Physics and Mathematics.[1]

At the end of November he wrote to Bishop Smith giving his first impressions of his new home.[2] Things were progressing pretty much to his satisfaction, "at least in the most principal points". The boys seemed tractable enough and he was quietly confident of them, though reluctant to be too lavish in his praise until he knew them better. But there was already a marked improvement in discipline, and he intended very soon to bring them gradually back to an exact observance of the *Rules*. He had put a floor into Mr Gray's old room and made it comfortable so that he and the boys could use it as their sitting room during the winter. Ann Greenlaw had agreed to stay on, for another year at least.

He had discovered that there were no inventories or records of the contents of the house, not even of the religious items. He planned to remedy this, and intended to start by checking and cataloguing the books, some of which were in a parlous condition. He had unearthed one irreplaceable volume, the *Fratres Wallemburgiei,* covered with mildew and sodden with rain water, and had had to dry it out leaf by leaf. He had also retrieved the original papers of the College from the bottom of an old press and brought them to safety. Lastly, he was able to reassure the bishop that Grant of Rothmais had promised him that their lease would be safe so long as he remained the tacksman.

The question of the lease had arisen because of the development of the land at the head of the Braes, and the granting of new tacks there, over the past three decades (see pp. 84f.). A survey of the area carried out for the

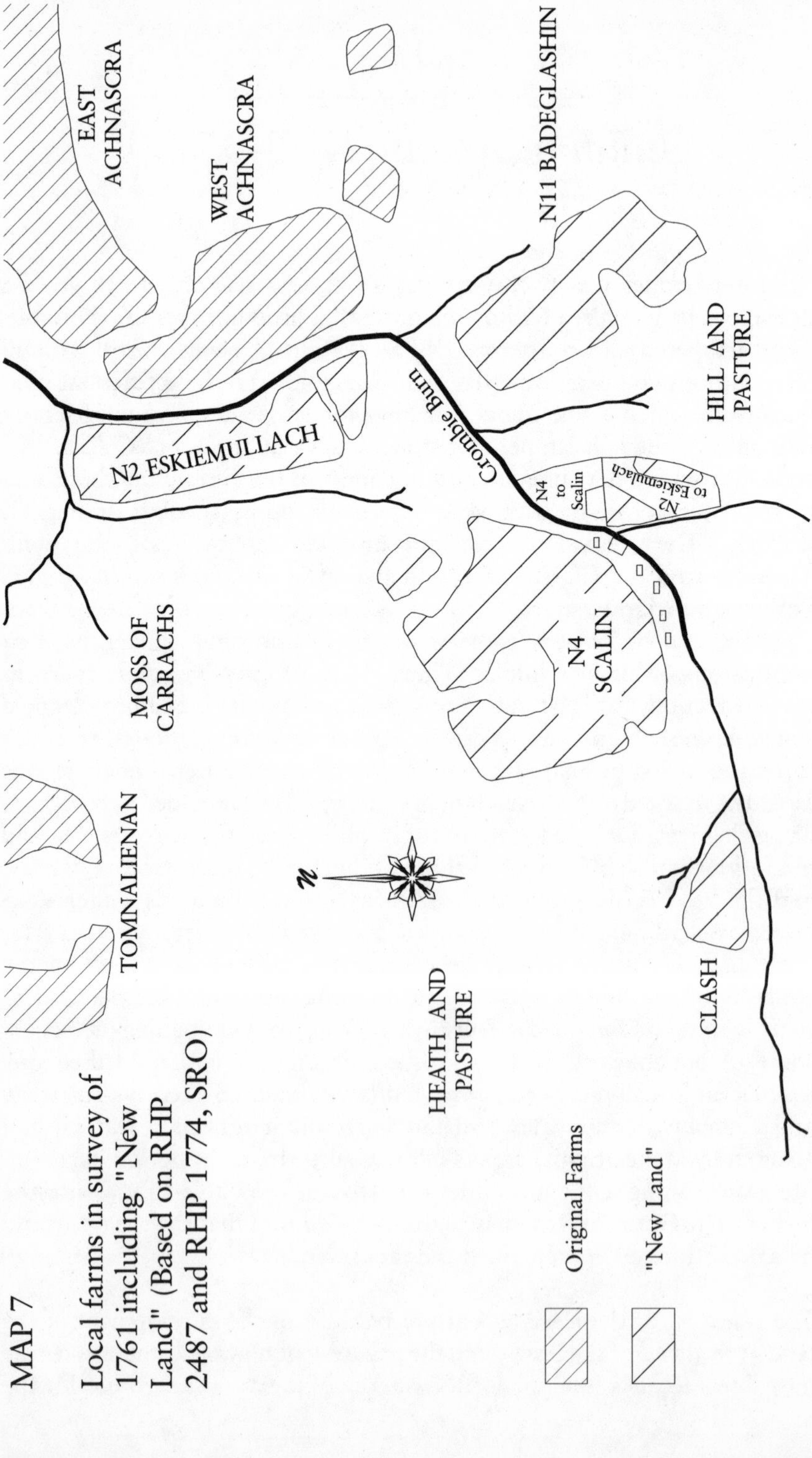

MAP 7

Local farms in survey of
1761 including "New
Land" (Based on RHP
2487 and RHP 1774, SRO)

EAST
ACHNASCRA

WEST
ACHNASCRA

N11 BADEGLASHIN

HILL AND
PASTURE

N2 ESKIEMULLACH

Crombie Burn

N4
to
Scalin

N2
to Eskiemullach

MOSS OF
CARRACHS

N4
SCALIN

TOMNALIENAN

N

HEATH AND
PASTURE

CLASH

Original Farms

"New Land"

Duke of Gordon in 1761 provides details of the extent of these developments to date. Scalan, Badeglashan, Eskiemullach and Clash are all
described in it as part of "the New Land that is lately taken Inn to Corn
Land off the Pasture And is not Incorporate with the old Plows But are in
Seperate Tacks & Crofts".[3] They had been progressively taken up and
subdivided among local tenants. Tack no. 4, 'the Scalin', included the Hill
of Scalan itself and the land at its foot as far east as the Crombie and the
Slochd burns, and that part of it not held by the seminary was now leased
to a number of tenants – James Mcalea, Peter Stuart, Alexander Grant,
Robert Rattray and Paul McPherson, who worked it in runrig. The Clash,
which had formerly been a shieling belonging to Lettoch farm and used
also by Calier, was now leased to Paul McPherson's brother John on
condition that he cultivated it, and three acres of it were already under
crops.

The survey also shows two plots on the east side of the burns. One was
the land originally gifted to the seminary, which had never been part of a
tack but which inexplicably was now defined as part of Tack no. 4,
belonging "to Scalin." The other lay immediately to the south and was
described as a croft or pendicle of the Eskiemullach tack. Map 7 is based
on the maps that accompanied the survey.[4]

Traditionally, tenants' leases were short-term, or even renewed annually, in many parts of the Highlands, and were often bound by no
written contract, so that security of tenure depended to a great extent on
the goodwill of the tacksman. His position was particularly powerful
when land was in demand, as was the case with the recently improved
lands on the Hill of Scalan. How would the tack be divided, when some
tenants were seeking to increase their portion? Grant of Rothmais had
promised to continue all the existing leases, including that of the seminary, so long as he remained the tacksman. And though he was himself a
Protestant he had always shown goodwill towards the College. But the
rumour was that he was planning to give up Tomnalienan, perhaps even
that Whitsun. If so, the other local tenants, and particularly the seminary's closest neighbour James Mcalea, had made it known that they
intended to bid for the vacant land.[5] Mcalea was likely to make a far less
friendly tacksman. Fortunately, however, Rothmais decided to hold on to
Tomnalienan meantime, in the knowledge that all the tacks on the Duke's
estates would be coming up for renewal in several years' time, and that
that would be his opportunity to make a move.

That spring Mr Geddes had a request from a family in Strathglass for
their son to join the College as a boarder, that is, a student paying board
since he did not intend training for the priesthood. The parents were so
anxious to enrol him that they were willing for him to be boarded out in

the neighbourhood if there was no room in the house. Mr Geddes was in favour of accepting him. He judged that he could now consider increasing the roll without attracting attention from their enemies, and that having a boarder would be "rather an advantage than a loss."[6] It was the first such request he had received, and reflected Scalan's growing good name under the new master.

To take in boarders when they were so short of funds and trying to rebuild was certainly a temptation, but it could bring them problems, and had done so before. And in fact as they received more requests over the next few years these problems would come to a head. How many lay students could the College accept without losing its real purpose and ethos? How could it resist pressure from wealthy and influential parents, without offending those valuable supporters of the Church? How ensure the true intention of students?[7] By the end of the decade these were nettles that the bishops would have to grasp, as we shall see.

Mr Geddes had been at Scalan less than five months, but the students had already made such progress under his care that he was able to send the Scots College Rome the names of two of them, Sandy Cameron and John Gordon, whom he would be recommending for transfer in the near future.[8] By the autumn of 1763 the student roll had doubled to six, and he had to advise Bishop Smith that to expand much further at this stage would be neither practical nor prudent -

> Untill the House shall be repaired, we can scarcely have Accommoda-
> tion for more than those we have or are expected; & tho' I hope there is
> no Danger, yet, in my Opinion, it is not proper to venture with many
> more, but very gradually.[9]

He was thinking particularly of the minister of Glenlivet, James Grant, whose malice the seminary had good reason to remember. But he must have been thinking also of his own workload. The nearby station of Strathavon was again without a priest, and much of the pastoral work among its 800 Catholics was falling to him and taking him from his duties at Scalan. Had he not been called away so often, or even if he had been able to entrust the seminary to a reliable assistant, he would have held "high hopes" for all his students, for they showed much promise. Apart from the youngest, Sandy Innes, who had only recently arrived, every one of them had already given evidence of a sincere desire to pursue his vocation.

Sandy Cameron was the most advanced, and the one with whom he had talked most seriously concerning the priesthood. When in March of the new year the oldest of the boys, Willie Gordon, decided not to continue at the College, Mr Geddes gave his bedroom to Sandy as the most senior student and unofficial 'Head Boy'.[10] He considered him the "most proper" of his boys for this distinction, a judgment well justified that he perhaps later remembered when in the year before his own death Alexander Cameron was consecrated bishop.

That spring also saw John Paterson of Coffurich return to Scalan. He had been at the College for a short time some three years before, when his piety, will to succeed and humility had impressed everyone around him. He had been a joy to teach, and it had been a blow to Mr Gray when he had left to join the Benedictine monastery at Würzburg.[11] But the climate abroad had not suited his health and he had been forced to abandon his hopes of the monastic life and return to Scotland. Now the bishop had given him permission to enrol at Scalan again, a decision that the seminary would thank God for in years to come. He was still the very same boy they remembered – perhaps even darker now, but with the same frankness, the same winning desire to please and innocence, that seemed almost incongruous in one now grown so tall.

On 4 August Mr Geddes saw the first fruits of his rebuilding when Sandy Cameron and John Gordon set out for Rome, and Sandy Innes for Paris. The boys were financed in part by a fund of £12 Sterling for students bound for the Scots Colleges, half of which came from a grant made by Pope Clement XII for this purpose, and the rest from interest on a bequest from James VIII to the Mission. The terms specified that it was to be distributed at the discretion of the Cardinal Protector. The new Protector, Cardinal Albani, who had only come to that office the previous year, was a punctilious patron and required a strict account of the students and their expenses as a condition of releasing the grant.[12] It was important that his demand be met, for outside help of this kind was crucial to the Church in Scotland and its hopes of sending boys abroad. We can gauge its importance from a break-down of the Mission's finances made about this time: its total holdings amounted to only £340, and – apart from priests' salaries – one third of the identified areas of outlay concerned students' costs.[13]

Given the poverty of the Mission and the draining cost of sending students abroad, it was essential that great care be taken in selecting suitable boys, because the bishops could not afford to waste money on failures. Care was doubly necessary in the case of Rome as the hub of the Catholic Church, and the news in 1765 was that the Scottish Mission's first two ambassadors, Sandy Cameron and John Gordon, had made a promising start there and were living up to expectations. Bishop Smith was in fact now pressing for more boys to be made ready for transfer. But Mr Geddes felt that he should wait until he was sure of their suitability and commitment. All of them showed promise, he explained, but none was yet fully tried, and he urged patience –

I am much of Opinion that none should be sent to Old Town [Rome] but such of whose embracing the Eccles. State there is great Probability.[14]

He reminded the bishop that other countries were careful to send only "their most hopeful Subjects to that common City of Christendom", and believed that he would wish to do the same, since it was from Rome that the Scottish Church could hope to receive "the greatest & most essential Favours."

In fact no boys were sent abroad that year, and with the student roll now standing at seven, and several other boys "begging" to join, Mr Geddes' energies were stretched to the limit. He was no longer covering Strathavon, but now had Glenbuchat to serve on the other side of the Ladder Hills, a task difficult enough for much of the year and almost impossible in winter. In May responsibility for the Cabrach mission also fell to him when Mr Charles Gordon left suddenly and without warning. He gave what support he could, and made arrangements for the upkeep of the priest's house, the rent of the croft and the harvest.[15]

But these calls were keeping him from his work at the seminary, and must inevitably harm it, he warned: "I hope you will not from what I here write infer, that I am uneasy here," he told the bishop; "No: I am happy enough, only it gives me some trouble to meet with so many Avocations from my proper business."[16] His words echoed the concerns of masters before him, and would be echoed by his successors, because rarely throughout Scalan's history could bishops afford to spare a priest solely for the College, without other outside duties. John Geddes never complained of the burden on his own account. But it was beginning to tell on his health.

Seven years before, while still a student at Rome, he had first vomited blood, and at that time a threatening Consumption was diagnosed, brought on it was believed by excessive study. The weakness was to stay with him all his life, and the symptoms would return whenever he was under unusual strain. Now the effects of his overwork were only too obvious. He was spitting blood again, and the pains had returned to his chest. Repeated blood-letting, the remedy used successfully on previous occasions, was having no effect. But his fellow priest Mr George Hay – the future bishop – who was trained in Medicine, recommended applying a poultice to the chest, and this brought some easing of the pain.[17] Mr Geddes himself found that exercise, especially walking and horse-riding, reduced the symptoms, and he hoped to ride down to the coast in the summer.

Bishop Smith would have liked to give him an assistant, and had one

MAP 8
Division of Scalan Tack in late 1760s
Based on RHP 1776 (date 1774), SRO

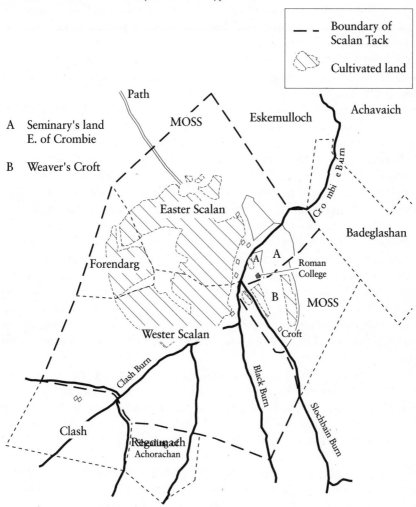

Boundary of
Scalan Tack

Cultivated land

A   Seminary's land
E. of Crombie

B   Weaver's Croft

Path

MOSS   Eskemulloch   Achavaich

Crombie Burn

Easter Scalan

Badeglashan

Forendarg

A   A   Roman College

B   MOSS

Wester Scalan   Croft

Clash Burn

Black Burn

Slochbain Burn

Clash

Ringorm
Achorachan

Note   Cultivated areas only marked for Scalan, for Seminary's land on
East side of Crombie (A) and for "Weaver's Croft" (B) which was
acquired in 1784.

The boundary of Easter Scalan, Wester Scalan and "Forendarg"
is close to the summit of the Tom (Hill) of Scalan. Note the
uncultivated corridors to allow access to the pasture at top of hill.

available in Alexander Kennedy, the same man whom he had previously considered sending to assist Mr Gray. Kennedy had just returned for the second time from the Scots College Rome with a less than satisfactory report, and the bishop was reluctant to bring him forward for ordination and at a loss how to use him. But Mr Geddes preferred to have no assistant rather than Mr Kennedy, because his previous stay at Scalan had ended "in a way not at all honourable", and if he returned the fear was that he would soon take up with his old acquaintances in the neighbour-hood, and the peace of the house would be destroyed.[18]

He was therefore "something mortified" when Mr Kennedy arrived at the end of the year, and his first impressions did nothing to ease his fears. Some of the students were very young and impressionable, yet he was constantly indiscreet in his talk in front of them and would not be silenced. He was critical of almost everything about the Church – especially the clergy in Rome, whom he called "despicable and ridiculous" – and open in his dislike of Scalan. He could see no fault in himself and believed that the master, the senior priests and the bishops were all against him. Mr Geddes had to warn him more than once against giving scandal, but found him unrepentant. "I have nothing to regret," he would reply, shrugging his shoulders. "Do you want me to lie to the boys, as you yourself do?" Faced with this reaction he had no choice but to write to Bishop Smith and ask that the young man be removed as soon as possible, suggesting that he might complete his studies under an experienced priest such as George Hay at Preshome, who might have more success with him.[19]

Mr Kennedy was in any case almost ready for ordination and the bishop took him out that summer.[20] He was accepted for the Highland Vicariate, ordained by Bishop Hugh MacDonald, and posted to the station at Arisaig, where however he served for only some seven years before his premature death in 1773.

By now they were "a family of fifteen", including ten students and three servants, and facing severe problems of space. But they had agreed that there was no sense in extending the house, or even repairing it, until the question of the lease was resolved.[21] This now seemed likely to happen one way or the other very soon, because the Duke of Gordon was having the long-awaited new tacks drawn up for all the properties on his estates. By Whitsun 1776 contracts had been agreed for all but ten of the farms of Glenlivet. But Tomnalienan-and-Scalan was not among them, and the seminary had to wait until the following year to find out what their situation would be.[22]

In the new arrangements Grant of Rothmais gave up his rights on Tomnalienan (including Scalan),[23] and the whole tack was signed over to

James Mcalea, who had been a tenant there for over twenty years. His seventeen-year lease was conditional upon his "Improving into Corn Ground Such pieces of Barren ground as were Improveable."[24] He had already shown himself a less than friendly neighbour to the seminary, and was likely to prove a far less sympathetic landlord than Rothmais, but since his tack covered not only himself but all the existing tenants it at least gave the seminary security of tenure until 1784.

Mcalea was now by far the biggest landholder in the Braes. His tack extended to some 499 acres and only the Gordons of Lettoch, whose farm totalled 407 acres, came anywhere near him. It included the 154 acres of Tomnalienan itself, and almost 345 acres in and around the Hill of Scalan. This latter ground was divided up shortly afterwards into three separate farms, East Scalan, West Scalan and Fuarandearg, all in his name, and appeared as such in the Gordon Estate *Contents and Estimates* of 1772.[25] West Scalan was easily the largest of the three, but it was mostly moorland. East Scalan, which included the seminary's tack, extended to ninety-five acres, of which twenty-eight were arable, fifteen under grass, and the rest moss or moor. The arable was divided into six lots or holdings, the largest of which was the seventeen acres that had been held by the seminary for the past half century.

An estate map of Glenlivet drawn in 1774[26] shows this division of the land into three farms, and reflects the situation as it must have been by the late 1760s (Map 8). Both it and the *Contents and Estimates* also identify the seminary's land on the east side of the Crombie as part of the farm of East Scalan. Strictly speaking the new contract of 1767 should not have applied to this piece of land, since it had never been part of any tack. But the previous survey of 1761 had unaccountably included it in the Scalan tack, as we saw, and this was repeated in the documents of 1772 and 1774. The ambiguity was of little consequence at the time, but would become a focus of dispute in 1784 when the whole tack of Scalan would come up for renewal and fall into new hands.

The security of tenure guaranteed by the new tack at last gave the bishop the chance to rebuild. He supported Mr Geddes' proposal that rather than simply patch and extend the old house they should seize this opportunity to build an entirely new one, and use a new site on the other side of the Crombie burn.

The site they chose was new only in the sense that no house had been built on it before, but it had in fact been laid out as a garden since before the '45 and probably as early as 1720 (see pp. 45 and 89f.). Modern aerial photography (Plate 16) shows clearly that the new house was built *inside* this rectangular garden. (The photograph also shows what remains of the outbuildings added later at either end of the house – on the north 'wing' in

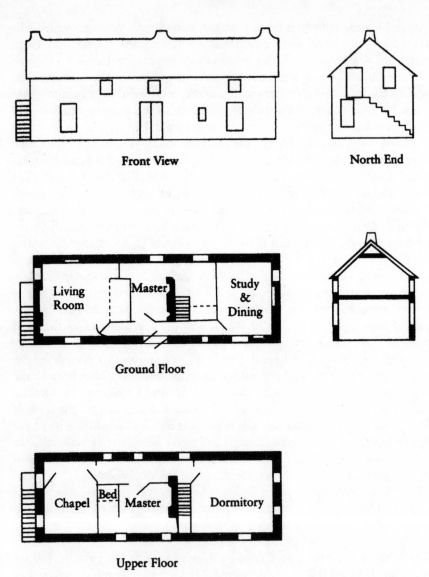

Front View

North End

Ground Floor

Living Room

Master

Study & Dining

Chapel

Bed

Master

Dormitory

Upper Floor

Fig. 2. Seminary House, 1767.

Based on Dean A. and Tait M. 'Scalan Reconstructed: Architectural and Documentary Evidence', *IR*, vol. xlvi, no.1, Spring 1995, espec. p. 38

the 1770s, and on the south at the same time and again in 1785 [27] – which when completed formed a rectangle within the garden.)

The building of 1767 still stands today, but with major modifications carried out twenty years later – described in Chapter 16 – and several further alterations and developments made in the nineteenth century after it ceased to be a seminary. Fortunately, restoration work carried out in 1992-4 has revealed a great deal about the original structure and allowed the restorers to draw firm conclusions as to its appearance and use.[28] The present description and illustration (Fig.2) are based on their findings.

The building comprised a ground floor of normal height, and upstairs rooms with walls about one metre high and lit by windows set at floor level. The front door let onto a short transverse corridor giving access to the two main ground floor rooms, the living room and the study/dining room, and to several smaller rooms between. The steep stairs led to a corridor on the upper floor, giving access to the boys' dormitory at the south end of the house, the chapel at the north end, and the master's study and bed alcove between. None of the rooms in the house had ceilings and in the dormitory, chapel and study/bedroom the thatched roof was visible through the rafters. The roof itself was apparently supported by a double ridge pole (Plates 9 and 10). The overall exterior dimensions of the house were approx. 54' x 18'.

The chapel was intended for use by the Catholics of the neighbourhood as well as the College community, and for this reason an exterior door and separate outside straircase were built, in line with the seminary's policy of segregating the students and keeping visitors within the house to a minimum (Plate 9).

There was no obvious provision for a kitchen in the original plan, and none of the rooms would have been suitable for the purpose. The restorers have suggested that the kitchen built adjacent to the old house on the west side of the burn continued to be used until about 1773, when a new kitchen was built on the north wing of the new site.[29] This is certainly a possibility, albeit a most inconvenient one especially in winter.

The new building stood as striking evidence of the advances in architectural practice that had taken place in the half century since the seminary moved into its first home by the Crombie burn. It was in every way more impressive than the earlier houses of 1716, 1738 and 1749-52. Unlike them it was the work of specialist tradesmen – masons, wrights and heatherers – and was built to a specified plan. Its outer walls were of limestone, almost two feet thick, and its internal party walls of well finished wattle and daub. The workmanship and high quality of the joinery in its walls, flooring and roof have surprised modern experts.[30]

The advance from traditional towards more modern building techniques and styles that was taking place in Scotland at this time had already reached the lowlands of the North-East by this date, and was beginning to extend into the upland areas, though it had not yet got the length of the Braes.[31] At the beginning of the decade, for example, the Commissioners of the Forfeited Estates had approved a semi-standard design for new combined school-and-schoolhouses within their areas – two-storey stone structures, limed and with slated roofs.[32] And on several estates in Lower Banffshire new Mains farms were now being built on the rectangular model, with the two-storey farm house forming one side and single-storey 'offices' on the two adjacent sides enclosing the farm yard, some of which bear a resemblance to the new seminary even in matters of detail.[33]

The designers of the 1767 house would no doubt have had such trends and models in mind, because Scalan was to be school, residence and farm, though in a combination unique to itself. The Church authorities intended it to be comparable with the best of the times, within the limits of their pocket. They wanted a building that would meet all the foreseeable needs of the seminary, and also serve as a national facility and meeting centre for the Mission, conveniently situated as it was almost at the boundary of the Highland and Lowland Vicariates. Not least they wanted a building that would, without provocation, be a visible symbol of their hard-won gains to date and of their hopes for the recovery of the Catholic Church in Scotland.[34]

Bishop Smith was now in his eighty-fourth year and in failing health, and his Co-adjutor was already having to consider what changes would be necessary if he should die. The Mission's finances were in urgent need of re-organisation and the task seemed beyond the present Procurator. Bishop Grant had already earmarked Mr George Hay for the post when word came of Bishop Smith's death on 21 August. He at once took Mr Hay from his station at Preshome in the Enzie and brought him to Edinburgh. Preshome was still one of the Mission's foremost stations and it was important that an able priest be sent to serve there. His choice for the vacancy was John Geddes. He judged that Scalan was now on a firm footing again, with standards restored, the lease secured and the new house rising, and that Mr Geddes' work there was done.

To take his place at the seminary he arranged to bring Mr John Thomson home from Douai, where he had been Prefect of Studies for the past few months following his ordination earlier that year. Mr Thomson arrived at Scalan on 7 December. The exterior of the new building was now virtually complete, and though only part of the interior was habitable the 'little family' had already moved in. Mr Geddes stayed with them for a further week to hand over the reins, and then set out for the Enzie.[34]

Bishop Grant was correct in his assessment of Scalan's recovery. Under John Geddes it had been built anew, in every aspect. In his five years as master he had brought to the task energy and determination, idealism, wise judgment, charity, courtesy and grace – those same qualities that would distinguish his work as a bishop in later years, and for which he would always be remembered.

Time would show, in fact, that his term of office had been a watershed for the seminary. Before it, Scalan's existence had so often been tenuous, makeshift and hand-to-mouth, with each new promise of progress almost always frustrated, whether by the hostility of its enemies or its own shortcomings. After it, despite occasional lapses of management, the College would enjoy a new stability and solidity, built on the firm foundations he had laid; and increasingly, as the memory of Culloden waned and society's attitude softened, a degree of security and even comfort (we could still hardly call it prosperity) hitherto unknown.

NOTES

1. Details of Rome courses and teachers in Bishop Geddes 'Dates of Some Things to be Remembered', entries for 1750-59, B JG 1/1, SCA. See also Goldie M. 'Common Sense Philosophy and Catholic Theology in the Scottish Enlightenment', *Studies on Voltaire and the Eighteenth Century*, no. 302, 1992.
2. John Geddes to Bishop Smith, 27. 11. 1762, BL.
3. 'Plan of Glen Livit Exhibiting the different Farms Contained in each Daugh', 1761, RHP 1774, SRO; and 'A Short Description of Glen Livet', 1761, RHP 2487, SRO; re Clash, 'Contents and Estimates, Lands of Glenlivat', 1772-3, CR 8/185, SRO.
4. RHP 2487, SRO.
5. John Geddes to Bishop Smith, 8. 3. 1763, BL.
6. John Geddes to Bishop Smith, 28. 2. 1763, BL.
7. Pressure from parents of the gentry or lesser gentry, and the fear of offending them, was always likely to be a problem for a Church that depended so much on them for support and protection. Cf. also Appendix III.
8. John Geddes to Bishop Smith, 28. 2. 1763, BL.
9. John Geddes to Bishop Smith, 12. 11. 1763, BL.
10. John Geddes to Bishop Smith, 15. 3. 1764, BL.
11. Re Würzburg, see Dilworth M. 'Scottish Benedictines at Würzburg', *IR*, vol. xv, no. 2, autumn 1964; and the detailed account of the monastery's foundation and early years in Dilworth M. *The Scots in Franconia* (Edinburgh and London, 1974). John Paterson's home, Coffurich, was in the Enzie in Lower Banffshire.
12. Bishop Geddes 'A Brief Historical Account of the Seminary at Scalan',

1777, CH 1/3, para 32, SCA. The original grant from Clement XII had been increased by Cardinal Spinelli c. 1760, and specified as being for the Scottish seminaries. It brought in £24 p.a., of which £12 went to Scalan. Re Cardinal Albani's requirements – John Geddes to Bishop Smith, 15. 3. 1764, BL.

13. George Hay to Bishop Smith, 12. 4. 1765, BL. Accounts for 1765.
14. John Geddes to Bishop Smith, 3. 3. 1765, BL.
15. John Geddes to Bishop Smith, 14. 5. 1765 and 14. 1. 1766, BL.
16. John Geddes to Bishop Smith, 14. 5. 1765, BL.
17. George Hay to Bishop Smith, 12. 4. 1765, BL. Re his first illness when at Rome – Bishop Geddes 'Dates of Some Things to be Remembered', B JG 1/1, entries for 1758-9, SCA.
18. John Geddes to Bishop Smith, 14. 1. 1766, BL.
19. John Geddes to Bishop Smith, spring 1766 (in Italian), BL.
20. John Geddes to George Gordon, 24. 8. 1766, BL.
21. John Geddes to Bishop Smith, 3. 3. 1765, BL.
22. Rentals, Duke of Gordon Estates, 1770-86, CR 6/1 f. 27 (Glenlivat), SRO. The contracts of 1765 were for 19 years, those of 1766 for 18, and those of 1767 for 17, in order that all would cease in the same year, 1784.
23. Rothmais took a share of the vacated tack of Tombreckachie in Lower Glenlivet – Tack, John Grant of Rothmaise and John Stuart on Tombreckachie, 1767, GD 44/23/3/74, SRO.
24. Tack, James Mcalea on Scalan and Tomnalienan, 1767, GD 44/23/3/77, SRO. The rental was £41/10/4, plus services.
25. 'Contents and Estimates', incl. Lands of Glenlivat, 1772-3, CR 8/185; and 'Descriptions of Tacks', 1774, CR 8/189, SRO.
26. Thomas Milne Map of Glenlivet, 1774, RHP 1776, SRO.
27. See pp. 146, 160, 179 and 182f.
28. Dean A. and Taitt M. 'Scalan Reconstructed: Architectural and Documentary Evidence', *IR*, vol. xlvi, no. 1, spring 1995, pp. 34-51. Reconstruction conducted by Taitt Building Ltd.
29. *Ibid.*
30. *Ibid.*
31. Walker B. *Farm Buildings in the Grampian Region* (Grampian Regional Council, 1979), pp. 61f. New styles and techniques were first adopted in the Mearns and the Laigh of Moray, and gradually worked their way inland from these coastal areas in a NW and SE direction respectively.
32. Cf., Report by Factor on Estate of Monaltry, 1761, with scale plans of proposed school, and estimate of costs (total cost £134/12/10): 'Schemes for Improvement', Forfeited Estate Papers, E 773/58/1-3, SRO. The upper storey comprised the sleeping quarters of the master's family.
33. Eg., Letterfourie Home Farm, Rathven, in Walker B. *Op. cit.*, pp. 23 (fig. 11) and 27f., and Fenton A. and Walker B. *The Rural Architecture of Scotland* (Edinburgh, 1981), p. 186: the wing appears to have floor-level windows upstairs strikingly similar to Scalan's 1767 building.
34. The house on the west side of the burn was probably not abandoned entirely, but used for a few more years along with the other outhouses for steading cattle and storing hay, grain, etc. No trace of the house itself remains, but

several thatched buildings – originally either outhouses of the seminary or part of the Scalan farm-town – were still in use in the 19C (see Plate 2), and the ruin of one of these is still standing. An archaeological survey might reveal further valuable information concerning the site.

35. House founded 19 June, inhabited from c. 30 Nov. J. Geddes departed 15 Dec.- Bishop Geddes 'Dates of Some Things', entry for 1767, B JG 1/1, SCA.

13

'Mr Paterson Indeed
Exceeds Expectation' (1767–1774)

In his last few months at Scalan Mr Geddes had started giving Catechism
lessons to a young boy from the neighbourhood, Paul McPherson. The
lad had been born at the Clash, half-a-mile south of the College, in 1756,
shortly after his father took on the new tack there. He had lost his mother
at the age of six, and had received only the most basic schooling, first at
the little Catholic school at Clashnoir, and then at a school run by an old
woman, who it is said taught Reading but not Writing since she could not
write herself. But Mr Geddes had found him intelligent and willing to
learn, and it was not long before he was teaching him the 3 Rs along with
his Catechism.

Paul had always expressed an interest in the priesthood, and when his
father realised how set he was against an apprenticeship or any trade he
had asked Mr Geddes to consider him for Scalan. At the time, of course,
they were still occupying the cramped house on the west side of the burn,
and it was impossible to take more students. But Mr Geddes had
promised to bear him in mind, and when he himself left Scalan he
particularly asked Mr Thomson to find a place for him in the new house
as soon as possible.[1]

His opportunity came the following spring (1768) when one of the
senior students, John Farquharson of Glen Conglas, left for the Scots
College Rome, and he was admitted in June. Many the day that summer
he must have woken in his dormitory bed, only to remember where he
was, and gazed out of the window in the gable end, trying to catch a
glimpse of his father moving about the farm. He was still only twelve.
But he was to have a great influence upon the Catholic Church in
Scotland, and even in Rome itself, in the course of his long and eventful
life; and after his death he would come to be revered as the most famous
ever son of the Braes.

Mr Geddes tried to retain an interest in Scalan from his station in the
Enzie, and to support his successor, who he felt had made a promising
start:

Mr Thomson is really, as I think, an excellent young man, [he wrote to Mr James Grant] but one may discover in him some of the effects of youth: yet it is surprising to see him do as well as he does.[2]

He believed, nonetheless, that Scalan could never be anything more than a junior seminary for the Scots Colleges under its present leader: to become an all-through seminary as originally envisaged would require a master of greater experience and standing; indeed, he believed it would require a permanent staff of two; but this was obviously beyond the means of the Mission at present. Meantime he suggested that a small committee of senior clergy be appointed, to take decisions "as to the Admission & Expulsion of the Boys, and every thing else relating to the Studies, Diet, Cloathes, and spiritual Duties", in view of the master's inexperience.

The "effects of youth" that he had discovered in Mr Thomson were a certain impetuosity, and a rashness in spending Mission funds. The new master had been trained entirely at the Scots College in Rome, and then had taught briefly at Douai, so that his only experience of seminaries had naturally led him to associate them with comfort and elegance. He had been shocked by the half-finished interior of Scalan, had already made improvements at considerable cost, and was anxious to make more. Mr Geddes asked Mr Grant, the Administrator for the North-East, to instruct Mr Thomson to hire no more tradesmen until he could visit Scalan and judge the needs for himself, and then sanction only what was absolutely necessary to be done.

Mr George Hay, whose place Mr Geddes had taken at Preshome, was now in his fortieth year. He had been born and raised a Protestant in Edinburgh, attended lectures in Medicine at the university there, and been apprenticed to a surgeon. While still a medical student he had joined the Young Pretender's army, after tending the wounded at the battle of Prestonpans, and only ill health had frustrated his hopes of following the Prince into England. He had been arrested and detained for a year after Culloden because of his support for the Jacobite cause. In 1748 he had been received into the Catholic Church, fully aware that his conversion would debar him from gaining a medical qualification at Edinburgh, and the passport to worldly success that this would have given him.[3]

Three years after his conversion he had entered the Scots College Rome, where he was ordained seven years later. Though he had come quite late to the priesthood it was clear that his strength of mind and character, and his formidable energy, would take him far. Now in the autumn of 1768, just nine years after his ordination, Bishop Grant nominated him to be his Co-adjutor, and before the end of the year the briefs for his consecration arrived back from Rome.

It was decided to postpone the ceremony until the following May, to be sure of good weather for travelling and to avoid the Church's busy Easter season. Mr Hay's present and previous stations, Edinburgh and Preshome, were both rejected as venues, being too much in the public eye, and the choice fell to Scalan. It was the first of only two episcopal consecrations ever held at the College.[4]

The ceremony brought together Bishop Grant, Bishop Hugh MacDonald of the Highland District, and his assistant Bishop John MacDonald, and we might well imagine their different thoughts that day. Bishop Grant's mind perhaps raced back nearly half a century to his own student days at Scalan, in the first turf house across the burn, under George Innes and then briefly under his own brother John Alexander. Bishop Hugh too was doubtless remembering his own ordination at Scalan, when he had knelt beside his classmate George Gordon, the first two 'heather priests' since the Reformation.[5]

Surely also he and Bishop John must have looked about with admiration at this fine new-built seminary of the Lowland Vicariate, and compared it with their own situation. They had a small, temporary house at Glenfinnan, opened only the previous year, but for twenty years before that they had been without any seminary at all. Bishop Hugh had been forced to send boys at his own expense into the Lowland District, where they had received their secular education at the public school at Fochabers, and their divinity from Mr John Godsman the priest at Auchenhalrig, and from where a few had graduated directly to the Scots Colleges abroad.[6]

Mr Hay had come up to Scalan for his consecration in the company of Robert Menzies of Aberfeldy, who had been studying with him in Edinburgh and was now to be admitted as a trialist at the seminary. And before he returned to the capital he made arrangements for John Paterson to come back to live with him at his home in Blackfriars Wynd, so that he could give him personal supervision during his final year's training before ordination. The young man may well have headed South at the same time that Paul McPherson left Scalan for the Scots College Rome.[7]

Robert Menzies' stay at Scalan was brief and far from happy. Mr Thomson seems to have neglected him and singled him out for criticism, and he, far from home and alone, completely lost his confidence. He became ill, and the Braes seemed like a prison to him. One day in early spring he suddenly walked out of the house and set out on foot for Edinburgh.

Only desperation could have made him think of such a journey. His path lay across some of the most desolate high country in Scotland, and he with no map or concept of the lie of the land, but only his wits and his prayers to see him through. He must have been on the road for over a week, and we can only guess at his loneliness by day, and at nights his terror of dangers real and imagined. At last he came to sights he recognised – the castle, and the town perched smoking on its ridge, and he made his way through familiar streets until he turned the last corner into Blackfriars Wynd. There he landed exhausted at the door of Bishop Hay, who took him in. And only then, perhaps, did the tears come that until now he had not dared to shed.

He told the bishop that Mr Thomson had dismissed him, but this is hardly to be believed: he had run away in a panic, certain that the master did not want him, and scarcely knowing fact from fantasy. Whatever the exact truth Mr Thomson could take no credit from the affair. Bishop Hay believed that Robert had "not had the least assistance" at Scalan, and that if he was given the fair trial he deserved he would probably make more progress in a month in Edinburgh "than he could have done in severals where he was".[8] Under his care the boy took up his books again with relish, and soon recovered his health.

The bishop had now almost completed John Paterson's training.[9] He was satisfied with his progress, and impressed by his "exceeding good dispositions of heart",[10] and both he and Bishop Grant were anxious to arrange his ordination as soon as possible. It had become clear that Scalan needed a change of master. Not only had Mr Thomson's treatment of Robert Menzies cast doubt on his fitness to look after boys; the bills that he had run up for building work at the seminary filled them with alarm. He had continued to spend on the exterior and interior, seemingly deaf to the instructions given him two years before, and they were of the view that he had now "gone too far".[11] They decided to ordain Mr Paterson on the week after Ember Saturday, then send him to Scalan immediately.[12]

John Paterson arrived at Scalan early in April, and his coming freed Mr Thomson to cover the Strathavon station, though he continued to live in at the College for the rest of the year.[13] Bishop Hay extended his visit for the Administrators' meeting that summer in order to make a thorough assessment of the situation at the seminary. Only then did he discover the extent of Mr Thomson's spending. The former master had "made a very commodious place of Scalan," he wrote to John Geddes, "& decorated it (perhaps too) much <u>without</u>,"

but I am sorry to tell you that by running such lengths, without advice or allowance, he has run me upwards of £30 in arrears, of the Scalan money . . . I believe poor M[r] Thomson was carried away with the delusion that many others are in, to imagine the Scalan funds are inexhaustible.[14]

Already that spring the Principal of the Scots College Paris was threatening to withhold the monies normally sent to the Mission, including the Scalan master's rent which Paris traditionally paid. Now with Mr Thomson's extravagance the position seemed so bad that Bishop Hay could "see no possible means to prevent shutting up doors for a time",[15] unless funds could be found from somewhere.

He wrote to Abbé Peter Grant, the Scots Agent, asking him to explore possible sources of assistance in Rome.[16] But he also believed that money could be found at Scalan itself. Savings could be made by more careful purchases and management of the accounts. The seminary already generated some income by sub-letting its surplus land to local farmers, but the rental for this could be increased. And the College should make a more rigorous distinction between its religious students and its lay boarders, and insist on full payment of fees from the latter.

He felt particularly strongly on the last point, and at Bishop Grant's request produced proposals for new *Regulations* covering the issue.[17] These argued that the chief reason for Scalan's failure to fulfil its purpose in recent years had been its readiness to accept unsuitable boys who had no intention of studying for the priesthood. Bowing to parental pressure to admit them had been highly damaging to the seminary, frustrating its main purpose, harming discipline, and consuming its income. To remedy this the *Regulations* should clearly distinguish three categories of student – Boarders, that is, lay students not intending studies for the priesthood; Members, boys definitely accepted for such studies; and Trialists – and apply different conditions for each. Boarders and Trialists should be charged an annual fee of £6, but Members would receive their education, board and lodging free. All should be required to supply their own clothing, footwear and blankets. And none should be admitted without an appropriate "attestation" from his local priest.

The purpose of these proposals was threefold – to vet applicants more rigorously, to limit the number of lay students, and to prevent parents gaining free education for their sons under false pretences. They were an attempt to clarify and tighten the rules, rather than actually change them, and as such were readily accepted by Bishop Grant and made the official *Regulations* of the College.

Bishop Hay also drew up several Guidelines in an attempt to draw in the reins at Scalan after the excesses and neglect of the Thomson régime, and to support Mr Paterson who had been thrown into his post without any priestly or pastoral experience whatever. The first, *A Plan for Some Points Relating to the Master*,[18] offered practical advice on the management of the house and its discipline. The second, *Accounts of Entry and Departure of Boys,* may well have been prompted partly by the experience of Robert Menzies. It required the master to keep a written record of every student, including date of entry and departure, destination, and (where applicable) reason for dismissal. The third, *A Plan of Rules for Keeping the Accompts,* was certainly inspired by Mr Thomson's prodigality. It was drawn up with Bishop Hay's customary meticulous attention to detail and included a ledger covering every conceivable item of income and expense.

Mr Paterson kept his financial record scrupulously to the last farthing, and at his first opportunity bought a handsome note book in Aberdeen to serve as an Account Book.[19] He was anxious not only to be exact, but to do all he could to economise, in order to keep Scalan open and at the same time to help and please Bishop Hay.

The bishop was universally respected, but not everywhere liked by his priests, for he had a reputation for severity and inflexibility. But to John Paterson he was his mentor, and he remembered with deep gratitude all that he had learned from him while in Edinburgh, "sitting within the Rails upon Sundays", without which he believed he could never have coped with the problems at Scalan. His letters to him at this date, in which he always addressed him as "Much honour'd Sir, & very Dear Father" and signed himself "your most obedient Child", touchingly reveal the affection and awe that he felt for him.

The bishop had requested that he send him an exact breakdown of Mr Thomson's debts, but this he was unable to do because Mr Thomson himself remained evasive on the matter, and whenever he travelled in the neighbourhood he learned of new ones unpaid.[20]

But he missed no opportunity of finding ways to make economies. Instead of buying yarn he bought wool and had it spun at Scalan. He made arrangements to take the horses and two 'quoys' [heifers] down to the Enzie for the winter, because fodder was only half the price there that it was in the Braes. He calculated precisely the house's needs for meal, based on a frugal diet of one peck per person per week (though he knew that two pecks was considered the normal consumption for adults). And where Mr Thomson had paid £9/10/-Scots per boll he managed to clinch a five-year deal for 40 bolls per annum at £7/10/- per boll, delivered to the door, by inviting the seller to supper and broaching the subject late in the evening when his guest was in good spirits.[21] He even contrived to make a saving on the decoration of the upstairs chapel, which had been begun before his arrival: the work was still not completed at the end of October,

but he laid off the wrights meantime, in order to save on candles in the
dark days of winter![22]

But to get bargains he needed cash in hand. He particularly needed
money at Martinmas, when the servants were to be paid and winter
provisions bought. Bulk items could always be purchased more cheaply in
Lower Banffshire, but no-one would carry them up to the Braes once the
winter set in. And he was not prepared to run up further debts: not only
did his honest and scrupulous nature abhor debt, but in the present
circumstances buying on credit was not to be thought of. In normal times
a very relaxed attitude to debt prevailed in the Braes, as throughout the
Highlands, but three bad winters had dissolved goodwill and made
everyone look after himself. He knew that when the time for payments
came at Martinmas, "one would be eating the other" , such was the "cry
for want". That first autumn, in fact, his neighbours many times tried to
borrow from him, hoping to appeal to his charity as a churchman, or his
inexperience as a young incomer. But he had nothing of his own, and
staunchly held on to the seminary money since it was not his to give.[23]

So insistently did he request money from Edinburgh that autumn that
Bishop Hay quite firmly reproved him for his impatience. He wrote back
with almost pathetic humility, admitting his "too great floughtiness" and
his lack of faith in God, accepting the reprimand as deserved, and asking
the bishop to correct him whenever he needed it in future.

> I shall endeavour to do better [he promised] but this also I must beg of
> you, when you write me something Severe, that you would soon after
> send me a Letter full of comfort, for I have need of that from time to
> time at any rate.[24]

And he assured him of his complete discretion in dealing with the finances
of the College: "My father tho' he were alive should not know what
money I have in my hands", he told him.

He believed in fact that Scalan's masters should be far more restricted as
to their spending power, and urged that Bishop Hay make this a firm rule:

> There is one thing I would wish to say, if it were not presumption in me
> to give advice. It is this, when this place is once in order (which I hope it
> will be pretty well against a few weeks hence) . . . I would have you
> make a Law at this place, that no more reformations should be made,
> until your consent were first ask'd, for if the Superiour here be allowed
> always to Cut & Carve as he thinks proper, money may be spent
> here . . . this is a law I know against my self at present, however it is a
> good one, as I know by experience.[25]

The bishop sent him enough money before Christmas to pay off his
outstanding debts. But old unknown debts were still appearing. Between

his poverty and his burden of work – for he had also been covering Glenbuchat that autumn – he begged to be sent no more students at least until the spring.[26]

The students he had inherited were a very mixed group. One he had high hopes for was young Tom Robertson from Edinburgh, for the little boy was always diligent at his studies, and "almost out of himself for joy" at the thought of soon being sent abroad. But that October Bishop Hay hired the boy's father to carry letters to Scalan, and during his overnight stay there he took his son aside and persuaded him to return to Edinburgh with him. The two of them devised a plan for Tom to abscond without the master's knowledge. When the father set out for home after breakfast the next morning Tom accompanied him "about two Ridge lengths" of the way, then returned and went to Mass as usual. Not until the afternoon did he slip away, unknown to anyone except his classmate Charles Geddes, who was in on the secret and went with him to where his father was waiting in the hills. As soon as Mr Paterson realised he was gone he sent John Cummin the servant lad after him, fearing for his safety, but there was no way of knowing which road he had taken.[27]

His departure left just three students at the seminary at the end of the year. Bishop Grant was pressing for four more to be admitted, but he gave no directions as to the terms on which they were to be accepted. Mr Paterson was sure that the boys' families would not be willing to pay the full fee for trialists as laid down in the new *Regulations*. He asked again for a moratorium on admissions, and particularly that no boys should be sent except those who had "even almost an absolute certainty" of completing their studies for the priesthood.[28]

Tom Robertson had given him every reason to be cautious of admitting boys, but he was not the only one. George Rankin had been flouting the spirit of the *Regulations* since his arrival the previous October. He was constantly telling the other boys how much he hated Scalan, and infecting them with his talk. Since he was showing no sign of making a decision as to his future Bishop Grant instructed that he should be asked to take an oath of commitment. But he countered with excuses – that he was still too young, that it would be a sin to take an oath and then break it, etc. He prevaricated through the winter, until finally the bishop lost patience and ordered him to be dismissed. Mr Paterson sent him home, taking care to have him accompanied by a senior student, and with a new pair of shoes and 5/- in his pocket, "on Purpose to stop the clamour of his mother".[29] He was glad to see the back of him, and would have preferred if his friend Charles Geddes had gone also. "Much has this house suffer'd this while past with keeping here very useless Creatures", he told Bishop Hay.[30]

* * *

He was far more happy with the servants. Janet Rae, whom he had taken on as housekeeper at Martinmas to replace the troublesome Annie Greenlaw, he pronounced "just to his liking". Young John Cummin the general servant lad also seemed promising. He was doing his best to please, anxious not to put his new job at risk, and worked well on praise and the occasional dram.[31] He was a skilled cobbler, and was making all the students' shoes. He was also helping to prepare a new kail yard on a barren piece of their existing land, allowing part of the old kail yard to be turned over to clover, and putting "a great deal more at the backside of the Kitchen" under the plough.[32]

Only the older servant, David Drummond, was unsatisfactory. He spent too much on snuff and whisky, had a malicious tongue, and was for ever complaining. He was a surly, quarrelsome man and seemed impervious to threats and warnings – "I can assure you I heat David's breast", Mr Paterson told the bishop, "but what does that signify, Within a little he will be just his old man again". He was giving the whole house a bad name, and so long as he stayed no housekeeper was likely to remain long.[33]

The winter of 1770-71 proved even worse than the three previous. From November one snowstorm followed another, until the houses and peat-stacks were barely visible. A woman perished in the snow quite close to the College, and Mr Paterson himself came very near to death when he strayed from his path and found himself in a peat bog. One farmer lost his entire twelve head of cattle. Many were still trying to cut their corn in February, at a time when they should have been sowing next year's, and even in April it was still almost impossible to get from farm to farm.

When Mr Paterson took on the wrights again after Easter to complete their work on the chapel, he learned that they had been working full-time since he laid them off, making coffins, such had been the mortality in the area. They finished their work at Scalan by the first week in May, by which date the weather had at last improved. The ploughing had begun every-where, but there was neither grain nor fodder nor grass to feed the oxen, and they were so weak that they could barely rise off their knees to draw the plough.[34]

When the bishops arrived for their Administrators' meeting in July they examined the College and assessed the progress of the students as usual. They were particularly interested to test Charles Geddes, whom Mr Paterson had described to Bishop Hay as "a Boy of no Genious" and "a triffling, lying sort of a pitiful creature", not fit to be a priest.[35] Their examination must have concurred with his report, because they decided that he should not continue with his studies. He left in August. (In later years he confounded their opinion, entering the Benedictine monastery at Würzburg, where he gained fame as a gifted scientist and was eventually elected prior.)[36]

Mr Paterson was now, in fact, erring on the side of caution in regard to students, determined to ensure that new applicants would only be accepted on the full agreed terms.[37] But this was not easy to enforce. When he admitted Donald Stuart in October he had great difficulty in getting the family to part with his fee. In the end he had to be content with £1 in hand, a bill of promise for £2 from the boy's uncle, and his "good word" to try to find another £1 later. Nor was this unique. He was unable to implement the *Regulations* to the letter at this date, not least because of Bishop Grant's failure to put the full weight of his authority behind them.[38]

By the autumn John Cummin had slipped far from his early promise, and turned out quite unsuitable to be about the seminary. He had shown himself to be a liar and a most unwilling messenger. He had taken to drinking heavily, and once when accompanying Mr Paterson to a funeral he took so much that he fell and ruined the master's greatcoat. He was insolent, and acted as if he was the master of the house, often inviting his friends in and feeding them at the seminary's expense. He was useful for making the shoes, certainly, but Mr Paterson did not think this benefit worth the friction he caused.[39]

He decided to end the young man's employment at Martinmas, hoping that his departure would also "chasten" David Drummond,[40] and arranged to take on an other local man, John Ross, to replace him. Ross was a much older man – he had been 'out' in the '45–and he had little appearance. "To look at him you would think it were Charity to give him a piece of Bread, Cloaths, or Shoes, and a Sin to seek any thing from him", Mr Paterson wrote, yet it was partly with an eye to 'seeking' that he took him on, for the man was in fact wealthy, single, and intending that his savings would go to a worthy cause at his death.[41]

But he was not so easily rid of John Cummin as he had hoped. The young man continued to hang about the farm, baiting his replacement whom he referred to as "old stinking Rossy". Annie Greenlaw was also trying to worm her way back into favour, under the pretext of wanting Mr Paterson to be her confessor. "You see how cunning the Creature is", he told his fellow-priest Mr Reid, but he knew better than to allow her back: Janet Rae was coping admirably, and under her care there was peace about the house, and his boys were once again "all <u>clean</u> [he underlined the word], tight, happy and content".[42]

They were all making good progress now too. With the departure of unsuitable boys and his careful vetting of new applicants, he felt that the

young crop he now had were the right kind of students at last. Bishop Hay
sent him cloth for uniforms, and he promised to have the boys "Genteel
and handsome with it" in time for the Administrators' visit in the
summer.[43] He chose 'Highland' uniforms – blue tartan waistcoats and
kilts (or alternatively breeches and hose) and blue coats. The bishop was
anxious to give his protegé whatever encouragement he could, and at the
same time to raise the ethos of the College. The religious schools and
seminaries of Europe, including the Scots Colleges at Rome and Paris, had
uniforms,[44] and a Scalan uniform would be among other things an
assertion of its right to be compared with the best.

To the same end Bishop Hay also gifted textbooks and other works to
extend the College library, which, following the legacy of Bishop Gordon,
had been progressively enlarged over the years. In his letter of thanks Mr
Paterson told him that the boys were "overjoyed" with them and had
taken "new life and Courage" from using them.He went on to describe in
some detail the lessons he was giving them, with all the quiet excitement
of a good teacher who sees his students progressing under his care. His
description is worth quoting at length, as it offers us a glimpse of the
Scalan of the '70s, and of the methodology and psychology of an
eighteenth century classroom:

> I have six of them now in one Class, making the Grammatical, and
> explaining the Cordery, and this is the way I go on with them. I
> myself first explain a short Lesson of the Cordery to them, then they
> learn to explain it, and to know every word, its derivation, and
> meaning, and when they come up and say this lesson, I ask every
> word at them, when this is done I make them get this short lesson by
> heart, and afterwards say it to me, the one beggining Salve Præceptor.
> the other answering Salvus Sis. &c and so on until they come to the
> end. I have these six into three pairs, the best and worst Scholar
> always together, so that the best can help the worst, every two by this
> means try to gain victories over their neighbours. You must write to
> me that you will give my Boys some reward, provided they do well,
> and answer you right next Summer – this I shall tell them, which will
> encourage them, & which they have need of, being all so very
> young.[45]

Young they were, and still relative beginners. It tells us much of the
education of the time that their Latin was well ahead of their English. One
or two had been close to three years at Scalan, yet could spell little more
than their names in their own language. The master was seeking to
remedy this, for which he needed an English Spell Book since there was
not one in the house.[46]

*   *   *

From the beginning he had never spared himself in his efforts to run the seminary as the bishops wished, and his work seemed endless: "From the moment that I rise, until night that I go to bed", he wrote from the heart that autumn, "there is no rest, but hearing Lessons, giving out ones, &c., &c.",[47] and most of his letters at this time conclude by his expressing himself too tired to write more.

The prospect of another horrific winter could only have added to his burden. In November he told a friend of his visit to a dying man, and how he believed that for many others in the Braes it would be better "that they were going the same road." People had already begun to forge bills in their desperation, and would soon be turning to stealing.[48]

At Martinmas many families sold their possessions and gave up house and land, because they had no means to pay their rent. Three families were to be seen begging "almost within a cry" of the seminary, while their creditors carried off all they owned. Mr Paterson appealed to Bishop Hay and the priest at Preshome for alms for the poor, and received a donation from both of them.[49]

The new year, 1772, started as the old left off. The first six weeks were one continuous storm, the greatest in memory. The snow lay as deep as ever and the priest of Glenlivet, Fr Bragan, very nearly perished in it on his return home from a sick call. He lost his path and succumbed to cold and exhaustion, and was only found by pure chance, lying in an old lime kiln, "preparing for death with his face amongst the snow". With the water-mills frozen solid men had turned to their querns to grind whatever little grain they could scrape together, and – incredible as it sounds – to give themselves and their families some heat by the friction and exercise. Not even the well-to-do were immune – "Even our Gentlemen, and Gentle-women are heating themselves with the hand of the Coorn or highland Mill", the master told a fellow priest. He believed that the people of this class would probably survive, but what would become of "the generality" was more than he could say.[50]

Bishop Hugh MacDonald, Scalan's first 'heather priest', was now in his seventies. He had been a bishop for more than forty years, for much of that time trying to administer his Vicariate while forced to live beyond its boundaries. His constitution had never been strong, even in his student days at the seminary. By the new year of 1773, as yet another ill winter brought distress to the Highlands, he had sunk so low that he could barely rise from his bed or bring himself to eat. In the March he died.

Bishop John MacDonald, who succeeded him, was immediately faced with a severe problem of manpower. Such was the shortage of priests that he could no longer afford to leave the master in the Highland seminary – sited since 1770 at Buorblach in North Morar – for he was one of the few young and able-bodied men still available to him. Having no priest to replace him there he would if necessary have accepted a lay master, but even this proved impossible. Much against his will and with great sadness, he was forced to close the seminary in May.[51]

The situation was little better in the Lowland District, and not likely to improve in the near future. The students at Scalan were young and none was due for ordination for some years, as Bishop Hay was painfully aware: "Before our young Recruits come to our assistance I fear we shall all be good for nothing with the increased Labour our straits lay upon us", he warned the Scots Agent that summer.[52]

But in the longer term Scalan remained the Mission's main hope. Mr Paterson had achieved a great deal there already. Over the past two years he had overseen major extensions to the property, building a new kitchen on the north wing of the yard (Plate 5), and a byre, barn and stable on the south wing.[53] He had cleared the debts and the problems that he had inherited, and put the house on an even keel. It seemed that the College could now even offer a partial solution to the loss of Buorblach, by taking some of its former students, an arrangement that Bishop MacDonald wished and Mr Paterson happily agreed to.[54]

The first Highland boy, Donald MacDonald, arrived in September, to be followed by Angus and Archie MacDonald shortly before Christmas. There were now twelve students in all, some of them beginners, and none advanced beyond the middle stages of Grammar. Mr Paterson was happy with them, and with his servants.[55] Bishop Hay for his part was delighted with the young master. "Mr Paterson indeed exceeds expectation", he told John Geddes,

> his attention & application to his present business gives great satisfaction, especially considering that he has no less than twelve boys in different classes, and to manage himself alone every thing about them both for soul & body, temporals & spirituals, and yet does all in such a manner that no fault can be found & does it with the greatest chearfullness and alacrity.[56]

He advised that most of the boys were still too young and untried to be considered for the Scots Colleges, and recommended that they should stay a year or two more with Mr Paterson, where they were doing so well.

As the new year of 1774 opened the Braes were again one uniform white, and moving even from farm to farm was next to impossible. The people had taken refuge in their last solace, Mr Paterson wrote, "only drinking down sorrow, and with the Husky Bottle banishing away the melancholy thoughts of hard times". He could not tell how the poor had survived the last two summers.[57] Thankfully the last harvest had been good, producing enough grain for a good sowing, and the prospects for 1774 seemed better at last.

But for many in the Braes, it had come too late. Over the past two summers, unable to eat or pay the rent, they had sold up and left.[58] Most had made for the Lowland towns, where they joined the hundreds of others from every part of the Highlands. Bishop Hay watched them tramping the streets of Edinburgh in the depth of the winter of 1774, seeking help and relief, but disappointed in their hopes through the sheer size of the problem they presented.[59] Many stayed on nonetheless, picking up whatever casual work they could find. (Two years later the bishop reckoned that some 400 Highland Catholics now lived in the capital alone, so many that he opened a Gaelic chapel for them, placing in charge of it Mr Robert Menzies, the boy whose vocation he had salvaged when he took him in from Scalan seven years before.[60])

In July 1774 the two most senior Scalan students set out for the new Scots College at Valladolid, which had replaced the Madrid College after its closure in 1767. Their places were taken by Murdo Shaw from the Highland District, and Thomas Bagnall, the son of a Staffordshire potter whose family had moved to Glasgow, the first boy to be admitted to Scalan from that city. The following November Lewis MacDonald of Morar joined the seminary direct from the public school at Fochabers.[61]

There were now more students on the roll than the house could accommodate, and several of them had to be boarded out in the neighbourhood. Among these were two of the Highland boys, Donald MacDonald and young Murdo Shaw, who were lodged with Paul McPherson and his family in the Scalan farm town. Their costs were met by their own Vicariate, of course. Mr Paterson kept a separate account for all his Highland students, which he sent periodically to Bishop John MacDonald for payment.[62] There were never more than four on roll at any one time, nor could there be with the limited space available. However much Bishop MacDonald wished it, any full-scale admission of Highland students, amounting to a kind of amalgamation of seminaries, was simply not feasible at this date.

NOTES

1. Biography of Paul McPherson in *Catholic Directory*, 1849, and printed in Gordon J. F. S. *Journal and Appendix to Scotichronicon and Monasticon* (Glasgow, 1867), vol. 1, p. 596.
2. John Geddes to James Grant, 22. 2. 1768, BL. The rest of the paragraph is also based on this source.

3. Scottish medics were in demand in England, the armed forces, and in many parts of the world; cf., details of distinguished 18C alumni of the Edinburgh University Medical School in Hamilton D. *The Healers: A History of Medicine in Scotland* (Edinburgh, 1981), pp. 128f. George Hay had attended the lectures of the renowned Professor of Anatomy and Surgery Alexander Monro ('Primus').

4. The second being that of the Highland Bishop Alexander MacDonald in March 1780 – see p. 166.

5. 'Heather priest' – ie., one who received his entire training in Scotland.

6. Bishop Grant to Bishop Smith, 6. 11, 1762. Before Glenfinnan there had been no seminary in the Highland District since the destruction of Gaotal by Government forces in 1746.

7. *Catholic Directory*, 1849, *loc. cit.* Paul McPherson travelled via Aberdeen and Holland.

8. Bishop Hay to John Geddes, 12. 10. 1770, BL.

9. Bishop Hay guided his reading, provided him with sermon notes for the whole liturgical year, and had him make copies of his own writings on the duties of a priest – Bishop Hay to Bishop Grant, 3. 2. 1770. And see Mr Paterson's transcriptions of Bishop Hay's writings, 28. 11. 1769, B GH 1/2, SCA.

10. Bishop Hay to Bishop Grant, 3. 2. 1770, BL.

11. Bishop Hay to ?, 3. 3. 1770, BL.

12. Bishop Hay to Bishop Grant, 3. 2. 1770, BL.

13. John Paterson to Bishop Grant, 27. 4. 1770, and to Bishop Hay, 25. 12. 1770, BL.

14. Bishop Hay to John Geddes, 13-16. 8. 1770, BL.

15. Bishop Hay to James Grant, August 1770, BL. Re the threat to withhold monies by the Scots College Paris – John Gordon (Principal), Andrew Riddoch (Procurator) and Alexander Gordon (Prefect of Studies) to Bishop Grant, 30. 4. 1770, BL.

16. Bishop Hay to Abbé Peter Grant, 13-16. 8. 1770, BL.

17. 'Regulations for Scalan', 1770, CS 1/1/5(1), SCA. A draft "sketch" was also sent to James Grant in Aberdeen on 14. 12. 1770.

18. CS 1/1/13, SCA: all three documents are from this source.

19. 'Account Book of Scalan,1771-87', CS 1/6 (a), SCA. He bought it while in Aberdeen for the annual blessing of the oils – John Paterson to Bishop Hay, 22. 3. 1771, BL.

20. John Paterson to Bishop Hay, 15. 8. 1770, BL.

21. John Paterson to Bishop Hay, 19. 8. 1770 and 11. 9. 1770, BL.

22. John Paterson to Bishop Hay, 8. 11. 1770, BL.

23. John Paterson to Bishop Hay, 19. 8. 1770 and 14. 9. 1770, BL. Re the normally relaxed attitude to debt in the Highlands, see Grant I. F. *Every-Day Life on an Old Highland Farm 1769-1782* (London, 1924), espec. pp. 79 and 146.

24. John Paterson to Bishop Hay, 14. 9. 1770, BL.

25. Ibid.

26. John Paterson to Bishop Hay, 25. 12. 1770, BL.

27. The father's part in the incident was particularly underhand, ungrateful and

disloyal, for not only had Bishop Hay trusted him as his messenger, he had subsidised Tom's schooling before he came to Scalan and had often helped the parents in times of need – John Paterson to Bishop Hay, 16. 10. 1770, BL.

28. John Paterson to Bishop Hay, 25. 12. 1770 and 19. 2. 1771, BL.

29. John Paterson to Bishop Hay, 19. 2. 1771, 11. 3. 1771, and 15. 4. 1771, BL.

30. John Paterson to Bishop Hay, 22. 3. 1771, BL.

31. John Paterson to Bishop Hay, 25. 12. 1770, BL.

32. John Paterson to Bishop Hay, 11. 3. 1771, BL.

33. John Paterson to Bishop Hay, 15. 4. 1771, BL.

34. John Paterson to Bishop Hay, above letters, and 6. 5. 1771, BL. The cattle may have been further weakened by the practice common among Braes farmers – and recalled from his childhood by Abbé Paul McPherson – of bleeding them to provide sustenance for their families in times of want.

35. John Paterson to Bishop Hay, 15. 4. 1771, BL.

36. Dilworth M. 'Scottish Benedictines at Würzburg – A Supplement to the Necrology', *IR*, vol. xv, no. 2, autumn 1964, p. 181.

37. In the case of one boy he gave the mother so strong a lecture on the improbability of his passing the trial period, and the mortification to his family should he fail, that she was reduced to tears and took him home declaring that "she would not trouble them with her son" – John Patertson to Bishop Hay, 8. 7. 1771, BL.

38. John Paterson to Bishop Hay, 20. 10. 1771, BL. Re Bishop Grant's authority, cf., by implication, 'Regulations', 1779, CS 1/1/5 (i), Afterword, SCA.

39. Mr Paterson calculated that shoes made by a hired cobbler would cost "three Babies" ($1\frac{1}{2}$ d) a pair at most, and that at four pairs per student per year this would amount to 3/- in all, plus the man's meat.

40. John Paterson to Bishop Hay, 20. 10. 1771, BL. He gave him a parting present of 2/- – Account Book for Scalan, Household Expenses for 1771, CS 1/6 (a), SCA.

41. Ibid. Re John Ross 'out' in '45, cf. List in Tayler A. and Tayler H. *Jacobites of Aberdeenshire and Banffshire in the Forty Five* (Aberdeen, 1928), p. 441.

42. John Paterson to John Reid, 17. 11. 1771, BL.

43. John Paterson to Bishop Hay, 20. 11. 1771, BL.

44. Re Rome, see McRoberts D. 'Scots College Rome: Students' Dress', *IR*, vol. ii, no. 1, summer 1951. Re Paris, cf. 'Statuta Collegii Scotorum Parisiensis' (in Latin), CA 10/2, SCA, cap. vii 'Regulae Generales': the uniform comprised *toga* and *pilleum*.

45. John Paterson to Bishop Hay, 20. 11. 1771, BL. [Salve Præceptor – Greetings Master; Cordery – The *Colloquies* of Maturinus Corderius, probably the selection *Colloquorum Centuria Selecta*, with translation into English by Clarke, published in York in 1718].

46. John Paterson to Bishop Hay, n.d., but probably Dec. 1771, BL.

47. John Paterson to Bishop Hay, 20. 10. 1771, BL.

48. John Paterson to John Reid, 17. 11. 1771, BL. Re price rises of wheat, barley and oats (in Lowlands) in 1771, cf. Hamilton H. *An Economic History of Scotland in the Eighteenth Century* (Oxford, 1963), Appendix II.

49. John Paterson to John Reid, 17. 11. 1771, and to Bishop Hay, 20. 12. 1771, BL.

50. John Paterson to Charles Cruickshank, 18. 2. 1772, BL. Though water-mills had long been in use in Upper Banffshire, they had not replaced the querns – cf., Shaw J. P. *Waterpower in Scotland 1550–1870* (Edinburgh, 1983), p. 24. The seminary itself apparently had no quern, according to the list of items sold off at the public roup at its closure in 1799 (CS 1/8/2 and 1/8/5, SCA).

51. Bishop John MacDonald to Bishop Hay, 18. 3. 1773, 20. 4. 1773, and 4. 5. 1773, BL. The master was Mr Angus MacGillis. The bishop's team was further depleted that July by the death at Arisaig of Alexander Kennedy, the man whose two spells at Scalan had brought such disharmony to the College.

52. Bishop Hay to Abbé Peter Grant, 13. 8. 1773, BL.

53. Entries for expenses re kitchen, barn, in 'Account Book for Scalan, 1771-87', CS 1/6 (a), SCA, Household expenses for 1772-3.

54. Bishop Hay to John Geddes, 13. 8. 1773, BL.

55. John Paterson to John Geddes, 25. 1. 1774, BL.

56. Bishop Hay to John Geddes, 9. 3. 1774, BL.

57. Since their staple diet was of cereals, the summer – the last few months before the harvest – was of course the hungriest season of the year. For livestock, on the other hand, the worst-time was the end of winter, before the spring growth.

58. John Paterson to John Geddes, 25. 1. 1774, BL.

59. Bishop Hay to John Geddes, 28. 1. 1774, BL.

60. Bishop Hay to Alexander Gordon, 14. 5. 1777, BL.

61. Student Register, in 'Account Book for Scalan, 1771-87', CS 6/1(a), pp. 161-4, SCA.; this has also been printed in Anderson W.J. 'The College for the Lowland District at Scalan and Aquhorties: Registers and Documents', *IR*, vol. xiv, no. 2, autumn 1963, Appendix III, pp. 116ff.

62. Account of expenses owed by Bishop J. MacDonald, accumulated from 23. 12. 1773 and paid 9. 9. 1775, Account Book for Scalan, CS 1/6 (a), pp. 175f., SCA. Paul McPherson was the brother of John of Clash, and the uncle of the future Abbé Paul; he charged £4/10/- p. a. for each boy.

14

How They Lived in the mid-1770s

The *Account Book* kept by Mr Paterson,[1] recording as it does every item of income and expenditure during his term as master, provides us with a striking and detailed picture of the day-to-day economy of Scalan, and an insight into how the little community lived.

The financial year ran from Whitsun to Whitsun, and was divided into two halves at Martinmas (11 November). This division reflected the age-old rhythm of rural society, for Whitsun fell after the end of the spring sowing, and Martinmas after the gathering of the harvest and at the time of stocking up for winter. Both were therefore the season for clearing debts and placing new orders. They were also the dates upon which servants and hired hands were paid their half-yearly wages.

Every Whitsun the master balanced his account, and had it audited and approved by the bishop, and the scale of the Scalan economy may be gauged from this annual auditing. In the decade 1771-81 the mean annual income – mainly from boarders' fees, but also from produce of the farm – amounted to a little over £92, while the average expenditure totalled some £89. When he first took up office Mr Paterson had been instructed to make every economy and to keep his finances in the black, and this he did, building a cumulative profit of £32/10/6 over the decade.

The total rent for the tack of Tomnalienan-and-Scalan had been fixed in 1767 at £41/10/4 per annum, plus specified sevices including carriages by horse and foot, and labour at the sowing and harvest seasons.[2] From the *Account Book* we learn that the seminary's share of the total was £1/13/4 (exactly £20 Scots) in cash, plus "a part of a days work for bondage cutting down the Duke of Gordon's corn upon the town of Lettoch." Tenants in fact had the option of paying extra money in lieu of these services, and Mr Paterson took this up, paying 4d as equivalent of the part-day's labour.

From several contemporary records and memoirs that have come down to us,[3] it would seem that the larger Highland farms were virtually self-supporting at this time. And certainly something of the old tradition of self-sufficiency still held good among the farmers of Glenlivet. For this reason it has usually been assumed that Scalan too was self-sufficient and lived entirely off its own farm produce. But this was not in fact the case. It was a community of scholars, students and servants, who we might expect would be less able to support themselves than their neighbours,[4] and the evidence of the accounts confirms that this was so.

As regards foodstuffs, for instance, they bought most of their requirements in. Although they sowed corn, they found it necessary to purchase large amounts of meal for the needs of the house – 30 bolls annually from Gordon of Aberlour, plus other smaller local purchases as need arose. And though they kept their own beasts, including at least one milch cow, they bought in most of their requirements for dairy produce, placing regular orders for butter at 8/- the stone, and cheese at 4/-. Occasionally they were able to use one of their own beasts for a mart – so called because it was slaughtered at Martinmas, to provide meat for the winter – but most years they had to purchase one locally, at a cost of about £2. And though they kept a few hens about the yard, these were obviously not enough for their needs at the table, for the accounts show regular payments for cooking fowls and eggs.

Meat and dairy products were generally reserved for Sundays and major feastdays. Similarly, fish was only eaten during Lent, and sometimes on Fridays: thus in 1772 Mr Paterson paid 13/- for "fourteen Big fish for Lent coming", and two years later £1/12/- "to fish great and small", again to be saved for Lent. The staple diet of the house on normal days was prepared almost entirely from cereals or kail.[5] Cereals formed the main ingredient of broth, and the accounts show that they were bought from the miller prepared for this purpose ("to the stricking three firlots of Bear for broth" is a typical entry). In meal form they were boiled into porridge and also made into bannocks on the girdle, generally using a mixture of cereals even including pease.[6] As to kail, this was prepared either as a cooked vegetable or as a broth (the term 'kail' was used with both meanings). It was home-grown in the yard, both from seed and seedling. Not only did the seminary provide for all its own needs, but, from the amount being grown by the end of the decade – 1500 plants in 1779 – it may be that it was actually selling some of its produce in the neighbourhood.[7]

Vegetables were in fact the one foodstuff in which the Scalan community were entirely self-sufficient. They planted their own carrots, onions, turnips, cabbage and leeks from bought seed, and produced their own seed potatoes on a regular basis.

Janet Rae the housekeeper was responsible for the purchase of food. She bought her sugar in quite small quantities, measured by weight and costing 5d per lb. Salt on the other hand was sold by volume. Great Salt, which she used for curing, she bought in bulk – a half-boll at a time was not unusual; but her Small Salt for the kitchen and table she purchased in much smaller amounts, by the peck. On special occasions she liked to add variety to her cooking by using spices, as the infrequent references to them in the *Account Book* show – "to Lb anise seeds – 8d", "to Spice, Ginger and Carvey – 1/2".

Tea was also something of a rarity at Scalan. Though it had been introduced into the North-East early in the century,[8] it was still a luxury in the Banffshire uplands at this date. Janet Rae certainly considered it a luxury – at 3/6 to 4/-, one lb cost the equivalent of six weeks of her wages! She bought it rarely, and – to judge from *Account Book* entries such as "Tea, not to be used for sometime to come" – she guarded it jealously. Coffee was only a quarter of the price, but it also was drunk infrequently: 1 lb would last the community half the year.

A sample of the entries for kitchen equipment gives some idea of the storage, preparation and serving of food at Scalan at this time:

To a Bouie for weighing meal – 9d
To Cupper [cooper] for ordering Cogs Barrels &c – 6d
To an iron hoop to a Beef stand [perhaps a pickling barrel] – 1/-
To a Knock and Mell for beating bear or barek – 1/3
To a Chopen Triancle – 9d
To an iron fire pan – 10/-
To tinning tea kettle – 1/6
To a Laddle – 3d
To timber bowls and Plates 1/-
To $\frac{1}{2}$ Doz China cups & plats 7/6
To the Tinker for making Spoons 1/6

The usual table drink for master and boys alike was ale, which, as Mr Paterson's purchase of "a Cock & peal for Bruing" indicates, was made on the premises. But he also made it his business to keep a stock of spirits and wine in the house. Blended or "mix'd" whisky cost 8d per bottle, and was kept mainly as an occasional treat for the servants or a refreshment for hired labourers. Malt whisky, which cost 1/- a bottle, was reserved "to keep the house for strangers". And brandy, at 1/11 per bottle, was kept for very special occasions, a visit from the Duke's factor, no doubt, and the summer arrival of the Administrators of the Mission.

The master always made special arrangements for the annual Administrators' meeting, when the bishops and other senior clergy were to be entertained. Then would be seen food and drink never normally set upon the Scalan table. His wording of the accounts sometimes gives us a hint of this: "to two Salmon on account of the Bps and other company being at Scalan – 6/8", for instance. And some years he actually kept a separate account of purchases made for the meeting. In 1774 his special account included the following: 4 pints "unmix'd" whisky; 1 lb "fine tea" at close to double the standard price; 1 lb coffee; 1 pint of Rum at 3/6; 2 dozen bottles of porter costing 7/-; a wedder, slaughtered on the farm; 3 hens from the yard; 4 bottles of wine at 1/2 each; and "3 pecks of the best kind of flour". The last item would have been wheat flour, which the seminary also bought from time to time for making altar breads. These Janet Rae shaped and baked herself, using the special bread-irons kept in the house (Plate 13).

At a time when many of the old tasks of the home were being handed over to specialist tradesmen, the *Account Book* shows that at least some of the processes involved in cloth making were still undertaken on the premises at Scalan. References to the purchase of "pirns & flights to wheels" prove that the seminary spun its own woollen thread; the purchase of potash suggests that some bleaching was carried out; and the fact that indigo was bought from time to time implies the dyeing of made-up cloth. Other entries suggest that the community bought in their flax and spun it themselves, but that the weaving process – whether of fine linen or the coarser harn cloth – was handed over to the local weaver.[9] And when best quality linen was needed – for shirts for students travelling abroad, for instance – it was always bought ready-made.

Similarly, when Mr Paterson introduced uniforms he purchased ready-woven cloth from which the garments could be made up, buying it either by the yard or the slightly longer ell. The tartan used for kilts, waistcoats, breeches and hose cost 1/- or more per ell. The cheaper plaiden was used for the linings, and heavy blue say cloth, at 2/10 per ell, for the coats. The local tailor, Tom Geddes, was brought in to make up the garments: it was normal practice at this time for a tailor to work at the customer's house, and for the customer to provide the cloth.[10] At 4d a day it was a worthwhile contract for him, for in a good year he might spend forty days at Scalan. Some accessories, such as knee buckles, could not be made, and these Mr Paterson bought when he had occasion to go to Aberdeen at Easter for the blessing of the oils.[11] But the only article in the boys' entire outfit actually bought off the peg was their bonnets.

While John Cummin was employed at Scalan he made all the students' shoes, even tanning the leather himself, as is clear from references to the purchase of "bark for hides" (that is, wood bark for curing the leather). After he was paid off at Martinmas 1771 there are no more such references, but instead entries for shoes made by the local cobbler. Though these were more costly, they were still surprisingly inexpensive: the cobbler only charged 2/2, for instance, for making eight new pairs and mending a further fourteen. He apparently provided the leather, but other items were bought in for his use, for separate entries for leather thongs, hemp, "tiers", and tackets all appear in the *Account Book*. John Cummin

continued to live in the neighbourhood, and was hired from time to time
as a messenger in Mr Paterson's day. And in later years under new
masters he was taken on as a full-time servant again, and would become
indeed a highly valued member of the Scalan community, as well as its in-
house shoe maker.

When students were travelling abroad they were thought of as ambassadors for Scalan and the Scottish Mission, and were clothed accordingly. When Joseph Hendry and John Gordon were sent to Valladolid in
1774 it cost the house £8/6/4 to kit them out. The tailor was brought in,
best quality fabrics were purchased, including silk for cravats and
cambric for ruffles, and each boy was provided with the following
comprehensive outfit: 1 "big coat", 1 "meat coat", 1 waistcoat, 1 pair
of breeches, 3 shirts, 2 pairs of stockings, 1 silk cravat, 1 night cap, 1 pair
of shoes with knee buckles, 1 pocket napkin, 1 pen knife, and 1 comb.

Like all the houses in the Braes the seminary community burned peat
for their heating and cooking. As tenants of the farm of Tomnalienan they
had always cut their peats on *Fèithe Bhadach*, the Vattich Moss. It may be
that the Moss was also still providing them with fir candles for their
lighting, from the huge resinous trees that lay buried in its depths, which
the local people plundered for many different needs. These slivers of fir
gave off a cosy glowing light, though not a particularly bright or steady
one, as well as a great deal of smoke. But since they do not of course figure
in the accounts we do not know if they were still being used. It is certain
on the other hand that oil lamps were in use for some purposes, for the
accounts record regular purchases of salmon oil "for winter light".
Several of these entries specify that they were "for giving light to the
Boys", which suggests that oil lamps were used mainly in those parts of
the house used by the students – particularly we may guess in the study,
where they would provide a steady light, and the dormitory, where they
would be safer than rush lights.

The community also made their own candles. The main season for
candle-making was November, because the mart slaughtered at that time
of the year provided the tallow, and the new stock was timely for the dark
months ahead. It would seem that large quantities were made, for use
throughout the year, because extra tallow had to be bought in quite
regularly. Their needs were not only domestic, of course, as the account
entry "to Cotten weecks [wicks] for Candles to the Altar" reminds us.
Wicks were supplied by merchants in response to the very widespread
demand of home candle makers at this date, and the candles were
fashioned round them, either in moulds or by a process of repeated
dipping, drying and rolling.

Some homes used their surplus tallow to make soap, but manufactured
soaps had also long been available even in the Highlands, and Scalan

preferred to buy in whatever was required, despite the exorbitant price: 1 lb of standard soap cost 7d, while the accounts record the purchase of soft soap for the first time in 1780, at no less than 17/- the half-firkin.

Arranging for the supply of soap, and every other aspect of hygiene and health, were also the responsibility of the housekeeper. She made sure that every boy were provided with his own napkins, horn comb, and chamber pot. She also kept a few basic medicines to hand – notably sulphur for use as a laxative, and alum for an astringent, as well as "vomits" and other "doses of physick" unspecified. Day-to-day ailments she dealt with herself, but the *Account Book* also records payment to the Glenlivet doctor for house visits and providing medicines, and on at least one occasion the payment of a student's travelling expenses down to Keith for specialist medical advice that could not be had locally.

The classroom and everything in it was of course the responsibility of the master. Writing paper was surprisingly expensive, 11/8 per ream in the early 1780s; but quill pens were (literally) ten-a-penny. Mr Paterson made his own ink from galls, possibly also using for the same purpose the copperas which occasionally figures in the accounts.

He believed in teaching by encouragement rather than fear. As well as persuading Bishop Hay to donate prizes he himself made regular use of Scalan funds to buy "rewards" – he bought prizes to the value of 6d three times a year on average, and also made other occasional purchases – "to something for the Boys to encourage them to do well – 2/-", "for sweet meats to Boys to make them behave well – 6d."

Nor did he forget them at Christmas. The "pins" that he always bought "for them to divert themselves with" must refer to skittles. And they must have been a great favourite, because the tradition lived on long after he left, and for over twenty years "pins" were the boys' expected Christmas present. Why new ones were needed every year is not clear.

If skittles were the standard winter amusement at Scalan, swimming was the favourite pastime in summer. There are places on the Crombie burn, both above and below the house, where the bend of the river has carved out a channel deeper and wider than elsewhere. In his second summer in charge Mr Paterson hired two men to build a dam at one of these places, to form a rough and ready swimming pool, as we read from the entry in his ledger – "to Dam Men for the Boys to Play, 1/-".

The original Scalan *Rules* had stressed the importance of recreation, but they had also insisted that the boys should undertake some regular tasks about the house, and Bishop Hay's instructions to Mr Paterson in 1770 had repeated this requirement. But whereas originally the main purpose of the chores had been their educative value, there is no doubt that the practice had been gradually increased over the years, and extended to include outdoor work, in order to reduce the need to hire local labour. How much the boys were now being called on to do we do not know: it would not be as much certainly as in the late 1780s and early 1790s, when their tasks would include up to ten days of farm work every year – digging, harvesting, and even shearing – at which time lessons were abandoned, to the detriment (some believed) of the boys' education.[12] But whatever the scale of their work, it could only be supplementary: it could never replace the need for domestic servants or hired hands on the farm.

The seminary employed three persons full-time at this date – a housekeeper, an under-servant girl, and a servant lad. Janet Rae, who took over as housekeeper from Annie Greenlaw in the autumn of 1770, was to remain in the post for no less than seventeen years, easily the longest of any of Scalan's housekeepers. Her starting wage was 16/8 per half-year, with board. The under-servant girl, who assisted her, was paid only 13/4 per half-year, and for this reason girls rarely stayed long in the job. Anna Roy (a daughter of 'Muckle' Peter Roy),[13] her sister Betty, and then Jean Davidson all held the post briefly between 1771-76, when Betty returned to it and this time stayed for eight years.

The servant lad was expected to work on the farm as well as acting as handyman about the house, for at this date the seminary did not yet employ a specialist farm supervisor. The title of the post did not imply that it should be held by a young man, and was used equally for young John Cummin and for old John Ross who succeeded him. Apparently the wage was negotiable: John Cummin was paid £3 a year, whereas John Ross accepted the post for only £2; when young Jamie Cuie took over from Whitsun 1773 the wage was restored to £3. Jamie remained three years at Scalan; Willie McKay who followed him stayed five; and his successor Johnny Roy (another of 'Muckle' Peter's family) stayed four.

In addition to their wages the servants received free footwear. Even John Cummin, who was a skilled cobbler himself, had his shoes bought for him. And Janet Rae was given "a pair of net leather shoes" on one occasion, which must have been fashion footwear because at 3/6 they were almost twice the price of a standard pair of shoes. The master also rewarded the servants with other bonuses from time to time: in the case of the men these usually took the form of tobacco, snuff or a dram.

The position of David Drummond was different from that of the other servants, and seems to have been based entirely on bonuses. He was already at Scalan when Mr Paterson arrived, and he stayed on as a general assistant and odd-job-man until at least 1778. In all that time there are no records of wages paid to him, but regular entries for payments in kind – shoes, stockings, breeches, a coat, bleached harden for his shirts, "soap to sheave", quite regular drams, and (by far the most frequent) snuff. In the seven years 1771-78 these gifts amounted to £7/4/7 in value, the equivalent of a part-time wage, and this must have been the arrangement under which he worked for the master.

The men were expected to run messages as part of their day's work, though only the servant lad would be called on if the message involved long distance travel, and for this he received special payment. John Cummin, for instance, was paid 6d for journeying down to the Enzie and bringing back two horses, a round trip of over 70 miles; at a later date Johnny Roy received 1/- expenses for meeting Bishop Hay at Aberdeen and accompanying him back to Scalan. But there were times in the year when the servant lad could not be spared from the farm, and then it was necessary to hire outsiders as messengers, at considerably greater cost. Thus Mr Paterson had to pay 5/- for "a man's mantinance and a horse including the mans wages" for bringing the bishop from Stobhall to Scalan, and a further 3/6 for taking him back.

By far the greatest outlay on hired outside labour was of course for work on the seminary's farm. Some tasks, such as building dykes or trenching, only occurred occasionally. But others came up every year.In particular, the master always had to hire in extra hands for work at the peats, and at harvest time.

The peats were cut in the *Fèithe Bhadach* in May, and enough hands were hired to finish the work in three days. In 1777, for example, Jamie McKay was hired as leader "at the flaughter spad", with six men at the digging under him, and a dozen women on "barrows", gathering and stacking. Jamie was paid 6d a day, the men 5d, and the women 4d, and all were encouraged in their back-breaking work by being kept well supplied with pipe tobacco. The peats were left to dry out until July, when a man was hired with two horses to bring them home, a two-day task.

There were a number of people to pay at harvest time. First, the hired hands who helped cut the corn. Then the proof man to gauge the yield of grain – his expertise might cost 6d. Then the miller, who was entitled to his multure or portion of grain in addition to his cash payment. The size of the latter may be judged from a typical entry in the *Account Book*: "for stricking at the Miln half a Boll of Barley – 1/6".[14]

The seminary sowed several different cereals (all generally termed 'corn') at this date. Entries for 'barley' refer to the new 'English' variety, with two rows of grain to the ear; 'bear' refers to the traditional hardy type, with four rows to the ear. Other entries show that oats were also sown, but on a limited scale, for half a boll of seed was a typical purchase.

We know too that the farm practised rotation. Every year small quantities of rye grass and clover seed were purchased – usually only about 5-6 lb weight of each – to refresh portions of the land after several seasons under corn. And the use of these crops further suggests that the land was being regularly fertilised as a matter of routine at this date, since in the soils of Upper Banffshire red clover could only be sown successfully after marling or liming.[15]

From the earliest days it had been the practice to keep a horse at Scalan, for farm work and travelling in the neighbourhood. Later, as the house had come to be used increasingly as a meeting venue, the horse had also been useful for bringing visitors up from the Lowlands; Bishop Smith, who always journeyed by horse, may have started the tradition, which – as we saw – was continued by Bishop Hay.

Cattle were kept at Scalan chiefly for their milk at this date, but they were also used for ploughing, as we know from the purchase of 'theats' [bands for harnessing]. There must have been an arrangement in the neighbourhood whereby draught cattle were shared at ploughing time. The traditional Scottish plough was still in general use in the Banffshire uplands at this date. A heavy, home-made implement, fashioned largely of wood, it required a team of up to a dozen beasts to draw it,[16] and the Scalan cattle – and the horse – would have taken their place in the local team.

According to the rules for 'souming' then in force, every farm was restricted as to the number of beasts it might keep by its acreage of grassland, from which was calculated its capacity to pasture them.[17] With only two cows and one horse, the Scalan farm was stocked far below capacity in the mid-'70s: twenty years later it would be maintaining a herd of seven cattle.[18]

Nor was it yet keeping sheep in any serious way. The flock must have been small, to judge from the scale of restocking – "two Ewes and 2 Lambs" was a typical purchase, almost certainly of the traditional Scottish breed. In the 1790s, when the new sheep economy was beginning to make its mark in Upper Banffshire, the seminary's flock would be systematically increased to over a hundred.

It is surprising that no reference occurs in the accounts to the keeping of goats. Since the time of Bishop Gordon goats' milk – as well as mountain air and clear burn water – had become something of a Scalan 'trademark' among Lowland clergy seeking a place to convalesce. (Bishop Hay and Paul McPherson were among those who drank it to recover their health and well-being). But it may be in fact that it was not actually produced on the seminary's own farm, but elsewhere in the neighbourhood.

A selection of *Account Book* entries from the 1770s gives an idea of the kinds and prices of agricultural equipment available at the time:

To an Iron Spad – 2/6
To three Corn hooks – 1/2
To a Syth – 2/6
For a wheel barrow – 2/10
To two juniper skulls – 1/-
A new Cart with the wheels 6/-
To a muck cart killoch and axl tree – 2/-
To hoops for tubs and for girths to cartwheels – 4/10
To Hooping cogs & kirns [churns]- 4d
To a Bear ridle – 1/-
To a Oat ridle – 8d

Hooping of the wooden cogs, tubs and churns, and fitting girths to the cartwheels, was the work of the local smith Lachlan Forbes. He was also responsible for fitting the ploughshare, shoeing the horse, and indeed pretty well all the seminary's metalwork jobs, even some of those that would normally have been given to the cooper. His account was settled at Martinmas, and it might run to as much as 17/6 for a year's work.

Finally, the accounts offer some record of the programme of building and repairs to the house and 'offices' in Mr Paterson's day. They show that in his second year he had a new barn built, purchasing three trees from which to cut the timber. The following year, 1773, he built a kitchen on the north wing of the yard – for, as we saw, there had been no provision for a kitchen in the 1767 design. He bought in two fir trees at a cost of 2/6, from which he had the roof cabers cut for the new building, and straw for thatching, at the same price.

Four years later, the accounts record his purchase of "one dozen of deals", and then "two fir trees for Cabbers to Kitchen and Barn": this must surely imply an extension to the kitchen wing, because it would certainly not have been necessary to re-roof the existing building after so short a time. That same year he also had a hen house put up, using the same building methods and materials as for the other outhouses.

By now the site was taking on the shape of a rectangle – with the house on the east side, and an entire north 'wing' and part of a south 'wing' completed. It was therefore probably at this date that a wall and gate were built on the west side, to complete the rectangle and enclose the yard. Today no sign remains of any wall, but ninety years ago Dom Odo Blundell saw one, and took it to be part of the original seminary complex.[19] His claim has been questioned, but is in fact confirmed by a nineteenth century photograph (Plate 5), which clearly shows the remains of the corner of a wall, and shows moreover that it was built integrally into the north wing and is therefore almost certainly contemporary with it.

Mr Paterson's building programme continued into 1778, when the records refer to wood being brought from Abernethy, a man hired for two days "at the arm saw", and a second man "eight days helping to order houses". Judging from the scale of the contracts, these were not major building works. But nor were they merely minor repairs, for the latter the seminary normally carried out for themselves, always – for example – buying in their own glass "losens" and putty to replace broken windows.

In 1774 the master sought permission to add ceilings to the upstairs chapel and the main lower-floor room, which like all the other rooms in the house had been built with open rafters. This was the one major interior improvement that he asked for during his term as master. Bishop Grant approved the plan, and gave him £1/10/- to cover it. With this he bought in the wood, some Prussian Blue paint, linseed oil for a mixer, and one paintbrush. But the rest of the paint, and all the labour, he had to pay for himself. He found he needed eight times as much paint as he had originally ordered!The joinery alone took James Mirin the local wright seven-and-a-half working weeks, and the paintwork a further three days. Before all was finished there was a shortfall of £1/12/6 to be found somehow from Scalan funds.

NOTES

1. 'Account Book for Scalan, 1771–87', CS 1/6 (a), SCA; kept by John Paterson, and after him successively by John Farquharson and Alexander Farquharson.
2. Tack to James Mcalea on Scalan and Tomnalienan, 1767, GD 44/23/3/77, SRO.
3. Cf., eg., Mrs Elizabeth Grant of Rothiemurchus *Memoirs of a Highland Lady* (London, 1898; Edinburgh, 1988 ed.), espec. pp. 235f. (Memoirs written in 1840s–50s, but referring to the 1800s).
4. Though it should be remembered that most of the boys and masters had been raised on farms.
5. Bishop Hay 'Costs and Inconveniences that the proposed unison of SSries [seminaries] would bring on H: V:', notes on back of letter dated 26. 6. 1778, CS 1/1/4, SCA.
6. At this date barley was the most commonly used cereal for consumption, oats still being chiefly a rent-paying crop: cf., Gauldie E. *The Scottish Country Miller 1700–1900* (Edinburgh, 1981), p. 2.
7. Sale of kail continued to the last days of the seminary: thus, eg., 900 plants were sown in 1789, and 1700 in 1795: 'Various Accounts', 1787-99, CB 6/1, pp. 6 and 40, SCA.
8. Tea had actually become fashionable in the Aberdeen area before Edinburgh, on account of that city's sea trade with Holland – Grant A. *Miscellany of the Spalding Club* (Aberdeen, 1841), vol. II, pp. 40ff.
9. Re the processes of linen making, see Durie A. J. *The Scottish Linen Industry*

in the Eighteenth Century (Edinburgh, 1979), pp. 2-6; re home spinning and weaving, by huge numbers for home use and to supplement family income, cf. *Ibid.*, pp. 38ff.

10. Cf., Plant M. *The Domestic Life of Scotland in the Eighteenth Century* (Edinburgh, 1952), pp. 195f.

11. John Paterson to Bishop Hay, 15. 4. 1771, BL.

12. Cf., the controversy over using the boys, p. 191 below. The Accounts for 1791-2 include an item "To Gingerbread for the boys, for shearing well" – 'Various Accounts', 1787-99, CB 6/1, p. 15, SCA.

13. This is very likely the Peter Roy Grant of Badeglashan who was 'out' in 1745 (Tayler A. and Tayler H. *Jacobites of Aberdeenshire and Banffshire in the Forty Five* (Aberdeen, 1928), list, p. 430; see also Mitchell S. 'Scalan in the Eighteenth Century: A Postscript – the 'Forty five', *Scalan News*, no. 14, June 1997, p. 18.

14. The nearest mill was at Refreish just the other side of the Bochel.

15. Cf., Grant J. and Leslie W. *A Survey of the Province of Moray* (Aberdeen, 1798), p. 330.

16. See the detailed description in Grant J. *Agriculture in Banffshire 150 Years Ago* (Banff, 1902), pp. 12-15. An entry in the Account Book for 1774 "to timber for a Plugh" shows that the seminary fashioned its own plough at this date: only the metal blade and coulter were purchased.

17. Bil A. *The Shieling 1600–1840* (Edinburgh, 1990), pp. 130ff.

18. The stock then consisted of "the old black cow; the belled quoy rising five; the gared Cromey cow; the brocket cow; the old cow designed for a Mart; the hacket quoy; the year old brown quoy; an old cow for a Mart" – 'Account of cattle Sold from Scalan & bought', 6. 8. 1792, 'Various Accounts', CB 6/1, p. 27, SCA.

19. Blundell O. *The Catholic Highlands of Scotland*, vol. 1 (Edinburgh, 1909), p. 39.

15

Highlanders and Failed Harvests (1778–1783)

In August 1778 Bishop Grant arrived back in Aberdeen exhausted by his journey to the Administrators' meeting at Scalan. He failed to recover his health through the autumn, and on 3 December he died. He was succeeded as Vicar Apostolic by Bishop Hay.

No-one had more knowledge of the Mission, and particularly of its financial affairs, than the new leader. He was especially aware of the "prodigious expences" involved in sending students to the Colleges abroad. His accounts showed an outlay of £184 Sterling for this purpose over the past five years, a figure which would have been even greater but for the generosity of some of the boys' parents.[1]

He was therefore anxious to make economies wherever possible, at home and abroad. In regard to Scalan, he was now in a position to implement the *Regulations* that he himself had drawn up in 1770, but which had never been fully observed under his predecessor.[2] He had the document re-issued and a number of copies made for the use of the College and the parents of would-be students. At the same time he raised the fees for boarders from £6 to £8 a year.[3]

A few months before, Bishop John MacDonald had put forward a proposal to unite the Highland and Lowland seminaries in a single establishment at Scalan, arguing that it would bring a financial saving to the Mission. The fact is that the rental of the farm of Buorblach, which he had acquired for the Highland seminary, was beyond the purse of the Highland District.[4] Mr Paterson shared his view that amalgamation would cut costs, but he considered this advantage as "trifling" compared with the "internal peace and contentment" of the house. He had admitted a number of Highland boys over the years and knew the problems at first hand. They and the Lowland students had always formed "two separate families", and he had often been hard put to make them agree. He even doubted whether a Highland and Lowland master together in the same house could refrain from unedifying disputes.[5]

Bishop Hay was equally conscious of the likelihood of friction. "It is too well known", he wrote in his notes regarding the proposal, "that Boys H and L . . . have a great mutual contempt for, and antipathy, to one another, and they stick not, when together, to express this contempt." The Lowland boys were wont to deride their Highland classmates as "bags of pottage", and they would retaliate with cries of "Bodach gaoithe!" [windy old fool], and the name-calling had more than once led to fisticuffs. He also believed that Highland students would not take to the frugal régime at Scalan, that they would be too far from home to return there in the event of illness, and that their Gaelic would inevitably suffer, since it would not be the medium of instruction in an amalgamated seminary, and "for obvious reasons" could not even be permitted during recreation. But he also saw financial disadvantages in the plan. Scalan would have to be either rebuilt or extended, and the cost would be a drain on both vicariates. He opposed the proposal, therefore, from every point of view.[6]

But more than this, he believed that amalgamation would be unwise in that the long-term future of Scalan itself was now in doubt. The College's situation "in as cold and stormy a place as is in Scotland" had been necessary at the time of its foundation, he explained:

As Scalan was begun in troublesome times it was the ruggedness and remoteness of its situation that made it be placed where it is. But as we are in hopes to have more liberty, it cannot be doubted but L.V. [the Lowland Vicariate] in some short time may see it convenient and necessary to bring down their S. to some part of the Low country where the cold is not so rigid and where provisions of all kinds can be easier got.[7]

His notes are the first written expression of a growing conviction among the leaders of the Church that Scalan was no longer suitable in the changing times, and of their intention to abandon it as soon as the political situation allowed.

There seemed every chance, in fact, that 1778 might be a year of real change for the Catholics of Scotland, for Parliament was debating bills to end the Penal laws throughout Britain and Ireland. The bishops reported to Rome that the Church had "never been more hopeful, never more prosperous." "The generosity of the King and ministers gives us great hope for the future," they added, "and we already enjoy far greater freedom than our forefathers ever had."[8] It must have seemed to them only a matter of time before the seminary itself could come in from the cold.

But by January 1779 there were ominous signs of a resurgence of popular anti-Catholic feeling, fuelled behind the scenes by persons and groups alarmed at the new liberality. On 2 February it erupted into mob violence in Edinburgh, in which the new priest's house in Chalmers Close was destroyed by fire, a second priest's residence was pillaged, and shops and houses of known Catholics were attacked and robbed.[9]

Everyone who could fled the city. But one old priest refused to leave. Allan MacDonald, who had been one of the original students on Eilean Bàn more than sixty years before, and had been sent home from Scalan by Bishop Gordon in 1730, was now in his eighties. He had seen much in a long life. Just three years after his ordination he had joined Charles Edward Stuart's army as a chaplain, and taken part in the entire '45 campaign. After the defeat at Culloden he had accompanied the Prince in his perilous escape to the Outer Isles, and was later captured and held in a prison ship on the Thames and in Newgate Gaol, and sentenced to banishment for life. He had spent twenty years in Rome, but had at last returned home in his old age. He was now living in Edinburgh, and after all his travels he had no mind to move house again for a mob. Tricking his enemies was nothing new to him. Telling his landlord that he was leaving town he called a coach, paid the driver to drive a mile or two out, and himself slipped back to his rooms and locked himself in, from where he watched the riot in peace.[10]

The following week Bishop Hay issued a pastoral letter urging his people to respond with courage and forgiveness, and reminding them of Jesus' words 'Blessed are you when men persecute you in my name.'[11] He must have been well aware even as he wrote it that any thoughts of giving up Scalan and opening a new seminary would need to be shelved meantime.

On 9 May Bishop John MacDonald died of a fever contracted while visiting victims of an epidemic sweeping through Knoydart. His sudden death left the Highland Vicariate without a leader and there was some delay before his successor, Alexander MacDonald of Bornish, was named. It was a controversial appointment and the cause of much ill-will within the Highland Church. One of the casualties of the dissention was the house and farm of Buorblach, the home of the Highland seminary, whose tack was cancelled through local spite.[12] Before the new bishop had even been consecrated the seminary was forced to close.

Mr Austin MacDonald, the deacon who was master at the time of its closure, was sent to Scalan to assist Mr Paterson, and he took with him Lachlan MacDonald, the first of a number of Highland students to make the journey over the next few years. Circumstances had brought about a kind of amalgamation, meantime, where argument had failed.

Lachlan, who was already well advanced in his studies, sailed for Douai in October. Austin MacDonald himself must have left at about the same time and returned for a few months to the West, where he at once began to run up debts.[13] He returned to Scalan the following spring (1780), perhaps in order to be present at the consecration of his bishop Alexander MacDonald there in March, the second and last episcopal consecration to be held at the College. By the time he left Scalan in July he had run up further debts in the neighbourhood, which remained unpaid even after he returned, and only came to light at his untimely death at the College towards the end of 1781. Mr Paterson was then forced to arrange a roup of his possessions, by which he managed to raise enough money to pay the local farmers what they were owed.[14]

By the spring of 1782 nine Highland boys had been admitted to Scalan, and five of these had gone on to the Colleges abroad. Only two now remained, but Bishop Alexander MacDonald was pushing to enrol more. Mr Paterson already had ten students, and his problem was space. He was expecting two more boys from the Lowland District in the spring, who would of course take priority, and he did not know how to respond to the Highland request. He appealed to John Geddes, the former Scalan master who had been appointed Co-adjutor Bishop of the Lowland District in 1780, and whose responsibilities included control of the Vicariate's funds. "This house can conveniently enough contain twelve Boys", he told him, "but more would rather throng us too much, for there is only proper room in the dormitory for twelve Beds, and twelve, too, need all the room about the fire."[15] He believed he could accept two more Highland boys "on a pinch", but only on the understanding that their admission would be temporary while they were awaiting a call from one of the Scots Colleges.[16]

Keeping Scalan financially above water remained his other chief anxiety. The accounts show that he lent the seminary sums of money from his own quota on numerous occasions at this time. He found this necessary, if ready cash was to be available for the prompt payment of bills, because the College grant only arrived from Edinburgh twice yearly.[17] He was still alert for any chance to save or make money, either for the seminary or the Mission. He had originally taken on John Ross as a general servant in 1771 partly because the man had spoken of donating a portion of his wealth to the Church. The matter had been taken no further at the time, but the two men were now discussing it again, and Mr Paterson believed he would "get him kept firm" to his word this time. John Ross proposed to donate 1000 Merks to the bishops, of which the annual interest would be paid to himself during his lifetime, and thereafter divided between the priest of Tombae and the poor of Glenlivet. The master warned the bishops that the old man's relatives did not share his views on good works, and would try to block any donation, so that if they liked the arrangement they would be well to conclude it at once. Not surprisingly, they agreed to the terms and took steps to receive the donation at Whitsun.[18]

That spring also Mr Paterson learned that the rental on the seminary's land was to be increased. James Mcalea's tack of Tomnalienan-and-Scalan now had only two years to run and he had been negotiating with Alexander Milne, the Duke's factor in the district, to have his tenants' leases re-assessed, in the hope that higher rentals would be fixed before the new contracts were drawn up in 1784. Milne's decision was that the tenants of Easter Scalan should pay £60 Sterling over the final two years of the current tack. Everyone in the neighbourhood believed that he had made a private deal with Mcalea, agreeing to the increase in the rents in return for a discreet backhander. As to Mcalea himself, the prospect of more money had given him "a new Swagger", and he was now to be seen strolling about the Braes "with, almost, the broad Side of his foot foremost." He was behaving as if he knew something that his tenants did not know, and Mr Paterson warned Bishop Geddes that he was not to be trusted, and that they would be wise to make early representation to the Duke to ensure that they retained their land come 1784.[19] Bishop Hay was at this time still on a prolonged visit to Rome, but he would be home in time for the Administrators' meeting at Scalan in August, and Mr Paterson intended to use that opportunity to give him news of the latest position.

The main business of the August meeting was financial. Bishop Hay had recently acquired money from several sources – compensation from the Government for damage to property during the Edinburgh riots of 1779, an additional grant from Propaganda, and profits from his own published works – and he informed his colleagues that most of it would be used directly for the benefit of the Church. He intended making a grant of £600 to the Mission and £400 to Scalan.[20]

Shortly before the bishops arrived at the seminary for their meeting three of the students had set out on the first stage of their journey to Rome. Jamie Sharp of Mortlach, and two Highland boys Ranald MacDonald and Johnny McDonell, left the Braes on 17 July and made their way on foot to Edinburgh. When they set sail from Leith dock in a ship bound for Ostend, they had no warning of the nightmare ahead. For eleven days they endured a ceaseless storm, and when at last they reached the coast of Flanders the ship could not venture in because of the wind. They had no choice but to wade ashore in waist-deep water, losing their shoes and hats in the process. From there they struggled barefoot to Douai. When they arrived at the door of the Scots College, exhausted and dispirited, Mr John Thomson was on the step to greet them.[21] The former Scalan master made them take a few days' rest, and then set out with them himself on the long overland journey to Leghorn, from where he escorted them by sea to Rome.

The boys' departure left nine students at Scalan. The oldest of them, at twenty, was Charles Durward from Glengairn. Bishop Alexander Mac-Donald had arranged his admission the previous December, with the intention of eventually sending him to Rome, despite never actually having met the boy. Mr Paterson found him to be "of such an odd kind of appearance" that he could not be sent anywhere abroad, much less to Rome. He considered that he should never have been allowed into Scalan, "either to touch Book or pen", and was certain that the bishop would not have recommended him if he had seen him for himself. He suffered him until October, and then sent him home.[22]

His presence had highlighted the general problem of Highland boys attending the Lowland seminary, and also the difficulty for Highland bishops to keep in close touch with the eastern outposts of their Vicariate. Nor had the presence of the Highland boys made Mr Paterson's financial management any easier. On the day of Charles Durward's departure he sent Bishop Geddes a final account of their expenses, to be forwarded to Bishop Alexander MacDonald for payment. The Highland District had sent no money for sixteen months, and the debt now stood at over £18.[23] It was not a burden that the seminary could readily carry, and he was at pains to have it cleared before the balancing of the books at Martinmas.

When Bishop Hay was given the latest news concerning the seminary's land that summer he at once made contact with Gordon of Glastirim, a second cousin of Bishop Gordon, and asked him to act on the Church's behalf in negotiations with the Duke. In October announcements were read out on behalf of His Grace in the chapels of Glenlivet and Stratha-von, inviting immediate offers from anyone seeking new tacks. Mr Paterson set out without delay for Fochabers, to learn the most up-to-date news from Gordon of Glastirim and arrange a meeting with the Duke's new chief factor Mr Tod.[24] He was conscious of a "great noise" and an "odd stir" of something approaching panic for land in the Braes. Above all, he distrusted James Mcalea and his friends: "Our Master, Scalan, is a Cunning man", he warned the bishop, "and I am afraid, has as Cunning, & more able folks, join'd with him".[25] He urged him to take action as soon as possible, and proposed that he might even consider bidding for the tack of the whole of Scalan, and then keeping as much as was needed for the farm and subletting the rest.

Bishop Hay did not support the proposal in its entirety, but he did send a *Memorandum* to the Duke by Gordon of Glastirim requesting some additional land on both sides of the Crombie.[26] On the west side he asked for a second plot, next to the seminary's existing land and equal in size. And on the east side he sought to acquire the "small stripe of mourish ground" at the back of the house known as 'the Weaver's Croft', which was at the time a pendicle of Eskiemullach farm. This plot, which extended to 35 acres and reached to within six feet of the seminary building, would be especially useful in that it would provide direct access to the grazing land beyond. His Grace received the *Memorandum* very favourably, giving the bishop every confidence that the Church's request would be met.[27] The land panic continued, meantime, with even small tenants putting in bids quite beyond their means.

The harvest was a disaster that autumn, portending another famine. The crop was late ripening, and frosts and snow in mid-October all but destroyed it on the ground. Mr Paterson urged that no more students should be admitted to the seminary, because there was no way to feed them. The old neighbourliness of the Braes had been "turn'd almost upside down" by the hardship and by each family's need to look after itself. There was now "no speaking to people", and no chance of persuading anyone to part with meal at any price, at least until Candlemas. The traditional source of comfort in times of famine, the "Husky Pots", were "almost laid aside" this winter, though whether through lack of barley, or the recent legislation prohibiting private stills, the master did not say.[28]

In the New Year (1783) he travelled down to the coastal plain in search of meal and succeeded in finding some, though not enough to last the house until the next harvest. He barely managed the return journey – "The Storm chas'd me all the way, & catch'd me by the heels just at Tombae," he told Bishop Geddes at the end of the month, by which time Scalan was "every way hemm'd in by mountains of snow."[29]

The weather remained unchanged until the end of March, delaying the ploughing again and setting back the sowing of the crop. Gordon of Glastirim had been in decline all winter, and that month he died.[30] His loss cast new doubt over the seminary's land, but fortunately for the Church his widow continued to represent their interest. She met the Duke in person in May and reminded him of their tack. His Grace readily recalled Bishop Hay's *Memorandum* and promised to discuss it with his chief factor. The two men were expected to visit Glenlivet in the summer, and the master hoped to meet them then, and perhaps even entertain them at Scalan itself.[31]

By the beginning of June the weather was much improved, though the harvest was still expected to be scant because the seed sown had been of such poor quality. For all the distress of the spring, Mr Paterson's little family were in good health and spirits: "They have not, as yet, thanks be to God, feel'd anything of this bad year," he was able to report.[32] He might have added that it was his own care, foresight and good house-keeping that had saved them from the horrors of the famine all around them.

The Catholics of the Braes received no poor relief from the Kirk parish at this time, and though they were sent some alms from Edinburgh by their own Church the amount must have fallen far short of their needs.[33] Mr Paterson himself was unable to help them in any but the smallest ways, and his helplessness, along with his ceaseless efforts for the seminary and his self-denial at a time of want, undoubtedly took their toll upon his own health, which had never been good. He was a man of childlike sincerity, whose one earnest desire was to become daily more perfect in fulfilling his duties as master and priest. As a youth he had chosen the monastic life, and as à man he had long had one eye on the next world, and "a kind of disgust" for "the Valley, here below" with its evil and its sorrows.[34] The distress of that year could not but have brought him low. Perhaps it even hastened the effects of his illness, which had grown steadily more severe through the spring, and was now diagnosed as advanced Consumption. By May the symptoms were all too clear to see.

At the beginning of July he took a turn for the worse, suffering severe colics and stomach pains all that month.[35] When Bishop Geddes arrived at Scalan for the annual meeting on 22 August he appeared somewhat improved and in good spirits. Bishops Hay and Alexander MacDonald were already there with Mr John Farquharson, and at supper Mr Paterson expressed his pleasure that the three bishops had arrived. "If I am to dy this Year", he added, "I hope it will be before you go away".[36] He repeated these words many times in the days that followed.

On the 28th he had a "long serious conversation" with Bishop Geddes, in which he told him that he did not expect to live long, and was very concerned for Scalan, and asked him particularly to go to Glenfiddich where the Duke was at his shooting lodge and speak to His Grace about the renewal of the tack. The bishop arranged for himself and John Farquharson to meet the Duke over breakfast the following day. They discussed their anxieties with him and his factor Mr Tod, and were reassured by their "favourable answer".

By the time they arrived back in the Braes Mr Paterson had already received the viaticum. He was still aware and alert, and remarkably cheerful and resigned. In the afternoon he "fell into a Lethargy", and between ten and eleven that night he died, the three bishops at his bedside as he had wished.

His funeral was arranged for 1 September. Timber was brought to the College, and his coffin was assembled in the upstairs bedroom where he lay. But he was a tall man, and when he was placed in it and the bearers made ready to bring him out of the house, they discovered that the coffin was too long to take the narrow corridor and staircase. So they carefully passed it through the small floor-level window of the bedroom, and lowered it to the ground. Then they shouldered the coffin and bore the body on foot down the glen, one at each corner and one to each side. The graveyard was some miles distant, and as they went every so often a man would step forward without a word from the following crowd to take one of their places. Perhaps, as was commonly the custom, when they reached the grave they made a circuit of it, sunwise, with the coffin. And no doubt, once Mr Paterson was in the earth and the prayers were said, the whole crowd raced one-another home, all but the oldest, as traditionally they always did after funerals in the Braes.[37]

When the Administrators dispersed from their meeting a few days later, the former servant John Cummin was hired to attend Bishop Hay on his journey back to Aberdeen. As he walked beside the horse, his shoulder close to the bishop's knee, he could see how distressed he was. He was wringing his hands with emotion.

"O John, John, we have lost our head!" he exclaimed.[38]

For Scalan they were true words. Mr Paterson was only in his mid-thirties when he died. He had been master for thirteen years, the second longest term of any master. None was more dedicated, prudent, humble, caring or devout in his leadership. And none was more fruitful, for no less than two dozen of the boys under his care went on to serve the Mission as ordained priests.

NOTES

1. Bishop Hay to Henry Innes, 24. 7. 1778, BL. The accounts for the year 1777-8 were in the red by £18.
2. Cf., by implication, his Afterword to 'Regulations', 1779, CS 1/1/5 (i), SCA.
3. Five copies in different hands, 1779, CS 1/1/6–CS 1/1/10. One of these (CS 1/1/7), which does not include the Afterword, was probably intended for in-house use at Scalan itself.
4. Buorblach had apparently been acquired against the advice of the ageing Bishop Hugh MacDonald – Austin MacDonald to Bishop Hay, 10. 10. 1779, BL.
5. John Paterson to William Reid, 14. 10. 1778, BL.
6. Bishop Hay 'Costs and Inconveniences that the proposed unison of SSries [seminaries] would bring on H: V:', notes on back of letter of 26. 6. 1778, CS

1/1/4, SCA. The "obvious reasons" were the need to discourage cliques, and more generally to prevent private conversations that the master could not understand. Scalan was first and foremost a Lowland seminary. How different the attitude to Gaelic from that of the *Rules* of 1722!

7. Ibid.
8. Bishops' Report to Propaganda, 1778, in Blundell O. *The Catholic Highlands of Scotland* (Edinburgh and London, 1909 and 1917), vol. II, p. 112.
9. At the height of the attack Bishop Hay himself arrived at Blackfriars Wynd, knowing nothing of it, and asked an old woman in the mob what was happening. "Oh sir, we are burning the Popish chapel," she told him, "and we only wish we had the bishop to throw into the fire!" – from the account in the biography of Bishop Hay in Gordon J. F. S. *Journal and Appendix to Scotichronicon and Monasticon* (Glasgow, 1867), pp. 158ff.
10. Alexander Geddes to ?, 8. 3. 1779, BL. Geddes refers to Allan MacDonald as "Mr Ronaldson" on account of his being a Clanranald. The letter gives a detailed account of the build-up of hostility as well as the riot itself. Even in March the Catholics were remaining indoors. Re the broader question of the fuelling of anti-Catholic feeling, see Donovan R. K. 'Voices of distrust: the expression of anti-Catholic feeling in Scotland 1778–1781', *IR*, vol. xxx, 1979.
11. Bishop Hay Pastoral Letter, Feb. 1779, printed in *The Scots Magazine*, Feb. 1779. Re whole episode, Forbes-Leith W. *Memoirs of Scottish Catholics During the XVIIth and XVIIIth Centuries* (London, 1909), vol. II, pp. 368ff.
12. Bishop Hay assumed charge of the Highland Vicariate, pending the appointment of a successor, and sought nominations for the position from the Highland clergy. Finding support divided equally between Alexander MacDonald of Bornish and Alexander MacDonald of Sandaig, he recommended the former as being the choice of the senior clergy. His decision aroused the anger of the younger priests and the family of Sandaig. Apparently as an act of spite against the Church, MacDonald of Sandaig persuaded Lord Lovat, the owner of North Morar, to grant the tack of Buorblach farm to himself, and not to the Highland bishop as promised. Cf., Gordon J. F. S. *Journal and Appendix to Scotichronicon and Monasticon* (Glasgow, 1867), pp. 176f.
13. Austin MacDonald to Bishop Hay, from Arisaig, 10. 10. 1779; from Ardnafuaran, 22. 12. 1779; from Moidart, 30. 1. 1780; from Arisaig, 2. 2. 1780; from Moidart, 29. 2. 1780; BL.
14. John Paterson to Bishop Geddes, 29. 12. 1781, BL.
15. John Paterson to Bishop Geddes, 12. 1. 1782, BL.
16. John Paterson to Bishop Geddes, 12. 4. 1782, BL.
17. He lent money on fifteen occasions between Feb. 1779–Sept. 1780 to a total value of £27/10/-, being repaid in three instalments; and again eleven times between Oct. 1781–March 1783 (total £18, repaid in two instalments): 'Account Book for Scalan', CS 1/6 (a), p. 178, SCA.
18. John Paterson to Bishop Geddes, 12. 1. 1782, 2. 3. 1782, and 12. 4. 1782, BL.
19. John Paterson to Bishop Geddes, 2. 3. 1782 and 12. 4. 1782, BL.
20. Bishop Geddes' detailed account, printed in Anderson W. J. 'The Autobio-

graphical Notes of Bishop John Geddes', *IR*, vol. xviii, no. 1, spring 1967, p. 48.

21. Bishop Geddes' account, in Anderson W. J. *Op. cit.*, pp. 48f.

22. John Paterson to Bishop Geddes, 16. 7. 1782; and to Bishop Hay, 5. 10. 1782, BL; and Student Register, in 'Account Book for Scalan', 1771-87,CS 1/ 6 (a), pp. 161-4, SCA.

23. 'Account Book for Scalan', 1771-87, CS 1/6 (a), SCA.

24. John Paterson to Bishop Geddes, 10. 10. 1782, BL.

25. John Paterson to Bishop Geddes, 5. 10. 1782, BL. ['Scalan' – i.e., James Mcalea].

26. 'Memorandum' to Duke of Gordon, March 1780, GD 44/23/6/3, SRO. He had originally drawn up the document in spring 1780, when it seemed that an amalgamation of the Highland and Lowland seminaries might be long-term. He now had a copy made and sent to the Duke.

27. John Paterson to Bishop Hay, 21. 10. 1782, BL.

28. John Paterson to Bishop Geddes, 1. 10. 1782 and 28. 12. 1782, BL. Re crop and harvest of 1782 in Highlands of NE, inflated prices, etc., see Report of Earl of Fife, in *2nd Report of Distress in Scotland*, presented to Parliament 28. 5. 1783, printed 7. 5. 1846, p. 2. Re whisky legislation – Act 19 Geo III cap. 50, 1781: cf., Moss M.S. and Hume J. R. *The Making of Scotch Whisky* (Edinburgh, 1981), p. 38; and Craig H. C. *The Scotch Whisky Industry Record* (Dumbarton, 1994). [Candlemas – 2 February].

29. John Paterson to Bishop Geddes, 31. 1. 1783, BL.

30. John Paterson to Bishop Geddes, 15. 3. 1783, BL.

31. John Paterson to Bishop Geddes, 7. 6. 1783, BL.

32. Ibid.

33. Cf., *OSA*, vol. xvi, p. 238, Parish of Inveravon, report by Rev. J. Grant (c. 1792). Relief to the poor was paid from parish dues, to which the Catholics did not normally contribute. Rev. Grant was always antagonistic to Catholics, but matters improved with the appointment of William Spence as minister in 1795, and parish money was thereafter given to Catholics also – cf., Dunnett H. *Invera'an A Strathspey Parish* (Paisley, 1919), p. 108, quoting a Kirk Session record of 11. 12. 1798.

34. John Paterson to Bishop Geddes, 25. 3. 1783 and 1. 10. 1782, BL.

35. John Farquharson to Bishop Geddes, 27. 7. 1783, BL.

36. Bishop Geddes to John Reid, 30. 8. 1783, BL. Details of illness, conversations and death in Bishop Geddes to John Thomson, 19. 12. 1783.

37. Re sunwise, Phillips J.G. *Wanderings in the Highlands of Banff and Aberdeen Shires* (Banff, 1889), p. 82. Re race home, McPherson J.M. *Primitive Beliefs in the North East of Scotland* (London, 1929), pp. 127f. Some of the funeral customs of the Braes were still practised at the end of the last century – cf., taped reminiscences of Jean Cameron, SA 1953/241/B, School of Scottish Studies, Univ. of Edinburgh.

38. Related by John Cummin to Rev. J. A. Stothert, and recounted by him in Gordon J. F. S. *Op. cit.* p. 230.

16

'Accompts Extravegant' (1783–1788)

Even before Mr Paterson's funeral the bishops had decided that Mr John Farquharson would be his successor.[1] The new master had been a classmate of John Paterson at Scalan, before leaving in 1768 for the Scots College Rome. One year later he had transferred to Douai, where he had completed his training and remained on after his ordination as Prefect of Studies. He had returned to Scotland in 1781 and been posted to Strathavon, the district in which he had been born and raised. Thus though he was now in his mid-thirties he actually only had two years' experience on the Mission.

He received the news of his appointment while still at the Administrators' meeting at Scalan, and left at once for Strathavon in order to conclude his affairs there, returning to take up his post on 1 September.[2]

His journey to Glenfiddich with Bishop Geddes to meet the Duke and his head factor had been time well spent. Mr Tod had proved a "very fast friend" during their discussions, and the Duke himself had appeared well disposed towards them, and anxious in fact to support all the priests on his estates.[3]

He agreed to renew the lease of all the seminary's existing land on the west side of the Crombie, though he did not allow them the extension requested in Bishop Hay's *Memorandum*. The other new land requested in the *Memorandum*, the Weaver's Croft on the east side of the burn, they did acquire, not as a direct lease from His Grace but through Mrs Gordon of Glastirim. She had continued to represent their interest after her husband's death, according to her promise, and now took the lease of the Croft in her own name and sub-let it to the seminary at the same rental.[4]

These arrangements were agreed in September 1783, to take effect from Whitsun the following year. This was the date when all the farms in Glenlivet were to come under new tacks, and it was a particularly important date for the tenants of Tomnalienan-and-Scalan. James Mca-lea, who was nearing sixty, was not renewing his tenancy, and the Duke's factor took the opportunity to split the two farms and create two separate tacks for them. He also decided to abandon the tacksman system on them: that is, where Mcalea had acted as tacksman or principal tenant, paying the entire rental to the Gordon Estate himself and in turn leasing portions of the land to his sub-tenants, from now on all the tenants were to be 'conjunct', sharing the rental according to the size of their holdings and each paying his portion direct to the estate.[5]

The factor also took the opportunity to raise the rental of the whole farm by one fifth, and between this and the extra land acquired by the seminary the master now found himself paying 30% more than before.[6].

During the winter of 1783-84 Mr Farquharson was already planning how he would improve the Weaver's Croft, once it came into his possession. He kept Bishop Geddes informed of his plans, since it was the bishop, as Procurator of the Mission, who would have to sanction the costs involved. His advice was that they should plough the whole area, which was at present nothing but "wild muir", and build a dyke around it since it lay open to the common pasture: the work would admittedly be expensive, but profitable in the long term. He also advised that it would be essential to buy a flock of thirty wedders to control the part of the holding that was left under grass.[7]

At the same time he warned the bishop of possible problems with the new tenants of Scalan – John and William Stuart, James Lamb, James and Paul McPherson, and John Barclay – concerning the 'Park' on the east side of the Crombie that the seminary had held since 1716. They were claiming, apparently on the word of James Mcalea, that the seminary had always paid rent for the plot, and that as such it was "a pendicle of the tack of Scalan by prescription". If their argument was upheld, of course, they would force the seminary to pay a larger proportion of the total Scalan rental. They were not for giving up, and he feared that the argument might yet come to "an open Rupture".[8]

He had hoped to discuss the issue with Bishop Hay at his home in Aberdeen, but for several weeks the weather made travelling impossible. So heavy was the snow at Christmas that hardly anyone managed to reach the College for Midnight Mass, and those who did were marooned there for several days. Worse was to come: on 2 January, the master reported,

> a furious easterly wind laid all level; several houses were overturned, others totally disappeared under mountains of snow; no less than 12 staks of corn were driven, God knows where, in this neighbourhood alone . . . I was the other day somewhat diverted at the melancholy sight, of people's seeking by means of long poles, a sheep cote which after an hour search they found out: only four of the sheep were lost tho' they were nigh four days buried under.[9]

The weather hardly improved through March and April, as if it was determined to make the people emigrate, the master joked; for his part, he would happily move anywhere, providing it was southward! One of his boys, Sandy Barclay, had taken ill with coughing fits in the autumn, and had been "bedfast" since Christmas, his health certainly damaged by the snell damp of the Braes. Mr Farqharson sent him home to Fochabers at the beginning of April to recuperate, fearing he was threatening Consumption,[10] and remembering Mr Paterson's death of TB at Scalan only the year before.

His own health too had "visibly decayed" since coming to the seminary, between the coughs and colds that never left him and the cares and trials of his work. At first he had "even dispair'd of ever putting up with Scalan," but he had gradually learned to cope with the conditions and ignore his cough, and by the summer he felt on top of the work at last. "Length of time has rendered me <u>myself</u> again, and I now begin to blush for what I then was", he confessed to Bishop Geddes; "my present situation has a deal of uneasiness attending it, but is far from being disagreeable to my turn of mind, could I but keep things right & tight".[11] The boys were a pleasure and making good progress, and, as the corn rose in the fields, he was coming to love his new life.

And then in July he received completely unexpected news. He was to be sent back to Douai, to be Rector of the College. It was a promotion, certainly, but one that he did not relish. "I dread much my happy days are over", he told the bishop. He left almost at once after the Administrators' meeting, and was in his new post by September.[12]

He was succeeded by Mr Alexander ('Sawney') Farquharson, a second cousin from Lower Glenlivet, where some of the family still lived at Minmore. Alexander Farquharson had received his early training for the priesthood under John Paterson at Scalan, and had then spent eight years at the Scots College in Rome, where he had been ordained earlier that year: Scalan was his first post on the Mission.

He immediately ran into trouble with his fellow tenants of Scalan farm. They had not given up their dispute regarding the seminary's share of the rental, and they perhaps thought that they would be able to squeeze more out of a newcomer. If so, they didn't know their man. He refused outright to meet their demands. They then presented a petition to the Duke against him, but His Grace – remembering his promises to Bishop Geddes – "threw their petition to the door" and reprimanded them severely, warning that if any of them raised any further complaint he would "not get a furrow in his intrest", and instructing the factor to "remove" any who gave the master trouble. At the same time he confirmed the status of the 'Park' on the east side of the Crombie as being a gift from one of his forebears, with security during his lifetime. Finally, he promised Mr Farquharson that whenever he had it in mind to slate the roof of the seminary he would instruct the local tenants to carry the slates up to Scalan from whatever quarry he chose.[13]

The Duke visited the seminary in January (1785), and the master no doubt discussed the slating of the roof with him then. The project would have had appeal to both of them: to His Grace, who made it his business to encourage improvements to the farms and property on his estates, and to the new master, whose mind was already running ahead to ambitious plans for Scalan. Mr Farquharson was aware that, in the freer atmosphere that now prevailed in Scotland, the bishops had begun a church building programme on the Mission and that slate-roofed churches were already being built or planned.[14] He must have felt that this was an opportune moment, armed with the support of the Duke, to approach them with his own plans for the seminary.

In April he made the first of a number of requests for money when he asked Bishop Geddes to send him £20 to buy in timber and other building materials.[15] He used them to build a new kitchen on the south side of the yard, most likely converting one of the existing barns there.[16]

At about this time Bishop Hay started a Mission building fund from a grant of £100 that he had recently received.[17] This gave him greater freedom to support projects, and he agreed to new proposals that Mr Farquharson now put to him, for further extensive work to be started in the spring of 1786, at an estimated cost of £50.[18] It was to involve interior work on the house, and slating of the outbuildings, including the one being converted into a kitchen on the south wing (Plate 6).[19]

By the time the work was due to start Bishop Geddes, as Procurator, was already becoming concerned at the rapid diminution of his funds, and Bishop Hay himself was beginning to fear that they had been "premature in undertaking too much at once, especially, the renewal of Scalan". He was even thinking of cancelling the work. But early in March a near-disaster at the seminary put the whole matter in a quite new light. It was a nightmare that the community had always dreaded. A spark from a chimney landed in the thatch and set it ablaze. Master, boys and servants ran for ladders and poles, and with hay-forks and their bare hands frantically tore away the heather. Only the good fortune that the fire was spotted early, and the winter dampness still lingering, prevented a tragedy, as Bishop Hay himself reported:

> had they been a few minutes later in observing it, it would have been impossible to save the house; as it was they tirred [tore off] all the thatch, & were glad to save the divets [turf underlay].[20]

The fire did little serious damage, in fact: the divets had protected the timbers, so that the roof itself remained untouched and only required to be rethatched. But it was a stark warning, and the risk of future fires to a thatched building convinced Bishop Hay that a new roof was now "most necessary". He authorised work to be started immediately on slating the new kitchen and the other inhabited outhouses – as well as the interior refurbishment that the master had requested – with the intention of sanctioning the slate-work on the house itself as soon as funds allowed.

The masons began their work after Whitsun.[21] But Mr Farquharson was evasive regarding what was being done and spent. In a scribbled note to Bishop Geddes he excused his brevity, due to his being "on great hurry, having a great number of work men at home", and promised, "I will write you soon all my doing".[22] In June he wrote that the building was "pretty well advanced", that the masons were due to finish their work within three days, and the slaters within ten at most. He was confident that the house would be in "a torlable way" in time for the Administrators' meeting, "tho' not all finished above stairs". He also mentioned that he had altered some of the plan, though he did not give details. His casual attitude must have irritated and worried the bishop, as must his peremptory and cavalier tone in regard to money:

> Bring a good deal of cash along with you when you come north, I will need a good deal of money then, I think I was moderate enough in my last draught, considering Circumstances.[23]

He would not have used such words to Bishop Hay.

Bishop Geddes cleared all the outstanding bills for work on the house, and left him enough cash in hand to cover work still to be done, according to Mr Farquharson's estimate of costs.[24] But the master's figure turned out to be a wild guess, and he soon exceeded it, continuing to write out bills of promise to local tradesmen in the bishop's name during the autumn. He remained evasive as to the size of these debts, excusing himself from putting pen to paper because of ill health, and promising to send an exact account "in a few days".[25] But it was December before he finally sent full details of the overspend, which by now stood at over £31, with a request that the money be sent at once:

> I must draw upon you immediately for it. for they are pleaging me for it; and for to answer my work men was obligded to delay paying my meal, which I must pay this incoming week. You'll perhapps think my account extravegant . . .[26]

No doubt the thought did cross the bishop's mind.

The autumn's harvest had been "extraordinary bad", and with the prices of meal and fodder higher than ever there was every prospect that the people would face ruin in the coming year. A number of tenants in the district had still not paid the grassum on their 1784 tacks, two-and-a-half years on, and they had been warned that they must pay up or face eviction the following Whitsun. If this happened, Mr Farquharson believed that "the most part of the Brair's of Glenlivet would sett a begging".[27] He himself had clinched a deal with Leslie of Balquhain which guaranteed a supply of meal for seven years at a fixed price,[28] so that the seminary remained largely untouched by the distress all around. He was able to maintain a full house, and feed his students well, throughout the winter. "I & they live pretty snogg and contented", he told Bishop Geddes early in the new year, "plenty of meat and fire, and I assure you we spare neither".[29]

But his self-satisfaction was not shared by Bishop Hay, who considered him a poor manager, far too free with money, and – as a local man – "too much in the midst of his friends". The bishop in fact wanted him out of Scalan before more harm was done. He already had in mind a successor, Andrew Dason,[30] a former student of the College and a graduate of Valladolid, who was now in his second year at Shenval. In May he paid a visit to the Cabrach, where he broached the subject with Mr Dason, who declared himself willing to give Scalan a trial if required.[31] This clinched his decision that Mr Farquharson would go that summer.[32]

He travelled to Scalan in mid-July, to give himself time to gain a precise idea of the situation at the seminary and the state of the building work, before the Administrators' meeting. It did not take him long to realise that Mr Farquharson's rosy and uninformative reports had been camouflaging the real state of affairs. The signs of neglect were all too obvious. Of the building work scheduled for the spring and summer – the conversion of the kitchen on the north side of the yard into a chapel for use by the College and the local people – "scarce a single article" had been completed.[33] And the finances were in disarray:

I have made a more narrow inspection into all particulars, and I am sorry to say that I have found matters in a most disagreeable situation. On ballancing house accounts, all is expended, & he at least £10 in house debt himself, besides house accounts unpaid. At the same time no provisions in the house, everything run out; meal scarce what will serve till Martinmass; paper, sugar, spirits, wine, &ca. &ca. all at an end: and what is still worse, £20 to pay at Martinmass to Capt[n] Lesley, according to bargain, for meal already expended.[34]

Worse still, he found several other "very disagreeable things", which he was unwilling to put in writing, and which we may guess perhaps concerned misappropriation of funds. They only served to confirm the wisdom of his decision. (His suspicions concerning Mr Farquharson were later more than amply justified when he was accused of several forgeries. He was deprived of his faculties and departed for Rome in 1794, to avoid conviction which could have resulted in the death penalty.[35])

*   *   *

On 27 August Andrew Dason arrived from the Cabrach, and two days later Bishop Hay sent Mr Farquharson to take his place at the Shenval station. He himself stayed with the new master for a further week to appraise him thoroughly of the situation at the seminary, and what would be required to restore it to what it should be. He wrote out an action plan which he left with him on the understanding that it would be given a trial for one year, at the end of which the two of them would assess its success before having it "enacted into a fixed Rule." He believed that it would bring major savings in the costs of board and lodging. Mr Dason found the plan acceptable, but pointed out that he could hardly carry it out until all the remaining debts were cleared and the current building work was completed.

The bishop was happy to comply, and before leaving paid off all the known debts and exacted promises from the wrights and heatherers to return and complete their work on the chapel.[36] He gave £18 into Mr Dason's hand for autumn house expenses, and then felt he could depart, confident that the seminary was in the care of an honest man, and even seeing the hand of Providence in recent events, as "the necessary means to put this poor place on a proper footing for the future." His only concern was that the new master seemed depressed at the thought of being left on his own, and reluctant to work closely with the boys. He asked Bishop Geddes to give him all the support he could.[37]

Mr Dason was pitched in just as preparations were underway for the harvest season. By early October the little money he had been given was spent, and there was "neither Meal nor Malt" in the house. The masons had now returned, but there were only two of them and they seemed to be making almost no progress. The wrights, for all their promises, were not seen until November, and then Mr Dason had to dismiss them after three days because they were demanding more money than had been agreed.[38]

He was especially shocked at the state of the boys. They were "mostly all overrun, both with Itch and Lice" (which explains his reluctance to give them too close supervision), and "very unruly and far gone in a dissipated way"; but he believed that some of them at least were "naturally well inclined" and with proper care might be made useful subjects.[39]

The problem of their hygiene largely solved itself when Janet Rae left in October. She had been housekeeper for nearly seventeen years. For the past two she had been threatening to leave, and had finally handed in her notice for Martinmas, to everyone's relief. But a month before her leaving date she had a fierce quarrel with Meggie the under-servant girl, which ended with her walking out, cursing and swearing like a Dragoon. Mr Dason later learned that she had gone over to the Cabrach to keep house for Alexander Farquharson. He was happy to see the back of her, not least because he was almost sure that she had been the person responsible for recent petty thieving at the seminary. After her departure the house, and the boys, became much cleaner under Meggie's care.[40]

Martinmas was the time for payments, and Mr Dason wrote to Bishop Geddes several weeks in advance, giving him details of what would be required at that date, and asking him to make money available. Between outstanding bills, servants' wages, and essential purchases, he calculated that he would need no less than £84 Sterling, but since the sum was so great he invited the bishop to cancel any items he considered unnecessary.[41] Bishop Geddes sent him £40: he did not dispute his list, but proposed that some items be bought on credit – the plough oxen and the marts, for instance, which accounted for £20 – and so spread the outlay into the spring. This was not the encouragement Bishop Hay had asked him to give, and it touched a nerve with a man struggling against the odds. The master's response was curt and to the point:

> I have neither leisure nor convenience at present of showing how extreemly much you are a stranger to Country business in supposing that Cattle may be bought from an unknown person in an open Market for Credit; the rest of your solutions are something of the same nature: however in short, when money and necessaries are wanting I shall either dismiss the Boys, or leave them myself to provide for themselves.[42]

He wrote again in the new year, providing an even more detailed account of costs, justifying every item, and reminding the bishop "one final time" that he was restoring order and "making discipline flourish again" after his predecessor's neglect, and that he could do without harassment.[43]

The tone of these letters was not at all in character. They were the words of a man who felt that his efforts were not appreciated and his problems not understood. And of a master – not the first – who felt himself alone, with children and servants but no peers for company, at the depth of the year, amidst a lonely landscape and a "multiplicity of unfavourable circumstances".[44]

They were the words also of a sick man. He had contracted a violent cough and cold before ever coming to Scalan, and had been unable to shake them off since. Bishop Hay knew enough to suspect Consumption, and when he sought the advice of Dr Levingston in Aberdeen the specialist's diagnosis confirmed his fears. Horse-riding exercise and a diet of goats' milk were prescribed, but despite these measures Mr Dason grew daily weaker.[45] He was finally forced to heed advice and take a rest in a less harsh climate. At the end of January he rode down to Huntly, and stayed there a fortnight.[46] The break certainly raised his spirits and he was able to joke about his health in a cheery note to a fellow priest on his return – "I am not dead yet", he told him, "altho' nearer that period than when I wrote you last".[47]

His jest was truer than he knew. Shortly after Easter his local doctor examined him again and sent his observations to Aberdeen, where Dr Levingston concluded that his Consumption was far advanced, and that he must be relieved of the burden of Scalan without delay. Bishop Hay decided to move him in the summer at latest, but could see no easy way to replace him. He even toyed with the idea of putting Mr James Carruthers, the priest of Glenlivet, in overall charge of the house, which would have involved his supervising the boys from Ceannakyle over three miles away.[48] This would have been a disastrous solution, and fortunately Bishop Geddes talked him out of it.[49]

Towards the end of June Mr Dason left Scalan, and went across to the Cabrach to stay at the farm town of Bracklach, where he would be close to his relations. Bishop Hay left Aberdeen at the beginning of July to look after the seminary for a week or two until he and Bishop Geddes could meet to decide upon a successor. His journey took him through the Cabrach, and he took the opportunity to call at Bracklach, where he found Mr Dason somewhat better, though still far from being out of danger. He was cheered by what he saw, and even held out some hope that the young man might in time be able to resume his work at the seminary.[50]

His first action on reaching Scalan was to re-engage the tradesmen to resume their work on the new chapel, the former kitchen on the north side of the yard: the conversion had lain half finished and untouched since the previous autumn.[51] He remained at the seminary until the Administrators' meeting in August, which because of the problems at Scalan was this year held at Gibston.

Discussion at the meeting confirmed that there was not a single priest, "fit or not fit", who could be spared for Scalan, and it was finally agreed that he himself would remain on at least for the summer. This would allow him to "get matters to rights" before the arrival of a new master, while his authoritative presence would ensure that the building work was finished promptly.[52]

Early in August Mr Dason moved into his relatives' home at Haddoch on the far side of the Cabrach, for it had become clear that he was dying. Bishop Hay realised that his own stay at Scalan was going to be more prolonged than originally planned. But this would at least bring certain benefits, as he explained to the Scots Agent in Rome:

Besides the necessity of the case, the advantages we expect from this plan are these. 1°. I will see from experience at what rate matters can be managed here so as to produce the ends we expect from it. 2°. By cutting off all superfluous expences, I shall lay a plan for future economy, & 3°. By paying a handsome board for myself, we will be better enabled to relieve its present burden.[53]

Under his eye the masons completed their work on the chapel walls that month, and the wrights and heatherers made a start on the roof. On 1 September he set out for Aberdeen to tidy up his affairs there, bringing Mr Guthrie up from Mortlach to oversee the tradesmen. This humble and much-loved priest was an old friend of the seminary from his days in Glenlivet and, as a trained and accomplished carpenter, the ideal man to keep an eye on the wrights.[54]

While Bishop Hay was still on the road he heard the news of Mr Dason's death; he was barely twenty-four.[55] He only spent eight days in Aberdeen, for he was anxious not to allow things to slip again at Scalan.[56] After a hurried visit to the Enzie he was back at the seminary by 19 September.

As bishop, his influence upon the seminary – his practical support for Mr Dason and Mr Paterson, for instance, and his decisive action in replacing John Thomson and Alexander Farquharson – had already proved crucial, enabling it to grow and to survive crises unscathed. No bishop, unless Bishop Gordon, had offered such telling leadership. Now he was to lead it directly, as master. He already knew that his stay would not be a matter of mere weeks as he had first thought. But he could hardly have imagined that he was to be tied to Scalan for the next five years.

NOTES

1. Bishop Geddes to John Reid, 30. 8. 1783, BL.
2. Student Register, in Account Book for Scalan, 1771-87, CS 1/6 (a), pp. 161-4, SCA.
3. Bishop Geddes to John Thomson, 19. 12. 1783, BL. The Duke also renewed the tacks of the priests at Ceannakyle, Findron, Mortlach and Gibston. He had been influenced by Abbé Peter Grant, who had returned earlier in the year after 45 years as Agent in Rome.
4. Arguments betwixt Duke and Tacksmen re lease of 19 years from 1784, Sept. 1783, CR 8/145, p. 29, SRO. Rental for the Croft was £2/10/- p. a. The arrangement involved no hardship to the previous occupier, William McKay, who was guaranteed land on Eskiemullach farm as one of the conditions of that farm's new tack. (Was this the same Willy McKay who had been the servant lad at Scalan from 1776-81?)
5. Ibid.; and Duke Gordon Estates, Rentals 1791-1803, Lordship of Glenlivet, CR 6/2, ff. 41-2, SRO.
6. Tack of 1767-84, GD 44/23/3/77, SRO; John Farquharson to Bishop Hay,

12 .3. 1784, BL; Tack of 1784-1803, Scalan, GD 44/23/4/36, SRO; and List of Grassums Payable on Duke of Gordon Estate, 1784, GD 44/51/194/1, SRO. The total rental for Scalan-and-Tomnalienan had been £41/13/4; the new rental for Scalan alone was now set at £30, plus one wedder, services, and £30 grassum. The seminary's total rental was £2/3/4 p. a.

7. John Farquharson to Bishop Geddes, 8. 1. 1784, BL.
8. John Farquharson to Bishop Hay, 12. 3. 1784, BL.
9. John Farquharson to Bishop Geddes, 8. 1. 1784, BL.
10. John Farquharson to Bishop Geddes, 5. 5. 1784, BL.
11. John Farquharson to Bishop Geddes, n.d. (summer 1784), BL.
12. John Farquharson to Bishop Geddes, 18. 7. 1784; and ditto, from Douai, 4. 10. 1784, BL.
13. Alexander Farquharson to Bishop Hay, 4. 2. 1785, BL.
14. Re churches recently opened, see Johnson C. *Developments in the Roman Catholic Church in Scotland 1789–1829* (Edinburgh, 1983), p. 153.
15. Alexander Farquharson to Bishop Geddes, 26. 4. 1785, BL.
16. Payments to masons and wrights in autumn 1785, 'Account Book for Scalan', 1771-87, CS 1/6 (a), SCA.
17. Bishop Hay to Bishop Geddes, 29. 4. 1786, BL.
18. Bishop Hay to Bishop Geddes, 20. 4. 1786, BL, quoting a letter from Alexander Farquharson.
19. Alexander Farquharson to Bishop Hay, 6. 3. 1786, re slating; and to Bishop Geddes, 8. 12. 1786, re liming walls; BL.
20. As for note 16.
21. As for note 17.
22. Alexander Farquharson to Bishop Geddes, 15. 5. 1786, BL.
23. Alexander Farquharson to Bishop Geddes, 19. 6. 1786, BL.
24. Ibid., and Bishop Hay to Bishop Geddes, 4. 6. 1786, BL.
25. Alexander Farquharson to Bishop Geddes, 19. 11. 1786, BL.
26. Alexander Farquharson to Bishop Geddes, 8. 12. 1786, BL.
27. Ibid.
28. Alexander Farquharson to Bishop Geddes, 24. 5. 1785 and 21. 6. 1785, BL.
29. Alexander Farquharson to Bishop Geddes, 19. 2. 1787, BL.
30. Bishop Hay to Bishop Geddes, 30. 1. 1787, BL. Re his criticisms of Alex. Farquharson, Bishop Hay to Bishop Geddes, 20. 6. 1787, BL. I use the spelling of Mr Dason's name that he himself used.
31. Andrew Dason to Bishop Geddes, 28. 5. 1787, BL.
32. Bishop Hay to Bishop Geddes, 20. 6. 1787, BL.
33. Bishop Hay to Bishop Geddes, 4. 8. 1787, and n.d. (August 1787), BL.
34. Bishop Hay to Bishop Geddes, 3. 9. 1787, BL.
35. Cf. Canon Clapperton's commentary on the *Book of Zaknim*, in Anderson W. J. (ed.) 'The College for the Lowland District of Scotland at Scalan and Aquhorties: Registers and Documents', *IR*, vol. xiv, no. 2, autumn 1963, Appendix V, pp. 148f. After years of wandering in Europe and South America Alexander Farquharson died in poverty in London in 1811.
36. He reckoned that the work would use up £10-£12 of the £30 remaining in his Mission Fund – Bishop Hay to Bishop Gordon, 3. 9. 1787, BL.
37. Bishop Hay to Bishop Geddes, 23. 9. 1787, BL.

38. Andrew Dason to Bishop Geddes, 18. 10. 1787; and to Bishop Hay, 8. 1. 1788, BL.
39. Andrew Dason to Bishop Hay, 28. 10. 1787, BL.
40. Ibid., and Andrew Dason to Bishop Geddes, 1. 11. 1787, BL.
41. Andrew Dason to Bishop Geddes, 18. 10. 1787, BL.
42. Andrew Dason to Bishop Geddes, 13. 11. 1787, BL. Re the £40: 'Various Accounts, 1787–99', entry for 13. 11. 1787, CB 6/1, SCA.
43. Andrew Dason to Bishop Geddes, 6. 1. 1788, BL. The bishop paid £30 promptly – CB 6/1, SCA, entry for 4. 2. 1788.
44. Andrew Dason to John Reid, 26. 11. 1787, BL.
45. Bishop Hay to Bishop Geddes, 23. 6. 1788; and to John Thomson, 11. 8. 1788; and Andrew Dason to John Reid, 30. 12. 1787; and to Bishop Hay, 8. 1. 1788, BL.
46. Andrew Dason to John Reid, 22. 1. 1788; and to Bishop Geddes (from Huntly), 4. 2. 1788, BL.
47. Andrew Dason to John Reid, 17. 2. 1788, BL.
48. Bishop Hay to Bishop Geddes, 23. 6. 1788, BL. He also planned to place John Anderson, who was not an ordained priest, in residence and in charge of the boys' studies.
49. By implication, Bishop Hay to Bishop Gordon, 11. 8. 1788, BL.
50. Bishop Hay to Bishop Geddes, 6. 7. 1788, BL.
51. Bishop Hay to John Thomson, 11. 8. 1788, BL.
52. Ibid.
53. Ibid. He did indeed pay a "handsome board" – £20 Sterling per annum: 'Various Accounts', CB 6/1, SCA.
54. Mr Guthrie had been sent to the less isolated station at Mortlach after having a leg amputated. There he did sterling work for some years, getting about as best he could on what he called his "tree leg" and always putting his own needs last. In his incapacity he was sometimes on the edge of starvation. Mr Paterson more than once slipped him money during his time as master – 2 guineas from his own quota in 1770, for instance (John Paterson to Bishop Hay, 25. 12. 1770, BL) – and even bought hand-made vestments from him (for Mr Guthrie was also a skilled clothes-maker) when the College had no real need of them, simply to put bread into his mouth.
55. Bishop Hay to Bishop Geddes, 4. 9. 1788, BL
56. Before leaving he gave precise instructions for the delivery of his effects, including bed and bedding, six leather chairs, table linen, his books, and a map of Cook's voyages for use in the classroom – Bishop Hay 'Furniture to be sent to Scalan', 1788, CS 1/1/15, SCA.

17

'Upon a Proper Footing' (1788–1793)

If Bishop Hay's first impression of Scalan had been one of shock at the damage caused by recent mismanagement, yet he immediately recognised its potential if managed well. "Since ever I came to this place," he later recalled,

> I have thought that it might be turned out to much better accor. that [*sic*] it has been; and that if we could get its income sufficient for twelve or upwards, we might both supply foreign shops and bring up some here also to the highest.[1]

As his words imply, he was already envisaging it as an all-through seminary (in accordance with Bishop Gordon's original intention), at least for some students. In this his thinking was certainly influenced by the situation at the Scots College Rome at this time. Since 1773, when the Society of Jesus had been disbanded, the College had been governed by a succession of ineffective Italian Rectors, and its teaching had been in the hands of Propaganda, whose syllabi ill matched the students' needs. In 1782 his own nominee for Rector, the former Scalan master Mr John Thomson, had been passed over by the Cardinal Protector in favour of the man in post, Francesco Marchioni. After the death of the long-serving Scots Agent Abbé Peter Grant two years later, Mr Thomson had remained in the city as his successor, where the simmering acrimony between himself and Marchioni further damaged the College. Its state had by now fallen as low as in the worst days at the beginning of the century,[2] so low that the bishops had been forced to stop sending students. The Cardinal Protector responded by withholding the legacy of King James set aside for Scalan.[3]

In this state of deadlock the College hardly seemed to have a future; and if not, might not Scalan be developed to take its place? It was a possibility that Bishop Hay shared with his Co-adjutor:

> Our boys at Prop^da [Propaganda] have had very ill luck; oh what a Change in our regard in that city! we miss the good old Gentleman [Abbé Peter Grant], that was always while he lived our friend & Protector; God's will be done! who knows but Scalan may yet turn out to be of some good service in its place?[4]

He knew that it would be at least three years before new ordinations would afford him the luxury of appointing a new master, and that in the meantime he himself would probably be tied there. But he resolved to make a virtue of necessity and use the time well. If Scalan was to fulfil the task he had in mind, it would need a "thorough reformation . . . both as to external & internal" to set it "upon a proper footing again", and he was determined to undertake this himself, however long it took.[5] He must have known that only he in all the Mission had the authority and the ability to achieve it, and this knowledge clinched his determination to stay.[6] It was a measure of the man, and to his great credit, that he saw the crucial importance of Scalan to the Scottish Mission so clearly and was ready to commit himself to it – even if (as we shall see) it also suited himself to do so.

He soon saw from personal experience that changes would be needed to the house, if it was to serve the purpose he had in mind. It was in fact during his first winter at Scalan – a mortally cold one, when the boys were hardly able to venture outdoors, and the lack of space tried everyone's nerves to the limit – that he decided to extend the building.

He may have had another issue in mind also. He must have been deeply concerned by the deaths from TB of two of Scalan's masters in the past five years, and – it has recently been suggested [7] – as a medical man he may have suspected that the house's low upstairs rooms, without ceilings and immediately under a roof of thatch, presented a health hazard.

His solution to both problems was to expand not outwards but upwards: to raise the roof, so creating much more space in the upstairs rooms by eliminating the sloping rafters, and allowing the addition of an attic to accommodate a new dormitory (Plate 8), (see Fig. 3). There is no conclusive documentary evidence for the date of this extension, but the date that best fits the circumstantial evidence is 1788-89, for the Accounts for this financial year record the purchase of quantities of wooden deals and window glass, and large-scale hire of masons and heatherers "helping with the roof."[8]

Since the time of the fire it had been his intention to have the roof slated, and this extension would have provided the obvious opportunity. But two major works were beyond the Mission's means, and a choice had to be made between them. He decided that slating was the lower priority and would need to wait. The kitchen, which presented the greatest fire hazard, was in a separate building, and already slated. And as to the house itself, his own experience that first winter, when fires, candles and crusie lamps were in fullest use, may have convinced him that it presented no real hazard, given strict safety regulations and good discipline. So the thatched roof remained, and would in fact serve the house without

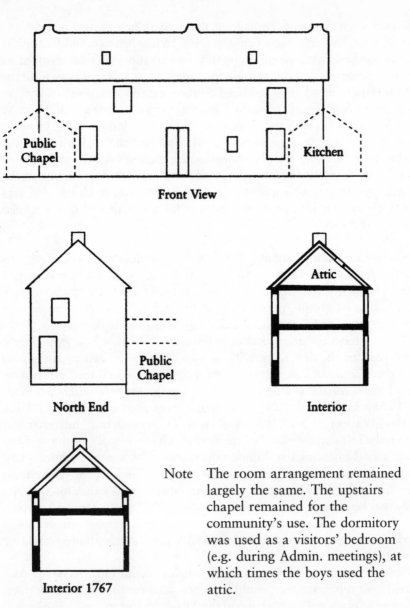

Front View

North End

Public
Chapel

Interior

Attic

Interior 1767

Note   The room arrangement remained largely the same. The upstairs chapel remained for the community's use. The dormitory was used as a visitors' bedroom (e.g. during Admin. meetings), at which times the boys used the attic.

Fig. 3. Seminary House, extensions of 1788–9.

Based on Dean A. and Taitt M. 'Scalan Reconstructed: Architectural and Documentary Evidence', *IR*, vol. xlvi, no. 1, Spring 1995, espec. p. 38

mishap for a further sixty years, until finally replaced with slates in the mid-nineteenth century, long after its seminary days were over.[9]

Bishop Hay was wont to call Scalan his 'Patmos', after the home-in-exile of St John the Evangelist, but if so it was a place of willing exile for him. Nearly a decade before, at the height of anti-Catholic fervour in Edinburgh, he had first used it as a retreat from the city, where he could find health and strength again walking in the hills and bathing in the Crombie. Now he welcomed the chance to make his home in it, after years living with the pressures of public life. And he found that the Braes climate suited his health admirably. If his first winter was wickedly cold, his second turned out to be the mildest in living memory, and after experiencing both he felt that his health was better at Scalan than it had been for many years.[10]

He discovered that he could fulfil his episcopal duties well enough from his upland retreat, and the care of the boys he found a "very agreeable amusement." At his time of life, in fact, Scalan seemed the very place to end his days in this world and ready himself for the next -

I have nothing else to apply to, but to prepare for the change which is daily approaching; and my present situation, is as much adapted to that as any other place I could be in, in the whole Mission.[11]

He had become deeply disenchanted with the world that man had made. The French Revolution in particular had been a profound shock to him, spreading a spirit of irreligion and iconoclasm throughout Europe. He confessed himself "more and more inclined" to believe that it was the beginning of the cataclysm foretold in *Revelation,* and that even now "preparation was making for the last Period of time".[12]

Meantime his "thorough reformation" of Scalan was progressing more quickly than he had dared hope. By the spring of 1790 his first two boys, William Catanach and John Gordon, were ready for the Scots College Rome, now open to students again. William was just turned thirteen, and John only ten, and they had only lately made their first Communions. They set out for Edinburgh in May, accompanied by old Robert Cummin, the father of John Cummin the Scalan servant. These were anxious times, and war with France threatening, and Army pressgangs were known to be out on the roads, ready to waylay boys even as young as these two. They were safe with Robert, and he was too old to be pressganged.[13]

In the autumn a third student, Sandy Badenoch, was sent to the Scots College Douai. But the French Revolutionary parliament had introduced measures against the Church that summer which cast doubt over the future of both Douai and Paris. With the situation in France uncertain, and less than ideal at Rome, Bishop Hay believed that it was time to set the Scottish Mission "on an independent footing", to ensure its survival whatever the outcome in Europe.[14] He wanted it to be independent not only in providing and training its own priests, but as far as possible financially, for he knew too well what it was to rely on grants that might be withheld at whim. His intention in future was to seek sponsors within Scotland, and make judicious investments with the Scottish banks, some of them specifically in Scalan's name.[15] It was a policy that the Mission would continue to pursue during his lifetime, and that finally began to lift the Church – and the seminary – out of the poverty that had dogged them until now.

His vision of making Scalan a model of excellence covered every aspect of college life, including what today would be called the living and learning environment. As well as extending the house he took steps to improve its interior, and in particular the new chapel as its spiritual hub. Almost his first act on arrival was to send for a painting of Christ, an *Ecce Homo*, from his old home in Blackfriars Wynd, to form the altar piece. Later he purchased a carpet, and had a large wooden tabernacle made up by a local carpenter.[16]

He also sought to enhance the land on which the College stood. There was a large, almost rectangular area within the Park that had been enclosed with a dyke some years before, as the estate map of 1774 shows clearly (Map 8). A walk-way was now created along the perimeter of this area, which later came to be known as 'the Bishop's Walk', because he took his exercise on it and, it is said, composed some of his published works as he strolled there. Its long straight lines and hedge of trees were more in keeping with the Park of a contemporary Lowland demesne than with the bare windy saucer of the Braes.[17] The remnants of it survive today (Plates 4 and 16).

The Accounts for 1789 record that he also purchased a sundial for the garden beside the house. This became the subject of an apocryphal story, which is worth retelling in that it seems to sum up the strange incongruity that the College must have presented in the district. It is said that once when he was deep in the study of his books he asked the servant girl to find out the time for him from the sundial. She went out to the garden, walked round it several times and considered it awhile, not knowing what to make of it, but knowing that his request must be obeyed. She finally picked it up and struggled indoors with it, so that he could read it for himself.[18]

He must have been deeply engrossed, for he apparently had not thought to refer her to the clock in the living room. It was a fine tooled brass alarm that had been in the seminary's possession for twenty years, and may now be seen on display at the Blairs Museum near Aberdeen (Plate 11).

He took an equal interest in the seminary farm and worked closely with John Williamson, his excellent and open-minded manager, in developing it.[19] He had himself studied the principles of agriculture in some depth, and actually wrote a lengthy paper covering every aspect of the subject while he was master. From it we learn that in his time Scalan became something of an experimental farm, where scientific "trials" were carried out with a view to improving productivity.[20] In the tradition of the medieval monasteries, the seminary was setting an example to its contemporaries in modern and efficient agriculture.

Advances in both horticulture and agriculture in eighteenth century Scotland – the creation of parks and landscaped gardens according to aesthetic canons, and the development of efficient farms on scientific principles – were part of the 'improving' impulse of the Enlightenment, in which the great landowners of the Lowlands were the vanguard.[21] Bishop Hay was himself a son of the Enlightenment, and the enhancement of the seminary's land in his time was, in small, driven by the very same purpose as theirs – to provide a gracious environment, to tame the wild, to make the land productive, and to create order and beauty in a barren place.

Limited though they were, these improvements would still have been beyond the Mission's pocket if they had all been carried out by specialist labour. But in fact he made use of the boys wherever possible, under the supervision of hired specialists, for new dyking, ditching and planting, for instance, as well as for the routine agricultural work of winning the peats, manuring, sowing and helping with the harvest. Each student was expected to give about ten days a year to such work, which he justified on the grounds that it was necessary in order to ensure a future for Scalan, but beyond the College's means if undertaken entirely by hired hands. Although he came in for severe criticism for these "avocations", he was able to prove that they did not interfere in the least with the students' academic progress.[22]

His first concern of all, indeed, was to raise academic standards. We can gain some insight into the curriculum in his day from his teaching notes,[23] his own works, and the textbooks in use. The core of the syllabus remained the four year course of Classics, with religious subjects including Scripture, Catechism and Spiritual writings, while 75 minutes per day were devoted to Arithmetic. The senior students (the 'Theology' class) were expected to supervise the Classics students, and to help, hear and test them. They also learned Italian, in preparation for Rome (as earlier generations had learned French in readiness for Paris).

Among the textbooks in use for the Divinity syllabus [24] were Ray's

Wisdom of God in the Creation and Durham's *Physico Theology* and
Astro Theology, which integrated the latest findings of Science within a
God-centred philosophy. These would have been used alongside Bishop
Hay's own writings on the subject, and in particular his manuscript
Elements of Metaphysics, which was written while he was master for use
as the standard general Philosophy text.[25] It was a wide ranging work, in
which Metaphysics was interpreted to include branches as various as
Ontology, Logic, Natural Theology and Psychology. Its breadth, and its
attempt to effect a synthesis of diverse elements, reflected his own
education, first at Edinburgh in the early days of the Scottish Enlightenment, and then in the progressive and stimulating milieu of the Rome of
the '50s, where John Geddes was his fellow student. The eclectic philosophy of his *Elements* and other works presented a synthesis of the two
traditions,[26] and the Scalan Philosophy syllabus based upon them was no
doubt similarly at once Scottish and Roman.

We can infer from the reference books and equipment in use that
History, Geography and Cosmology were also taught. Bishop Hay's
course notes for the latter have survived, and we know that he had an
astronomical ring dial sent to Scalan as a visual aid for them. For
Geography he purchased a globe, to add to the map of Cook's Voyages
that he himself brought with him.[27] And among the historical texts in use
were source books of ancient and also modern (including Scottish)
history.[28]

The approach to the curriculum was probably not noticeably different
from that of seventy years before. Its secular elements still mirrored those
of the traditional Scottish Grammar Schools, and were little touched by
the new Academies that had opened in several parts of the country in the
past two decades, where courses were being offered in Applied Mathematics, Physics, Chemistry and Technical Drawing. The Academies were
also developing new teaching methods, including the use of such visual
aids as solid Geometric shapes, and it was perhaps through their influence
that Bishop Hay ordered a set of Conic Sections for Scalan.[29]

We know something of the Scalan library also, because many of its
holdings have survived and form part of present day collections. From the
inscriptions on them there appears to have been a tradition of masters
bequeathing some of their own books to it when they left, which must
have been prompted by Bishop Gordon's bequest of his own books and
those of Bishops Nicolson and Wallace in 1745 (cf., p. 89). William
Duthie bequeathed at least twenty-three volumes, John Geddes some
fourteen, and John Thomson, John Paterson, William Gray and John
Farquharson all made smaller bequests. The library now contained
several hundred volumes in all, the greatest number of them in Latin,

but with French well represented and a smaller number in Italian and English. Some were rareties even in Bishop Hay's day, for the earliest were incunabula from the sixteenth century and many others had been printed before 1700.[30] As might be expected, most were religious or spiritual, but secular subjects were not neglected: Rossi's *Engravings of Antient Rome*, Cornelius Nepos' *Lives of Illustrious Men*, the Works of Erasmus and Isaac Newton, Johnston's *Delitiae Poetarum Scotarum*, and a Hebrew Dictionary are among the many texts that have survived. They give some small hint of the admirably broad, catholic learning that was fostered at Scalan – as indeed it was in the Scots Colleges abroad at this time – and which would remain a hallmark of the Scottish seminaries that succeeded Scalan in the nineteenth century.[31]

Just as it is impossible to compare Scalan exactly with contemporary Scottish Grammar Schools or Universities, or with the senior seminaries abroad, since it was none of these yet had something of all of them, so we cannot make any exact comparison of its library with contemporary libraries. It was certainly far superior to almost all the Grammar School libraries of its time. An idea of the small size of the latter may be gained from the grants of £10 made by the burgh councils of Dunfermline and Kirkudbright to establish libraries in their schools in the eighteenth century, while even in an institution of such antiquity and prestige as the Aberdeen Grammar School the library remained small and neglected until well after 1800.[32] By comparison, Scalan's excellent library was quite remarkable for its time and place. It was a tribute to the enlightened educational philosophy, the devotion, and the sheer love of learning of successive masters. And it symbolised, perhaps as well as anything, that "strange blending of culture and poverty, of city and croft" that for over eighty years was the Scalan in the Braes.[33]

The standards of behaviour were also tightened at this time. We know that a monitor system was in use in Scalan's last years, and it would be in character that this was introduced, or certainly developed, in Bishop Hay's time. We know too that the boys' traditional household tasks were now put on a more formal rota basis: they included serving at table, sweeping, tidying the dormitory, and ringing the bells which divided the day. There was apparently also a rota of *ex-lectors*, that is (presumably) boys deputed to read aloud at meal times.[34]

But if life under the strict and sometimes dour Vicar Apostolic was perhaps not just such fun for the boys as under several of his predecessors, he certainly did not neglect their recreation. After the first winter, when they had been cooped up in the house for days on end, he sent for games equipment suitable for use indoors – a set of shuttlecocks and battledores, which Bishop Geddes bought at one of the new toy shops in Edinburgh.[35]

They must have converted the main study into a court by pulling the furniture to the walls, and at first they had to make do with chairs for a net. But the game proved so popular that a proper net was purchased for them later,[36] which suggests that they may also have played outside in the summer, probably in the shelter of the yard, or even on 'the Green', the grassy area bounded by 'the Bishop's Walk'.

Bishop Hay was himself an example for the students to aspire to, whether in scholarship or in pursuit of their daily lives. Tall, lean and ascetic, he was always the first to rise and the last to retire at night. His narrow box-bed with its thin mattress, which was said to resemble a coffin, seemed to sum up the man.[37] His day was divided between work and prayer, with a frugality that matched his frugal diet. The one 'weakness' that he allowed himself was chewing tobacco, and even this was not for pleasure: he had long been a martyr to violent headaches, and having tried every possible remedy to no effect he had discovered that chewing eased the pain. But he considered it an ugly practice.

Endowed with a powerful intellect and formidable energy, he wrote prolifically during his days at the College on subjects both practical and speculative. But he allowed neither his studies nor any other duty to come before his supervision of the boys. If any of them was sick he thought it no trouble to sit for hours at his bedside. And at nights he would sit in the candle light in his long blue and red tartan reading gown, and have the boys pull the benches forward and gather round for stories, of the old days or perhaps of his memories of tending the wounded at the battle of Prestonpans.[38]

In setting standards for every aspect of life at Scalan he was following the principles of his predecessor Bishop Gordon, whose vision was always that the seminary should be a match for the Colleges abroad, but now with added urgency, since there seemed to be a real chance that it might soon have to take their place. If he was not the first he was certainly an outstanding example of a Church leader who believed in excellence in education, in its secular as well as its religious aspects. To him, only the best was good enough – a concept and a tradition that can still find echoes in Scottish Catholic education today. His term as master was Scalan's apogee.

But his influence also extended far beyond the boundaries of the College. There was probably no-one in the Braes other than himself trained in Medicine at this time. The health of both humans and animals had always been a matter of self-help, based on traditional herbal remedies, or in the case of serious and lingering disease, recourse to the folk healers and the supernatural.[39] When in need, the people had been used to visiting the holy wells of St Michael or St Fergus in the neighbouring parish of Strathavon, or even the famed healer and diviner Gregor Willox, who lived at Tomintoul and whose medical aids included a charm stone and a kelpie's bridle ring.[40] Now they could visit Scalan and receive scientific help from the bishop, and without having to pay, because when he had first decided on the religious life he had made a vow never to take money for his medical knowledge. The poor, indeed, often went away from Scalan with money in their pocket, and it was said that some came with feigned illness in order to return home with alms. Many came from far beyond the Braes, for his fame soon spread.

Local traditions survived long after his death, of remarkable cures he performed at Scalan on victims of madness and possession,[41] and though no doubt embroidered over time they were in fact based on truth. There is certainly reliable evidence for two exorcisms carried out by him. In one a man was brought to him bound with ropes, whose guardians refused to untie him because of his violent fits. Bishop Hay released him, and performed the Rite of Exorcism, during which the man, who knew only Gaelic, was heard speaking to him in several languages. He was completely cured, and soon after converted to the Catholic faith. The second case concerned a woman brought to him by her husband. She is said to have remained calm throughout the rite, until the moment when he addressed her possessor in Latin with the formula 'Tell me your name', when she at once began to thrash about and struggle furiously, but subsided when he commanded her to kneel in the name of Jesus Christ. The same question, response, and command were repeated several times, until at last she was quiet. When the rite was over she walked home healed, and she also later embraced the Catholic faith.[42]

Down in Edinburgh Bishop Geddes was now overrun with work. Most of the pastoral duties in the city were falling to him, he was Procurator of the Mission, and he had episcopal responsibility as far afield as Galloway, Perthshire and Angus. For some years he had also been serving the small but growing Catholic communities in the Glasgow, Paisley and Greenock areas, where there was now urgent need for a resident priest.[43] He made his visits to these Western districts on foot.

He was in fact a wonderful walker, even for those days. In the summer of 1790 – despite his duties, or perhaps to escape them awhile – he undertook a journey to Orkney and back, alone and on foot. He carried with him little but a pack and a folding umbrella, the latest thing from the city. He took in Scalan on his return, and seems to have covered the road from John O'Groats to the Braes in ten days.[44] He arrived at the door of the seminary, where no doubt an admiring crowd of local children and grown-ups gathered to gaze wide-eyed, not at the bishop (for they could see one of those every day) but his folding umbrella.

His weeks on the road probably marked a turning point in his health, which began to decline that autumn. His burden of work was only made the heavier by Bishop Hay's being tied at Scalan. He saw the necessity of the arrangement, and made no complaint, but by the spring of 1791 the danger signals of exhaustion could be read between the lines of his letters.[45] Bishop Hay ruled out placing a priest in Glasgow, for there was none to be spared, but proposed to relieve him of some of his duties in Edinburgh. Meantime he advised him to cut down on his pastoral work, even if this meant reducing his effectiveness. "Your health is of too much importance to be exposed even to the danger of being hurt", he told him.[46]

The Scots Colleges at Paris and Douai were by now under severe threat. The Revolutionary Government were looking for an excuse to take them over, but Bishop Hay believed that they might yet be saved if an experienced and senior negotiator could be sent to Paris from Scotland. Bishop Geddes was the obvious choice, for his powers of gentle diplomacy had been amply proved in the past, and if anyone could charm the French authorities and soften the difficult Scottish Rector it was he. Much against his will he was unanimously appointed by his fellow Administrators, and Bishop Hay travelled down to the capital to take his place.

It was impossible to spare a priest to take his own place at Scalan, because the Lowland District already had eight stations unmanned. He was therefore forced to leave the house, the farm and the boys' welfare in the care of the servants, and put John Ingram, the most senior student whom he was grooming as an assistant, in charge of lessons.[47] He was all too well aware that with such makeshift arrangements standards were bound to slip. He had no idea how long Bishop Geddes would be away, nor was there any prospect of newly ordained priests returning from Rome or Valladolid to give him room for manoeuvre.[48] Within weeks his problem was made worse by the untimely death of Robert Menzies, the Scalan old-boy who was priest of the Edinburgh Gaelic chapel. Without his help Bishop Hay feared that his own burden in the capital might be beyond him: "How far I shall be able to undergo this Charge, I can not say," he warned the Scots Agent in Rome; "but undertake it I must, and if I fail, God's will be done".[49]

It was in fact seven months before Bishop Geddes' return freed him to resume at Scalan. On reaching the Braes he discovered – as he had feared – that the standards had slipped badly in his absence. One of the boys in particular, Jamie MacIntyre, had let himself down. He had been enjoying a close association with the under servant girl. When the bishop learned of it he had no choice but to dismiss her, and severely warn Jamie and some of his friends.[50]

Under the circumstances he decided to release John Ingram,[51] and wrote at once to Douai to ask for a replacement. Several of the students were in fact already on their way home from that College, where the situation was now precarious. One of those travelling was Andrew Carruthers, a younger brother of Mr James Carruthers the local priest at Ceannakyle. The family hailed from the small Catholic community that had existed for generations in the neighbourhood of New Abbey, beside the Solway Firth. Even as a little boy Andrew had seemed destined for the priesthood, and was referred to affectionately as 'the young priest' by his neighbours because of his serious and pious disposition. These qualities he now brought with him to Scalan when he joined the community as senior student and Assistant teacher.

Bishop Geddes' frail health had been further damaged by his travels in France, and now for the first time he was troubled by a severe rheumatism. His doctor believed that his only hope of improvement was to leave the cramped and smokey wynds of Edinburgh, and he strongly recommended that he do so without delay. Bishop Hay accepted the need, but pointed out the difficulty of moving him: one priest could hardly be left to cover the city alone; and besides, since Bishop Gordon's day it had always been the tradition that one of the bishops should have his residence in the capital. If not Bishop Geddes, then it must be himself. And if so, what would become of Scalan?

> At present it is only in embrio, and needs an attention to bring it to a bearing, which I fear could not be expected from any but one of ourselves. Even during my late absence at Edin^r. it suffered more than I could have expected.[52]

The only solution that he could suggest was for the two of them to exchange places. His Co-adjutor would certainly benefit from the country life, and he could have as much or little responsibility as he pleased "as the boys would be rather an amusement, having Mr Andrew [Carruthers] to take the drudgery part". He asked him to give the idea thought at least.

The two of them were also looking for a suitable successor for Mr John Thomson, the Scots Agent in Rome, who had recently died – his death apparently hastened by the bitter quarrels concerning himself and the Scots College. Their choice was Paul McPherson, the ex-Scalan boy from the Clash, who was at this time serving as the second priest in Edinburgh, and had recently taken on the responsibilities of Procurator of the Mission. The need to replace him in this duty, and Bishop Geddes' unfitness to take on the work, probably clinched the decision for them: the only possible solution was for the two bishops to change places.

It was important that Bishop Hay be in Edinburgh in good time to brief Paul McPherson before he set sail for Rome,[53] and because of this there would be a gap of a few weeks between his leaving Scalan and Bishop Geddes' arrival. There was no choice but to leave Andrew Carruthers in charge, though the young man did not relish the prospect of having sole responsibility, especially of the farm and the running of the house, for which he had no experience.

As to the farm, Bishop Hay reassured him that John Williamson would look after it from day to day, and simply keep him informed. He also arranged for the manager not to sow corn that spring, but turn the whole farm over to grass, which would "take most of the trouble off him".[54] The herd of cattle was kept on, but the concentration was on sheep. For the past four years the farm had been building up its flock, until now sales of wool and animals accounted for almost a third of the total income. With the outlay on sheep minimal – merely the seasonal hire of a herd-boy and occasional payments for shearing[55] – the profit margin was greater than in traditional agriculture, and Bishop Hay must have been tempted to concentrate permanently on sheep-rearing, in line with current thinking on farm economy.

He also convinced Mr Carruthers that he could leave domestic matters in the good hands of the housekeeper Annie Gerard, and that once Bishop Geddes arrived he would assume overall responsibility for everything.

Having reasonably satisfied his stand-in he felt he could leave with an easy mind. He drew up an account of the finances, exact to the last farthing, ready for his successor. He had always kept his own expenses scrupulously separate from the main account, and these he now squared, adding £2 Sterling by way of a parting donation.[56] At the end of July (1793) he set out for the South.

For all his precautions, things did not work out as planned in his absence. John Williamson took ill soon after his departure, leaving the farm in Mr Carruthers' inexperienced hands. The young master also ran into difficulties with the boys. The last of the Douai students had left France, and six of them had moved into Scalan to complete their studies there. It had been expected that their arrival would benefit the seminary, and that they would easily settle in, since five of them had begun their student days there. But they turned out to be a disruptive influence, contemptuous of the Spartan life of the Braes and resentful of the summer farm work that was expected of them.[57] Mr Carruthers had no idea how to handle them, and only fuelled their truculence.

He also succeeded in upsetting the servants, and especially Annie Gerard. With his earnest and devout idealism went a somewhat dogmatic and inflexible concern for how things ought to be, as yet untempered with the realism and discretion of experience, which easily created resentment in those under his authority. Annie Gerard, for her part, had firm ideas as to home economy – her menus were famed for their frugality – and she was not easily to be deflected from them.When Mr Carruthers wrote to Bishop Hay just days after taking charge, asking if it was "proper there should be any female power in a place of this kind", the bishop easily guessed that all was not well between him and the housekeeper, and warned his Co-adjutor in advance.[58]

When Bishop Geddes arrived, therefore, he had a few problems to tackle. Between the farm, ill-disciplined students, and a dissatisfied housekeeper, it must have reminded him all too closely of the first time he had arrived to replace Mr Gray as master thirty years before. Fortunately, John Williamson now returned to work. And Bishop Hay agreed to take the Douai students away, before they infected the rest of the boys.[59] The domestic problem was more difficult to solve, but Bishop Geddes spent the summer discreetly and patiently working on it, making allowances on both sides and careful not to undermine anyone's position. By the autumn he was able to report that as far as he could tell the disputes were at an end and "perfect harmony" reigned in the house.[60]

These things were achieved despite his own infirmity. His rheumatic pain was now severe and constant, affecting the side of his head as well as his limbs, and requiring the application of plasters twenty-four hours a day.[61] And the theory that he would rest at Scalan was simply not working. It was not in his nature. Even when there was no work to be done he created it. He took to busying himself with the seminary documents, which he wished to research and put into some order. Bishop Hay urged him to take more care of himself:

> I beg & beseech you for God's sake to lay aside all these projects, to lock up all your old papers, & to follow the plan I have always had in view for you.[62]

It would be enough if he confined himself to looking after the boys, and influencing them simply by his presence.

But his health continued to fail. His arms were stiffening , he could only with great effort hold his spoon or "put in or out a button", and his legs barely carried the weight of his body, so that he often had to hold onto the wall to save himself from falling. He could no longer dress himself. Pulling on his breeches, which for modesty's sake he was still determined to do for himself, would take him twenty minutes. He who three years before had walked the length of Scotland could now manage just a few steps for exercise in the garden, and that only if he kept his eyes facing straight ahead.[63]

On 29 September there occurred an incident that made a deep impression on him and was to be a watershed in his life. Since coming to Scalan he had been celebrating public Mass in the downstairs chapel, and this day, the feast of St Michael, he was ready and vested as usual. He spoke a few words to the congregation, but then felt his legs so weak and his left arm so stiff that he dared not proceed with the Mass. There was nothing he could do but send the people away to the chapel at Tombae.[64] He knew then that his own days as an active pastor were as good as over.

It was at this difficult time that the best side of Andrew Carruthers' character came into its own. His idealism and devotion showed themselves in his gentle, unstinting care of the sick man. He attended him "extremely to his satisfaction", acted as his amanuensis, and took on all the teaching work of the College without demur.[65]

Bishop Geddes was actually beginning to "fall into some thing of a method" at Scalan, and would have been content to live there to the end of his days, had his own happiness been the only issue to consider. But he believed that his presence was already more of a burden than a benefit, and that if he stayed he could only become "a considerable embarrassment to the place".[66] He also feared the Scalan winter, and felt that he should be nearer a Physician, though he frankly believed himself beyond medical help. Mr Carruthers could not be faulted, but he really needed a "person of a nursing disposition", able to give him constant care. He thought his own nephew John Gordon would be ideal for the task, if he was willing, and his home in Aberdeen as suitable a place as could be found.

John Gordon promised to do all in his power to make him comfortable if he came to stay in Aberdeen, and Bishop Hay supported the move and urged him to make it before the winter set in. Bishop Geddes therefore made arrangements without delay for a chaise to be sent out to Scalan. He knew he was racing the clock, and that it would only be a few weeks before he was entirely bedridden. Despite his pain he took trouble to draw up an exact account of the finances, after which he felt free to leave.

A week before the end of October the chaise was brought to Tombreckachie, eight miles down the glen, and he was carried to it in a cart. He departed knowing that the seminary was in a state of order and harmony, and happy in the thought that his own illness was a great blessing, since it gave him the chance to suffer penance for his sins and prepare for death. His only regret was that he had become so useless to his Vicar Apostolic and his country.[67]

*   *   *

Bishop Hay's own choice for his successor was James Sharp of Mortlach, who had studied at Scalan in his early teens under John Paterson – he was one of the trio who had endured the nightmare voyage to Flanders *en route* for Rome in 1782. After eleven years at the Scots College he had been ordained there that spring. The bishop thought him "an agreeable and sweet tempered lad", the kind of master the seminary needed after the experience of Mr Carruthers. He was presently serving in Edinburgh, but could be spared. Bishop Geddes was doubtful about the appointment, and counselled that he be kept for some time longer in the capital: he felt he lacked experience, and might not take easily to the stern life at Scalan so soon after his long sojourn in Rome.[68] But despite his Assistant's recommendation Bishop Hay decided to send him to Scalan at once.

As to Mr Carruthers, if sharing office with him had been delicate for Bishop Geddes, it was likely to be quite beyond an inexperienced new man. And if he stayed the servants would always suspect that Mr Sharp was being influenced by him.[69] Bishop Hay decided to send him to Aberdeen, to complete his training under the former Scalan master John Farquharson.[70] That way the new master would be given a clean start and the chance to put his own stamp on the college.

NOTES

1. Bishop Hay to John Thomson, 26. 10. 1790, BL.
2. Abbé Paul McPherson 'The History of the Scots College Rome (1600-1792)', 1810, CA 3/18, pp. 335ff., SCA (and printed by Anderson W. in *IR*, vol. xii, 1961, pp. 138ff.).
3. Ibid., pp. 349f. in MS. They also threatened to withhold the legacy set aside for Scalan's counterpart in the Highland District.
4. Bishop Hay to Bishop Geddes, 6. 10. 1788, BL.
5. Bishop Hay to John Thomson, 28. 7. 1789 and 2. 11. 1789, BL.
6. Knowing that he was to stay he took the opportunity to transfer the 'Weaver's Croft' from Mrs Gordon of Glastirim's name to his own, so strengthening the Church's hold on it by having it based on a contract – Parish of Inveraven, Rental of Croft of Eskmulloch to Mr Hay, 1791, GD 44/ 51/745/4/9, SRO.
7. Dean A. and Taitt M. 'Scalan Reconstructed: Architectural and Documentary Evidence', *IR*, vol. xlvi, no. 1, spring 1995, p. 49; my illustration of the extension (Fig. 3) is based on Dean and Taitt's account and illustration (p. 38).
8. 'Various Accounts', 1787-99, CB 6/1, SCA. Expenses recorded for 1788 include £6/15/- for heatherers, £8/-/- to the mason, and 12/1$\frac{1}{2}$ for glass and putty.
9. The roof was still thatched when Rev. J. Stothert visited in the 1840s, but slated when Canon W. Clapperton saw it c.1860.

10. Bishop Hay to Bishop Geddes, 6. 10. 1788; and to John Thomson, 28. 7. 1789 and 6. 4. 1790, BL.
11. Bishop Hay to John Thomson, 6. 4. 1790, BL.
12. Bishop Hay to John Thomson, 2. 11. 1789, BL.
13. Bishop Hay to Bishop Geddes, 24. 5. 1790, BL.
14. Bishop Hay to Bishop Geddes, 26. 10. 1790, and to Cardinal Albani, same date, (in Italian), BL.
15. Bishop Hay to Bishop Geddes, 23. 6. 1791, BL.
16. Re *Ecce Homo*, Bishop Hay to Bishop Geddes, 4. 9. 1788, BL; re carpet and tabernacle, 'Various Accounts', 1787-99, July 1790 and May 1791, CB 6/1, SCA.
17. It was still called 'the Bishop's Walk' when visited by Rev. J. Stothert in the 1840s.
18. Phillips J. G. *Wanderings in the Highlands of Banff and Aberdeen Shires* (Banff, 1881), p. 93; probably related to him by the tenant McGregor, who liked to tell visitors stories (some of them tall) regarding Scalan. Re purchase of sundial – 'Repairs of house and Place about Scalan', entry for 10. 6. 1789, 'Various Accounts', CB 6/1, SCA.
19. Bishop Hay to Bishop Geddes, 9. 8. 1793, BL.
20. Bishop Hay 'Notes on Agriculture', written in a Bell's 'Commonplace Book'; chaps. on vegetation, ploughing, harrowing, soils, manures, vegetables, grasses, grain, hay, oxen, etc. Re "trials", see p. 89; B GH 2/7, SCA.
21. See further pp.207f. below.
22. Bishop Hay to Bishop Geddes, 18. 8. 1793 and 30. 9. 1793, BL, where he justified the farm work, and 'proved' that it had had no ill effect on the boys' academic progress. The practice was however not continued at Aquhorties, the College that replaced Scalan, where it was expressly forbidden even during holidays or recreation time – cf., *Regulations for the Administration of the College of Aquhorties* (Edinburgh, 1799), p. 41. But something similar was re-introduced in later years at Blairs, the College that replaced Aquhorties in 1829, whose last Rector recalls boys being expected to help at the 'tattie howkin' ' on the farm, up to the time of its closure in 1986–verbal communication by Mgr J. McIntyre.
23. Bishop Hay 'Distribution of the Hours for Scalan', n.d., CS 1/1/14, SCA.
24. Re textbooks referred to in the present account, see 'Books to be sent to Mr Hay', CS 1/1/15, SCA; and Bishop Hay to Bishop Geddes, 4. 9. 1788 and 8. 2. 1791; and to John Thomson, 28. 7. 1789, 2. 11. 1789 and 6. 4. 1790; and Bishop Geddes to Bishop Hay, 24. 10. 1789, BL. Other texts included works of controversy such as *Butler Against Bower*; Antoine's *Moral Theology* and *Dogmatick*; spiritual writings including the works of Teresa of Avila in Italian; and more popular works such as *Pious Christian*, *Garden of the Soul* and *Spiritual Combat*.
25. Bishop Hay 'The Elements of Metaphysics', B GH 2/1 and 2/2, SCA.
26. Goldie M. 'Common Sense Philosophy and Catholic Theology in the Scottish Enlightenment', *Studs. on Voltaire and the Eighteenth Century*, no. 302, 1992; his article includes a discussion of Hay's 'Elements', and an appendix with a summary of its contents.

27. Bishop Hay to John Thomson, 6. 4. 1790; and Bishop Geddes to Bishop Hay, 24. 10. 1789, BL.
28. Including the *Selectae Historiae* of sacred and profane history; Rollins' *Antient History*, Goldsmith's *History of Rome* and Plutarch's *Lives*; and Knox's *History of Scotland*.
29. Bishop Hay to John Thomson, 26. 10. 1790, BL. Re the Academies, Scotland J. *The History of Scottish Education* (London, 1969), pp. 104ff.
30. Doughty D. 'Chapeltown, Braes of Glenlivet, and Tombae, the Debris of the Old Scalan Library', *Deeside Field*, 19, 1987; also, Cherry A. 'The Library of St Mary's College, Blairs, Aberdeen', *The Bibliotheck*, vol. 12. no. 3, 1984; and Ross A. 'Book Hunting in the Highlands', *St Peter's College Magazine*, vol. xix, no. 74, June 1950. Many of the surviving Chapeltown volumes, including 89 from the Scalan library, are now held at the Bishop's House, Aberdeen. Valuable items among the latter include Plutarch's *Lives* (parallel Greek and Latin texts; Lausanne, 1572); a 1543 edition of Cicero's *De Philosophia*; a 16C *Opuscula Quinque* of St Gregory of Nyssa; the *Homilies* of Johann von Eck (Paris, 1566); a text of Erasmus printed Antwerp, 1551; and a 16C edition of Suetonius' *Twelve Caesars*. The above are mentioned here merely to offer a taste: it would be a worthwhile task to build upon the work of Doughty, Cherry and Ross and attempt a more comprehensive listing of surviving works from the Scalan library, many of which are to be found among the 27000 volumes of the Blairs Collection on long-term loan at the NLS.
31. Re the Scots Colleges, cf. Moran P. A. 'The Library of the Scots College Douai', *IR*, vol. xliii, no. 1, spring 1992; and Halloran B. *The Scots College Paris 1603-1792* (Edinburgh, 1997), pp. 177-93. (Halloran describes the Paris library as "a magnificent achievement"). Re Scalan's successors, cf. Cherry A. *Op. cit.*, p. 66.
32. Grant J. *History of the Burgh Schools of Scotland* (London and Glasgow, 1876), pp. 436ff.
33. Doughty D. *Op. cit.*
34. John Gordon to ?, 5. 8. 1799,BL, comparing the régime at Aquhorties to that at Scalan: "We have no ex-lectors no serving at table no sweeping of the house &ca &ca, nay our beds are even made for us and I hear that the maid servants are also to ring the morning or first bell".
35. Bishop Hay to Bishop Geddes, 14. 9. 1789, BL.
36. 'Sundries', Complete Account, June-Nov. 1793, CS 1/1/7, SCA.
37. Based on Rev. A. Cameron's 'Life of Bishop Hay', Valladolid 1829, B GH 5/ 3, SCA.
38. Ibid., and evidence of the student Donald Carmichael; and memories of local people related to Rev. J. Stothert, in Gordon J. F. S. *Journal and Apppendix to Scotichronicon and Monasticon* (Glasgow, 1867), pp. 277 and 419.
39. Masson D. 'Popular Domestic Medicine in the Highlands Fifty Years Ago', *TGSI*, vol. xiv, 1887–8; there is an excellent summary of the most common contemporary Highland illnesses in Sinclair J. *Analysis of the Statistical Account of Scotland* (Edinburgh, 1825), pp. 127ff.
40. McPherson J. M. *Primitive Beliefs in the North East of Scotland* (London, 1929), espec. pp. 37ff. re local holy wells, and 260ff. re Gregor Willox.

41. Phillips J. G. *Op. cit.*, p. 92, from oral traditions related to him from 1820s.
42. Gordon J. F. S. *Op. cit.*, p. 278. The first case occurred when Hay was master, recalled by eye-witnesses; the second when he visited in 1795, recalled by Rev. D. Carmichael, one of the students.
43. Bishop Geddes to Bishop Hay, 30. 11. 1786, BL.
44. Bishop Geddes 'Plan of a Journey to the Orkneys and a Journal', 9 June – 13 July, 1790, BJG 1/5, SCA.
45. Espec. Bishop Geddes to Bishop Hay, 17. 3. 1791, BL.
46. Bishop Hay to Bishop Geddes, 12. 6. 1791, BL.
47. Bishop Hay to Mr Fryer, 17. 12. 1791, BL.
48. Bishop Hay to John Thomson, 7. 10. 1791, BL. The Rome students had only recently begun Divinity. And Valladolid, where the Rector seemed determined to hold on to his students, had not produced a priest in the past four years.
49. Ibid.
50. Bishop Hay to Bishop Geddes, 22. 8. 1794, BL.
51. John Ingram returned to Edinburgh to take up a teaching post there.
52. Bishop Hay to Bishop Geddes, 11. 2. 1793, BL.
53. Bishop Hay to Paul McPherson, 7. 8. 1793, BL.
54. Bishop Hay to Bishop Geddes, 9. 8. 1793, BL.
55. Sheep Accompt, 1793, CS 1/7/6, SCA; Scalan Account, 24. 11. 1793, CS 1/7/ 5, SCA; and Complete Account, June-Nov. 1793, CS 1/1/7, SCA.
56. State of Scalan Accounts, 1 Nov. 1792–7. June 1793, as left by Dauley to Mr Marroch [Bishop Hay to Bishop Geddes], CS 1/7/2, SCA.
57. Bishop Hay to Bishop Geddes, 9. 8. 1793, 18. 8. 1793 and 30. 9. 1793, BL. The other three students were stranded at Bruges.
58. Bishop Hay to Bishop Geddes, 9. 8. 1793, BL. Andrew Carruthers felt that he was trying his best to guide ill-mannered students and overweening servants – Andrew Carruthers to Bishop Hay, 3. 9. 1793, BL. Apparently in Andrew Carruthers' case, the years did not bring a softening, but rather a gruffness – cf. the stories in Gordon J. F. S. *Op. cit.*, p. 647.
59. Bishop Hay to Bishop Geddes, 26. 8. 1793, BL. Four were sent to Valladolid; one was lodged at Ceannakyle and continued to take his lessons at Scalan under Mr Carruthers; the sixth – Andrew Scott the future bishop – was brought to Edinburgh to study under Bishop Hay.
60. Bishop Geddes to Bishop Hay, 30. 9. 1793, BL.
61. Bishop Hay to Bishop Geddes, 18. 8. 1793, BL.
62. Bishop Hay to Bishop Geddes, 26. 8. 1793, BL.
63. Bishop Geddes to Bishop Hay, 30. 9. 1793, BL.
64. Ibid.
65. Ibid., and Bishop Geddes to Bishop Hay, 11. 10. 1793, BL.
66. Bishop Geddes to Bishop Hay, 11. 10. 1793, BL.
67. Bishop Geddes to Bishop Hay, 20. 10. 1793, BL.
68. Ibid.
69. This was the view of the Glenlivet priest, Alexander Paterson, who knew Andrew Carruthers well, being his near neighbour and previously his Prefect of Studies at Douai. Mr Paterson also advised that to leave him at Scalan

would be "of no service with regard to the union and harmony there" –
Alexander Paterson to Bishop Hay, 17. 11. 1793, BL.

70. Bishop Hay sent Andrew Scott (see note 59) to be his companion. The two
boys were ordained together in 1795. Andrew Carruthers, his fellow Andrew
Scott, and his critic Alexander Paterson (see note 69) had all begun their
careers at Scalan, and all were to end them as bishops and Vicars Apostolic.

18

Changed Days, Changed Needs

James Sharp arrived at Scalan in the late autumn. How different must his coming have been from the arrival of George Innes seventy-seven years before! Not alone was the seminary unrecognisable from the original turf house, but the whole environment had been transformed – the Braes, the Banffshire Uplands, Scottish society itself, and the place of the Catholic Church within it.

Communication within the Highlands, and between the Highlands and the Low Country, had improved beyond belief. The impetus for change, where earlier legislation had so signally failed, had been the Jacobite risings of 1715 and 1745.

After the '15 George Wade had been commissioned to develop a network of roads across the Highlands, to allow the swift movement of Government troops in the event of further insurrections. In the Grampians his teams completed the road between the barracks at Fort George and Ruthven in 1728, extending it South almost to Dunkeld the following year, and adding a link road to Crieff in 1730.[1]

The '45 had prompted a second wave of construction, including, in the North-East, the military road built in 1754 from Braemar via Corgarff and the Lecht to Tomintoul and Grantown, which passed within two miles of Scalan and opened up communication to Strathspey and to the South.[2] In later years this route was extended in several directions[3] – north-eastwards to Fochabers, where it linked with the coastal post road, and north-westwards to meet the same post road closer to Inverness. It was this latter branch that Bishop Geddes used just three years before Mr Sharp's arrival, on the last leg of his journey from Orkney to Scalan.[4] It was also extended at its southern end, from Braemar over into Glenshee and beyond the Highland Line to Blairgowrie and Perth. This was now the most direct route between Scalan and Edinburgh. Bishop Geddes had used it the previous summer, riding in the Huntly chaise from Tomintoul to Perth, from where the fly could be taken all the way to the capital.[5] Such a journey now took only three days, for these military roads were built for fast travel. They were at least 20ft in breadth, and could carry every kind of wheeled carriage. They were maintained annually, and had staging posts providing overnight lodging at regular intervals.[6]

To the east of the Grampians there were now two major roads linking the North-East with the Lowlands. The coastal route from Inverness had been progressively extended, and now ran via Aberdeen and Stonehaven to Dundee. And diverging from this road at Fochabers was a second route, which followed an inland course skirting the eastern edge of the uplands through Keith, Huntly, Alford-by-the-Don, and on via Brechin to Edinburgh. It was on this old road, now upgraded to carry wheeled traffic, that the Scalan mail was brought from the capital.[7]

The trauma of the '45 had also given a new impetus to the building of local roads within the counties. Magistrates were now obliged to exercise a far tighter control to ensure that the existing legislation was implemented, while at the same time new and more demanding laws had been introduced, culminating in the Road Act of 1771.[8] Upper Banffshire had benefited from the new resolve like everywhere else. In the 1770s a vehicular road was built down Glenlivet to Inveravon, giving the glen direct access to Strathspey and the North; and the old Tomintoul-Tomnavoulin-Glenrinnes bridle path was developed into a road able to take carriages, thus linking Glenlivet directly with the South, the West, and the post roads of the North-East.[9]

As yet, no road had been built in the Braes themselves:[10] carts were in use on the farms, but the usual means of travel between farms was still by horse or on foot (though, as we saw, Bishop Geddes was taken from Scalan down to Tombreckachie on a cart).

Map 9 summarises the road system as it was in the North-East at this date.

When Scalan first opened Tomintoul had been no more than a farm. But in 1778 a model village had been built on the site, with terraced streets laid out in a grid pattern, and within two decades it became the main centre of population in Upper Banffshire. It was only one of a number of 'new towns' built in the North-East over the previous thirty years. All were sited on the estates of the great landowners, and they stood as visible symbols of the changes that were taking place in the old rural society.[11] One or two – such as Grantown on the Spey, and Gordonsburgh further west in Lochaber – by their very names reminded the world of the driving forces behind their creation, and of the part played by the landed gentry in transforming the old way of life.

Early in the century these titled men had begun to improve their lands, by introducing more productive methods of agriculture based on scientific principles. And when the country finally 'settled' after Culloden they had encouraged their tenants to follow their lead. Everywhere they had promoted projects for the conversion of barren land to arable – through enclosure, drainage, preparation and fertilisation of the soil, and rotation of crops – by offering incentives, and often (as we saw in the Braes) by making such improvements a condition of granting or renewing tacks. The new methods had prompted the invention of new farm machinery, which in turn accelerated the adoption of the latest methods.[12] At the same time, supported by their capital, new agriculture-based industries arose, in particular thread manufacture, which had become a widespread cottage and factory industry in Banffshire by the 1770s.[13]

Greater productivity had in turn led to a higher quality and greater variety of farm produce becoming available in the country as a whole. And at the same time rising wages, which outstripped prices in the forty years after Culloden, had resulted in a generally improved standard of living, and particularly of diet. By 1790, in the Lowlands certainly, meat dishes, dairy foods and wheaten bread were everywhere on the table.[14]

The improved road system allowed foodstuffs and other goods to be brought from afar. And at the same time it opened the eyes of travellers to how people lived elsewhere, and so raised their own expectations for life. Some began to despise the old penurious way of living to which they had been raised. Even some of the priests of the Mission were now beginning to expect certain 'luxuries' as the norm, and as their right.[15]

As we saw, the seminary farm had been among the first in the district to embrace the new methods. Almost from the beginning its lands had been enclosed, and the now out-moded runrig had never been practised, though it was the system still used by the rest of the tenants on the tack of Scalan until the late 1760s. For the past twenty years at least the soil had been marled and limed, and enriched with clovers and rye grass, as a matter of course. Root crops and a wide variety of vegetables had been grown at least since Mr Paterson's day. And more recently John William-son had been brought in as a specialist farm supervisor,open to the latest developments in the Lowlands, and with Bishop Hay's enthusiastic support had turned Scalan into something of an experimental farm.

But it must have been well ahead of most of its neighbours. The trend towards more productive methods was by no means uniform across the country, and the Banffshire uplands were among the last to adopt the new improvements. And in addition, a gulf was growing between the practices of the wealthier and poorer farmers there. Some of the former were already practising commercial farming; all were now growing root and green crops; the new factory-made machinery was to be seen on their land; many had introduced the Linton breed of sheep, and a few were moving entirely over to sheep-rearing. The poorer tenant farmers in contrast were only now beginning to sow clover, and occasionally flax and rye, along with the traditional crops; their few sheep were of the old

MAP 9

Vehicular roads in North East Scotland c. 1790

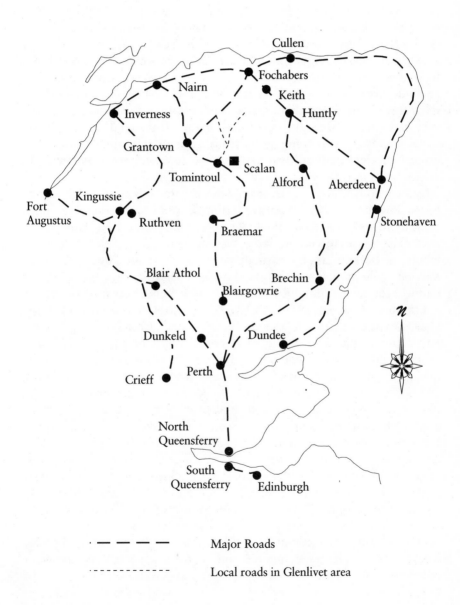

- – – – – Major Roads

········ Local roads in Glenlivet area

Scottish breed; they still used the kellach; and their tools were still – in the words of a contemporary report – "for the most part fabricated by themselves, in their pristine rudeness".[16] The reasons for the gulf are not far to seek: the preconditions for improvement were the possession of resources and of will; and each required the other. The commercial farmer had both, the subsistence tenant neither. And so the gulf widened.[17]

The famines of the 1770s and 1780s had demonstrated all too starkly how vulnerable the upland farmer was. They had driven Highlanders to beg on the streets of the cities. The second had caused waves as far away as Westminster, prompting an official enquiry (in which Upper Banffshire figured prominently) and, for the first time ever, Government intervention and aid.[18] For the small farmers, it proved a watershed. On the one hand, it left them in no doubt that the new methods were now essential to their very survival.[19] On the other, it forced many off the land entirely. In the Braes – as we saw – some had already gone in the famine of 1772-4; others who had held on then had become destitute ten years later; still others had faced eviction in 1787.

Some who had given up their holdings became labourers on the larger farms. But as less labour-intensive farming – and notably sheep-rearing – came more and more to dominate the upland landscape, many among this new class were forced to look for work further afield. Migratory labourers became an increasingly familiar sight on Highland roads, making their annual way to the Lowland harvest, carrying a bag of oatmeal for their food and their clothes in a bundle on their back.[20]

Britain had been at war with France for more than a year when Mr Sharp arrived at Scalan, and the conflict had actually brought some temporary respite to the Highland poor, offering employment in the ranks of the army to some, and helping to keep others on the land by raising the demand for beef.[21] Ironically also, Government legislation enacted in the 1780s, which had aimed to eliminate private whisky distilling by outlawing small stills and prohibiting all exports from the Highlands, had had quite the opposite effect. By driving the private Highland stills underground it had turned a respectable pursuit into a lucrative black market industry.[22] And nowhere was it more thriving than in Glenlivet. The "aquavite pots" that Mr Duthie had feared might draw attention to the seminary after Culloden, and the "husky bottles" that had been the people's solace in the hungry spring of 1774, were now the secret source for a systematic smuggling operation to the Lowlands. Scores of men were now making the journey to the South or the East Coast, travelling by night, and distributing their wares among a network of agents. Their road led over the Ladder a mile to the east of Scalan, or over to the Lecht past its very door.[23] Their trade was their means of surviving in the glens where they were born.

But whatever the short-lived respite, for many the ultimate effect of the new agriculture was permanent migration, whether abroad or to the towns. The population of Glasgow doubled in the last two decades of the century, while some observers estimated that in many parts of the Highlands it was halved or worse.[24] The shift accelerated the trend towards wage labour, whether of the specialist tradesman or the unskilled general worker. It accelerated the emergence of a landless, wage-earning population, dependent on purchasing the necessities of life, and the decline of the subsistence farmer and the old self-sufficiency.Ironically therefore, despite the improvements in transport and communication, life in the remote uplands was becoming in some ways harder, and harder to sustain.

The migrations were also changing the demography of the Scottish Catholic Church. A census taken in the early 1760s had shown that the Highland Catholic population was perhaps twice as large as that in the Lowland Disctrict.[25] But when Bishop Hay had sent his estimate of numbers to Rome in 1780 a swing had already begun: he calculated that there were now 9000 communicants in the Highlands, and 8000 in the Lowlands.[26] This was in fact the last time that the Highland figure would exceed the Lowland. Emigration was shifting the balance away from the remote areas, and from the West in particular.[27]

After the famine of 1772-4 Bishop Hay had opened a Gaelic chapel in the capital to serve the new arrivals. And following the famine of the early 1780s Bishop Geddes had argued for a permanent priest in the Glasgow-Paisley-Greenock area, where he believed there were now some two hundred Catholics, between Lowlanders, Highlanders and Irish.[28] His letter was one of the first references to the immigration from Ireland, which at that date was still only a trickle and overshadowed by the influx from the Highlands, but which in the next forty years would become a flood that would quite eclipse the latter in scale, and turn the demography of Catholic Scotland on its head.

Not all the changes were due to migration, however. The Enzie, once the home of Bishop Nicolson, had declined somewhat as a Catholic stronghold, especially in the neighbourhood of Fochabers, the seat of the Dukes of Gordon. When the Episcopalian Bishop Pococke visited the area in 1760 he was told that many of the Duke's tenants had by then converted to Episcopalianism, the religion adopted by the laird's family some thirty years before.[29]

Nor had the Church in Aberdeen been greatly affected by new arrivals. The city had in fact only grown by some 25% in the second half of the century, far less rapidly than the towns of the West-Central belt. But the small Catholic community there and in the Garioch was of long standing. Bishop Hay had made his home in the city for most of the 1780s, and Bishop Geddes was now living there and would remain there until his death. One modern commentator has argued that for twenty or thirty years around the turn of the century Aberdeen could lay claim to being – as much as anywhere – the national headquarters of the Church.[30]

Changed also beyond recognition was the standing of Catholicism in Scotland. The reader will not have failed to notice the virtual disappearance of coded language and aliases – a sure barometer of the times – in the correspondence of Scalan's masters with their fellow clergy over the previous three decades.[31] And even the few examples still to be found were now more used by habit than necessity. This once clandestine College had for some time felt free to be quite open, though still discreet, as to its business. Despite the Edinburgh riots of 1779 and brief outbreaks in Glasgow and Aberdeen, the old hatreds and suspicions were melting.

Why the change? First and most fundamentally, religion itself was no longer the burning issue that it had once been,[32] and the storms of confessional controversy that had blown across Europe in the sixteenth and seventeenth centuries had much abated in the eighteenth.

The Catholic Church itself had changed. Internationally, it had adopted reforms and a new openness and willingness to co-exist, especially under Popes Benedict XIV (1740-58) and Clement XIV (1769-74). At home too, it had sought to throw off its old image. It had severed its close association with Jacobitism, the threat of which had now in any case all but evaporated. After James' death in 1766 the pope had pointedly refused to recognise Charles Edward as the legitimate heir to the British crown. Charles himself was now five years dead, but even before his death the Scottish bishops had publicly expressed their recognition and support of the reigning monarchy. And as evidence of the loyalty of their people they could point to the thousands who had fought for their country in the Seven Years War of 1756-63 and in America, and to the hundreds now enlisting for the war against France.

At the same time, Bishops Hay and Geddes in particular had deliberately involved themselves in Scotland's intellectual circles, through their writings, and in the case of Bishop Geddes through the contacts he cultivated, and by doing so had helped to bring Catholicism closer to the mainstream of national life.[33]

Given the rôle of the Church's leaders, and the proven loyalty of its people, it was becoming difficult for its enemies to continue to write it off as the embodiment of backwardness, superstition and treason.

And in any case, those enemies had themselves changed. Many of Scotland's leading figures, and particularly the intellectual élite, were now genuinely committed to moderation and the concepts of justice and tolerance.[34] In London the Government was already committed in Law to the principle of religious freedom in England, Ireland, and those mainly Catholic colonies annexed from the French. Moreover the establishments in both London and Edinburgh shared something of Bishop Hay's own horror of the French Revolution and the wave of iconoclasm apparently sweeping Europe, and these erstwhile enemies of the Church now preferred to make common cause with it in face of the greater enemy, irreligion. They needed their Catholic citizens, of course, never more than now. And this was a card that Bishop Hay had long since learned to play.[35]

The new relaxation was felt too in the field of education. It was almost half a century since the parish schools had abandoned their old rule of weekend attendance at the kirk as a condition of enrolment,[36] and Catholic children could now usually attend with a clear conscience. And more recently the SSPCK had shown itself even more accommodating. Just two years before, Bishop Geddes had held discussions with Mr Kemp, an official of the SSPCK, concerning the possibility of excusing Catholic pupils from catechism in the Society's schools, and found him most sympathetic. Kemp had suggested that a catechism without set answers be compiled for the Catholics, and was even happy to use standard Catholic handbooks in preparing it.[37] Up at Scalan Bishop Hay let it be known that, if these arrangements went ahead, he would be willing to recommend the SSPCK school at Badevochel to Catholic parents, and even close the existing Catholic school in the Braes.[38]

Despite all these changes the Act of 1700 remained in force, by which attendance at Catholic worship was still technically punishable by banishment, or even death. The Law was ridiculously out of kilter with the real world, and with the rest of Britain, a dead letter and an anachronism waiting to be abolished.

For more than a decade, in fact, the Catholic Mission had been building new churches in the North-East. The most recent one, completed at Preshome between 1788-90, with its striking and unambiguously ecclesiastical facade, was the first in Scotland since the Reformation to be designed quite openly as a church. Like the others it was built in expectation of an imminent change in the Law.

That change came in the spring of 1793 when the Scottish Catholic Relief Bill became Law, effectively (as its name implied) relieving Catholics from the penalties of the 1700 Act.[39] The bishops at once took the required oath of allegiance, as an example to their flocks, and instructed the clergy to urge their people to follow suit, even in the traditional Jacobite strongholds where they could expect resistance and suspicion.[40] At the same time they informed the pope of the joyous news:[41] after two centuries, they told him, the new Act at last gave the Catholics of Scotland the right to profess their faith in freedom.

They themselves now had the opportunity to revive the plans that they had been forced to shelve since the riots of 1779. Among other things, they could start to look seriously for a more suitable replacement for Scalan.

The seminary's shortcomings which Bishop Hay had pointed out in 1778 – its harsh climate, and its remoteness – had not gone away. Indeed, events in the intervening years had only served to confirm them: the hardships of its climate had been brought home as never before by the deaths from TB of Mr Paterson and Mr Dason, while the discomforts of its remote situation had become even more apparent with the growth of the money economy and the rising aspirations of the priests of the Mission.

And to these disadvantages could now be added others. Shortly before Mr Sharp's arrival the Scots Colleges at Paris and Douai were finally lost.[42] Their closure, and the real possibility of losing Rome also, made it likely that Scalan (with its Highland counterpart at Samalaman) would need to take on a new and larger rôle for the foreseeable future as an all-through seminary and with more students. But it was clearly too small for such a task. In addition, maintaining a farm in the Braes was a constant struggle against the odds and uncertain at the best of times, and, as the past decade had shown, even the tenure of the land was at risk and likely to remain so. Whatever the short-term respite due to the artificial conditions of war, Bishop Hay must have seen the writing on the wall for the Banffshire uplands. Nor could the illicit whisky convoys, which now passed Scalan's door, have impressed him as setting the right example for the upbringing of growing boys. Lastly, with the Church's centre of gravity shifting from the Gaelic Highlands towards the centres of population, it now had the opportunity to move away from the periphery, figuratively as well as geographically, and to play its part in the mainstream; but Scalan was too out-of-the-way to prepare its future priests for such a rôle.

From every point of view, therefore, this must have seemed a good time to leave; to find a larger and more suitable home in a gentler, more accessible place. Already before Mr Sharp walked in the door, Scalan had lost its reason to be. Just when it had at last been raised to the acme of its fortune under Bishop Hay, the builder himself was preparing to abandon it.

NOTES

1. Salmond J. B. *Wade in Scotland* (Edinburgh, 1934), p. 140; also Taylor W. *The Military Roads in Scotland* (1976; Colonsay, 1996 ed.), pp. 46f.
2. Grant J. *Records of the County of Banff 1660–1760* (Aberdeen, 1922), pp. 380ff.
3. Details of all the road extensions in Grant J. and Leslie W. *A Survey of the Province of Moray* (Aberdeen, 1798), pp. 333ff.
4. Bishop Geddes 'Plan of a Journey to the Orkneys and a Journal', 9 June – 15 July 1790, B JG 1/5, SCA.
5. Bishop Geddes to Bishop Hay, 27. 8. 1792, BL.
6. Shaw L. *The History of the Province of Moray* (c. 1780), enlarged and updated by Gordon J. F. S. (Glasgow, 1882), vol. ii, p. 134.
7. For over half a century Huntly had been the seminary's nearest post office, but a nearer and more convenient one had later been opened at Keith. George J. Gordon to Bishop Gordon, 19. 2. 1736, BL, gives news of PO at Huntly, with weekly departures. The earliest ref. to the Keith PO that I have found in the correspondence is Bishop Hay to Bishop Geddes, 8. 2. 1791, BL, but the context does not suggest that it was very recently established. The master could either have letters uplifted from there or delivered by runner to his door at extra charge. By the evidence of the Accounts he usually did the latter. Such arrangements were normal practice at the time – cf. Haldane A. R. B. *Three Centuries of Scottish Posts* (Edinburgh, 1971), passim.
8. Re legislation, responsibilities and implementation, see Whetstone A.E. *Scottish County Government in the Eighteenth and Nineteenth Centuries* (Edinburgh, 1981), pp. 81ff.
9. Grant Rev. J., Parish of Inveravon, *OSA* (c. 1792-5), vol. xvi, p. 240. The first was built by General Grant, the second by the Duke of Gordon. As a caveat, it should be added that Donaldson described the roads linking Upper to Lower Banffshire as "impassable" for several weeks every winter at this time – Donaldson J. *General View of the Agriculture of the County of Banff* (Edinburgh, 1794), p. 26.
10. The first vehicular road in the Braes was built in the 1840s, through the influence of the parish priest Fr James Glennie.
11. For details of Tomintoul see Gaffney V. *The Lordship of Strathavon: Tomintoul Under the Gordons* (Aberdeen, 1960), espec. pp. 42ff. For the broader picture – Lockhart D. G. 'The Evolution of the planned villages of North-East Scotland', unpublished Ph.D. thesis, Univ. of Dundee, 1974; also Smout T. C. 'The Landowner and the planned Village in Scotland 1730–1830', in Phillipson N. T. and Mitchison R. (eds.) *Scotland in the Age of Improvement* (Edinburgh, 1970). Examples of new towns were Fochabers beside Gordon Castle; and Rothes, Portsoy and Old Deer, all on the estates of Lord Findlater.
12. Re date, lead given by Lord Findlater, inducements to tenants, and importation of tools and machinery, see Donaldson J. *Op. cit.*, pp. 7f., 12, 14, 20. For a general modern account, see Handley J. E. *Scottish Farming in the Eighteenth Century* (London, 1953), pp. 210ff. The same source (pp. 120ff.)

gives details of the scientific treatises upon which the new methods were based.

13. The flax grown on the Gordon estate around Fochabers was said to be of the finest quality and highest yield in Scotland – Lock D. *Tour Through Most of the Trading Towns and Villages of Scotland* (Edinburgh, 1778), pp. 57 and 60. Lock also attributed the development of the industry to the lead given by Lord Findlater.

14. Hamilton H. *An Economic History of Scotland in the Eighteenth Century* (Oxford, 1963), p. 377. Prices had risen by c. 50% for meal, and by up to 100% for meat and dairy products. For details of more local prices for cereals and meal see *Miscellany of the New Spalding Club*, vol. II, (Aberdeen, 1908), 'Fairs Prices of Aberdeenshire', pp. 27-30 (for years 1747–1806).

15. Bishop Hay to Bishop Cameron, 9. 6. 1804, comparing priests' expectations re housing, furniture, etc., at the turn of the century, with those of the 1770s.

16. Grant J. and Leslie W. *A Survey of the Province of Moray* (Aberdeen, 1798), pp. 323-330; and Grant J., *OSA*, vol. xvi, pp. 239f.

17. Kay G. 'The Landscape of Improvement – a Case Study of Agricultural Change in North-East Scotland', *Scot. Geog. Mag.*, vol. 78, no. 2, Sept. 1962.

18. Walton K. 'Climate and Famines in North East Scotland', *Scot. Geog. Mag.*, vol. 68, no. 1, April 1952, p. 19; re official enquiry, *Second Report of the Distress in Scotland*, presented to Parl. 28. 5. 1783, Bill passed 18. 6. 1783, printed 7. 5. 1846 (espec. pp. 2f. re Banffshire uplands).

19. As a result, changes soon began to appear on even the poorest land – Souter D. *General View of the Agriculture of the County of Banff* (Edinburgh, 1812), p. 98 etc.

20. Garnett T. *Observations on a Tour Through the Highlands and Part of the Western Isles of Scotland* (London, 1800), vol. II, p. 36. Migratory labour was not new – men and women had been seeking seasonal labour on Lowland farms since early decades of the century at least – but its scale had now greatly increased.

21. Devine T. M. 'Highland Migration to Lowland Scotland', *Scot. Hist. Rev.*, vol. lxii, 2, no. 174, Oct. 1983. Among the privates and NCOs of the Northern Fencibles, raised by the Duke of Gordon between 1778-83, 13 were from Inveravon and 19 from Kirkmichael – nine of the former being labourers and the rest small tradesmen; among those raised from 1793 and whose birthplaces are known, 13 (of 101) hailed from Glenlivet or the Braes; in the ranks of the Gordon Highlanders, raised in 1794, were 16 men from Inveravon parish, 13 of them described as labourers. Cf., Bulloch J. M. (ed.) *Territorial Soldiering in the North-East of Scotland During 1759–1814* (Aberdeen, 1914), pp. 119ff., 152ff. and 236ff. respectively. For a detailed account of the circumstances leading to the raising of the Highland regiments, and the foundation, organisation and history of the Gordon Fencibles, see Mackintosh H. B. *The Northern or Gordon Fencibles 1778–1783* (Elgin, 1929).

22. Moss M. S. *The Making of Scotch Whisky* (Edinburgh, 1981), espec. pp. 33-46. A more detailed catalogue of the acts may be found in Craig H. C. *The Scotch Whisky Industry Record* (Dumbarton, 1994). Before the end of the

decade the Government had become sufficiently alarmed to set up a commission on the issue – cf., *Reports Respecting the Distilleries in Scotland by Committees of the Honourable the House of Commons appointed in 1798 and 1799* (London, 1799).

23. For a striking description of the smugglers, and their brazen defiance of the Law, see Thomas Guthrie's *Autobiography* (London, 1874-5) vol. i, pp. 70f., referring to the period c. 1812. See also the excellent and fully illustrated account in Cooper D. and Godwin F. *The Whisky Roads of Scotland* (London, 1982), which includes photographs of the Ladder road and the road from Well of Lecht to the Braes. Cooper, who describes Glenlivet as "the heartland of illicit distilling", refers specifically to ruins beside the Slochd burn above Scalan which almost certainly housed illicit stills.

24. Eg., Newte T. *Prospects and Observations on a Tour in England and Scotland* (London, 1795), pp. 235f. Newte identified the new sheep walks as the greatest cause of depopulation; "Where these prevail," he wrote, "the people have been diminished a half, or two thirds."

25. Bishop Smith to Abbé Peter Grant, Account of the Mission, 1763, SM 4/13/9, SCA.

26. For an account of the change see Darragh J. 'The Catholic Population of Scotland Since the Year 1680', *IR*, vol. iv, no.1, spring 1953.

27. "Emigration here without end, and more in bud," the priest of Knoydart reported in 1791 (Augustine MacDonald to Bishop Hay, 11. 7. 1791, BL). He believed that 4000 Catholics had left the area in the past few years, and that another 1500 might follow that year. Elsewhere the trend was similar, if less spectacular.

28. Bishop Geddes to Bishop Hay, 30. 11. 1786, BL. By 1794 the number had risen to c. 500.

29. Pococke R. *Tours in Scotland 1747, 1750, 1760* ed. Kemp D. W. (Edinburgh, 1881), Letter xxxvii, 28. 7. 1760, p. 193.

30. Anderson W. J. 'The College for the Lowland District of Scotland at Scalan and Aquhorties – Registers and Documents', *IR*, vol. xiv, no. 2, autumn 1963, General Introduction, p. 91.

31. Interestingly, recent research has also shown that the use of aliases by Catholic families in the Braes of Glenlivet (particularly when recording the baptism of children) virtually ceased in the mid-1770s, it being now no longer necessary to preserve anonymity – Mitchell S. 'Hidden Families: Aliases and Patronymics in Upper Banffshire', *Aberdeen and N. E. Scotland Family Hist. Soc. Journal*, nos. 66 and 67, 1998.

32. This was also literally the case: when Scalan first opened witches were still being burned, but it was now close to seventy years since the last such burning.

33. Goldie M. 'The Scottish Catholic Enlightenment', *J. Brit. Studs.*, vol. 30, no. 1, Jan. 1991. Also Kidd C. 'Antiquarianism, Religion, and the Scottish Enlightenment', *IR*, vol. xlvi, no. 2, autumn 1995.

34. Re thinking of Scottish intelligentsia, including attitude to Catholics, see Sher R. B. *Church and University in the Scottish Enlightenment – the Moderate Literati of Edinburgh* (Edinburgh, 1985), passim, espec. pp. 278ff. Re the general growth of toleration for religious minorities through the century, cf.

Smout T. C. *A History of the Scottish People 1560–1830* (London, 1969; 1985 ed.), pp. 214ff.

35. See for instance Bishop Hay 'Reflections on the State of the Rom: Catholicks in Scotland' (spring 1779), SM 4/17/1, SCA, warning that Catholics would emigrate if the Penal Laws were not revoked.

36. MacInnes J. *The Evangelical Movement in the Highlands of Scotland 1688–1800* (Aberdeen, 1951), p. 243.

37. Bishop Geddes to Bishop Hay, 17. 3. 1791, BL.

38. Bishop Hay to Bishop Geddes, 12. 6. 1791, BL. He was also prepared to supplement the school master's salary from his own pocket.

39. Conditions were set – that Catholics take an oath of allegiance to the Crown, renounce obedience to any Pretender, and deny the temporal claims of the papacy. The oath itself was covered by a separate Act – *An Act Requiring a certain Form of Oath of Abjuration, and Declaration, from His Majesty's Subjects, professing the Roman Catholick Religion, in that Part of Great Britain Called Scotland*, 3 June 1793, 33 Geo III, cap. 44.

40. Cf., eg., Alexander MacDonald to Reginald McDonell, Morar, 28. 8. 1794, OL.

41. Bishops to Pope, 8. 7. 1793 (in Italian), copy 4/74/5, BL. They expressed the hope that their news would be of some consolation to him in those "calamitous times for Holy Church".

42. The circumstances of their loss have been described in detail in Johnson C. *Developments in the Roman Catholic Church in Scotland 1789–1829* (Edinburgh, 1983), chap. 12 'The Revolution in France'.

19

Seeking a New Scalan (1793-1799)

The new master was barely in the house when Bishop Hay sent him instuctions to have the stock of wine delivered down to Aberdeen. It must have been a considerable stock, because it was to be sent in several separate deliveries, a dozen bottles at a time, to avoid the requirement of a permit. Bishop Hay wanted it away from Scalan for reasons that he preferred not to put in a letter.[1] Did he doubt the boys? Was he remembering petty pilfering by servants in the past? Was he uncertain of the master's authority?

Mr Sharp himself was keenly conscious of the problems he faced. His first impressions of the boys and servants were good, certainly: he found them "very tractable and submissive." But he was all the time afraid of "being imposed upon for want of experience", and particularly asked Bishop Geddes to send him some guidelines on the rôle of a master.[2]

There is no record of the bishop's reply. But we do have a paper, *Observations Relating to the Catholic Missions of Scotland,*[3] composed by him in Aberdeen about this time, which may well have been expanded from notes he wrote to Mr Sharp. Despite its title, this ninety page document was almost entirely concerned with the seminary, with sections on its aims, courses of study, the selection of students, and 'the Qualifications desirable in the Master': the last probably based closely on his guidelines to Mr Sharp. It was written from personal experience, and showed all the qualities we would expect from its author – insight, sensitivity, vision, and practical good sense.[4]

The *Observations* were intended for Bishop Hay's notice, and Bishop Geddes took the opportunity to express his opinion on matters he considered crucial to Scalan's wellbeing. Among other things he argued against ever again appointing a young, unproven man as master, in view of the responsibilites of the post ; he in fact urged the need for two masters, for the same reason; and (conscious of Scalan's hybrid rôle) he even recommended the establishment of a separate Academy, run by priests for boys not intending the priesthood, as soon as resources allowed. In so doing he was identifying perhaps the three most central and recurrent issues relating to Scalan throughout its history.

Mr Sharp meantime was finding some problems with the boys' discipline. Jamie MacIntyre, especially, showed little respect for him and refused to obey the house rules. He appeared to have forgotten the severe warning he had received only the year before, when his behaviour had led to the dismissal of the young maid, and had now struck up a more than platonic friendship with the new girl May. The relationship was not discovered until the spring, and then May agreed to end her employment at Whitsun and move out of the district "without any noise about the matter". Jamie was sent home on Bishop Hay's orders.[5]

The bishop seemed to have found the ideal site for his proposed new seminary when the farm of Oxhill came up for sale in the autumn of 1794. It was down in the Enzie, and struck him as "an excellent place for a Scalan, near the Sea, near the Moss, and a good field well grazed . . . under His Grace's wings & in a Catholic Country".[6] There were others interested in buying, but the Duke preferred to give first option to the Church.[7]

Though he found the prospect very attractive Bishop Hay was daunted by the cost, and not at all sure that he should take a risk that might jeopardise the whole financial standing of the Mission. Bishop Geddes believed that he should: the land was excellent, with ample marl and lime; and money could be recouped by renting part of it out, as well as from the slate quarry that lay upon it; if the decision was his, he "would have no scruples".[8] Mr John Farquharson shared his view, and thought it less of a risk in those uncertain times to put money into property than into bank shares.

But Bishop Hay remained doubtful. Neither his Co-adjutor nor Mr Farquharson had considered the disadvantages, he felt. Whatever the long-term income there would be an immediate outlay, of which the land itself would only be a small part. The costs of the house, furniture, staff and students would all be greater than at Scalan. Though the benefactions he was seeking might cover a portion of the cost, there was no doubt that he would have to borrow a substantial sum, and the interest would hang like a millstone on the Mission.[9]

His discussions with Mr Tod, the Duke's factor, confirmed his doubts, and gave him figures to argue from. The price of the land alone had now risen to an exorbitant £2800; the house would cost between £300-£500 to build, and its plenishing a further £200; so they would need to spend at least £3300 "before they could even sit down upon the place". Even if they drew in £500 from subscriptions, and added the bank shares held in Scalan's name, this would still leave a shortfall to be borrowed, with a crippling annual interest of over £74.[10]

In the event he had very little response to his appeal for subscriptions,[11] and though Mr Tod held the sale up for him until 21 December, he was still undecided when the deadline expired, and Oxhill was lost. Bishop Geddes greatly regretted the missed opportunity, which Providence had seemed to put in their way.[12] He had favoured the deal throughout, always putting the case with his customary tact. But some senior clergy made no secret of their opinion that the Vicar Apostolic had lost Oxhill through stubbornness, and a rather hurt Bishop Hay later told the Scots Agent in Rome how much he had been "blamed & bullied for not making the purchase".[13]

If little was to be had from private benefactions, the bishops believed that the British Government itself might perhaps now offer a more promising source of support, judging by the willingness it had recently shown in supporting new Catholic seminaries in England and at Maynooth in Ireland. But first it would need to be fully convinced of the loyalty of the Scottish Catholic Church. They themselves had already given a lead in declaring loyalty. But such declarations were still anathema, and deeply suspect, to many of their flock in the Western Highlands and the North-East whose hearts remained Jacobite. To demonstrate the unequivocal loyalty of the official Church at least, they asked again for prayers to be said for the King and Queen at all Masses,[14] and this time by name so that there could be no doubt as to which royal house was intended!

In autumn 1795 they wrote to Henry Dundas, the Lord Advocate, asking him to support the re-imbursement of the Scottish Mission for the loss of its Colleges in France, and received "a most friendly answer".[15] The following January Bishop Hay met the MP Alexander Brodie while he was on a visit to Edinburgh, and discussed their needs with him. Brodie promised support and asked for written details to strengthen his hand when he took the case to London. Bishop Hay compiled a *Memorial* for his use, explaining that the loss of the Colleges had deprived the Mission not alone of a supply of priests but of an annual income of 3000 Livres. He included a detailed account of the Colleges' revenues to substantiate his argument, and guaranteed that any re-imbursement received through the Government's good offices would be spent solely on establishing new seminaries in Scotland.[16]

On the same day he sent a letter to the Scots Agent in Rome with news of the negotiations, expressing cautious optimism as to their outcome. "If this succeeds", he wrote, "we will be in no straits for Seminaries; at hoc tibi soli per interim."[17]

Alexander Brodie was as good as his word in arguing the financial case among his London colleagues, and within three months Bishop Hay was able to give Rome much firmer news -

Our friends at Court have promised to procure us re-imbursement for our two Colleges lost as soon as peace comes; It is upon this that our expectations of getting a proper one at home are grounded.[18]

Though Mr Sharp had now settled in to Scalan, and experienced all its seasons, he was still struggling with the discipline and the workload, and Bishop Hay was glad to have the opportunity of sending him an assistant in the summer. James MacDonald had just returned from Rome, where he had been ordained earlier in the year. He had forgotten some of his English while abroad, and the bishop felt that a few months at Scalan would give him the chance to recover it before going on the Mission, and at the same time take some of the burden off the master. Mr Sharp's own younger brother John, who had begun his training at Scalan, had been ordained at Valladolid the previous autumn and was now on his way home. Bishop Hay decided to send him to Scalan as an assistant also. It was a decision, he told his Co-adjutor, "necessary for several reasons . . . on both [the brothers'] accounts", which he would explain when they met.[19] He clearly believed that the staff needed to be strengthened because there were now twelve students on the roll, and they covered a wide age-range.[20] The plan was that John Sharp would only stay at Scalan for a year, but in fact he was to remain at the College until it closed.

This larger staff was now necessary since, with the closure of Paris and Douai and the threatened closure of Rome, Scalan was now at last taking on the rôle of all-through seminary (a development that made the search for larger premises the more pressing).

For decades past, the luxury of sending a second – let alone a third – priest to Scalan would have been unthinkable. But Valladolid was bearing fruit at last, and the Lowland Vicariate now found itself with what must have seemed something close to an embarrassment of riches. "You will be surprised when I tell you that by this years supply I have more hands than places where to put them", Bishop Hay wrote to Rome that November. "But," he added, "if our new Scalan succeeds we shall find them work".[21]

The 'new Scalan' to which he referred was the estate of Aquhorties, which had just become available. It lay among the beech, birch and whin of the Aberdeenshire lowlands, just twenty easy miles from Aberdeen itself, in the lee of rocky Bennachie Hill the Highlands' last eastern gesture to the sea. John Leslie of Balquhain, to whom it belonged, was a Catholic and on friendly terms with Bishop Hay – the bishop had bought Scalan's meal from him during his time as master, sometimes stayed at the family home at Fetternear, and had baptised five of his children.[22] Leslie had recently bought up all his tenants' leases, so that the whole estate of 600 acres could be let out as a single unit, and was prepared to offer it to the Church on a lease of 99 years at a moderate rental. It was an arrangement that appealed to Bishop Hay, for there would be no outlay on a purchase, yet the length of the lease would meet all the Mission's foreseeable needs. In all, he thought it "far preferable to Oxhill".[23] He decided to seize the opportunity while he had it, in the hope of money to come.

Acquiring Aquhorties now gave him a good reason to press the Government anew, and he sent a carefully worded letter to Sir John Hippisley in the spring.[24] The estate was rather beyond the Mission's means, he explained, but they had taken it because they could never expect another such offer. The need for a seminary in Scotland was even more urgent than before, in view of France's expansionist policy in Europe which now also threatened their College in Rome. Unlike their brothers in England, the Scottish Catholics were too poor to make any serious contribution. But he believed there might be staunch friends of the Government who would be willing to subscribe, "knowing our Attachment to King and Country", and he also hoped that the Ministry itself might make a donation.

His letter spoke of a "new seminary" in Scotland, but it was in fact his intention to establish two, to serve the Highland and Lowland Vicariates respectively. It was a hope not shared by his counterpart in the Highlands, Bishop John Chisholm, whose own District was already in debt to the Mission and in no position to finance a new house of the size that would be required.[25] Bishop Chisholm's preference was for Aquhorties to serve the needs of both Vicariates, but this Bishop Hay rejected outright. He then proposed that his present college at Samalaman in Moidart should continue as a junior seminary meantime, with Scalan performing the same function for the Lowlands, and that Aquhorties serve as the senior seminary for both Districts until he could open his own, which would be as soon as possible.[26]

Again, Bishop Hay resisted the proposal. He was determined to keep the Highland and Lowland seminaries separate. His reasons were the ones he had advanced twenty years before – the expense, but more particularly the fact that Highland and Lowland students could never live together in harmony. And he now had a third reason also: to open a single, national seminary, far larger than the existing ones and in a far more visible location, might not be prudent so soon after the Act of 1793.

It was this last reason that he stressed to the Lord Advocate the following year, in a letter of consummate diplomacy, when explaining to him the Mission's need for two seminaries and arguing the case for Government funding: the Catholic Church, he assured him, would prefer not to place all its students in a single College, "least too many in one place should give umbrage to certain classes of people, which we always wish to avoid".[27]

The first one was now built at Aquhorties, he informed him, but at a cost that had far exceeded the subscriptions received, and the second planned by his colleague bishop for the Highlands was also sure to exceed any donations they might expect. Some might perhaps argue that the Church should train its future priests abroad without needing to build seminaries at home at all: this might still be possible – he agreed – despite the recent closures, and no doubt would cater adequately for the ecclesiastical part of their training. But it was only in Colleges in Scotland itself that they would receive something more – "those principles of Government and Loyalty, which are congenial to the constitution of our Country". And if the Government was seen to be supporting those Colleges, this could only further strengthen the loyalty and gratitude of the Scottish Catholic Church.

It was a masterly letter, which skilfully touched two of the more sensitive nerves of the London Establishment – its lingering doubts as to the loyalty of Scotland's Catholics, and its fears that in their new-found freedom they might already be getting above themselves – and used these to persuade it to hand over money not just for one new seminary but two.

NOTES

1. Bishop Hay to Bishop Geddes, 3. 1. 1794, BL.
2. James Sharp to Bishop Geddes, 8. 1. 1794, BL.
3. Bishop Geddes 'Observations Relating to the Catholic Missions of Scotland', (manuscript by several amanuenses), CS 1/4, SCA.
4. This little-known document would be well worth publishing. It still has relevance, and its idealism, wisdom and sanity would be an object lesson to those engaged in education (Catholic or otherwise) today.
5. Bishop Hay to Bishop Geddes, 22. 8. 1794, BL.
6. Bishop Hay to Paul McPherson, 8. 10. 1794, BL.
7. John Farquharson to Bishop Geddes, 6. 11. 1794, BL.
8. Bishop Geddes to Bishop Hay, 19. 11. 1794, BL. Oxhill was said to have produced the best crop in the Enzie in the disastrous harvest of 1782.
9. Bishop Hay to Bishop Geddes, 3. 11. 1794, BL.
10. Bishop Hay to Bishop Geddes, 24. 11. 1794, BL. The Scalan bank shares were currently worth £1309.
11. Bishop Hay to Paul McPherson, 1. 11. 1796, BL.
12. Bishop Geddes to Bishop Hay, 27. 1. 1795, BL.
13. Bishop Hay to Paul McPherson, 1. 11. 1796, BL.
14. Bishop Geddes to Bishop Hay, 27. 1. 1795, BL.
15. Bishop Hay to Paul McPherson, 16. 1. 1796, BL.
16. Bishop Hay to Alexander Brodie MP, 19. 1. 1796, BL.
17. Bishop Hay to Paul McPherson, 19. 1. 1796, BL.
18. Bishop Hay to Paul McPherson, 16. 4. 1796 and 4. 5. 1796, BL.
19. Bishop Hay to Bishop Geddes, 27. 6. 1796, BL. James MacDonald was a native of Glenlivet. After several months at Scalan he was sent to Aberdeen, and in later years served at Mortlach, Huntly, Edinburgh and Traquair before ending his days as Rector of the Scots College Rome. He died in 1822.
20. Nine of the boys were at various stages of Grammar; three were advanced students at the stage of Philosophy.
21. Bishop Hay to Paul McPherson, 1. 11. 1796, BL.

22. See Roberts A. 'The Leslies of Balquhain and the Burial of Bishop Hay', *Recusant History*, autumn 1995.
23. Bishop Hay to Paul McPherson, 1. 11. 1796, BL.
24. Bishop Hay to Sir J. Hippisley, 14. 3. 1797, BL.
25. Bishop J. Chisholm to Bishop Hay, 5. 5. 1797, BL.
26. Bishop J. Chisholm to Bishop Hay, 30. 1. 1798, BL.
27. Bishop Hay to Lord Advocate, 26. 2. 1799, BL.

20

Taking Their Farewell

As Bishop Hay had stated in his letter to the Lord Advocate, the house at Aquhorties was now built and furnished. The sandstone building stood four floors high, imposing in its square, unadorned symmetry (Plate 14); with spacious accommodation for thirty students and three teachers; boasting two dormitories, individual cubicles for seniors, a purpose-built library, indoor recreation room, and a two-storey chapel. The time had come to prepare for the move.

The bishop decided not to appoint James Sharp onto the staff. It is possible that he was influenced by adverse criticism of Mr Sharp by third parties, as the young priest himself believed,[1] but it is more likely that he based his decision on his own observation of him during several visits to Scalan. Aquhorties was to be a new beginning, he wanted it to get off to the best possible start, and he did not believe James Sharp was the man for the job. Instead he took his brother John from Scalan, and appointed three other priests to create a staff of four, with the intention that he would also live there himself and teach some of the courses.

It was decided that James Sharp would remain at Scalan, to serve as missioner for the Braes and maintain the farm. He would have preferred a teaching post at Aquhorties, and thought his new charge "a very gloomy prospect". He had formed no great opinion of the local Braes people. He thought them "buried in profound ignorance" and indifferent to the Church's teaching. They neglected the Sacraments, and contributed their dues with the greatest reluctance if at all. To work among them in the face of such difficulties held no attraction for him, nor would it – he supposed – for any priest.[2]

A week before the move a public roup was held of all the surplus contents of the house and farm: the herd of four cows and two calves; the farm equipment – tools, harrow, coulters, ploughs, yokes and grindstones; and the plenishings of the house – beds, tables, presses, kail box, meal barrel and chists. The appointed officials were William Gordon of Lettoch farm and William Grant of Tombreckachie, and credit was offered to all of good security making purchases of 10/- or above.[3] The sale amassed over £50 in all, though barely more than £6 of this was in cash. By far the largest purchaser was James Sharp himself, who bought house furniture and other items to the value of £21/9/10, all on credit, to supply his needs for his new life in the Braes.[4]

There were six boys transferring to Aquhorties, and they left Scalan in three separate parties over a period of nine days. It was a hard time to leave, in mid-July and the Braes at their best. The earth was warm under their feet, the land alive, and behind them Ben Rinnes cutting the blue sky. Almost out of memory were the dark, sodden seasons, and the long frost-bound months.

The first party arrived at their new home on 15 July. Waiting for them were the three staff members, John Gordon, Alexander Badenoch and George Gordon, who had been getting the house ready since the beginning of the year. Bishop Hay himself arrived on 24 July with the last of the students, Willie Sloan, accompanied also by John Sharp and two maid servants whom he had brought from Scalan.[5] He had not yet received written confirmation of a Government building grant – this would not arrive for another two months, and the first instalment itself not until December[6] – but he confidently expected it. The change of heart from the riot days of 1779 was not lost on him: "O how wonderful are the workings of Divine Providence!" he wrote to Rome; "twenty years ago they were burning our houses and chapels, and now they are helping us to build chapels and colleges!"[7]

The change that Aquhorties represented could hardly have been lost on him either, or on the boys, as they came down out of the hills and caught their first sight of it. How much bigger and grander it was than Scalan! And how utterly different from the first Scalan that they had been taught about, and which had met those first students when they came down out of the hills in 1716. This new house pointed to the future, and seemed to symbolise their Church's gradual and hard-won recovery from the body blow of the Reformation: how far it had come already, clawing its way painfully back from the dark days of its near-extinction!

Three days after the last boy arrived Bishop Hay sent word to the Procurator of the Mission that they had moved in:

We are now safely come down to this place, bag and baggage, as they say, and have taken our farewell of Scalan as a School.[8]

With this brief and unsentimental valediction he closed the door on eight decades of endeavour – of struggle often kept alive by little but faith, hope and love – and drew to an end a chapter in the history of the Catholic Church in Scotland.

NOTES

1. James Sharp to Bishop Hay, 16. 11. 1798, BL.
2. Ibid. The incidence of problems concerning marriage, dispensations, etc., (cf.

chap. 10, note 12); the numerous references to fornication and illegitimacy in the Inveravon Parish records (MF A In 1 55, ECL) – which also include some Catholics – and in the RC parish Obituaries for Glenlivet (MF A In 3 56 a, ECL); and the explicit and implicit references to non-practice in *Status Animarum* (from 1814, held at St Michael's Tomintoul), all offer a caveat against any over-sentimental view of the Braes community at this time.

3. Announcement of Sale by Public Roup, CS 1/8/1, SCA.

4. Sale by Public Roup, CS 1/8/2 and 1/8/5, SCA. The smallest purchaser was the former servant, John Cummin, who spent just 4d (cash).

5. 'Names and dates of the Arrival of Boys to Auchorthies', CS 2/14, SCA; also, 'De Schola Aquortisiana &c.' (in Latin), CS 2/11, SCA. One of the staff members, Mr John Gordon, had actually been in residence since Whitsun 1798.

6. Bishop Hay to Charles Maxwell SJ, 14. 9. 1799, BL, telling him of letters from Lord Advocate and Sir J. Hippisley confirming PM Pitt's order to the Treasury. Bishop Hay expected the money early in October. The total sum was £1600, of which £600 was designated for the building of seminaries.

7. Propaganda Archives, Scozia, 16. 8. 1799, quoted in Bellesheim A. *History of the Catholic Church of Scotland* (Edinburgh and London, 1890), vol IV, p. 262 (in Italian).

8. Bishop Hay to Charles Maxwell SJ, 27. 7. 1799, BL.

21

The Achievement of Scalan

In those eight decades Scalan had been home and school to scores of boys. Within its walls all sorts had studied – the intellectually gifted like Alexander Geddes, the many of "middle genius", the plodders like George Duncan, and even the disabled. There had been biddable boys, like Johnnie Gordon; and trouble makers – Jamie McIntyre, who had finally been sent home, or Alexander Kennedy, who came good in the end; and others who had promised well but later brought only disgrace to the Mission – John Gordon of Birkenbush who apostatised, Francis MacDonell who did the same and far worse, and Alexander Farquharson who narrowly escaped the hangman's rope. Some had been the sons of lairds and tacksmen, others from families who could not pay their board. All sorts too had taught and guided them: a succession of masters, equally diverse in their skills, virtues and failings. With this great diversity of talent, commitment and condition, yet driven by a single aim and ideal, what had Scalan achieved in those eighty-three years?

The chief touchstone for its achievement must be its success in training priests for the Mission, since this was its *raison d'être*. Unfortunately it is virtually impossible to put an exact number to this. Because the records are far from complete it is difficult to compile a definitive list of Scalan students, particularly for the early years. We have registers for the years 1762-66 and 1770-85[1]. And we can make inferences from the admissions lists of the Scots Colleges, which are extant for Rome, Douai and Spain, and have been calculated in the case of Paris.[2] Bishop Geddes' *Brief Historical Account of the Seminary at Scalan*[3] is particularly useful up to the 1760s, though he did not claim to have recorded all the students who later served the Mission, and declared himself particularly uncertain in regard to the last few years before the '45. Beyond these sources we have to rely on contemporary correspondence. But again this source is far from complete and, partly because of its need to camouflage events (especially in the early years), not always clear either in regard to students' names or as to their definite association with Scalan.

Within these limitations I have identified in Appendix I sixty-three Mission priests who certainly spent time at Scalan, to which may be added at least three 'possibles',[4] and perhaps up to three others who though ordained for the Mission never actually returned to serve on it.[5]

Of these, only three – George Gordon, Francis MacDonell and John Gordon[6] – received their entire training at the seminary, in accordance with its founder's "first dessign", and all three attended during its first forty years. Two others, John Gordon and James McLachlan, were already senior students and within about three years of ordination when the College closed. And a further six students either completed or received much of their senior training there after beginning elsewhere.

For the rest, Scalan was a junior seminary only. For a few, like the Douai students who arrived in 1793, it provided a temporary home for several months between one Scots College and another. And for John Godsman, James Leslie and James Duffus in 1720, and three Highland lads sixty years later, it was really no more than a staging post for a few weeks before they were sent abroad. While these boys can arguably be included as Scalan students for the purpose of number gathering, they were in no serious sense Scalan-trained. The average length of attendance of all students subsequently ordained was in fact only about two years and ten months.

Whatever the real total, it would fall well short of the 'upwards of a hundred' Mission priests generally claimed for Scalan, a figure which seems to have started as a round-number guess and to have become established through frequent repetition.[7] The actual total, if an exhaustive list could be compiled, would certainly not exceed seventy-five.

But this itself is surely impressive enough. It amounts to some eight or nine priests for every decade of Scalan's existence. And it becomes the more so when we recall the seniority to which some rose in later life: Hugh MacDonald, James Grant, Alexander Cameron, Alexander Paterson, Andrew Scott and Andrew Carruthers all became bishops and eventually Vicars Apostolic, and as such had a profound influence upon the Scottish Church in the eighteenth and nineteenth centuries; and Peter Grant and Paul McPherson, who held the post of Scots Agent in Rome for forty-six and forty-four years respectively, perhaps exerted an even wider influence.

Others who never rose in the ranks of the Church were deeply influential simply by their record of dedicated service. We immediately think of Mr Lachlan McIntosh, for sixty-four years priest of Glengairn, who was still visiting his far-flung Highland flock by pony until well into his nineties; or George Mathison, who served the people of Bellie, his birthplace, for close to half a century; Christopher MacRae, who laboured in remote Kintail for some fifty-five years; Anthony MacDonald, who covered his Small Isles station by boat for more than fifty; and the combative Charles ('Priest') Gordon, who stood up to bishops, and spent the entire sixty years of his priesthood in Aberdeen, where he was recognised and held in affection by all for his charity, good humour, and sharp wit.

At the other extreme were the surprisingly large number who died tragically young: Dugald MacDonald; John Gordon, whose only fault in an innocent life was neglect of himself; Donald MacDonald; Andrew Dason, whose brief spell as master at his old College had been so promising; and Angus MacDonald, who caught the illness that killed him while visiting the sick. All these men were dead within five years of their ordination. What their influence might have been, had they lived, can only be guessed at.

Because Scalan served as seminary for the Lowland District after the division of the Mission into two Vicariates in 1732, it was only during the years 1716-32, and for brief periods after the closure of Buorblach in 1774 and 1779, that Highland boys were admitted. Probably only about fourteen Scalan students from the West Highlands and Islands went on to serve the Mission, with a further five from those parts of the Grampians such as Upper Deeside that formed an eastern outpost of the Highland Vicariate. But if the College's contribution to the Highland Church was numerically small, measured in real influence it was crucial, since it gave it Hugh MacDonald who as its first bishop drew the blueprint for its future.

And for the same reason perhaps Scalan could even claim to have had some indirect influence upon Catholicism in the New World, through the thousands of Highland Catholics who emigrated there in the thirty years after Hugh MacDonald's death, though the chaplains who went with them were all trained in the West and/or abroad, and only one of them – William MacDonald – actually spent any time in the College.[8]

All but one of the rest of Scalan's students came from the Lowland District. As we might expect, their birthplaces reflect quite closely the areas of strength of the Catholic Church in the eighteenth century (Fig. 4):[9]

Fig. 4. Birthplaces of Scalan students
from the Lowland District ordained for the Mission

Lower Banffshire (Enzie and neighbourhood)	20
Upper Banffshire (Glenlivet and Strathavon)	12
Other North-East (Strathbogie, Mortlach, Cabrach etc.)	9
East Highlands	3
Edinburgh	2
Glasgow	1
Other	2
Unidentified	4

These boys were trained for the Lowland District and at its expense, and almost all went on to serve in Lowland stations, mainly those same traditional Catholic areas from which so many of them had sprung.

It is true that (except briefly at the beginning and at the very end) Scalan was never really the all-through seminary that Bishop Gordon, had hoped it would be – with hindsight, this was always going to be a pipe dream – and that it remained for the most part a junior seminary for the Scots Colleges. But if its rôle was therefore to a great extent determined by their needs, and its *Rules* modelled on theirs, the influence was not all one-way. A number of their most senior members of staff had their early training at Scalan, including several rectors: Robert Grant and John Farquharson at Douai; Alexander Cameron and John Gordon, for half a century between them at Valladolid; and Paul McPherson for twenty-seven years at Rome.

Nor should we forget the influence that Scalan must have exercised upon its own masters. The demands of looking after a small and close community, and the diverse responsibilities, surely had a lasting formative effect on them, especially those who were at or near the beginning of their priestly lives. If we omit Bishop Hay, George Duncan and the deacon William Gray, the average age of Scalan masters at the time of their appointment was under 29 years, and their length of experience as priests only 2 years 7 months. The seminary was Alexander Smith's first real posting, and his fifteen months in charge must have taught him much that he would later put to use in his long career as a bishop (though apparently it failed to teach him financial acumen). Between 1716-27 George Innes probably learned all that was needed in his later work as Prefect of Studies, Procurator, and finally Principal of the Scots College Paris. Mr John Geddes was only three years a priest when he was appointed master at Scalan, and one would like to think that the many calls upon his patience, charity and discretion during his five years there honed those natural virtues that so distinguished his later career. And – as we shall see below – the trade that young James and John Sharp learned as Scalan's last master and assistant, they would later put to use in the seminaries that were set up after it closed.

As the demography of the Catholic Church began to change towards the close of the eighteenth century, Scalan alumni were called upon to serve the new needs. The new station in the Glasgow-South Inverclyde area, established in 1792, was served by John Farquharson from 1794, and after him by Andrew Scott, who remained in the city for over thirty years, latterly as bishop. But by 1808 the Catholic population in the area had grown so large that the station had to be divided. Separate parishes were created in Greenock, Paisley and Ayr, and again in establishing all of them Scalan men played a vital part. The first three priests at both Ayr and Greenock were all former students, as was Alexander Paterson, who served at Paisley from 1812-16 and returned there as bishop in 1818-28.

Dundee was also made a separate station towards the end of the eighteenth century, reflecting its rise as an industrial centre, and it was Scalan-trained Mr Donald Stuart who was sent to serve there in the early years of the nineteenth. And at the other end of the country the little Catholic community at Dumfries, which had always been under the care of the chaplain at nearby Terregles House, became a parish in its own right in 1816, with Mr William Reid the first parish priest.

How well suited these men were for their new task we might wonder, sons of traditional rural North-East Catholicism as most of them were.[10] But, ideal or not, it is very doubtful whether the Church could have coped with the demands of its new urban flocks without these Scalan men, who played a key rôle in the crucial first few decades. But for them, the pattern of the seventeenth and early eighteenth centuries would most probably have been repeated, when hundreds or thousands had been lost to the practice of the Faith simply through lack of pastors.

The move to Aquhorties in 1799 represented an attempt to meet the needs of this growing, changing Church. But if it was a new beginning, it was also a continuation – a "new Scalan" in Bishop Hay's words – a continuity of aims and methods, and even of personnel. Bishop Hay himself lived and taught at the new college until his death in 1811, and several Scalan-trained men joined the staff, including John Sharp, James Sharp who was made Procurator in 1807 (see p. 242), and Alexander Badenoch who was appointed Rector in 1826.

As it turned out, Mr Badenoch was Aquhorties' first and last Rector, for by 1829 the college had itself become too small to meet the ever-increasing demand for priests. It was closed that year, and removed to larger premises at Blairs near Aberdeen.

And again there was continuity: James Sharp continued as Procurator of the new seminary, and his younger brother John was appointed its first President. John held the presidency of Blairs for eighteen years, after which he continued to live there until his death in 1860. He thus played a crucial part in setting the pattern for the new college, which was to remain Scotland's national seminary for 157 years, spanning the period from Catholic Emancipation to the post-Vatican II Church and the pontificate of John Paul II. Blairs in time built its own unique traditions, but it built them on the foundations of its predecessors. It was the direct descendant of the first turf house by the Crombie Burn.

*   *   *

It was the confluence of the old native and the new immigrant streams that became the nineteenth century Scottish Catholic Church, and which in time gave us the Church of today. Considering Scalan's vital rôle in regard to both those traditions, we can fairly claim that without it the Church in our country, on the threshold of a new Christian millenium, would have been very different in both size and character from the one we know.

But the full story of Scalan's achievement goes beyond the training of Mission priests. What of the students who did not pursue this vocation to the end? Or of those lay students who never planned to? Scalan nonetheless exerted an influence upon them, and through them upon society.

Six of them – John Geddes, Charles Geddes, John Anderson, John Ingram, Peter Sharp and John Dawson – followed a monastic vocation in Scots Benedictine houses abroad, the first four at Würzburg, and the other two at Ratisbon, where Fr Dawson rose to the position of prior.[11] At least one other boy, Charles Farquharson, joined the Society of Jesus.

Others made a particular contribution to their Faith as laymen. Thus John Skene opened a school in Glasgow in 1786, at a time when the tiny Catholic community was beginning to grow through the influx of Highland immigrants, but a full seven years before it could be spared a priest of its own. He went some way to filling the gap, instructing the children in Christian doctrine on Sundays, and providing a contact for Bishop Geddes, who was still covering the Glasgow area from Edinburgh.[12] His work is cited here as just one example among many, known and unknown to us; to represent all those whose careers were not specifically religious, but who through their Christian education in the Scalan community, and the ideals they learned there, influenced society for the good.

Quite a high proportion of Scalan boys, and especially its lay students, came from prominent local families. Among them were the sons of the tacksmen of Lettoch, Minmore, Auchriachan, Blairfindy and Auchnarrow. And this serves to remind us that the seminary also exerted an influence upon the local community. Not only did it provide schooling for some of its leading members, but it set standards of scholarship and a love of learning that must have had an effect upon the community as a whole. The high reputation of the remote schools of Glenlivet and Kirkmichael through the nineteenth century and beyond [13] surely owed something to the example of the seminary, remembered there with pride and affection long after its closure. And perhaps, even, its influence lies somewhere behind the love of words and verse-making that has long been an unexpected tradition among the down-to-earth farmers of the Braes.

In agriculture Scalan was always among the leaders in the Upper Braes. It was bringing barren land under the plough as early as 1717 when perhaps only Demickmore was doing so, and its success in cultivating on the *Tom* of Scalan encouraged others to follow suit and take out new tacks there. It had introduced new crops and scientific methods by the 1770s, ahead of all but the largest farms. Its willingness to run a progressive farm probably helped to ensure that its own tack was successively renewed, and may have prompted its neighbours to look to their own methods to safeguard their leases also.

In one respect, however, it is possible that the seminary may actually have had a damaging effect upon the local community; that is, in hastening the decline of Gaelic as a spoken language. Its presence certainly coincided with a critical time for Gaelic in Upper Banffshire. When it opened in 1716 the language was still spoken almost everywhere; but by the time of its closure in 1799 it was already in retreat. The decline followed the classic pattern – a gradual melting, disappearing first in the lower ends of the valleys, lingering longest in their upper reaches; a shift of habit and loyalty, part of a more general anglicisation of life-style introduced from the South; a change in which schooling played a vital part, and which therefore most affected the young.

There is fairly clear evidence that decline came earlier to Glenlivet than to neighbouring Strathavon. In 1750 Mr Duthie felt that his lack of Gaelic would have made him "useless" in the latter station, but not in the first. By the 1790s the language was "growing daily more corrupted" and the Kirk stopped using it for its services in Inveravon parish, nearly a hundred years before it finally abandoned its use in Kirkmichael (Strathavon).[14] By the 1870s there were only about a dozen persons in the whole of Glenlivet still speaking Gaelic, whereas in Upper Strathavon above Tomintoul it remained the language of the majority of the people.[15]

There were no doubt a number of reasons for its earlier decline in Glenlivet and the Braes, but one of them may well have been the presence of Scalan, with its community of incomers whose language of discourse was English, its English-speaking masters who often also served as priests to the local congregation,[16] and its many other contacts with the community.

In religion, it goes without saying, Scalan had – and has had since – a profound effect upon its local community. As a college it was at different times that community's fellow outlaw, its focus of solidarity, its Mass centre, its symbol. And for a century-and-a-half after its closure it was held in fond memory by the local people, though largely forgotten elsewhere.

In the first half of the present century writers such as Odo Blundell and Peter Anson[17] did invaluable service in helping to revive the memory. Visitors began to seek out the old seminary again, among them the students of Blairs College, whose outings to the site from the 1960s onwards (Plate 15) were organised to give them an insight into the conditions faced by an earlier generation of students, and to let them see their own vocations as part of an ongoing tradition. More recently still, through the efforts of the Scalan Association,[18] the College has been re-discovered by a wider public. Restored by the Association as a monument and pilgrimage centre, it has again become a focus of pride, spirituality, and a sense of religious history, not only locally but nationally. It is now held in regard by many – and not alone by Catholics – as a precious part of Scottish heritage.

It would be fruitless, and in a sense idle, to attempt to gauge Scalan's 'success' in achieving the aims that its founders had for it. No doubt there were times when it might have taken in more students, and when the community fell below the number supposedly required to be 'academically viable'. And for most of its days the student roll was probably lower than the ideal number for a seminary as a spiritual community. Perhaps also it might have hoped for a higher ordination rate among those whom it did admit. It was regrettable, if inevitable, that successive masters felt the need to spend such energy on making ends meet, and latterly so much care on holding onto the lease (for which reason the present work has also frequently dwelt on these issues).

It could and should have been given a higher priority as to resources, though the Mission was for most of the time severely constrained in these matters by circumstances largely beyond its control. Several of its masters felt quite bitterly that they were not given the encouragement they needed, and certainly the seminary did not enjoy the wholehearted support under some bishops that it had received from Bishop Gordon. Apart from John Geddes, perhaps none of the bishops entirely understood the difficulties of its management until Bishop Hay experienced them for himself. And, with little room for manoeuvre, their choice of master was in a few cases less than ideal. This last circumstance was of more consequence than any other shortcomings because at Scalan, as in education everywhere, good practice and standards were ultimately a question of people. It is no coincidence that the seminary's most fruitful years – under John Geddes, John Paterson and George Hay – were periods when very special men were in charge.

Ironically, at the very time when it had attained a stability, a degree of comfort, a level of organisation and staffing, and a capacity to fulfil its original mission never possible before, the Church deemed it obsolete and ready for closure.

When the two Kirk ministers visited Scalan in 1760, at its very lowest ebb, they expressed surprise at the stir caused by a place that seemed of so little consequence, and this must have been the impression it gave throughout its early days. Had they returned in later years, even at the high-water mark of its fortunes and resources, these men of the Establishment would probably still have considered it a rather poor place compared with the seats of learning to which they were accustomed, and they would have been surprised to find it thriving, indeed still surviving at all, in its retreat among the hills.

And even today it is just such a feeling of surprise that most strikes the visitor, when he or she comes upon it for the first time. What an incongruous place for a college! Here was a house, dwarfed by the huge, intractable landscape, remote, poor and unobtrusive, not a part of respected society, indeed breaking the laws of respected society by its very existence, surviving at all only through dogged determination and courage. Its influence and achievement seem quite out of proportion. Whatever its shortcomings, and quite against the odds, it vindicated the original vision of its founder, and achieved as much as he and his successors could have hoped for, and more.

It is perhaps above all this quality of strength-in-weakness that has won the respect, admiration, and affection even of those who have no close affinity with its aims.[19] And for those who share its ideals, and understand what a keystone it was in the survival and recovery of their Faith, it is remembered with love, and mentioned – as Bishop Geddes predicted – with veneration. His judgment, with which we began Scalan's story, is a fitting place to end it.

NOTES

1. Register for 1762-66 in John Geddes 'Memorie della Casa di Scalan', MS (copy made 1909), CS 1/2/2, SCA. Register for 1770-85 in 'Account Book for Scalan', CS 1/6 (a), pp. 161-4, SCA. Both also printed in Anderson W. J. 'The College of the Lowland District of Scotland at Scalan and Aquhorties: Registers and Documents', *IR*, vol. xiv, 1963, Appendix III.

2. Re Rome, see Brown W. E. et al. *The Scots College Rome* (London and Edinburgh, 1930), Register of Students, pp. 114ff. Re Madrid and Valladolid, see Taylor M. *The Scots College in Spain* (Valladolid, 1971), Appendix III, pp. 304ff. Re all the colleges except Paris, see *Records of the Scots Colleges at Douai, Rome, Madrid, Valladolid and Ratisbon* (Aberdeen, 1906), vol. I, *Register of Students*. Re Paris, see Halloran B. M. *The Scots College Paris 1603–1792* (Edinburgh, 1997), Appendix II, pp. 206ff.

3. Bishop Geddes 'A Brief Historical Account of the Seminary at Scalan', 1777, CS 1/3, SCA, also printed in Anderson W. J., *Op. cit.*, pp. 93-105.

4. Possibles: Angus MacGillis, b. North Morar, at Scots College Rome 1730–1740, ordained Rome 1740, served as chaplain in '45 and later at Lochaber; may have attended Scalan briefly before Rome. Alexander MacDonald, b. 1719 Kinlochmoidart, at Scots College Rome from 1737, ordained Rome 1746, served at Knoydart, d. 1797; may have attended Scalan briefly in 1737 before travelling from there to Rome with Dugald MacDonald. Alexander MacDonald, who attended Scalan Dec. 1775–Nov. 1776 before transferring

to Douai – not certain if he can be identified with one of several priests of this name (confusion and ambiguity in clergy lists).

5. Ordained for Mission but did not return to serve on it: Definite: William Gordon, b. 1722 Strathbogie, who graduated to the Scots College Rome, and was ordained there c. 1749, remaining in Rome 1749–51, at Loretto from 1751. Possible: William Farquharson, b. 1712 Auchriachan, to Scots College Paris 1726, expelled but ordained at Troyes 1735. Received pre-Paris education at Catholic school at Auchriachan, but may have attended Scalan briefly c. 1726. Possible: Andrew Riddoch, b. 1700, at Scots College Paris from 1721, returned to Scotland, to Paris again 1734, ordained there 1740, remained all his life as Procurator of College, d. 1772; may have been at Scalan briefly c. 1732.

6. John Gordon only remained at Scalan because the conditions in the years after the '45 made it impossible to send him to Paris as planned. We could almost add Hugh MacDonald to the list, since he moved to Scalan after twenty months at the seminary on Eilean Bàn.

7. Early in the present century Dom Odo Blundell asserted that "over a hundred missionaries were educated wholly or partially within its walls" – Blundell O. *The Catholic Highlands of Scotland* (Edinburgh, 1909 and 1917), vol. I (1909), p. 24. The popularity of his book gave the figure currency, and his (deserved) authority gave it unquestioned acceptance.

8. Mr William MacDonald served for twenty years in Glengarry County, Upper Canada. He actually only spent a few months at Scalan after his escape from Douai in 1793, before being sent to Valladolid.

9. A complete list of students, including lay students who were usually quite local, would reveal an even greater dominance of Banffshire.

10. Cf., Aspinwall B. 'Scots and Irish Clergy Ministering to Immigrants, 1830– 1878', *IR*, vol. xlvii, no. 1, spring 1996.

11. Re Peter Sharp and John Dawson, see Dilworth M. 'Two Necrologies of Scottish Benedictine Abbeys in Germany', *IR*, vol. ix, no. 2, autumn 1958; re John and Charles Geddes and John Anderson, see Dilworth M. 'Scottish Benedictines at Würzburg, A Supplement to the Necrology', *IR*, vol. xv, no. 2, autumn 1964.

12. Bishop Geddes to Bishop Hay, 30. 11. 1786, BL. John Skene had actually been dismissed as "unfit" by Mr Paterson in 1778.

13. Barclay W. *The Schools and Schoolmasters of Banffshire* (Banff, 1925), pp. 166, 170 and 180f. Barclay himself does not point to the influence of Scalan.

14. Re corruption, see OSA vol. xviii, p. 454; (the return for Inveravon parish does not refer to Gaelic at all). Re Kirk abandoning Gaelic in Inveravon at end of 18C, cf. Douglas T. (Earl of Selkirk) *Observations on the Present State of the Highlands of Scotland* (Edinburgh, 1806), Appendix V; re Kirkmichael parish finally giving it up c. 1893, see Calder R. H. *Glenlivet Gleanings* (Banff, 1914), p. 27. But we should not draw too firm conclusions from the Kirk's arrangements, since in both Inveravon and Kirkmichael the Protestant population lived mainly at the lower (more English-speaking) ends of the parishes.

15. Ravenstein E. G. 'On the Celtic Languages in the British Isles: a Statistical Survey', *J. Royal Stat. Soc.*, 1879, p. 597. Recordings were made as late as

1956 of the last surviving native Gaelic speaker in Glen Avon, who recalled that Gaelic was the only language she spoke as a young child in the 1880s – Jean Ann Cameron, taped reminiscences, SA 1956/41, School of Scottish Studies, Univ. of Edinburgh.

16. Of all Scalan's masters only John Farquharson of Glen Conglas, and probably his cousin Alexander Farquharson from Minmore, as well as Francis MacDonell of Glengarry, were fluent native speakers of Gaelic. They were in charge for less than five years between them. John Alexander Grant had reasonable command of the language, though not born to it.

17. Blundell O. *Op. cit.*, and Anson P. *The Caravan Pilgrim* (London, 1938), pp. 163f. It was Anson who first suggested that the old building should be acquired and its history made better known.

18. The Scalan Association was founded in 1946 by three priests, Frs Peter Bonnyman, David McRoberts and Alexander MacWilliam, with the stated aim "to restore and maintain Scalan as a place of pilgrimage and a national monument for the Catholics of Scotland." The house was purchased for £50 the same year. The Association has restored the exterior and much of the interior. In its early years it had a small membership, mainly clergy, but in the present decade interest has burgeoned – thanks in no small measure to its lively and informative biannual magazine *Scalan News* – and membership now stands at over 600.

19. For example, the warm accounts by Church of Scotland ministers, Stark J. *Priest Gordon of Aberdeen* (Aberdeen, 1909), pp. 16ff.; and Dunnett H. *Invera'an, a Speyside Parish* (Paisley, 1919), pp. 114ff.

Postscript: Scalan After They Left

After the seminary closed James Sharp continued to live in a house that was now far too large for his needs. The furniture was his own, and Bishop Hay supplied him with other items including his bed and blankets. He farmed the land and increased its yield.[1]

The 'Weaver's Croft' had been transferred into Bishop Hay's name around 1789,[2] and this arrangement lasted until 1803 when all the tacks in Glenlivet were renewed. It was then subsumed into the rest of the Church's holding, and the whole leased to Mr Sharp as a single tack in his own name, at an annual rental of £6.[3] The lease was binding for one year only, to be reviewed and if need be extended annually. This arrangement, which applied also to the other tenants of the Scalan tack and elsewhere, in effect allowed the Duke to increase his rentals at will. And the very next year he did so, in the case of Scalan farm from £49 to £56. Mr Sharp was able to meet this sum, and was given the opportunity to acquire the whole tack – Easter and Wester Scalan, Fuarandearg, and the Eskiemullach ('Weaver's') Croft – on a long-term lease.[4] As was normal in the case of Catholic clergymen holding leases on the Gordon estates, his lease was dependent on his not being moved from the district, and was thus defined in the contract as "Dur^g Incum [during his incumbency] or 19 years." He in effect became the tacksman, with the other tenants paying their rent to him and continuing to farm their strips of land as before.

Serving the people of the Braes, and celebrating Mass for them in the 'downstairs' chapel on Sundays, he came to know his congregation better, and in time grew fond of them and began to feel at home among them. And they for their part gave warm evidence of their acceptance of 'the Professor' and of their growing affection for him.[5] It was a relaxed life he had now, and free of care.

Then unexpectedly in the spring of 1807 he received word from Bishop Cameron that he was to join the teaching staff at Aquhorties. Eight years before, the post would have been just what he wanted, but now – compared with his present work – he could only see it as "a very laborious and at the same time a very precarious station."

He warned Bishop Cameron that his leaving might well jeopardise the Church's possession of the land. The Duke had granted the lease to him and allowed him to acquire the whole of Scalan farm because he knew him personally, but it was doubtful whether he "might be disposed to grant the same Indulgence to another." The factor had told him frankly that "had it been B.Hay who had to transact, the Mission would have lost every furrow of it."[6] The contract only covered his own incumbency, after all, and the latest word from the Castle was that his neighbours in the Braes had made application to have the land recovered as soon as he vacated. In that case the bishop would have to apply to the Duke himself, as soon as possible, and take his chance in competition with other would-be tenants.[7]

Bishop Cameron's main concern was to keep possession of the house, with its chapel, and the ground on which it stood – the 'Park' on the east side of the Crombie – which he felt would be ample for the Mission's needs in the area. His plan was not to replace Mr Sharp, but to have the neighbourhood served in future by the priest from Tombae visiting the chapel occasionally; and to give his own unmarried sister Helen occupancy of the house, in the hope that the country air would be kinder to her health than Edinburgh.[8]

But though the farm was less important he was confident that the Church would be allowed to keep it also, if the lease was renewed in his own name. As he understood it, the Duke's practice when leasing land to priests of the Mission had always been to grant it to the current incumbent *and his successors in office*. There would be no successor to Mr Sharp, of course, but the factor would surely agree to grant the lease to him, as a bishop of the Mission, in preference to any other applicant.[9] In fact his argument was accepted and the lease was transferred to him, with security until 1823, but again with no guarantee in regard to a successor.[10]

Mr Sharp held a roup of his effects on 10 June. Most of the furniture and the other contents of the house were bought by Miss Cameron, and she was able to move in at once, while he was still in occupation.

Since the farm offered no long-term prospects for the Mission, Bishop Cameron believed it would be wasted effort and expense to continue to work it themselves. His real purpose in holding on to it was to sub-let it locally, to bring in money for the upkeep of the house and the general funds of the Mission. He asked his sister and Mr Sharp to be alert for offers, and when one came from John Stuart of Balevlair, on terms that seemed too good to miss, he urged them to accept.[11] Stuart was promising £25 rental for the coming year, and to match any rival offer in future years. In addition he guaranteed to graze Helen Cameron's milch cow, lead and thatch her peats, tend her garden, provide her with a horse, and keep the Park in grass for visitors. The deal would give him part-occupancy of the house,[12] but this would actually be an advantage because Miss Cameron could not possibly upkeep it all herself. He seemed willing, in fact, to do everything that she in her circumstances could not do. His offer was gladly accepted.

Early in September Mr Sharp left to take up his teaching post at Aquhorties. He had already learned, to his surprise and rather against his will, that he was to take charge of the Aquhorties farm also,[13] but he soon found out that he was in fact to become Procurator of the whole establishment. It was a post he would hold for nearly twenty years: so his new station turned out to be quite as laborious, but by no means so precarious, as he had feared.

Helen Cameron lived on in the house, supported by her brother. He helped her with money and food parcels and was in fact a lifeline to her, her "great and only benefactor", for she felt herself lonely, isolated and friendless in the big house. Alexander Paterson, the priest at Tombae, kept his cattle and horses on the land, and had meal delivered to her regularly,[14] but he was an infrequent visitor, only appearing when he had occasion to collect his beasts. Left on her own, she was the prey of local children who trespassed and caused damage.[15] John Stuart had forgotten his promises. He rarely provided her with a horse, which would have been so useful in her isolation, and refused even to feed her hens. He had not moved into the house, which as a result, she told her brother, had in two years become like one of the slums below his house in Blackfriars Wynd. She believed that Stuart was planning to use the ground floor as a byre, which indeed could hardly be worse than it was. And around the yard things were no better:

> All is going to wreck, office houses, Gardens and dykes. they were to have been vallued at last martinmass, it was never done as yet, the sheep coat is fallen & the door & wood stolen and no one to look after or care how things Go.[16]

Despite the conditions she continued to live in the house, never coming to terms with the life of the Braes and always the outsider. She was still occupying part of it when the local priest at Tombae began keeping parish records in 1814.[17] By then she perhaps felt that she was too old to face the upheaval of a flitting, and had reconciled herself to ending her days there, whatever the hardships. She lived eighteen more years, and was buried in the parish in 1832.[18]

The whole tack of Scalan remained in Bishop Cameron's name until it expired in 1823. When new tacks were drawn up that year the Church gave up tenancy of nearly all the land, which was again divided up into Easter and Wester Scalan and Fuarandearg and redistributed to local people. One of the new co-tenants of Easter Scalan was John Cummin, the servant lad who had been taken on at the seminary more than half a century before, and who was now approaching seventy.[19] His and all the other leases were extended annually and held by the same tenants or their families throughout the 1820s and 1830s.[20]

The Church retained its land on the east side of the Crombie – the old Park, with the adjacent Eskiemullach (or 'Weaver's') Croft. It was held in the name of Alexander Paterson, the former priest of Glenlivet who was now Assistant Bishop of the Lowland District and living in Paisley.[21] The records name James Michie, John Lamb and the Widow Gordon as his sub-tenants from Whitsun 1823. Michie, who was master at the local school at Achnascra (before he turned to whisky-smuggling), had the largest holding, three-quarters of the whole;[22] Lamb took over the widow's portion in 1825.[23]

Among the other local contracts drawn up in 1823 was one for a new tack at Faevait, a plot of barren land $1\frac{1}{2}$ miles down the Braes that formed a corner of the Vattich Moss. It was taken up jointly by John Stuart and John Williamson, the old Scalan farm manager in the days of Bishop Hay.[24] Williamson must have been an old man by this date, and three years later the Rentals show Stuart as the only tenant.[25]

Since Mr Sharp's departure the Scalan chapel had never in fact been used as planned, and the local people had been making a seven mile round trip to the church at Tombae for Sunday Mass.[26] When the one-time Scalan student Abbé Paul McPherson returned to his birthplace from Rome in 1827 he was determined to bring Mass back to the Braes. At first he considered building a new church on the land of the former seminary, which was still held in Bishop Paterson's name. But when the Duke offered him the lease of Faevait [27] he readily accepted, since it was far more central to the Braes than Scalan. In 1829 he erected a church and presbytery on the newly acquired land, and three years later added a boys' and a girls' school.[28] His church was the forerunner of today's parish church, which stands on the same site.

Since the new property amply covered the Mission's needs, the Church's interest in the old seminary land and buildings now finally ceased, and Faevait – or Chapeltown, as it came to be called – replaced Scalan as the centre of Catholicism in the Braes. Bishop Paterson gave up his tenancy of all the land beside the old college – the Park and the Croft – which now passed directly to his sub-tenants John Lamb and James Michie.[29] As to the house itself, there were at this time some fifty-five tenant families living on the lands of Scalan and Tomnalienan,[30] and several were eager enough to take up residence in it. Shortly after Helen Cameron's death in 1832 they began to do so.

Their story, and that of their neighbours and descendants, falls outside the scope of the present history, and in any case will shortly be told elsewhere.[31] But it is good to know that great-grandchildren of John Cummin, the Lambs and the McPhersons were still farming the land in the area at the end of the nineteenth century,[32] and that some of their descendants are still to be found in the Braes of Glenlivet to this day.

NOTES

1. James Sharp to Bishop Cameron, 26. 5. 1807, BL.
2. Parish of Inveravon Rental, 1799, GD 44/51/741/5/3, SRO. Cf. Chap. 17, note 6.
3. Minutes of Factor's meeting re Rentals, at Hardhaugh 7. 7. 1803, Crofts of Eskemulloch, GD 44/23/7/2, p. 46, SRO.
4. Rental Book 1804-09, Lordship of Glenlivet, CR 6/3, f. 72, SRO. Rev. Alexander Innes had a similar tenure at Shenval; Mr John Gordon's lands at Haddoch and Kirktown were for his incumbency or 7 years; Mr Alexander Paterson had an unqualified 19 year tack at Tombae.
5. James Sharp to Bishop Cameron, 26. 5. 1807, BL. The next paragraph also from this source.
6. James Sharp to Bishop Cameron, 30. 5. 1807, BL.
7. James Sharp to Bishop Cameron, 4. 6. 1807, BL.
8. Bishop Cameron to James Sharp, 3. 6. 1807, BL.
9. Bishop Cameron to James Sharp, 10. 6. 1807, BL.
10. Bishop Cameron to James Sharp, 9. 9. 1807, PL.
11. Ibid.
12. Helen Cameron to Bishop Cameron, 3. 9. 1807, PL.
13. James Sharp to Bishop Cameron, from Aquhorties, 10. 6. 1808, BL.
14. Helen Cameron to Bishop Cameron, 15. 9. 1812, PL.
15. Helen Cameron to Bishop Cameron, 8. 1. 1808, PL.
16. Helen Cameron to Bishop Cameron, 9. 9. 1809, PL.
17. 'Status Animarum', record kept by Mr James Gordon from 1814, now held at St Michael's Tomintoul.
18. Glenlivet RC parish Obituaries (from 1817), MF A In 3 56a, ECL.
19. Rentals, Lordship of Glenlivet, 1825 (but from Whitsun 1823), CR 6/4, p. 91, SRO.
20. Rentals 1826-37, GD 44/53/24/43, SRO; and General Rental, Gordon Estates, Lordship of Glenlivet, 1838, CR 6/5, SRO.
21. Factor's Report, Strathavon, State of Arrears of Rent, 6. 7. 1824, GD 44/23/8, SRO.
22. Rentals, Lordship of Glenlivet, 1825, CR 6/4, p. 91, SRO. For a full account of James Michie and his contemporaries in the neighbourhood, see Roberts A. 'Tombae and Scalan: *Status Animarum*', *Scalan News*, no. 10, June 1995.
23. Rentals 1826-37, GD 44/53/24/43, SRO. The Glenlivet RC parish Obituaries (MF A In 3 56a, ECL) record the death of a Margaret Gordon at Scalan farm in 1832.
24. Rentals, Lordship of Glenlivet, CR 6/4, p. 91. 'Faevait' is an anglicisation of

Féithe Bhad ('the Moss of Tufts'), as 'Vattich Moss' is of *Féithe Bhadach* ('Tufty Moss').

25. Rental 1826, GD 44/53/24/43, SRO. Unfortunately the obituary list in the Old Parish Record of Inveravon is incomplete around this date, and includes no reference to John Williamson.

26. Mass was also occasionally celebrated in the kitchen of Lettoch farm.

27. Rental 1830, GD 44/53/24/43, SRO.

28. Abbé Paul returned to Rome in 1834 but the land continued in his name until 1838, when it was transferred to the tenancy of Bishop Kyle. (The Scottish Mission had been re-organised in 1827, the old two-fold division of High-land-Lowland giving way to a three-fold division into East, West and North Districts. Bishop Kyle was the first Vicar Apostolic of the new North District.) Cf., Rentals 1833, 1835 and 1837, GD 44/53/24/43, SRO; and General Rental 1838, Lordship of Glenlivet, CR 6/5, item 149, SRO. It is possible that the tenancy was transferred to Bishop Kyle because the priest who had succeeded Paul McPherson at Chapeltown, William Dundas, was dying of smallpox. He died that December.

29. Rentals 1826-37, GD 44/53/24/43, SRO. Lamb and Michie continued in possession throughout the 1830s; James Michie died in 1853.

30. Abstract of Report regarding District of Strathavon and Glenlivet, 19. 1. 1832, Glenlivet Legal Papers, GD 44/23/24, no. 8, SRO.

31. Roberts A. (ed.) *Tales of the Braes of Glenlivet* (forthcoming, Edinburgh, 1999?).

32. Cf., Census of 1891; also, signatures of donors of Album to James MacLachlan Smith, head teacher of St Mary's School Chapeltown, on occasion of his retirement, 25. 5. 1896, copy given to author by Veronica Gordon Smith, Edinburgh.

APPENDIX I

Scalan Masters

Note: in a few cases months are approximate

George Innes ?	Sept.–Nov. 1716
Alexander Smith	Nov. 1716–Jan. 1718
George Innes	Jan. 1718–June 1722
J. Alexander Grant	June 1722–Sept. 1724
John Tyrie	Sept. 1724–Feb. 1725
J. Alexander Grant	Feb. 1725–Dec. 1726
George Innes	Dec. 1726–June 1727 (from Balnacraig)
George J. Gordon	June 1727–Aug. 1738
Alexander Gordon	Aug. 1738–Sept. 1741
William Duthie	Sept. 1741–Sept. 1758
George Duncan	Oct. 1758–May 1759
William Gray	May 1759–Sept. 1762
John Geddes	Sept. 1762–Dec. 1767
John Thomson	Dec. 1767–Apr. 1770
John Paterson	Apr. 1770–Aug. 1783
John Farquharson	Sept. 1783–Aug. 1784
Alexander Farquharson	Sept. 1784–Aug. 1787
Andrew Dason	Aug. 1787–June 1788
Bishop George Hay	July 1788–July 1793
(John Ingram acting	Oct. 1791–May 1792)
(Andrew Carruthers acting	July–Aug. 1793)
Bishop John Geddes	Aug.–Oct. 1793
James Sharp	Nov. 1793–July 1799

APPENDIX II

Scalan Students Who Became Priests of the Scottish Mission

(See also Chapter 21 note 4 for names of other 'possibles', and note 5 for one definite Scalan student and two 'possibles' who though ordained for the Mission did not return to serve on it.)

Note: Chronological by date of admission.
    Date and place of birth in ( );dates at Scalan in **bold**; college to/ from which graduated in [ ]; date and place of ordination in *italics*; some details of later careers included.

Hugh MacDonald (1699, Morar); [from Eilean Bàn];**1716–1725**; *1725 Scalan*; Moidart (1725–6), Morar (1726–46), bishop (1731–1773), d. 1773.

George J. Gordon (1699, Fochabers); **1716–1725**; *1725 Scalan*; Glenlivet, Scalan Master (1726–38), Aberdeen (1739–66), d. 1766.

James Leslie (?, NE); **summer 1720**; [to Rome]; *1729 Rome*; Uist (1729–c.1740), Traquair (1740–45), Flanders (1747–80), d. 1780.

James Duffus (1703, Fochabers); **summer 1720**; [to Rome]; *1730 Rome*; Strathavon (1731–4), Deeside (1734–62), d. 1762.

John Godsman (1699, Dallachy, nr. Speymouth); **summer 1720**; [to Rome]; *1729 Rome*; Auchinhalrig (1734–69), d. 1769.

James Grant (1706, Wester Boggs, Enzie); **1724–1725**; [to Rome]; *1733 Rome*; Lochaber, South Uist and Barra (1736–47), Preshome (1748–59), bishop (1755), Lowland Vicar Apostolic (1767–78), d. 1778.

Peter Grant (1708, Blairfindy, Glenlivet); **c. 1724–1725**; [to Rome]; *1735 Rome*; Glengarry (1735–7), Scots Agent Rome (1737–83), d. 1784.

George Duncan (?, Edinburgh); [from Paris]; **1726–1732**; *1732 Scalan*; teacher in Highlands (1732–3), Scalan Assistant Master (1733–4), Angus etc. (1734–46), Traquair (1748–52), Edinburgh (1752–8), Scalan Master (1758–9), d. 1761.

Francis MacDonald (or MacDonell) (c. 1716, Kiltry, Glengarry); **1727–1736**; *1736 Scalan*; Scalan Assistant Master (1736–7), Moidart (1737–40), suspended (1742), apostatised (1743), Church of Scotland minister Strontian (1744), other posts in Highlands, d. 1784.

Allan MacDonald (1696, Stoneybridge South Uist); [from Eilean Bàn (1714–15), Rome (1715–1721), Douai (1727–1728)]; **1728–1730**; teacher in Highlands (1730–42); *1742 Highlands*; companion of Charles Edward Stuart, imprisoned; abroad (1746–68); latterly resident in Edinburgh, d. 1781.

William Reid (1713, Wester Boggs, Enzie); **1728–1733**; [to Rome]; *1739 Rome*; Mortlach etc. (1739–69), Aberdeen (1769–73), d. 1785.

Alexander Gordon (1710, Coffurich); [from Paris]; **1729–1730**; [to Paris, then returned]; **1732–1734**; *1734 Scalan*; Deeside (1734–5), Scots College Paris (1735–8), Scalan Master (1738–41), Edinburgh (1741–63), Stobhall (1763–76), Edinburgh (1778–93), d. 1793.

John Gordon (1706, Birkenbush, Enzie); [from Paris]; **1732–1734**; *1734 Scalan*; Preshome (1735–42), Aberdeen (1742–5), Buchan (1747–50), deserted Mission (1750), apostatised and later married, d. 1783.

Dugald MacDonald (1720, Uist); c. **1735–1737**; [to Rome]; *1746 Rome*; Rome (1746–8), Uist (1748–51), d. 1751.

Robert Grant (c. 1720, Blairfindy, Glenlivet); c. **1736–1740**; [to Paris, then Rome]; *1748 Rome*; 5 stations (1749–64), Rector Scots College Douai (1765–84), d. 1784.

John Gordon (1729, Glenlivet); **1743–1754**; *1754 Edinburgh*; Glenlivet (1755–7), d. 1757.

Alexander Geddes (1737, Pathhead, Enzie); **1755–1758**; [to Paris]; *1764 Paris*; Traquair (1766–8), Auchinhalrig (1769–79), dismissed from Mission (1779) and went to London, noted biblical scholar, d. 1802.

Alexander Kennedy (?, Perthshire?); **1756–1759**; [to Rome, returned as subdeacon]; **1765–1766**; [to Rome, and returned]; **1767**; *1767 Scalan*; Arisaig and Small Isles, d. 1773.

Alexander Cameron (1747, Auchindryne, Braemar); c. **1760–1764**; [to Rome]; *1772 Rome*; Tomintoul (1772–80), Rector Scots College Valladolid (1780–98), bishop (1798), Lowland Vicar Apostolic (1811–25), d. 1828.

John Gordon (1747, Clashnoir); c. **1761–1764**; [to Rome]; *1774 Rome*; Aberdeen (1774–6), Vice Rector Scots College Valladolid (1776–1802), Rector (1802–10), d. 1810.

John Paterson (c. 1747, Coffurich, Enzie); c. **1761–1762**; [to Würzburg, and returned]; **1764–1770**; *1770 Edinburgh*; Master Scalan (1770–83), d. 1783.

Alexander Innes (1750, Balnacraig); **1763–1764**; [to Paris]; *1777 Paris*; Drummond Castle (1780–1), Prefect of Studies Paris (1781–1792), Procurator (1792), d. 1803.

John Farquharson (1748, Glen Conglas); **1764–1768**; [to Rome, then Douai]; *1776 Douai*; Prefect Studies Douai (1776–81), Strathavon

(1781–3), Master Scalan (1783–4), Principal Scots College Douai (1785–93), 5 stations (1793–1814), Paris (1815–7), d. 1817.

James Cameron (1755, Dalbreckie?); **1764–c. 1769**; [to ?]; *c. 1778, ?*; 4 stations (1778–89), insane at Stobhall (1789–1813), d. 1813.

William Hay (1751, Flanders); **1765–1769**; [to Rome, then Douai]; *1776 Douai*; Stobhall (1776–83), dismissed from duties (1783), teacher, to America as tutor (1786), d. ?

George Mathison (1756, Bellie); **c. 1767–1770**; [to Valladolid]; *1778 Valladolid*; Auchinhalrig (1779–1828), d. 1828.

Peter Hay (? , ?); **c. 1767–1770**; [to Paris]; *1777 Paris*; Prefect of Studies Paris (1777–81), Auchinhalrig (1781–83), d. 1783.

Paul McPherson (1756, Clash of Scalan); **1768–1769**; [to Rome, then Valladolid]; *1779 Valladolid*; 4 stations (1779–93), Scots Agent Rome (1793–8), Huntly (1798–9), Agent and Rector Scots College Rome (1800–27), Glenlivet (1827–34), Agent and Rector Rome (1734–46), d. 1846.

William Reid (1758, Fochabers); **1768–1769**; [to Douai]; *1780 Douai*; Cabrach (1780–84), Kempcairn (1784–1825), d. 1825.

Robert Menzies (?, Aberfeldy); **1769–1770**; [later to Douai]; *1776 Douai;* Edinburgh Highland chapel (1776–91), d. 1791.

Lachlan MacIntosh (1753, Braemar); **July – Nov. 1770**; [to Valladolid, left and returned there]; *1782 Valladolid*; Glengairn (1782–1846), d. 1846.

John Anderson (1758, Glenbuchat); **1771–1772**; [to Ratisbon, left 1781]; **1788** Assistant Master Scalan; [to Würzburg]; *1792 Würzburg*; Würzburg as ordained Benedictine priest (1792–1828), d. 1828. (Not on Mission, but included here as having briefly served as Assistant Master at Scalan).

Alexander Farquharson (1758, Minmore, Glenlivet); **1771–1775**; [to Rome]; *1784 Rome*; Master Scalan (1784–7), Cabrach (1787–93), dismissed (1793), wandered in Europe and South America, in poverty in London, d. 1811.

John Gordon (1760?, Landends, Enzie); **1771–1774**; [to Valladolid]; *1784 Edinburgh*; Aberdeen (1785–97), Procurator Aquhorties (1799–1807), Eastlands and Factor Blairs (1808–23), d. 1823.

Donald Stuart (1756, Strathavon); **1771–1772**; [to Rome]; *1781 Rome*; Tomintoul (1783–1804), Dundee (1804–18), Elgin (1818–20), d. 1820.

Andrew Dason (1764, Haddoch, Cabrach); **1772–1777**; [to Valladolid]; *1785 Valladolid*; Shenval (1785–7), Master Scalan (1787–8), d. 1788.

Donald MacDonald (? , ?); **1773–1776**; [to Douai]; *1782 Douai*; Master at Samalaman (1783–5), d. 1785.

Angus MacDonald (?, Retland, South Morar); **1773–1776**; [to Valladolid]; *1782 Valladolid*; Kintail (1782–4), d. 1784.

Thomas Bagnall (1761, Glasgow); **1774–1778**; [to Douai, then Valladolid]; *c. 1787 Valladolid*; Professor Valladolid (1789–94), Kirkconnell (1795–1822), New Abbey (1822–6), d. 1826.

James Catanach (?, Gairnside); **1775–1776**; [to Buorblach, then Paris]; *1788 Paris*; served at Braemar, Barra, Lismore, Campbeltown, d. 1836.

Alexander Cameron (1767, Braemar); **1777–1779**; [to Valladolid]; *1792 Edinburgh*; Edinburgh (1794–8), Vice Rector Valladolid (1798–1809), Rector (1809–33), d. 1833.

John Davidson (?, Enzie); **1777–1779**; [to Valladolid]; *1792 Edinburgh*; Buchan (1792–3), Tombae (1793–4), Auchindoun (1794–1804), Professor Aquhorties (1804–8), Greenock (1808–15), d. 1815.

William Reid (1766, Enzie); **1778–1779**; [to Valladolid]; *1792 Edinburgh*; Stobhall (1792–1812), Terregles (1812–16), Procurator of Mission Edinburgh (1817–29), Dumfries (1829–45), d. 1845.

Anthony MacDonald (? , ?); **1778–1779**; [to Douai]; *1790?, ?*; Small Isles – with some time at Samalaman – (1790–1843), d. 1843.

Austin MacDonald (? , Drimore, S. Uist); [from Valladolid]; Master Buorblach (1777–9); Assistant Master Scalan **1779**, again **1780**; *1780, Scalan*; Strathavon (1780–1), d. 1781.

Alexander Paterson (1766, Pathhead, Enzie); **April – Oct. 1780**; [to Douai]; *1791 Douai*; Prefect of Studies Douai (1791–3), Tombae (1793–1812), Paisley (1812–16), bishop (1816), Paisley (1818–28), Edinburgh (1828–31), d. 1831.

Roderick MacDonald (1763, Garrfluich, South Uist); **June – July 1780**; [to Valladolid]; *1791 Edinburgh*; Badenoch (1791–1803), Uist (1803–28), d. 1829.

Christopher MacRae (1764, Kintail); **July – Sept. 1780**; [to Valladolid]; *1787 Valladolid*; Kintail (1787–1842), d. 1842.

James Sharp (1768, Mortlach); **1781–1782**; [to Rome]; *1793 Rome*; Edinburgh (1793), Master Scalan (1793–99), Braes Glenlivet (1799–1807), Procurator Aquhorties (1807–26), Preshome (1826–9), Procurator Blairs (1829–37), d. 1837.

Angus MacDonald (1762, ?); **Aug. – Sept. 1781**; [to Rome, then Douai]; *1791 Douai*; Professor Samalaman (1795–1802), Barra (1804–25), Rector Scots College Rome (1827–33), d. 1833.

James MacLachlan (1771, Cabrach); **1782–1786**; [to Rome]; *1795 Rome*; Banff (1795–1815), Huntly (1819–27), dismissed (1827), Rome and England, re-admitted (1832), Preshome (1832–46), d. 1846.

William Wallace (1767, Kinnore, Strathbogie); **1784 -1788**; [to Douai]; c. **May – Sept. 1793**;[to Valladolid]; *1798 Valladolid*; Professor and Procurator Valladolid (1798–1808), Professor Aquhorties (1808–9), 4 posts (1809–22), Traquair and Borders (1822–54), d. 1854.

Charles Gordon (1772, Landends, Enzie); **1785–1786**; [to Douai, then completed studies at Aberdeen]; *1795 Aberdeen*; Aberdeen (1795–1855), d. 1855.

George Gordon (1776, Fochabers); **1785–1788**; [to Valladolid]; *1797 Valladolid*; Professor Valladolid (1797–8), Foggyloan (1799–1805), Professor Blairs (1805–8), Auchindoun (1808–25), Dufftown (1825–48), d. 1856.

Andrew Scott (1772, Chapelford, Enzie); **1785–1786**; [to Douai]; **c. May – Sept. 1793**; [completed studies at Aberdeen]; *1795 Aberdeen*; Deecastle (1795–99), Huntly (1799–1805), Glasgow (1805–36), bishop (1828), Western District Vicar Apostolic (1832–45), Greenock (1836–45), d. 1846.

John Sharp (1772, Mortlach); **Jan. – June 1785**; [to Valladolid]; *1795 Valladolid*; Assistant Master Scalan (1796–99), Professor Aquhorties (1799–1801), 3 stations (1801–28), President Blairs (1829–47), retired at Blairs (1847–60), d. 1860.

Alexander Badenoch (1773, Keith); **1787–1788**; [to Douai]; **1793–1794**; [to Valladolid]; *1798 Valladolid*; Professor Aquhorties (1799–1802), Tomintoul (1804–8), Edinburgh (1808–17), Preshome (1817–26), Rector Aquhorties (1826–9), Edinburgh (1829–36), d. 1836.

James MacLachlan (1774, Strathavon); **1788–1799**; [to Aquhorties]; *1802 Aquhorties*; Professor Aquhorties (1802–3), 4 posts (1803–11), d. 1811.

John Gordon (1779, Tullochalum); **1790**; [to Rome (arrived 1792), then returned]; **1798–1799**; [to Aquhorties]; *1802 Aquhorties*; Professor Aquhorties (1802–15), Greenock (1815–33), d. 1833.

Andrew Carruthers (1770, New Abbey); [from Douai]; **1792–1793** (Acting Master Scalan July – Aug. 1793); [completed studies at Aberdeen]; *1795 Aberdeen*; Traquair (1797–1800), Munshes (1800–14), Dalbeattie (1818–33), bishop and Eastern District Vicar Apostolic (1833–52), d. 1852.

William MacDonald (?, ?); **c. May – Sept. 1793**; [to Valladolid]; *1798 Valladolid*; Deecastle (1799–1801), Professor Aquhorties (1801–4), Auchindoun (1804–9), left Mission (1809), in London (1810–26), Glengarry County Canada (1826–47), d. 1847.

Donald Carmichael (1782, Millhole); **1795–1799**; [to Aquhorties]; *1808 Aquhorties*; Tomintoul (1808–37), Procurator Blairs (1837–52), d. 1854.

William Thomson (1785, Braes of Enzie); **c. 1796–1799**; [to Aquhorties]; *1807 Preshome*; Deecastle (1808–22), Ayr and Ayrshire (1822–57), d. 1859.

APPENDIX III

A Note on the Issue
of Students' Social Backgrounds

The strategic importance of persons of influence (particularly the Highland chiefs and tacksmen) in protecting and fostering the Catholic Church
in the seventeenth and early eighteenth centuries, and the attention paid
to them by the Church leaders, were noted in Chapter 1.

The Church's endeavours in education were mainly aimed at this section
of society, since Bishop Nicolson knew that according to their schooling the
sons of chiefs and tacksmen were likely either to maintain the Faith or lead
their "dependants" into heresy (Chapter 1). Thus the pupils at the Catholic
school at Arisaig, for example, comprised "above thirty schollars off the
best Gentlemens children of the Highlands" (Chapter 2).

In the early eighteenth century the bishops deliberately selected well-
born boys for Scalan and the Scots Colleges, on the grounds that boys of
low birth would be despised if sent back as priests to their own people (cf.
the letter of Bishops Gordon and Wallace to Cardinal Falconieri, 13. 11.
1731, Chapter 6).

In Scalan's case the issue of students' social backgrounds arose at least
twice more in later years:

1) In 1763 when John Geddes wrote references for Sandy Cameron and
John Gordon his inclusion of details of their family backgrounds was
questioned by Bishop Smith, who argued that such information was
irrelevant to their suitability for the priesthood. Mr Geddes justified
himself on the grounds that the Scots College Rome had required him to
state their "conditionem"; and having himself studied at the College and
being familiar with Italian customs, he knew that to have omitted any
reference to parents' social standing would have been taken as implying
that they were of the lowest rank. He agreed that there was no recent
tradition of giving such information – and in some cases, including his
own, "there was little to be said on that head" – but pointed out that
Bishop Gordon had usually included some indication at least of students'
social origins, and that he himself had heard Bishop Smith criticised for
not doing so. (Letter, John Geddes to Bishop Smith, 28. 2. 1763, BL).

The difference in attitude between master and bishop, and particularly Mr Geddes' remark regarding his own humble birth, reveals much about the two men. Unlike the bishop, the master certainly *did* consider birth a relevant factor to a boy's suitability for the Mission priesthood. But it also reflected the changing times, away from the traditional pattern of vocations coming almost exclusively from the sons of the gentry.

2) It was this changing pattern that lay behind the criticisms levelled against Bishop Hay by some of his senior clergy in the 1780s, concerning his admission policy for students to Scalan. The criticism came to a head at a meeting at the seminary in autumn 1785, when objections were raised to admitting low-born boys, boys who had previously been servants, and boys in cases where a close relative had given scandal. The challenge prompted Bishop Hay to send his Co-adjutor Bishop Geddes a memo, *Reflections on the Present State of This District with Regard to the Providing and Admitting Boys to the Seminary* (MS, 9. 3. 1787, CS 1/1/ 11, SCA), the main focus of which concerned the question of students' social backgrounds. Bishop Hay noted that whereas in the past most vocations had come from the "Catholick Gentry", the situation had now changed – there were now fewer Catholic gentry, fewer still with sons, and none willing to forward their sons for the priesthood. Furthermore, the next class ("the better sort of farmers") – previously a rich source of recruits – was now in decline and few candidates were emerging from it. The "principal supply" from now on was in fact likely to come from the "inferiour rank of farmers" – those who worked their own small farms, subtenants, and those who combined crofting with a trade. Despite the changing social scene he still looked to the rural areas for his priests, and discounted merchants and tradesmen from the towns, since "little supply has ever been got from them".

Against the specific objections of his opponents he argued that the Scalan student body had always included some boys of low birth; that the "infamy" of a close relative who had given scandal, though a genuine consideration, should not be a decisive one; and that several former students, now priests, had previously been servants. On the last point, he recalled that it had actually long been a tradition at Scalan itself for the master to choose one of the boys "to run at his foot & take care of his horse when he went from home, as his foot servant", and that this practice had only been stopped later on account of the possible dangers and not through any sense of disgrace.

More generally he pointed out that God Himself has often chosen the low-born for His work, and that the Catholic Church has never throughout its history considered any factors other than personal qualities as relevant to the priesthood.

On these grounds he re-affirmed that the Mission's admission policy for Scalan was to be based on the same principles, and only where these were in doubt should any consideration be given to the issue of birth.

Glossary

Including Scots and other terms, but not Gaelic words, code words, or aliases, which are explained as they occur in the text.

Anise	aniseed
Axle tree	axle
Babie	half-penny
Balk	untilled strip between ridges
Bannock	oatmeal girdle cake
Belled	bald – i.e., white headed (?)
Bear	four-rowed barley
Boll	a dry measure, the value of which differed from place to place, and also according to whether it was used for grain, meal or flour. (A typical value when measuring grain was c. 1 Cwt.)
Bouie	small barrel
Brocket	with markings
Byre	cattle shed
Cabers	poles laid from top of house wall to ridge of roof, between the larger rafters or 'couple arms' (q.v.), as part of frame for thatch
Candlemas	feast of Purification of Blessed Virgin Mary, 2 February
Carvey	caraway
Chist	chest
Cock and peal	tap and pail
Cog	wooden vessel for holding liquid
Conjunct tenants	tenants sharing a 'tack' (q.v.) and paying rent direct to the landowner
Coulter	iron blade on plough, which cuts soil vertically
Couples	poles set vertically in foundation of a house, typically spaced 6–10 ft. apart, forming internal frame for walls
Couple arms	main rafters of roof, attached to top of 'couples' (q.v.) and ridge of roof
Coy	heifer

Cromey	with crumpled horn
Cruck	see 'couple'
Crusie lamp	hollow, open oil lamp with wick
Deal	plank of wood, usually 6 ft. or more in length
Dominie	school master
Dyke	wall of field or garden, usually built of turf and/or stone
Ell	measure of length, slightly longer than a yard
Farm town	the grouped houses of a farm shared by a number of tenants; also, the farm itself
Feal	turf cut large (usually applied to the turf used for building a house wall)
Fir candle	a house light made from a sliver of resinous fir
Firkin	small container (also a measure of capacity)
Firlot	a dry measure, equal to one quarter of a 'boll' (q.v.)
Floughtiness	flightiness
Gared	streaked
Garron	small, hardy breed of horse
Girth	metal band round the rim of a wheel
Grassum	initial payment by tenant to landlord on taking or renewing a 'tack' (q.v.)
Hacket	white faced
Harn	coarse linen cloth
Head dyke	the wall that formed the boundary between a farm's cultivated land and its grazing land
Infield	the cultivated land nearer to the farm house(s), which was enriched by rotation of crops, periods of fallow, and (latterly) fertilisation with marl, lime, etc., in contrast to the 'outfield' (q.v.)
Juniper skull	shallow basket made with twigs of juniper
Kail	curly leafed variety of cabbage; also, broth made from same
Kellach (killoch)	old type of cart, with one pair of wheels (at back end), long shafts, and container made of wickerwork
Kelpie	horse of folklore, supposed to live in rivers and lochs
King's Evil	scrofula (so called because believed to be curable by the king's touch)
Kirn	see 'quern'
Knock	wooden hammer
Lambin	slow to learn (Fr.)
Lead and thatch	gather and stack (peats)
Longsome	slow to learn
Losen	pane of glass

Lye	alkaline solution
Mains farm	chief or home farm of an estate
Mart	beast killed and salted about Martinmas (q.v.), for eating through the winter
Martinmas	feast of St. Martin, 11 November
Mashlum	mixed grain; also, meal made from same
Mell	wooden hammer
Merk	two-thirds of £1 Scots (see Note on Scots money at end of glossary)
Muckle	large
Office houses	the outhouses of a farm
Outfield	the cultivated land further from the farm house(s), which was sown annually without rest or fertilisation until the yield fell below a level that was economic
Patmos	island in Aegean to which St. John was exiled
Peck	a dry measure, equal to one quarter 'firlot' (q.v.)
Pendicle	a croft or small piece of land, attached to a larger
Pirlins	sticks laid horizontally across 'couple arms' and 'cabers' (q.v.) to form support for roof thatch
Pirn	bobbin or reel for winding yarn or thread
Plaiden	coarse woollen cloth
Plenishing	contents of a house
Pot	small private whisky still
Press	cupboard
Quern	hand mill for grinding corn
Quoy	see 'Coy'
Ridge pole	main timber that runs the length of the roof ridge
Rig	ridge or furrow
Rood	one quarter of an acre
Roof tree	ridge pole (q.v.)
Roup	sale (usually by auction)
Runrig	system of cultivation in which each tenant of a farm was allocated several strips of land interspersed among those of his fellow tenants
Say	woollen serge cloth
Scudo	coin of value c. 4/- (Ital.)
Shiel (v.)	take the cattle (and other farm animals) to summer grazing
Shieling	grazing land (distinct from and of better quality than rough pasture)
Soum	the amount of pasture that would support one cow
Stranguary	illness characterised by difficulty and pain in passing water

Sunwise	in the direction taken by the sun (in effect, clockwise)
Tack	the lease of land; also, the leased land itself
Tacket	hobnail
Tacksman	chief tenant of a 'tack' (q.v.), who paid the rental directly to the landowner and himself leased portions of it to sub-tenants
Tass	goblet
Theat	leather band fastened round horse, to which ropes or chains were attached in order to draw a plough
Tirred	tore (past tense of 'tear')
Viatic	money to cover the cost of a journey
Viaticum	the Eucharist given to the dying (in fact the same word as the previous, both meaning 'provisions for the journey')
Wattle dyke	wall made of woven sticks
Wedder	wether
Whin	gorse
Wynd	narrow alley off street

A Note on Scots Money

1 d. (penny) Scots = 1/12 d. (penny) Sterling
1 sh. (shilling) Scots = 1/12 sh. (shilling) [ie., 1 penny] Sterling
£1 Scots = £1/12 [ie., 1sh. 8 d.] Sterling
1 Merk Scots = £2/3 Scots [ie., £1/18 or 1sh. 1 1/3d. Sterling]

Bibliography of Sources referred to in the Text

PRIMARY SOURCES

MANUSCRIPT

Scottish Catholic Archives (SCA)
  Bishop Hay Papers (B GH)
  Bishop Geddes Papers (B JG)
  Blairs Letters (BL)
  Documents relating to Blairs College (CB)
  Documents relating to Church History (CH)
  Documents relating to Scalan College (CS)
  McPherson, Abbé P. 'History of the Scots College Rome' (CA 3/18)
  Oban Letters (OL)
  Preshome Letters (PL)
  Scottish Mission Papers (SM)
  Thomson, Rev. J. 'Some Account of the Mission in Scotland' etc.(TH/10)

  Archives of Scots College Rome: Catalogue (Flanagan)

Scottish Record Office (SRO)
  Church of Scotland: General Assembly Records (CH 1)
    Synod of Moray Records (CH 2)
    Parish of Inveravon Records (CH 2)
    Presbytery Records (CH 2)
    Copies of Reports (CH 8)
  Crown Estate Commissioners: Glenlivet Estate Office Records (CR 6)
  Forfeited Estate Papers, 1745 (E 700–88)
  Gordon Castle Muniments (GD 44)
  SSPCK Records (GD 95)
  Register House Plans (RHP)

National Library of Scotland (NLS)
  Church of Scotland, Report 1714 (MS 976)
  James Robertson, Journal 1771 (MS 2508)
  Church of Scotland G. A. Commission, Representation 1722 (MS 3430)
  William Roy Map of Scotland (from 1748) (Sheet 28. 2)

Elgin City Library
  Parish Register: Inveravon (MF A In 1 55)
  RC Parish Records – Glenlivet Obituaries (1817 -) (MF A In 3 56a)

School of Scottish Studies, University of Edinburgh (SSS)
  Tape Recordings, Reminiscences (SA 1953 and SA 1956)

Royal Commission on the Ancient and Historical Monuments of Scotland
(RCAHMS)
  Aerial Photographs 106 G/Scot/UK 130 (1946)
                         16 88 261 (1988)

RC Church, Tomintoul
  'Status Animarum': Records relating to receipt of Sacraments (1814 -)

In Private Ownership
  Retiral Memorial Album, Chapeltown, 1896

PRINTED

Contemporary Works
  Belches A. *An Account of the Society in Scotland for Propagating
    Christian Knowledge* (Edinburgh, 1774).
  Blaeu J. *Atlas Novus,*vol. v, including Scotland, (Amsterdam, 1654).
  Burt E. *Letters from a Gentleman in the North of Scotland* (London,
    1754).
  Defoe D. *A Tour Through the Whole Island of Great Britain* (1724;
    London, 1769 ed.).
  Donaldson J. *General View of the Agriculture of the County of Banff*
    (Edinburgh, 1794).
  Douglas T. (Earl of Selkirk) *Observations on the Present State of the
    Highlands of Scotland* (Edinburgh, 1806).
  Garnett T. *Observations on a Tour Through the Highlands and Part of
    the Western Isles of Scotland* (London, 1800).
  Grant J. and Leslie W. *A Survey of the Province of Moray* (Aberdeen,
    1798).
  Guthrie T. *Autobiography*, 2 vols. (London, 1874–5).

Innes T. *Critical Essay on the Inhabitants of the Northern Parts of Britain or Scotland*, 2 vols. (London, 1729).

Lists of Popish Parents and their Children in Various Districts of Scotland as Given to the Lords of the Privy Council and to the Commission of the General Assembly MDCCI – MDCCV (Edinburgh, 1705).

Lock D. *Tour Through Most of the Trading Towns and Villages of Scotland* (Edinburgh, 1778).

Macky J. *A Tour Through Great Britain* (London, 1723).

Martin M. *A Description of the Western Islands of Scotland* (London, 1703).

Newte T. *Prospects and Observations on a Tour in England and Scotland* (London, 1795).

Popery Reviving (Edinburgh, 1714).

Regulations for the Administration of the College of Aquhorties (Edinburgh, 1799).

Reports Respecting the Distilleries in Scotland by Committees of the Honourable the House of Commons appointed in 1798 and 1799 (London, 1799).

The Scots Magazine: 1747, Appendix for Year MDCCXLVII – 'Papers found in a Popish Chapel', No. II 'Instructions for Mr John Tyrie, etc.' (1735).

The Scots Magazine: Nov. 1766 – 'Report of Drs. Hyndman, Dick, et al. to General Assembly' (1761).

The Scots Magazine : Feb. 1779 – Bishop Hay, Pastoral Letter.

A Seasonable Warning by the Commission of the General Assembly Concerning the Danger of Popery (Edinburgh, 1713).

Second Report of the Distress in Scotland (presented 1783; publ. London, 1846).

Shaw L. *The History of the Province of Moray* (c. 1780; new enlarged ed. Glasgow, 1882).

Sinclair J (ed.) *The Statistical Account of Scotland* (Edinburgh, 1795).

Sinclair J. *Analysis of the Statistical Account of Scotland* (Edinburgh, 1825).

Souter D. *General View of the Agriculture of the County of Banff* (Edinburgh, 1812).

Wight C. *Present State of Husbandry in Scotland* (Edinburgh, 1784).

Manuscript, Subsequently Published

Allardyce J. (ed.) *Historical Papers Relating to the Jacobite Period 1699–1750* (Aberdeen, 1895), Vol. I.

Anderson W. J. (ed.) 'Ambula Coram Deo: The Journal of Bishop Geddes for the Year 1790', *IR*, vol. vi, 1955.

Anderson W. J. (ed.) 'Abbé Paul McPherson's History of the Scots College Rome', *IR*, vol. xii, 1961.

Anderson W. J. (ed.) 'The College for the Lowland District at Scalan and Aquhorties: Registers and Documents', *IR*, vol. xiv, no. 2, autumn 1963.

Anderson W. J. (ed.) 'The Autobiographical Notes of Bishop John Geddes', *IR*, vol. xviii, no. 1, spring 1967.

Bellesheim. A *History of the Catholic Church of Scotland* (London and Edinburgh, 1890), Vol. IV, Appendices: VI: Report of Bishop Nicolson to Propaganda, 1697; VIII: Report of Bishop Nicolson to Propaganda, 1700; XIII: Report of Bishop H. MacDonald to Propaganda, 1732; XVI: Report of Bishop Smith to Propaganda, 1747; XVII: Report of Bishops H. MacDonald and Smith, 1753; XVIII: Report of Mgr. Lercari to Propaganda, 1737.

Cramond W. *Extracts from the Records of the Synod of Moray* (Elgin, 1906).

Forbes R. (ed. H. Paton) *The Lyon in Mourning*, 3 vols. (Edinburgh 1895–6; Edinburgh, 1975 ed.).

Giblin C. (ed.) *Irish Franciscan Mission to Scotland 1619–1646: Documents from Roman Archives* (Dublin, 1964).

Grant A. *Miscellany of the Spalding Club* (Aberdeen, 1841), Vols. I and II.

Grant E. of Rothiemurchus *Memoirs of a Highland Lady* (London, 1898).

Grant J. *Records of the County of Banff 1660–1760* (Aberdeen, 1922).

Pococke R. (ed. Kemp D. W.) *Tours in Scotland 1747, 1750, 1760* (Edinburgh, 1881).

Records of the Scots Colleges at Douai, Rome, Madrid, Valladolid and Ratisbon: Registers of Students (Aberdeen, 1906), Vol. I.

Ruvigny and Raineval, Marquis of, (ed.) *The Jacobite Peerage, Baronetage, Knightage and Grants of Honour* (Edinburgh, 1904).

Acts of the Parliaments of Scotland (APS)

'Act Anent nobilmen who sendis thair sones oute of the cuntrie', Acta Parliamentorum Jacobi VI, 1609, *APS*, Vol. IV, p.406.

'Ane act anent the childrene of noble men and otheris remaning in seminaryis of popishe religioun beyond sea', etc., Acta Parliamentorum Caroli I, 1625, *APS*, Vol. V, p. 177.

'Declaration of the Estates of the Kingdom of Scotland', etc., Acta Gulielmi et Mariae, 1689, *APS*, Vol. IX, p. 39.

'Act for Preventing the Grouth of Popery', Acta Parliamentorum Gulielmi, 1700, *APS*, Vol. X, pp. 215ff.

Acts of Parliament of Great Britain (SAL)

'An Act to oblige all Persons, being Papists, in that Part of Great Britain called Scotland . . . refusing or neglecting to take the Oaths . . . to Register their Names and Real Estates', etc., 1723, 9 Geo I c. 24.

'An Act for the more effectual disarming the Highlands in Scotland . . . and for restraining the Use of the Highland Dress', etc., 1746, 19 Geo II c. 39.

'An Act for taking away and abolishing the Heritable Jurisdictions in that part of Greatt Britain called Scotland', etc., 1747, 20 Geo II c. 43.

'An Act Requiring a certain Form of Oath of Abjuration, and Declaration, from His Majesty's Subjects, professing the Roman Catholick Religion, in that Part of Great Britain Called Scotland', 1793, 33 Geo III, c. 44.

SECONDARY SOURCES

BOOKS

Anderson M. L. *A History of Scottish Forestry* (London, 1967).

Bannerman W. *On the Extinction of Gaelic in Buchan and Lower Banffshire* (Banff, 1895).

Barclay W. *The Schools and Schoolmasters of Banffshire* (Banff, 1925).

Barnes A. S. *The Catholic Schools of England* (London, 1926).

Bellesheim A. *History of the Catholic Church of Scotland* (London and Edinburgh, 1890), 4 vols.

Bil A. *The Shieling 1600–1840* (Edinburgh, 1990).

Blundell O. *The Catholic Highlands of Scotland* (Edinburgh, 1909 and 1917), 2 vols.

Brown W. E. et al. *The Scots College Rome* (London and Edinburgh, 1930).

Bulloch J. M. *Territorial Soldiering in North East Scotland During 1759–1814* (Aberdeen, 1914).

Calder R. H. *Glenlivet Gleanings* (Banff, 1914).

Cooper D. and Godwin F. *The Whisky Roads of Scotland* (London, 1982).

Cox E. H. M. *A History of Gardening in Scotland* (London, 1935).

Craig H. C. *The Scotch Whisky Industry Record* (Dumbarton, 1994).

Dealy M. B. *Catholic Schools in Scotland* (Washington, 1945).

Dickie G. *The Botanist's Guide to the Counties of Aberdeen, Banff and Kincardine* (Aberdeen, 1860).

Dilworth M. *The Scots in Franconia* (Edinburgh and London, 1974).

Donaldson G. *Scotland: the Shaping of a Nation* (1974; Nairn, 1993 ed.).

Dunnett H. *Invera'an, a Strathspey Parish* (Paisley, 1919).

Durie A. J. *The Scottish Linen Industry in the Eighteenth Century* (Edinburgh, 1979).

Dwyer J., Mason R. A. and Murdoch A. (eds.) *New Perspectives on the Politics and Culture of Early Modern Scotland* (Edinburgh, 1982).

Fenton A. and Stell G. *Loads and Roads in Scotland and Beyond* (Edinburgh, 1984).

Fenton A. and Walker B. *The Rural Architecture of Scotland* (Edinburgh, 1981).

Forbes A. *The 'Black Watch', the Record of an Historic Regiment* (London, 1896).

Forbes-Leith W. *Memoirs of Scottish Catholics During the XVIIth and XVIIIth Centuries* (London, 1909), 2 vols.

Fuller R. C. *Alexander Geddes 1737–1802, A Pioneer of Biblical Criticism* (Sheffield, 1984).

Gaffney V. *The Lordship of Strathavon: Tomintoul Under the Gordons* (Aberdeen, 1960).

Gauldie E. *The Scottish Country Miller 1700–1900* (Edinburgh, 1981).

Gibb W. G. *The Flora of Banffshire* (Aberdeen, 1912).

Good J. M. *Memoirs of the Life and Writings of the Reverend Alexander Geddes LLD* (London, 1803).

Gordon J. F. S. *Journal and Appendix to Scotichronicon and Monasticon* (Glasgow, 1867).

Grant I. F. *Every-Day Life on an Old Highland Farm 1769–1782* (London, 1924).

Grant J. *History of the Burgh Schools of Scotland* (London and Glasgow, 1876).

Grant J. *Banffshire Roads During the First Half of the Eighteenth Century* (Banff, 1905).

Grant J. *Records of the County of Banff 1660–1760* (Aberdeen, 1922).

Haldane A. R. B. *Three Centuries of Scottish Posts* (Edinburgh, 1971).

Halloran B. M. *The Scots College Paris 1603–1792* (Edinburgh, 1997).

Hamilton D. *The Healers: A History of Medicine in Scotland* (Edinburgh, 1981).

Hamilton H. *An Economic History of Scotland in the Eighteenth Century* (Oxford, 1963).

Hanley J. E. *Scottish Farming in the Eighteenth Century* (London, 1953).

Hay M. V. *The Blairs Papers (1603–1660)* (London and Edinburgh, 1929).

Johnson C. *Developments in the Roman Catholic Church in Scotland 1789–1829* (Edinburgh, 1983).

MacInnes J. *The Evangelical Movement in the Highlands of Scotland 1688–1800* (Aberdeen, 1951).

Macintosh H. B. *The Northern or Gordon Fencibles 1778–93* (privately printed, 1929).

McPherson J. M. *Primitive Beliefs in the North East of Scotland* (London, 1929).

McRoberts D. (ed.) *Essays on the Scottish Reformation 1513–1625* (Glasgow, 1962).

Moss M. S. and Hume J. R. *The Making of Scotch Whisky* (Edinburgh, 1981).

Paul J. Balfour (ed.) Douglas R. *The Scots Peerage* (Edinburgh, 1907), vol. iv.

Phillips J. G. *Wanderings in the Highlands of Banff and Aberdeen Shires* (Banff, 1881).

Phillipson N. T. and Mitchison R. (eds.) *Scotland in the Age of Improvement* (Edinburgh, 1970).

Plant M. *The Domestic Life of Scotland in the Eighteenth Century* (Edinburgh, 1952).

Pryde G. S. *Scotland From 1603 to the Present Day* (London and Edinburgh, 1962).

Roberts A. (ed.) *Tales of the Braes of Glenlivet* (forthcoming, Edinburgh, 1999?).

Salmond J. B. *Wade in Scotland* (Edinburgh, 1934).

Scotland J. *The History of Scottish Education* (London, 1969), 2 vols.

Scott H. *Fasti Ecclesiae Scoticanae* (Edinburgh, 1926), 6 vols.

Shaw J. *Water Power in Scotland 1550–1870* (Edinburgh, 1984).

Sher R. B. *Church and University in the Scottish Enlightenment – the Moderate Literati of Edinburgh* (Edinburgh, 1985).

Simpson H. F. M. (ed.) *Bon Record – Records and Reminiscences of Aberdeen Grammar School* (Aberdeen, 1906).

Smout T. C. *A History of the Scottish People, 1560–1830* (London, 1969; London, 1985 ed.).

Smout T. C. 'The Landowner and the Planned Village in Scotland, 1730–1830', in Phillipson N.T. and Mitchison R. (eds.) *Op. cit.*

Stark J. *Priest Gordon of Aberdeen* (Aberdeen, 1909).

Steven M. W. *History of the Royal High School of Edinburgh* (Edinburgh, 1849).

Tayler A. and Tayler H. *Jacobites of Aberdeenshire and Banffshire in the Forty Five* (Aberdeen, 1928).

Tayler A. and Tayler H. *Jacobites of Aberdeenshire and Banffshire in the Rising of 1715* (Edinburgh and London, 1934).

Taylor M. *The Scots College in Spain* (Valladolid, 1971).

Taylor W. *The Military Roads of Scotland* (1976; Colonsay, 1996 ed.).

Walker B. *Farm Buildings in the Grampian Region* (Aberdeen, 1979).

Waugh H. L. *George Watson's College: History and Record 1724–1970* (Edinburgh, 1970).

Whetstone A. E. *Scottish County Government in the Eighteenth and Nineteenth Centuries* (Edinburgh, 1981).

Withers C. W. J. *Gaelic in Scotland 1698–1981* (Edinburgh, 1984).

JOURNAL ARTICLES

Anderson W. J. 'The Edinburgh Highland Chapel and the Rev. Robert Menzies', *IR*, vol. xvii, no. 2, autumn 1966.

Aspinwall B. 'Scots and Irish Clergy Ministering to Immigrants, 1830–1878', *IR*, vol. xlvii, no. 1, spring 1996.

Blundell O. 'St Vincent of Paul and the Highlands of Scotland', *Dublin Review*, cxlix, July-Oct. 1911.

Blundell O. 'Bishop James Gordon and the Highlands of Scotland', *Dublin Review*, clix, July-Oct. 1916.

Cherry A. 'The Library of St. Mary's College, Blairs, Aberdeen', *The Bibliotheck*, vol. 12. no. 3, 1984.

Darragh J. 'The Catholic Population of Scotland Since the Year 1680', *IR*, vol. iv, no. 1, spring 1953.

Dean A. and Taitt M. 'Scalan Reconstructed: Architectural and Documentary Evidence', *IR*, vol. lxvi, no. 1, spring 1995.

Devine T. M. 'Highland Migration to Lowland Scotland', *Scot. Hist. Rev.*, vol. lxii, 2, no. 174, Oct. 1983.

Dilworth M. 'Two Necrologies of Scottish Benedictine Abbeys in Germany', *IR*, vol. ix, no. 2, autumn 1958.

Dilworth M. 'Scottish Benedictines at Würzburg, A Supplement to the Necrology', *IR*, vol. xv, no. 2, autumn 1964.

Dilworth M. 'The Scottish Mission in 1688–1689', *IR*, vol. xx, 1968.

Donovan R. K. 'Voices of distrust: the expression of anti-Catholic feeling in Scotland, 1778–1781', *IR*, vol. xxx, 1979.

Doran W. 'Bishop Thomas Nicolson, First Vicar-Apostolic 1695–1718', *IR*, vol. xxxix, no. 2, autumn 1988.

Doughty D. 'Chapeltown, Braes of Glenlivet, and Tombae, the Debris of the Old Scalan library', *Deeside Field*, 19, 1987.

Durkan J. 'Education in the Century of the Reformation', *IR*, vol. x, no. 1, spring 1959.

Goldie M. 'The Scottish Catholic Enlightenment', *J. Brit. Studs.*, vol. 30, no. 1, Jan. 1991.

Goldie M. 'Common Sense Philosophy and Catholic Theology in the

Scottish Enlightenment', *Studs. on Voltaire and the Eighteenth Century*, no. 302, 1992.

Hay M. 'Too Little and Too Late', *IR*, vol. vi, no. 1, spring 1955.

Innes T. 'The Inneses of Balnacraig', *The Deeside Field*, vol. 5, 1931.

Kay G. 'The Landscape of Improvement – a Case Study of Agricultural Change in North-East Scotland', *Scot. Geog. Mag.*, vol. 78, no. 2, Sept. 1962.

Kerr J. 'Old Grampian Highways', *TGSI*, vol. xlix, 1974–6.

Kidd C. 'Antiquarianism, Religion, and the Scottish Enlightenment', *IR*, vol. xlvi, no. 2, autumn 1995.

Lockhart D. G. 'The Planned Villages of Aberdeenshire: the Evidence from Newspaper Advertisements', *Scot. Geog. Mag.*, vol. 94, no. 2, Sept. 1978.

MacDonell A. and McRoberts D. 'The Mass Stones of Lochaber', *IR*, vol. xix, 1966.

McGoldrick W. 'The Scots College Madrid', *IR*, vol. iv, no. 2, autumn 1953.

McLaren R. 'Father Thomas Innes: Lost Papers', *IR*, vol. v, 1954.

Macmillan J. 'Scottish Catholics and the Jansenist Controversy: the Case Re-opened', *IR*, vol. xxxii, no. 1, spring 1981.

Macmillan J. 'Thomas Innes and the Bull *Unigenitus*', *IR*, vol. xxxiii, 1982.

Macmillan J. '"The Root of All Evil"? Money and the Scottish Catholic Mission in the Eighteenth Century', *Studies in Church History*, vol. 24, 1987.

Macmillan J. 'Jansenists and Anti-Jansenists in Eighteenth Century Scotland: the *Unigenitus* Quarrels of the Scottish Catholic Mission, 1732–46', *IR*, vol. xxxix, no. 1, spring 1988.

McRoberts D. 'Scots College Rome: Students' Dress', *IR*, vol.ii, no. 1, summer 1951.

MacWilliam A. ('Glenlivetensis') 'Scalan 1717–1799', *Claves Regni (St Peter's College Magazine)*, vol. xvii, nos. 67 and 68, Dec. 1946 and June 1947.

MacWilliam A. 'The Jesuit Mission in Upper Deeside 1671–1737', *IR*, vol. xxiii, 1972.

MacWilliam A. 'A Highland Mission: Strathglass 1671–1777', *IR*, vol. xxiv, 1973.

Masson D. 'Popular Domestic Medicine in the Highlands Fifty Years Ago', *TGSI*, vol. xiv, 1887–8.

Mitchell S. 'Scalan in the Eighteenth Century: A Postscript – The 'Forty Five', *Scalan News*, no. 14, June 1997.

Mitchell S. 'Hidden Families: Aliases and Patronymics in Upper

Banffshire', *Aberdeen and North-East Scotland Family Hist. Soc. Journal*, nos. 66 and 67, 1998.

Moran P. A. 'The Library of the Scots College Douai', *IR*, vol. lxiii, no. 1, spring 1992.

Ravenstein E. G. 'On the Celtic Languages in the British Isles: A Statistical Survey', *J. Royal Stat. Soc.*, 1879.

Ross A. 'Old Highland Roads', *TGSI*, vol. xiv, 1887–8.

Roberts A. 'The Leslies of Balquhain and the Burial of Bishop Hay', *Recusant History*, autumn 1995.

Roberts A. 'Tombae and Scalan: *Status Animarum*', *Scalan News*, no. 10, June 1995.

Ross A. 'Book Hunting in the Highlands', *St. Peter's Coll. Mag.*, vol. xix, no. 74, June 1950.

Stewart J. A. 'The Clan Ranald and Catholic Missionary Successes, 1715–1745', *IR*, vol. xlv, no. 1, spring 1994.

Szechi D. 'Defending the True Faith: Kirk, State, and Catholic Missioners in Scotland, 1653–1755', *Cath. Hist. Rev.*, July 1996.

Walker B. 'The Vernacular Buildings of North East Scotland: an Exploration', *Scot. Geog. Mag.*, vol. 95, 1979.

Walton K. 'Climate and Famines in North East Scotland', *Scot. Geog. Mag.*, vol. 68, no. 1, April 1952.

UNPUBLISHED WORKS

Clapperton W. *Memoirs of Scotch Missionary Priests* (MS, transcribed Wilson G., Elgin, 1901).

MacWilliam A. S. *The Scottish Seminaries – Loch Morar to Aquhorties*, 1714–1829 (typescript, 1977, SCA).

THESES

Dorrian G. M. 'Hugh MacDonald 1699–1773 – First Vicar-Apostolic of the Highland District in His Religious and Social Context', unpublished M. Phil. thesis, Univ. of Strathclyde, 1990.

Halloran B. M. 'The Scots College Paris, 1653–1792', unpublished Ph. D. thesis, St Andrews Univ., 1996.

Lockhart D. G. 'The Evolution of the Planned Villages of North East Scotland, c. 1700–1900', unpublished Ph. D. thesis, Dundee Univ., 1974.

McHugh M. 'Kirk, State and the Catholic Problem in the Western Highlands and Islands of Scotland 1690–1760', unpublished M. Litt. thesis, Univ. of Strathclyde, 1982.

Index